The Showgirl Costume

The Showgirl Costume

An Illustrated History

JANE MERRILL

McFarland & Company, Inc., Publishers

Jefferson, North Carolina

Unless otherwise indicated,
illustrations are from the author's collection.

LIBRARY OF CONGRESS CATALOGUING-IN-PUBLICATION DATA

Names: Merrill, Jane, author.
Title: The showgirl costume : an illustrated history / Jane Merrill.
Description: Jefferson, North Carolina : McFarland & Company, Inc.,
2019 | Includes bibliographical references and index.
Identifiers: LCCN 2018052600 | ISBN 9781476671741
(softcover : acid free paper) ∞
Subjects: LCSH: Showgirls—Clothing—History. | Costume design—
History. | Costume—History.
Classification: LCC PN2067 .M38 2019 | DDC 792.702/6—dc23
LC record available at https://lccn.loc.gov/2018052600

BRITISH LIBRARY CATALOGUING DATA ARE AVAILABLE

ISBN (print) 978-1-4766-7174-1
ISBN (ebook) 978-1-4766-3433-3

Front cover photograph © 2019 iStock

Manufactured in the United States of America

McFarland & Company, Inc., Publishers
Box 611, Jefferson, North Carolina 28640
www.mcfarlandpub.com

To Emma, whose study of New York laws
regulating the burlesque seeded my interest in showgirl history,
and Burton, her twin, our knight in shining armor.

Table of Contents

It's been said a woman dresses for other women because if she dressed for men she would not dress at all. Certainly when it comes to the glamorous costumes of the showgirl extravaganzas, the truth is more nuanced. Men and women alike were inspired by beautiful female bodies adorned like silvery angels. What could be a better backdrop to raise the mind above the reality of gambling tables and slot machines?

It is easy for staged nudity to look awkward. Instead, thanks to sparkling costumes and stately choreography, the shows dazzled, projected magical qualities. The audiences responded to the harmonious colors and movement and assemblage of bodies on display. The tradition itself is artful and ingenious, the revues often original, if long, and—what was it that people said after going to the Lido in Paris?—tasteful.

Those showgirls were beautiful performers. Their extinction is hard to believe.

—GAY TALESE

Introduction

"Sex is one of the nine reasons for reincarnation.
The other eight are unimportant."—Henry Miller

Finding the Terms

When Sally Bowles belted out "Life is a cabaret, old chum," she knew what cabaret meant because she was in one. Showgirls have known that they are performing as sexual objects—lightly clad showpieces of an aesthetic based in rhinestones, sequins, and feathers. And yet the nomenclature about them has been vague. First of all, the words surrounding the productions where the showgirl costume icon took shape are themselves diaphanous.

The word cabaret comes from a French Picard (before that, Dutch) word "camberete," meaning small room. According to the *Oxford English Dictionary* (OED), the cabaret was in the 1600s a wooden dwelling, shed, or any joint for gaming and drinking. Samuel Pepys in his diary of September 23, 1662, noted that "in most Cabaretts in France they have writ upon the walls 'Dieu te regard,'" and Dryden in *Marriage à la Mode* (1662) mentioned a song "sung, two or three years ago in Cabarets."[1] In contemporary Québecois, a tray in an eating establishment or at home used for carrying glasses, etc., is a cabaret.

In English, cabaret has a foreign twang. Nicolas Thibout's *Prières et Instructions Chrétiennes* (1737) decried cabarets as places to ruin one's health, as frequenting them led to gambling and intoxication. Henri de Saint-Simon in his memoir used the connotation to define a side table on which to put alcohol, coffee or tea for self-service. The idea of a gathering place for men of letters and artists and where parodies were presented began with Le Chat Noir, a "man cave" in Montmartre opened by the charismatic Rodolphe Salis in 1881.

The center of cabarets was Berlin during the Weimar era, until, writes theater historian Laurence Senelick, "Within a few years of Hitler's rise to power in 1933, the Nazis effectively suppressed all hints of cabaret subculture in Germany."[2] The European cabaret was a business but with the atmosphere of a club. The artists, poets and writers in Paris gravitated to the cabarets. The habitués created posters and published minor literary genres that advertised their chic by mocking the status quo. They hung their work on the walls of where they drank. In keeping with the fact that patrons cast themselves as

1

Photograph from a 1920s Paris show.

outsiders, "cabaret" continued to have a non-native appeal. A Persian or Arabic origin has thus also been suggested.

Once the stage lights went on in Paris, variety shows with dancing girls, and later professional dancers, semi-nude, became a popular indoor spectacle, eclipsing the traditional cafés-concerts. Most of the venues of this sort were known by the English term music-hall, a rubric imported from London, usually hyphenated. Meanwhile the word cabaret passed into many languages for drinking establishments with entertainment and was often retained as evocation. Further complicating the lexis, music-halls also called themselves theaters. As for the floor show that became the distinguishing characteristic of the music-hall, it began on the floor but moved to the stage. The context of the showgirl, the music-hall, stood at the top of the entertainment pyramid in the fin de siècle and the Jazz Era, yet the English word stuck. In the post–World War II era, the gaudy frivolities, influenced by the influx of English-speaking tourists, also were referred to as *boîtes de nuit*, or nightclubs.

The word nightclub may conjure up a palm tree décor and Miami or Havana but it appeared early in the OED with an 1871 reference from *Appleton's Journal*: "For billiards, and the best night-club in London, Pratt's." Thus in London at the turn of the century the nightclub was distinct from both cabaret and music-hall (the first was opened by Charles Morton in 1952), and not yet home to showgirls. It was after Prohibition was repealed in the U.S. in 1933 that big fancy nightclubs with showgirls, and supper clubs with their little sisters, the cigarette girls, proliferated. You were, Frank Sinatra said, a "show business nobody" until you did three shows a night at the Copacabana, and at big nightclubs like this one, showgirl numbers provided titillation.

A quintessential spot for showgirls in the U.S. was for a long time New York City. Writes Broadway theater historian John Kenrick, "In the United States, cabaret developed along more glamorous and less intellectually ambitious lines.... When a 1913 ordinance forced Manhattan's cabarets to close by 2:00 a.m., members-only clubs sprang up and stayed open for dancing till all hours—the first 'nightclubs.'"[3] Soon anyone looking for striptease and line dancers would check out the cabarets.

F. Scott Fitzgerald, no stranger to nightclubs, with wife Zelda, has a "famous cabaret star" at the next table in *This Side of Paradise* (1920), and an English newspaper in 1923 broadcast a big jazzy show at the Hotel Metropole in London as a "super cabaret."

Harold B. Segel makes a sensible distinction between cabarets and nightclubs. The nightclub conjures up a physically large venue whereas the cabaret is small and intimate, and the nightclub tends to offer gaudier entertainment in the tradition of the revue— raised stage, orchestra, troupe of dancers, and "singers and a standup comedian or two." The contemporary cabaret, notes Segel, will have certain of these features "but in scaled down form; it is, in effect, a miniature nightclub."[4]

Charles Rearick remarks, "For me, 'nightclub' brings to mind a 1930s–1950s Holly-wood movie scene with little tables, a singer in front, men in dark suits and women in gowns. The Paris places for 'showgirls' were more like our vaudeville or variety shows. The term 'music-hall' was used to describe the Olympia (the first French one) in the 1890s and a bunch of others afterwards."[5]

Florenz Ziegfeld created the spectacular girlie shows in New York, using the French word *revue* for a quick moving series of tableaux and acts. Showgirl costume design blossomed towards the end of World War I when Paris music-halls—most notably the Folies Bergère—introduced the "revue à grand spectacle" with a bigger cast of women dancers and background figures, elaborate costumes with changes for dozens of different tableaux, and typically a stairway effect where the star and others paraded down onto the stage (initiated at the Ziegfeld Follies). The French impresarios were, Charles Rearick explained to me, getting lots of ideas from English music-halls and from Broadway vaudeville. "In the 1930s, the 'girls' in a Paris revue were looking just like Busby Berkeley."

This was a type of entertainment that casinos continued in Las Vegas. People from the Hollywood film industry drove over to Nevada to behave more freely and watch scantily clad women on stage. French meant classy and playfully sexy and nude meant topless. From now on, the revue in the U.S. was often known as a showgirl spectacular. Now the Lido publicizes itself as a cabaret and burlesque show, thereby sending out feelers as both edgy and bawdy, as those terms respectively suggest.

In this way, music-halls supplanted cabarets in Paris, and some of the music-halls became supper clubs or nightclubs; and when hotel-casinos had showgirls, the terms for their venues were plucked, for descriptive or publicity purposes.

The word showgirl has been fluid, too. For a century of her history, a showgirl has been someone employed to appear onstage in the numbers of a revue. If the show is parody she is a burlesque dancer. If her act is striptease then she is a stripper or *stripteaseuse*. If she carries a prop she may be a fan dancer, for which there was a vogue in the first decades of the twentieth century. The showgirl as a member of the cast is sometimes called a chorister, and from the time Paul Derval took over as director of the Folies Bergère in 1918, there were *danseurs en ligne*. The distinction between chorus girls and showgirls broke down in the spectacular revues of the 1920s and 1930s for the reason that the entire company might take part in a tableau. Given the icon's universal appeal, most of the showgirls have had feathers, sparkles, high heels, and some level of undress.

For this book, the showgirl, dancer or "girl" dancer is the expositor of female glamour, usually but not always in a revue, who originated in the heart of Paris and kept her Frenchness in transcontinental settings as far away as Havana and Las Vegas. It turns out that the showgirl was the poster girl of glamour itself. Glamour, theorizes Stephen Gundle, emerged between 1900 and 1914 in a capitalist climate of the Third Republic, where "entertainment and display became more developed and systematic, as well as more varied. They opened up what appeared to be a utopia of desire in which all could to some degree participate."[6] In the first modern metropolis and a center of world economy, consumerism and entertainment, "the reputation for frivolity and licentiousness, which had been confined to the margins, came to be identified with the city as a whole."[7] French to the world has meant luxury and sensuality, and women on display in couture or on stage advertised the image of the city.

It is as much in female nature to have a fantasy showgirl self, to show off her physicality for an imagined audience within a paradise of safety, like a stage, as for a young man to parade his muscles. She turbans her hair in one towel, her body in another, and feels like Botticelli's Venus walking in the waves. Showing off is one way the healthy self-image forms. At two or three, my youngest daughter, Rosalind, would jump up on her parents' bed, gaze into the double mirror of the dresser opposite it, and cry out, "Je suis belle. Comme je suis belle." Shouldn't all of us feel we are miracles?

In the eighteenth century, if a young woman acted in a showy way to garner male attention she was called a showgirl in England. By 1814, Maria Edgeworth observed, "The girls are mere show girls—like a myriad of others, sing-play-dance, dress, flirt, and all that." By 1836 the showgirl was singing and dancing in variety acts or similar shows; a novel by G. Soane called *Lilian, Show Girl* disparaged "the tinsel dress of the poor showgirl." In the *Sporting Times* of September 1885 was the commentary that "it is perfectly heart-breaking to be confronted with nothing less antique than a Gaiety chorister, less hideous than a Drury Lane show girl." And by 1976 even the convention of fiery red lipstick and hair or wig color (bright red and blond) were quite set; L. St. Claire's *Fortune in Death*, cited in the OED, had "showgirls ... in plumed headdresses and rhinestone G-strings."

Photograph from a 1920s Paris show.

Cancan dancer by Janicotte, c. 1920–1950.

The showgirls in the revues have also been called kickers, line dancers, and choris-
ters, or just "girls." "Girls" is French stage lingo and not pejorative; if it were "filles" that
would have the undertone of tarts. Still, in this text I avoid calling adult female dancers
girls.

A French archives cataloguer told me that she would stick with dancer for the performers whether they danced or just stood pretty as mannequins, also called *figurantes*. "We French always judge. So, we hear in the word showgirl not a performer but someone sleazy, as in 'C'est une vraie cochone.'"

The person effectively disappears into the showgirl icon. The costume is the message of fantasy and the wearer is the show. Even if she appears for under a minute in a scene, the showgirl brings the glamour. Her costume is a defining and central element of a complex and floating field of entertainment, the revue. As producers of the shows confirmed again and again, the attraction for this type of entertainment was the troupe of pretty females and not the juggling seals or the headlining stars. A showgirl costume is not just any costume—it has endured over a hundred years as an eidetic societal image. Whether seen as sexual imperialism or "fun girl" masquerade, its power comes from being an international symbol of carefree, commercially proffered, chic seduction. Today showgirls are alive and well in Montmartre and on the Champs-Elysées. Some showgirls appear as window dressing in Las Vegas and some vibrant boutique burlesque shows, but a showgirl without a glamorous revue is a goldfish outside a tank, and Paris has the traditions both of spectacle and costuming.

The saucy Parisienne is the leitmotif that merges and embodies the many influences. Her showgirl icon passes like a flamboyant float through the throngs of them—all the different art styles and dress fashions that designers trafficked in. The spirit—Frenchness and sexiness—brings them all together con brio and beauty.

An Etiology of the Look

With the wearing on of decades, the cancan ceded to subtle and slick choreography, the action became more ritualized, the lighting multifarious, and the exposure of the female body more or less accepted. Yet, while the nature of fashion is to change, the elements of the iconic showgirl costume remained unchanged much longer than those of any day fashions, and gained a nostalgic and reverential quality. The ways the costumers have solved issues of clothing undress have continued to appear in avant-garde designs, e.g., by Jean-Paul Gaultier or Christian Lacroix. In America, where many showgirls migrated to dance in shows on the monumental scale (the scale natural to them), showgirls are extinct, given that the last spectacular on the Las Vegas Strip, *Jubilee!*, closed in 2016 after a 34-year run. Only in the dozens of old movie musicals that feature them do showgirls still stride aglitter up and down the American stage. Yet in Paris, there are four venues to choose from for a night out to see a showgirl spectacular.

When did the costume typifying showgirls originate and from what? Whereas fashion implies change, the iconic showgirl costume stabilized into feathers, sparkle and revealing clothes by 1910. By 1920, the revues in which the showgirls figured were arguably the world's most celebrated entertainment, the array of costumes catering to both voyeur and middle-class escapism and reflecting every epoch of France's glory and self-narrative.

There are, I have concluded, plausible visual sources for the iconic look of the showgirl costume. My approach is to encircle rather than define, to explore how the showgirl in her costume both signified prevailing culture in Paris and had a rapprochement with shows in the United States. The icon's true identity lies in an immense and rapid crosspollination by which the costume of feathered headdress, artfully displayed flesh, sparkling accessories, high heels and dramatic makeup came to be a preeminent Gallic symbol.[8]

"L'envers du music-hall," *La Vie Parisienne*, May 17, 1930, drawing by Hy Fournier.

The icon was a vision of men and women involved in the stage where beauty was enough; the ultimate value and the stage offered a tremendous platform for personal expression. These costumes have celebrated French culture around the world and have had stereotypical features that people recognized as looking French.

This book relays the idiom from which the costume derived, at what point it defined itself and became a reliable currency, and how it froze in time. The costumes are a paradox in many ways. They first figured in intimate settings where the women interlaced with the audience of mostly men; then the stages grew until the female performers entered on the wings of a jet plane at Bally's in Reno. The French light touch with artifice became predictable nostalgia in later iterations, often with literally huge costumes vis-à-vis material and the space they occupied. The music-halls reframed the erotic purpose of what *filles de joie* wore to solicit customers. A revue aimed at a display to overwhelm the senses, so over the top that the sultry femmes in the old posters of the French music-hall sometimes look in drag. There is a paradox of ever new tableaux, excess and transformation being the law of revues yet an emblematic costume that was a purposeful cliché. The cancan itself was considered *vieux jeu* by the time the first choreographed petticoats were flung up at the Moulin Rouge.

Being able to look at clips of showgirl revues and old photographs online is like having a telescope to gaze back in time. We can't follow the Magi and watch the Vikings sail their ships, but we can view precious records of popular entertainment. We can see Shirley MacLaine wrapping up a Paris show singing "Merci beaucoup," and various renditions of the French cancan from different periods. We see how the early showgirls wanted to be seen in their racy off-stage photographs.

The first chapter of this book opens a peephole on historically relevant sources for the costume. It traces the costume prototypes back to powerful influences including popular festivals, Renaissance Europe's royal masques and festivals, ballets de cour, Bourbon court folies, the French reputation for the risqué, the attire of demimondaines, the circus, ancient imagery of the dance, sexy interpretations of foreign costumes, public balls, the proliferation of luxury goods (e.g., at department stores in Paris), and the *féerique* as recounted in French fairy tales.

The plurality of elements that contributed to the icon made it as indelible as the Great Sphinx. Creative designers kept to a model of objectifying females at a lighthearted distance from reality, so showgirl "undress" has proclaimed exclusively external femininity. As Philippe Garner has said, the costumed nightclub revue is "a sophisticated amalgam of the camp, the exotic, and the erotic."[9]

The second chapter is about the context of bohemian artiness, especially in raffish Montmartre, and the costuming of the evolving revue in the music-hall. In chapter three, experts inform on the comparison of early Broadway. Chapters four and five describe the costumes of semi-nude shows during the Golden Age of music-hall, from 1918 until the Stock Market Crash of 1929 and the beginning of the Great Depression. After some details of plumes and spangles in chapter six and the Weimar revues in Berlin in chapter seven, chapter eight sums up the fixed icon in Paris, and chapter nine the French connection to entertainment in Las Vegas in the second half of the twentieth century, when the scanty French cabaret clothes translated to American nightclub revues. The costume lineage, a couture of risqué and spirit of hedonism, traveled both ways as early as the 1920s, resulting in the midcentury showgirl spectaculars of the hotel-casinos on the Las Vegas Strip. Showgirl fashions subsequently crossed over to sports, which is the subject of chapter ten. In the Appendix, Cassidy Zachary treats the influence on fashion and Tracy Jenkins Yoshimura guides us into showgirl costumes in the movies.

Throughout, conversations with experts, dazzling in their own fields of French and American culture, are intrinsic to the story.

ONE

Influences

A Glimpse of Ancient Dance

The *cocottes* (coquettes) who starred on the fin de siècle stages of French music-halls tended to be curvaceous; slender Liane de Pougy, who lunched on two egg yolks sautéed with deer sweetbreads, and a dish of strawberries in cream was an exception to the rule.[1] *Cocottes* wore opulent clothes well but also were cinched in by undergarments. All that changed in the decade before the Roaring Twenties when *danseuses* with slender, toned bodies replaced the cocottes. A close look at the ancient version of the showgirl costume shows no precedent for distortion of the body. Rather, among the ancients, form followed purpose and they made a boyish model for the more athletic feathered showgirl in skimpy clothes of the Paris music-hall during the Jazz Era.

The *khener*, professional dancers of ancient Egypt, performed at rites to guide the deceased into the afterlife and to celebrate the birth of nobles and to entertain at parties. A high-status family had its own dancers. In Egyptian art, like third millennium BC bas-reliefs at the Saqqara necropolis, lines of female dancers walk in procession or sway, or, at the other extreme, do flips or kick their legs high as they lean backwards in a bridge.

The *khener* wore specialized dress. The long ankle-length garment would have obstructed movement so from the Sixth Dynasty they wore crossed bands on their chest and skirts that ended at the thighs and left the legs free. These skirtlets were either a narrow strip of fabric that hung from a belt, and was fastened around the hips, or were an apron, cut round in the front. The outfit, white and plain, showed off the body. Ornamenting the dancer were narrow or broad collars, bracelets, earrings, flowers and ribbons. A headdress is described by Irene Lexova in *Ancient Egyptian Dancers*: "A very peculiar ornament was a cone made of semi-solid fat, saturated with scent, which was fastened on top of the head, so that the grease dissolving on the surface, trickled down the hair, and dress, passing on to them its scent."[2]

Dancing was part of the ecstatic rites for the Greeks. The maenad with her divine kinetic energy twisted and twirled so that her skirts could keep up with her body. In the pottery decoration in the Karlsruhe museum, Persephone returns from Hades and the maenads act out the rebirth of the year, a wild frolic taken up again in Europe in dances like the saraband, and eventually the cancan.

Greece also had show dancers, in a class with acrobats and jugglers. The fifth century historian Xenophon wrote in his *Symposium* that Socrates praised the performance of a female dancer and dancing boy, "and then got up and emulated their movements."[3] Female

Banquet scene, 18th Dynasty, from the tomb of Nebamun, c. 1370 BC (the British Museum).

show dancers in ancient Greece were *hetairi,* enslaved, not citizens. They danced naked or semi-naked, a contrast to being clothed in the loose folds of the peplos. The light garb accentuated their gymnastics and, presumably, demonstrated their vulnerability, the same as women in moments of peril do in Greek mythology—Helen baring her breasts before Menelaus, or Cassandra covering her defenseless body in advance of Ajax's attack. In the French movie *Les Enfants du Paradis* the courtesan Garence is going to be put on display naked but wiggles out of it; nevertheless it makes her more vulnerable to the audience. Thus it was that the goddess Ishtar in the Gilgamesh Epic descends to the underworld, and at each of the seven gates, her jewels and ornaments are taken away. At last, to her shame, her loincloth is removed.

According to the authority on Greek dress, Larissa Bonfante, "The Akkadian phrase for the loincloth is 'robe of shame' sometimes euphemistically rendered as 'robe of splendor.' There was evidently all the difference in the world, to ancient eyes, between a gloriously, divinely named figure wearing jewelry, a crown, a loincloth, even a belt, and one not wearing anything. Being 'stark naked' means poverty, as well as shame."[4]

In around the seventh century BC, the Etruscans on the Italian peninsula and the Cypriots had the same sort of attractive, minimal attire for women performers as the Minoans had in a previous millennium. It was called the *perizoma,* "thong," activewear that is significant as a showgirl costume because it was so well crafted, and because the Etruscans, luxury- and fun-loving, doubtless donned their *perizomas* and put on a good show. It was sewn according to a pattern, with a set-in crotch, seams and decorative borders. The thong could be pinned, buttoned (with wood or metal buttons), self belted or tied in place with a leather belt and perhaps a metal buckle. Vases show women doing a handstand or sword dance in the *peri-zoma.*[5]

In dramatic terms, the use of handsomely presented feminine partial nudity had power. The trial of Phryne, a beautiful courtesan in the fourth century BC, in which she disrobed before the jurors of a court, dazzled them, and as a consequence was released, is no myth. Moreover it indirectly influenced Western law. At that trial her attorney Hyperides tore off some of her garment to excite the jurors' pity. Hyperides also wept to show how Phryne's beauty moved him personally. Clearly the tactic on the part of the attorney was powerful because after that a ruling of no weeping by the defense in court was implemented.[6]

Perhaps the most naturalistic of the depictions of ancient Greek dancers are the mold-cast terracotta figurines known as Tanagras. Many are of fashionable women and they originally had red lips, pinkish skin and blond hair; some had sunhats and fans. But there are also statuettes running and dancing in tightly wrapped gowns with skirts and veils flying.

Hydria. The Judgment of Paris, Attic, 410-400 BC (photograph by Thomas Goldschmidt; courtesy Badisches Landesmuseum Karlsruhe).

The Greeks, though, considered semi-nudity for women and public exposure indecent. Writes Bonfante, "There was little difference, in their eyes, between such a costume and total nudity, and in real life dancing girls dressed this way were likely to be confused with courtesans."[7] She gives an anecdote of out of towners to Athens from Arcadia who saw for the first time girls in topless suits, Thessalians who danced, as was their custom, naked, wearing only some type of loincloth. According to Athenaeus, who wrote about culture from dining to courtesans in about 200 BC, the men could not restrain themselves

but "started up from their couches and shouted aloud at the wonderful sight they were seeing."

Importantly, Cleopatra was considered not a beauty but an ambitious diva who employed theatrical effects like splashing herself with gold and riding on a golden barge with silver oars, surrounded by sexy handmaidens, to impress Marc Antony.[8] The sensual excesses of imperial Rome were also imbued in European culture. One thinks of Valeria Messalina, wife of Claudius and cousin of Nero, who, in a blond wig and with her nipples painted gold, went to do shifts in a low-class brothel.[9]

The signs of skimpy costumes/showgirl attire are faint but exist. Classical scholar Adrian Goldsworthy points to the frequent mentions of gold dust/powder in ancient sources, wall paintings that show dancers in "almost a bikini type costume—bra band and little pants," and specific findings at sites in England in Roman times: "There may also have been similar garments in other fabrics less likely to survive—a few statuettes of goddesses that now seem nude may originally have had decoration painting or embossed on them to suggest simple outfits. Who wore them is very hard to say."[10]

Western Europe had no showgirls in the medieval period. If some belly dancers and snake charmers came from the Mediterranean or Western Asia to ply their trade, they were not perforce showgirls. Had they performed in public they would have been burned as witches. It is therefore to the Roman period that one looks, as Professor Goldsworthy has indicated, and where proof of well-sewn, very skimpy outfits for sporty girls and performers has been found.

Six examples of bikini briefs have been found around London beginning with the Queen Street bikini, excavated from a well, in 1953. They are closely fitted and laced with a single eyelet, made of vegetable tanned goatskin, and decorated with punched out openwork. They may have been worn by dancing girls and acrobats or have been a special version of an undergarment, worn for support or visits to the bathhouse. In any event, these briefs span the entire Roman period of Britain and were carefully hemmed and decorated. A similar garment was inventoried in the Landesmuseum at Mainz in the mid–nineteenth

Terracotta statuette of a dancing girl. Greek, Corinthian, fourth century BC. The dancer wears a flaring striped headdress, or *kalathiskos,* and chiton. A stripe on her right leg may be the remnant of a red boot (The Metropolitan Museum of Art).

century, and while now lost, was illustrated by the museum director; its openwork was elaborate, very pretty abstract tiny designs.[11]

Sicily has beautifully preserved mosaics of outfits that could go unnoticed on the beach today. One site is the Villa del Casalo (circa fourth century BC) in central Sicily, which is still being excavated. The scene for the bath of the extensive villa is known as "Bikini Girls," a large mosaic of not one but nine (one edge had been destroyed, thus originally there were ten) scantily clad women in colorful bikini briefs and bandeau tops, doing a variety of sports. They clearly represent an elegant competition, as their hair is done in different elaborate styles of braids and each individual has a slightly different outfit—mostly in colorful bands and neatly cut to show off the thighs.[12]

The outstanding precursor of ancient female dancers stands out in the little that can be historically known about Empress Theodora. Before her marriage to Justinian, Emperor of Byzantium, Theodora danced for all-male audiences in small showplaces. The dance numbers were bawdy and she had next to nothing on. She wore some type of little shorts for a dance she may have invented which can be called the Barley Dance.[13] The rags to riches, trashy dancer to Christian empress trope was in the European memory; it stands out unequivocally that the nearly nude could enliven a stage.

Procopius's Eyes: How a Sophisticated Historian Looked at the Empress Who Had Been a Starlet

PAOLO CESARETTI[14]

Often even in the theater, under the eyes of all the people, she stripped and remained naked on the stage, wearing just a thong around her sex and groin (… in Byzantium nobody could show themselves on the stage completely naked…); in that state she stretched out on her back flat on the ground. Certain slave-workers threw barley grains at her pubis, and suitably trained geese begged for them one at a time. As for her, far from feeling ashamed, she rose up very satisfied with her performance. She was more than shameless….

The passage describes a sort of pantomime parodying the union of Zeus (in the myth a swan, here represented by trained geese) with Leda, here played by a "shameless" actress that is no other than Theodora, the future bride (from 525 to 548, when she died) of the Roman Emperor in Constantinople, Justinian (he reigned from 527 to 565).

The passage is found in chapter 9 of the *Secret Stories* (Greek "Anekdota"), by Procopius of Caesarea, the greatest historiographer of the time, heir and continuer of the millennial Hellenic tradition with Herodotus and Thucydides. The author succeeded in carrying out an authentic literary prodigy: to quote Edward Gibbon, he "successively compiled the history, the panegyric, and the satire of his own times," respectively in his *Wars* (in eight books—written in about 550–553), in his *Buildings* (in six books, after 555) and in the aforementioned *Secret Stories*, which the most recent critics ascribe to 550.

We cannot address here many of the issues investigated by scholars in thousands of pages through the centuries: let us just remember that Procopius wrote his *Secret Stories* not only after the death of Theodora, proclaimed the *Augusta* (in 548, she was about 50) but above all that the author never saw the scene that he so effectively describes. The daring performances of Theodora—a starlet on the theatrical scene of Constantinople—occurred around 515–520, when she was 15–20 years old; at the time, Procopius, who was

La Dame au Masque on a postcard postmarked 1907.

roughly her age, was studying rhetoric in the best schools in the Mediterranean Levant, thousands of miles away.

The literary representation is effective: according to the ancient dictates of visualization (Greek "enargheia," rendering the events vivid, as if they were present) Procopius induces his readers—no less today than in his 6th century—to "see" the scene with their own eyes. But the pantomime with Theodora protagonist, had it ever been so, had taken place at least 30 years before he wrote about it. And he had not been an eyewitness. The most he could draw on was oral reports of dubious reliability, trivial "gossip." The most probable thing is that the passage in the *Secret Stories* reproduces a sort of "inner film" by Procopius that attributes to Theodora a racy representation that he saw himself, in Constantinople or elsewhere—or that he only imagined.

So, the text does not tell us so much about the "reality" of Theodora as about the way Procopius looked at trivial episodes and the "horizon of expectations," according to which at that time a theatrical scene was considered vulgar and infamous for the reputation of a woman. Because one of Procopius's intentions in the *Secret Stories* (in other works, as already mentioned, he wrote differently) is to dirty Theodora's image forever, in front of the court of history.

From the beginning, we first understand that in the 6th century "Byzantine" pantomimes of this genre, which presuppose the existence of a theatrical life, were possible and practicable, and this is a distinguishing feature of the Mediterranean East—Christianized and Christian—compared to its western counterpart. In the East, "ancient" urban life, with theaters, circuses and spas, had continued for a longer time, and had a wide audience. Theodora is the witness of this continuity at the threshold of the Middle Ages, although in the mosaics of Ravenna her image as imperial *Augusta was* already evolving towards a medieval iconic dimension.

Moreover, Procopius himself, in order to blame her, gives credit to the "ancient" image when he writes (in chapter 15) that she liked to linger in the bath for a long time, in the context of body care "more than necessary, but less than she would have wanted." Furthermore, he emphasizes that Theodora liked to sleep and even oversleep: sleep as a beauty care is still a habitual practice, and had its effects if Procopius conceded that Theodora "had a beautiful face and was gracious" with "an always vivid and frowning expression."

In Procopius' description of the pantomime of Zeus and Leda with Theodora protagonist, she wore no more than a thong. It is easy to represent the scene also on the basis of the evidence provided by the pictures of the "bikini girls" in the mosaics of the Villa del Casale in Piazza Armeria. On other private occasions it is likely that her clothing would have been more daring, as Procopius himself wrote (if with or without a real foundation, we cannot say). But it remains true that we can set this as well as other women's activities in an oriental imperial context where continuity with the ancient world is emphasized. See, for example, the scenes of everyday life in the "Megalopsychia" mosaic (Antioch, 5th century).

As the Church's authority decreased in Europe, the seductive face of womanhood surfaced from the hellfires where sacred art had confined it. From the mid–nineteenth century actresses/showgirls were singled out as having the gift of beauty and being unafraid to reveal their bodies to strangers. Often they were called nude, which is a state more aptly described in showgirl costume history as any level of undress.

Not only did the European showgirls wear body stockings and gauzy coverings for the first half-century or more of music-halls, but also they would virtually never be stark naked. Such a guise would project a subliminal message of poverty and servitude. The showgirl as a creation of Western tradition has, just like in a Western painting, had a scrap of covering at least, often and some materially rich ostentatious detail of attire, a jeweled collar or belt. Costume completes the showgirl's undress and has since ancient times. Often described as nude, nudity on stage has been a remarkable example of false advertising. When the French designer of high-end lingerie was guest directing and costuming for the Crazy Horse Saloon, she spoke of the dancers as "très très nues." She realized that she had to qualify the word which means anything from a show of gams to the merest G-string. What it always has meant, from ancient times, is nakedness as art.

Dancing and showgirls have also been associated with a luxurious lifestyle as far back as the Roman philosopher Cicero. In Rome in 63 BC, Cicero defended a military man named Murena from accusations of disreputable living while in Asia. Cato, prosecuting Murena, said he was a dancer. It was disgraceful among the Romans for an individual to entertain a group—this was fit only for a hired actor. First Cicero jabbed at Cato for getting drunk when a colleague danced naked at a banquet in his house. Continuing his defense, Cicero argued that Murena stayed aloof from all excess during his military command in Asia. How, then, could Murena be a dancer when such a thing went with drunken revels and lewdness?: "Do you think that you will find the shadow of luxury in that man in whom you cannot find the luxury itself?"[15]

A Line of Rose Girls

Showgirls tend to come in a troupe, and dance in a line. This allows them to be precious stones, rivers of the world, soldiers on parade, and so forth. As with a beauty contest, or girls being lined up by an emperor of China or Rome, the plurality added piquancy. This was seen in the mid–twentieth century in the Rheingold Beer contests in the eastern U.S. The images of contestants were displayed in local grocery and liquor stores where shoppers voted for their favorite who was crowned the Rheingold Girl. This ad-campaign-created beauty contest was the second biggest democratic U.S. election ever after the presidential one. People liked to discuss and pick their choice as French villagers had at a festive contest of pre-modern France called the *Fête de la Rose*. Catholic Europe abounded in name-day and religious festivals but the *Fête de la Rose* lay outside the church year. Held in a thousand towns and villages across France, this ritualized beauty contest involved all levels of society, embodied fecundity and secularity, and showed off a line of pretty girls. Even when it lived on as only a theme for romantic melodramas on the nineteenth century stage, it left a shadow of the vassal-suzerain rites such as *droit de seigneur* and a noble's role in choosing husbands for commoners.[16]

Nothing like the Fête de la Rose occurred in English-speaking countries. The only similar phenomenon was established long ago in Sweden, St. Lucia's Day, which has a signal difference. The Fête de la Rose featured older girls, of marriageable age, and had none of the holy solemnity of Luciadagan. The girl chosen as the sweetest and prettiest, the two being conflated, marched through the village in a procession of 12 "roses" dressed

Postcard, 1904: Laridan and Selva at the Folies Marigny.

in white with blue ribbons. When they arrived at the nobleman's castle there were verses and a ceremony. The ethos of the scene, the happy simple society, is akin to Jean-Baptiste Greuze's *Village Bride* (1761).[17]

It was during the restive politics of the Enlightenment that the Fête de la Rose evolved into a full-fledged theme. One thinks naturally of the Versailles court, where Louis XIV could play Cupid or the Sun in an allegorical dance, and Marie Antoinette put on shows at Le Hameau with a countrified ethos. Ironically, while playing an innocent lass, Marie Antoinette became to the French people a symbol of wickedness. Meanwhile nobles, increasingly sick of the decaying court culture, developed a passion for private theatrical entertainments, and the celebration of the line of rose girls and the climax of crowning one of them flowered. For the whole of the eighteenth century it provoked on-stage parodies of the studied decorum of the upper class.

By this time another convention of a line of girls was prevalent at concerts, of a sort of ground floor dress circle. As in the rose fête the girls were purely decorative. The old Fair of St. Ovid in Paris was by 1772 reduced to an entertainment spot called the Café des Nymphes. According to a volume called *Old Paris* by Henry Shelley, the young women sat in a gallery dressed in garments intended to caricature the fashions of the day.[18]

The private theater gave a platform for antiestablishment humor as the Revolution approached. While life at court was an unended performance, in their private estates and townhouses in the capital, people were relishing private theatricals—of the kind the Bourgeois Gentilhomme put on for his guests in Molière's comedy.

Non-royal, non-ecclesiastical festivities fused skits with interludes of singing and dancing. Writes Sarah Maza, they "were usually set in somewhat prettified village.... The rosiere theme provided an ideal vehicle for the standard [tropes] of the opera-comique: cottages, shepherds, cleverly engineered storms, and choirs of beribboned villagers."[19]

The Fête de la Rose as a dramatic theme became as common as china figurines of shepherds and shepherdesses. It was usable for disparaging the old order while celebrating the health of the nation. The charming troupe had only the task of appearance, like showgirls in the music-hall revues in a later era when the Fête de la Rose remained a stock memory. Garbed in costume, viewable and untouchable, the "roses" and the "danseuses" paraded and offered to the dominant male to be judged. The first night deflowering by the suzerain, alluded to in so many sources including a Jean de La Fontaine fable, may be a myth.[20] Still, the noble's controlling the sexuality of his female subjects was very real. By one custom, the governing noble positioned his leg on the bed of the newly married subjects. So it was with the Fête de la Rose that presented village girls like a bouquet of undifferentiated sex objects. The church rituals involving women, including confirmation and baptism, were weighty but the Fête de la Rose witnessed sheer superficiality, the look of prettiness of a dozen village girls on display. The music-halls would evolve the line of girls into an entertainment art.

Ballets de Cour

Dressing up extravagantly (in a persona different from one's native one) to perform has a long history, e.g., masquerade and Mardi Gras attire, or the "pearly costumes" on poor street performers in Victorian London, covered in old buttons. Showgirl costumes have looked back in time, half-idealizing, half-mocking the French court, and to when clothes were fur-lined, and hairdos two feet high, or the shoes of satin and the skirts too wide to get through the door. Masquerades at feast days and carnival time are direct antecedents of the music-hall revues, and occasions for medieval French nobility literally to put on plumage, and sources to be mined for showgirl revues in modern times.

Dramatic dances as interludes in entertainment also involved costumed masquers on floats bearing pagan gods and allegorical figures. The steps were not formalized and the costumes were elaborate. How showgirls move at the Lido seems like a page out of the dance manual of a fifteenth century Ferraran dance master, the first known by name, Domenico da Piacenze, in 1416: "with smoothness, appear like a gondola that is propelled by two oars through waves when the sea is calm as it normally is. The said waves rise with slowness and fall with quickness."[21] At the marriage of the

White City Arts, New York, 1906 postcard.

Duke of Burgundy in Bruges in 1468, mermaids and male sea creatures emerged from a whale and danced and leapt about. The balls and masquerades dazzled young (and aesthetic) King Charles when he crossed into Italy in 1489. At one wedding banquet, the allegorical entertainment for the meal included ladies dressed as Neptune and sea sprites to bring in the fish course. It is remarkable that both Niccolò Machiavelli and Leonardo da Vinci did the costumes and sets for the north Italian extravaganzas.[22] In 1502, Isabella d'Este, noblewoman of Mantua who patronized the arts and led fashion, remarked that the play staged at Lucrezia Borgia's wedding was dull except for the intermezzo.[23] Guglielmo, an early choreographer, put on a spectacle to fête the marriage of Constanzo Sforza and Camilla of Aragon in 1475. Clarke and Clement describe a mythological figure who served the meal and wine and a model of an elephant bearing the Queen of Sheba who entered with two other elephants behind which carried towers filled with ladies. After the spectacle came a dance in geometric patterns of 120 young men and women.[24] A court banquet given by the Duke of Milan in 1489 matched up the "ballets" with the courses:

> the serving of roast lamb was heralded by a portrayal of the legend of Jason and the Golden Fleece; the course of wild boar was introduced by Atalanta, while the fruits were accompanied by the appearance of Pomona. Attendants to the main characters danced appropriate measure during each of the episodes.[25]

The costumes at these Renaissance events evoked faraway lands. Received knowledge provided a rationale for boundless and fantastical exaggeration. Thus Native Americans galvanized Europe's interest in particular, as, from the accounts of conquistadors and their booty of bird feathers, jewelry, and animal pelts, the native population of the Americas was reimagined in bizarre headdresses.

The succession of tableaux to keep an audience distracted and impressed began with the French ballet de cour—a royal show of choreographed movement and costumes over 300 years before the music-hall revues. Yet the idea of lightening up the Renaissance spectacle with horse ballet, allegory, water fêtes, fireworks and masquerades was a clear progenitor: this level of blockbuster entertainment could be done.

Catherine de Medici ordered the ballets de cour to show the unity of France and royal power. She brought her appreciation of the grand costumed spectacle from Italy. For the *Ballet des Polonais*, presented in honor of Polish ambassadors to Charles IX's court (1573), a room at the Tuileries was converted into a temporary theater and 16 ladies were dressed up as the 16 provinces of France.

French ballet master, c. 1770.

The greatest and most exorbitant of the spectacles, by her Italian valet and dance master Baltazarini (in France renamed Beaujoyeulx) was the *Ballet Comique de la Reine Louise*, October 15, 1581, staged for the betrothal of Catherine's sister. It has been considered the first ballet. In terms of royal dress-up and costumes generally, it had also the importance that it was the first published and illustrated libretto: "The event was memorialized with drawings," which were sent in remembrance to all the courts of Europe like a party favor.[26] The narrative had Circe the enchantress who cedes her authority to the king at the end. Catherine participated and cavorted on a huge stage set around a fountain with her lady court dancers as nymphs. The formation and intricate patterns of the dance and the matching costumes of the dancers characterize the ballet de cour. Writes Trenton Hamilton in the *History of Western Dance*,

> The performers, recruited from nobility, moved on the floor more like animated costumes than individual dancers. They came together in strikingly designed groups, and they set up geometrical floor patterns that had highly symbolic meanings. To audiences of the period, for example, three concentric circles represented perfect Truth, and two equilateral triangles within a circle stood for Supreme power.[27]

The scenes in the illustrations of this greatest ballet de cour cannot be precisely equated with the event but we can presume they were quite like. Decorations on garments and masks created the effects of the supernaturals, and there is a row of damsels who wore stars on their gowns, and rays made of feathers on their heads. Headdresses were all the more emphasized because they relieved the sameness of masked performers viewed from some distance.

Catherine was bolstering her position as queen by giving the lavish entertainments for nobles, allies, and adversaries. The ploy seems to have met with success as after her husband's death she continued the festivities while reigning as regent for her son Henry III for 30 years.

Ladies at court were not raiding their wardrobes for the ballets de cour. Directors created the designs and had charge of the consummate coordination of costumes to sets and also music (lute or small ensemble; Beaujoyeulx was a member of a band of violinists before he became valet to Catherine). It is not known how the men as ensorcelled beasts (a dog, lion, tiger, hog, and so forth) were costumed but if the outdoor sculptures in the Renaissance castles inspired Beaujoyeulx they were fantastical.

By 1641, when Nicolas Saint-Hubert wrote instructions for other masters of ballets de cour in a treatise called *La Manière de composer et faire réussir les ballets* (How to compose successful ballets), there had been many ballets de cour. He advised about dance steps, scenery, story and costumes. What he wrote could have been written by a producer of a showgirl revue centuries later. Make careful sketches because tailors and headdress-makers follow sketches to the letter. Dress the dancers in character but embellish. Go for realism but short of burning Troy. Use ordinary clothes as well as silks. Saint-Hubert had designed ballets where real silver and gold bedecked the costumes yet he maintained that illusion could be created at a mere fraction of such great expense: for five pennies he could bespangle a costume to look as impressive by candlelight as a richer one "chamaré [heavily ornamented with] d'or et d'argent."[28]

Reuse characters in costumes in a new show, Saint-Hubert advised, but let's have no more of Ovid's *Metamorphoses*.[29] How prescient this sternly given advice was. Transformation from animal (or tree or stream) to human and back again is to French letters what tragic heroines are to Italian opera. The French had a genius for raising an audience into the realms of fairy tale. In the apex of fairy tales, by Charles Perrault (also an architect) and women writers such as the Comtesses de Ségur and d'Aulnoy at the French court in 1700, a monkey princess (Babiole) or La Chatte Blanche would be clothed in gems and feathers. Transformation would be a leading costume theme for the Jazz Era revues.

It is within reason to suppose that the ladies who danced carried their roles as nymphs, sirens, and goddesses to the extent of semi-nudity. The School of Fontainebleau was the French version of Mannerism. Certain fine portraits of aristocratic women showed them placidly bare-breasted. The royal mistress to Henry IV, Gabrielle d'Estrées, is depicted along with her sister the duchesse de Villars, in an anonymous painting known as *Gabrielle d'Estrées et une de ses soeurs*, 1594; Gabrielle's earrings make her flesh look real. And *The Lady at Her Toilet*, from the same period and at the Musée des Beaux Arts in Dijon, has a Mannerist dreamlike quality with an erotic sheen. The lady who sits before her mirror might have been preparing for a showgirl revue. She adorns herself with more jewels while she already has them in her hair, on her arms and fingers; particularly massive is the big gold jeweled collar she wears, as if she were a royal pet. In the background, the servant is doing something with the clothes of the lady which are stored in a large chest. The message is that I have plenty of togs but I choose to exhibit my fine breasts to the court.

Francois I invited Leonardo da Vinci to stay and other artists came to please the king. Toplessness combined in the Fontainebleau paintings with veils and jewels and evening big hats: In an anonymous Fontainebleau painting, *Bathing Beauties,* women stand around a bathing pool, undressed except for their fancy hats. While female nudity was not on the stage but very much in art during the Renaissance, a minor fashion drew attention to the breasts by rouging nipples. This appears in Venetian and Florentine paintings and was taken up by some courtiers as late as eighteenth-century France.

Europe's First Risqué Tableaux

A performer who dressed like a goddess and moved with stately grace wasn't pretending, she was testifying to her high-born status. From an early age, children of the nobility trained in dance and wore aristocratic clothes. Appearance defined them. In the masques at the English Renaissance court the nobles did not take speaking roles—that was left to professional actors. They were gorgeous mannequins. As a commoner never would, the elite female masquers displayed their breasts and a glimpse of their legs. The focus on physical bodies sexualized the performance. Aristocratic females were by definition high above the masses, and were showing their beauty only to their relative equals at court.[30] What makes the ladies who performed in Jacobean masques at Queen Anne's and King James's court prototypical showgirls is that a designer designed the clothes, an overarching manager, the queen, approved them, and that the costumes were not just fancy clothes but risqué fancy clothes, possible because the shows were private-public performances. (The Elizabethans and Jacobeans liked their secret elite entertainments, and "closet dramas" for one's intimates were popular.)

The Palladian style of architecture in England is identified with a cloth maker's son who rose to be royal surveyor and the queen's right-hand man for her entertainments. Inigo Jones traveled abroad before and after 1600. The trip he made in 1613–1614 was as cicerone to Thomas Howard, 21st Earl of Arundel, and his family. Howard was an early and huge collector of European art whose portrait was painted by Rubens and Holbein. The sensibility that Jones brought back from Italy had another influence additional to his architecture, as Jones designed the sets and costumes for the court masques that were Anne of Denmark's favorite occupation during her reign with her husband James I. Texts had been coming out on shows during Elizabeth I's reign but illustrated treatises on how to put on a really great show could be brought from Italy. When a Florentine artist was designing "balletti" for the son of William and Anne, Prince Henry of Wales, he asked for designs from home. Later, in about 1613, he requested the designs a second time, for a wedding commission. Prince Henry promised to return them quickly and asked for discretion.[31]

Another type of borrowing related to how to dress allegorical and mythological figures so that they would be instantly recognized by spectators. Jones found a "Book of Symbols" from Italy useful and was inspired by costumes for the Medici extravaganzas designed by Bernardo Buonatalenti, who both dazzled his fellow Florentines with exciting

intermezzi in the Uffizi court; and added milk and eggs to a Persian *sharbat* (sorbet) recipe, thereby creating the first ice cream. Naturally such an entertainment celebrated the ruler. Regarding Elizabeth I, Jean Wilson in *Entertainments for Elizabeth I* explains, "The queen's arrival at a country house transformed it into a world in which mythology came alive—satyrs serenading her, tritons swam in artificial lakes, nymphs granted her sovereignty over their dominions, and spring, like her youth, was everlasting."[32]

King James liked to watch dancing but not to step out on the floor himself. Anne, lithe and attractive, loved to dance. At Whitehall Palace at Christmastime, she and her ladies made a splash. Anne put her heart, soul, and the royal treasury into costuming the masques at a time when no actress performed on the London stage—not until a female played Desdemona in *Othello* in 1660.

"Le Décolleté de la Renaissance," an original drawing by Freddy Wittop (MS Thr 113426-28, courtesy Houghton Library, Harvard University).

It is known that Jones loved the intricacies of design because he oversaw the materials used for the costumes. His watercolor sketches of costumes for the courtiers are genius. One character is garbed like a dainty nymph; another is made mysterious and imposing. That the witches in their strange outfits are so effective gives one a chill, as James had conducted a witch hunt in Scotland when big storms had delayed the arrival of his bride from Denmark.

The themes of these Stuart court masques were similar to the French court festivals. Renaissance historian Roy Strong writes that the spectacles on both sides of the Channel "expressed" the power of the monarchy to bring harmony and bring the natural world into obeisance.[33] The spectacles move from initial statements of disorder and cosmic chaos towards revealing the royals as abstracted gods and goddesses, sun and stars, and so forth.

Like Catherine de Medici's ballets, the Stuart masques were progenitors of the stage revue. With thematic costumes decorated with layered mirrors, sequins, glass jewels and feathers, they brought the realm of fairy tales alive. Costuming became so much a part of myths that Peau d'Ane, Beauty of *Beauty and the Beast*, or Cinderella is defined by sparkle.

The royal entertainment known as the court masque began in 1604 when Queen Anne commissioned the poet Ben Jonson to devise a masque that her ladies could perform for the court at Twelfth Night. She requested a scenario of "female blackamoors" so that she could transform herself and present dramatic fantasy African costumes and have lustrous dark skin at night. The sets for *The Masque of Blackness* (1605) had machines. Heavenly visitants would lower and move forward as if riding a cloud, or sail in gondola-like boats. The Moon wore silver, certain women were barefooted, the Daughters of Niger (including Anne) were painted in blackface, and sea nymphs were wheeled in on the half-shell. The nymphs wore gauzy gowns made of lace extending a few inches past their knees with half-skirts over them of silver cloth. At the climax, as at all the masques, Anne and her ladies danced in fabulous gowns.

Royal inventories show that the costumes did not merely copy fashion. A bodice might be overlain with white satin, gold plate and pearls, and a double satin skirt embroidered with silver thread and lined with "sarsnet" in a contrasting color.[34] For a costumey effect there was a scalloped hem edged with silver fringe or a pair of wings. On Jones' designs for the masques of both Anne and her grandson Charles I, these jagged filmy skirts, leafy overskirts, and insect wings exhibit a strobe effect, merging antiquity, Renaissance and organic. Some of the ladies have complex sandals with straps going up the calf; others have *bottines* with the same motif as the dress. The colors followed festival iconography, e.g., dark blue for Night, Fancy in rainbow colors, or Diana in a green cape embroidered with silver stars.

The costumes were playthings of the moment, usually not worn again; although the wardrobe master could remove theatrical accoutrements he would not let the costumes go to the secondhand market. The costumes Anne of Denmark commanded from Jones were blamed for nearly bankrupting the realm. Sometimes it was several years before the tailors, shoemakers, and merchants were paid for their contribution to the extravaganzas. Only at the onset did Anne content herself by raiding the wardrobe closets of the dead Queen Elizabeth.

Anne had a mania for theatrical glitter. Buskins exposed under "barbaresque mantels to the halfe leg" (a show of legs being more shocking than cleavage) were encrusted with jewels. Anne insisted on the regalia of farthingales as proper attire under the gowns of ladies at court but her masques were private; here she could flout convention. In *The Vision of Twelve Goddesses*, 1604, Anne played Athena in a daring gown. A contemporary observer, Dudley Carlton, described her to a friend: "Pallas had a trick by herself, for her clothes are not so much below the knee that we might see a woman had both feet and legs, which I never knew before."[35]

The dresses had ribbons, crystals, jewels and sequins, gold, silver and copper trim, ermine, velvet, brocade and silk. Headdresses were a focal point and typically three-tiered, starting with a Roman helmet or a crown, then curling plumes or tassels, then feathers or stiffened fabric. Veils might flow from the headdress as well.

William Davenport wrote a text for a masque called *Luminalia* put on for Henrietta Maria, wife of the doomed Charles I, in 1638. Davenport rhapsodized about her dress, which evokes the kind of excess of a showgirl extravaganza in Paris in the 1920s. The description exists because contemporary printers published the texts of Renaissance entertainment at court or at country houses; evidently such texts sold well. The ladies in the spectacle of *Luminalia* wore close bodices, open before the breasts, of Aurora color, richly embroidered with silver. About the waist ran a short bias-cut garment in starlike beams of white, and under these were lower labels, large at the bottom and cut in a trefoil, tacked together with small twists of gold; the ornament at the shoulders coming down the bowing of arm was of the same color and form as the basis, their arming-sleeves and skirts of their gowns are that of the bodies; they wore well-proportioned ruffs and on their hair stood a small band or diadem of jewels and stars between, which in the hinder part had a scroll, large at the bottom and narrow toward the top, to which their falls of white feathers were fastened.

Although Elizabeth I in portraits and when she met envoys wore gigantic ruffs and a multitude of jewels, the clothes for the masques were something apart, gorgeous but not stiff, and single purpose for one evening's show. It is noted by Renaissance historian Barbara Ravelhofer that Henrietta Maria was a symbolic universe in *Luminalia*. She wore nativity stars, which had not been used in church ceremonies since the Reformation, and sunbeams on the waistline and sleeves of red and yellow, her aurora. The queen, who as a child had participated in one of the French ballets, sat in a fairy's seat adorned with more rays. Her appearance as a star-sun predated Louis XIV's epiphany as Sun King in a French court ballet.[36]

It must have been magical to dance in a masque, whose world was a perfect Arcadia. The concept is identical to the French revue of the twentieth century, where the showgirl steps down the staircase from heaven and brings the starlight of oblivion. Like the show-girls on stage in Paris or Las Vegas, the Jacobean queen and her ladies wore costumes more revealing than what they or peers wore in other circumstances. Like in the modern revues there was a lauded designer who pushed the envelope, e.g., raising hemlines to up over the ankles. In his charming and revealing costume designs, Jones was surely say-ing this is how the ladies in theatrical roles ought to look. But just as the posters for a revue spectacular may have seized on and exaggerated nudity, there is a question whether the masques displayed thighs or bosoms through sheer fabric, as in the watercolor pro-totypes.

Often in his drawings, Jones showed ladies' chests. The open bodices projected gracefully to a point near the abdomen, skirts were flounced and revealed lower leg, and sleeves were full. Four of Anne's masquers for the 1609 show had corsets that either ended below the breasts, or with transparent tops. It is unknown (though it is conceivable) whether Jones toned down the display of ladies' breasts from the allegorical figures to the wearers in performance.

Whereas French entertainment captured the world's imagination as ultra risqué, some frontal nudity in the masques predated the Folies Bergère and Casino de Paris by three centuries, and the English used female nudity for effect while cross-dressers still played women at the Globe Theater.

Jones could, according to Ravelhofer, have been inspired by a contemporary English taste for a liberal décolleté. In 1616, the wife of an English citizen caused a tumult in Paris because of her "nude" cleavage and white shoulders, an incident sufficiently memorable to be credited with an entry in Bayle's dictionary. Yet pushing the risqué was the same as what a music-hall producer would do to draw a crowd without paying for a top star. Showing female undress put forth that the women were objects of desire and unfamiliar creatures, not like the rest of us. At this time, German students from prosperous Protestant families traveled to Italy to broaden their horizons. They kept friendship albums as souvenirs, on the blank pages of which friends contributed coats of arms, mottos and pictures. Ulinka Rublack was able to generalize, after looking at hundreds of such little books in the British Library, that the traveling young German men of 1600 looked at the Italian women as sensuous and seductive compared with marriage material back home. The subtext was that foreign women are more seductive because of their very unfamiliarity. In these vignettes, writes Rublack, "Italian women were imaginary complements of confident elegance, ease, and often sexual appeal."[37] Their breasts were usually depicted uncovered, and were even more accentuated if dark veils were worn over the face. In the depictions of Italian sophisticates in the friendship books, in the costumes for allegorical feminine figures by Inigo Jones, and in the Parisian nightclub revues, bare breasts were a playful touch, turning mortals into appealingly supernatural symbols.

On stage in the light of torches and candles, a trompe l'oeil convention could also give the semblance of nudity to the upper torso. Through the early seventeenth century in European courts, fake breasts were worn by cross-dressing male actors and women. The men wore what the English called "skin coats," flesh-colored tissue which could cover body and legs. Fakes were made of fabric, papier-mâché, or plaster. These theatrical accessories, originating in Italy, were a type of "vizard" or molded mask. Early versions, crafted in Venice, were made by soaking leather and then fixing it on a live model for a day. Vizards were colored, polished and refined. According to Ravelhofer,

> While evidence indicates the use of false breasts in disguises for cross-dressing male masquers, we should not rule out the possibility that Jonesian lady masquers too resorted to such means in light of Continental conventions; furthermore, masques projected an idealized version of courtly femininity. Masques may well have aimed at a symbolic rather than naturalistic representation of female courtiers.[38]

Claire McManus points out that the naked breasts or breasts covered with gauzy material in Inigo Jones' designs were not themselves an innovation. If you were rich and elite you were one step down from a goddess. To show your shoulders would break with decorum but you could show off your breasts under certain circumstances. "Aristocratic female breasts were often bared in the Jacobean masque … and the French and Elizabethan court fashions of exposed female breasts continued into the Jacobean reign."[39] This included Anne herself with her bosom naked to the abdomen. On some gowns the breasts' shape was outlined by the costume and corsetry.

The Jacobean masques required a bevy of tailors, shoemakers, and merchants, and might well run over budget. The medley of costumes was a carefully crafted part of the effect. The masquers were only lightly acting, as the masques were more in the order of tableaux. This made the look all the more important; the tableaux were expressions of royal dignity but also homages to female beauty. The costumes of Medici festivals, French ballets de cour, and English court became a vocabulary, a cadre of elegant taste for artists, choreographers, and ultimately directors of music-halls to draw on.

Showgirl at the Court: Marie Antoinette

Aristocrats who found Versailles stifling had the ability to be somebody else in amateur theatricals or to live it up in Paris where they had *hôtels*. The class hierarchy was dismissed not only at Carnival time but at these high society revelries. Louis XV set out to seduce a commoner who, in spite of her maiden name Poisson, was rumored to be a gem. He arranged to make her acquaintance at a masked ball, to which he came not as a single character but a topiary yew bush in a group of man-sized yews. Even if the gossip mill exposed his imprudence, he could manage a tête-à-tête with the lady and exit from the crush with her. The bourgeoise, already prepped for her potential as court mistress, enflamed him. A divorce was neatly arranged and if she lost her financier husband's title, the king ennobled her as the Marquise de Pompadour, the incarnation of wily grace. Amateur theatricals were popular with the Marquise.

French royalty were forever putting themselves on display while finding ways to flee from the public eye for shade and absence. For Marie Antoinette (1755–1793), this meant the Petit Trianon or the theater adjacent to it, both of which her husband Louis XVI built for her. The performances were viewed as harmless trifles or bagatelles. No one visited her play house and play farm except by order of the queen, not even her husband, and the premises were designed so that servants were practically unseen. Sophia Coppola's movie, an extraordinary recreation of the life of Marie Antoinette, shows accurately that before the queen and her children went to the henhouse to gather eggs, the eggs were dusted off by unseen hands. Here Marie Antoinette played roles, as biographer Antonia Fraser writes, that "had absolutely nothing to do with the gorgeously attired stately role she played day by day at Versailles. She played shepherdesses, village maidens and chambermaids."[40]

The Empress of Austria choreographed her daughters' spun sugar lives. Marie Antoinette and her sister the Queen of Naples took to the opulence which compensated for inner insecurities. The Queen of Naples built the ultimate English garden in the dry southern Italian soil and changed her opulent dresses throughout the day to impress her visitors. As dauphine, Marie Antoinette out dressed her father-in-law's mistress the comtesse du Berry. Marie attended masked balls and likely dallied with her Swedish officer at one, but she took "Let's Pretend" to a new level when she created a sort of stage set on the grounds of Versailles where she could retreat and play the country lass with her entourage. While the Bourbon rule lasted, she had the best of both worlds for a showgirl, where she could alternate from dressing up in her queenly role to dressing down as a dairymaid. Details of Marie Antoinette's look when she acted in her private theater are as follows: no heavy makeup, panniers or trains; the plain pale dress, often muslin, drawn over the head, with a drawstring neckline, embellished with a few ruffles and

Postcard of a masquerade tableau, by Jean Gilles, b. 1925.

ribbons; a silk sash around her waist of pale blue or striped, with a straw hat. This, explains Fraser,

> was the costume of Marie Antoinette immortalized in 1783 by the brush of Madame Vigée Le Brun. The following year, when Mrs. Cradock, wife of a wealthy Englishman, was shown the Queen's Robes of State, it was as though she was inspecting museum pieces. In a sense, that was true, even if those concoctions of rose satin and blue velvet, heavily embroidered with pearls and other jewels, garnished with lace and gold and silver tissue, were still let out of the museum from time to time.[41]

Yet the music-hall producers and costumers would cast exclusively the most extravagant, cake topper-like fashions of the Bourbon court time and again.

A large part of France's greatness has derived from style and fashion, ever since the Duc de Burgogne traveled far to fairs to purchase his furs and fine cloth. But a fashionista needs someone to propel her into full-flung materiality. The most significant of the relationships between celebrity and dressmaker was Marie Antoinette and Rose Bertin. Rose didn't make the basic dress, which was the work of an anonymous tailor. Rose tacked on the masses of froufrou, the swags, lace and gold and silver embroidery.

A country girl who made good in Paris, Rose had ambition. Not long after setting up in the capital she moved her shop from a byway to the kind of prestigious address that has been crucial in luxury trades. Her shop window was her advertisement, and though there was no showroom as Frederick Worth would install, her association with the Queen guaranteed her success. The coronation dress she created was so heavy with its jeweled embroidery that Rose suggested to the duchesse de Cosse, Mistress of the Robes, that it be conveyed to Rheims Cathedral on a stretcher. Fraser deems Rose Bertin "extremely domineering; she was nicknamed 'the Minister of Fashion,'" and twice a week she was ushered into the inner cabinet to cater to the Queen's whims and play with her mind.

Bertin had provided the comtesse du Barry with silk and laces that cost a fortune but these expenses were a mere fraction of what Marie Antoinette spent. Their shared goal was to present the Queen as the most dazzling spectacle at Versailles, a work of art vanquishing all competition. The Queen was half a million livres in debt by the end of 1776; many of Rose Bertin's royal customers would of course never be in a position to pay their bills.

The resale of the King's banquet table was a major business; so were the clothes the Queen ordered and may never have put on. Fraser points to an expenditure of three yards of new ribbon daily to tie the royal peignoir and two yards of green taffeta daily to cover the basket in which the royal fan and gloves were carried: "The extraordinary amount of new outfits ordered annually—twelve court dresses, twelve riding habits and so forth and so on—was in part explained by the privileges of her household to help themselves to these garments once discarded but hardly worn." Fraser evokes the compelling picture of the Wardrobe Book being presented to the Queen each morning on a pincushion by the Mistress of the Robes, to make her choices for the day.[42]

A lady-in-waiting to the Queen, Madame de La Tour du Pin, related in her memoirs how social dancing almost disappeared at Versailles because of fashionable attire, especially the theatrical poofs depicting ships, scenery, and, incredibly (and presumably in a death knell for the poof), the storming of the Bastille:

> There were fewer balls than in later years [1778–1784], for the ladies fashion of that day made dancing a form of torture: narrow heels, three inches high, which kept the foot in the same position as if standing on tiptoe to reach a book on a highest shelf in the library, a pannier of stiff, heavy whalebone spreading out on either side; hair dressed at least a foot high, sprinkled with a pound of powder and pomade which the slightest movement shook down on the shoulder, and crowned by a bonnet known as a "poof" on which feathers, flowers and diamonds were piled pell-mell—an erection which quite spoiled the pleasure of dancing.[43]

The Queen's popularity at court waxed and waned but was never considerable. It is striking that she chose to sing and act in tableaux before the courtiers, which she did at Fontainebleau and in the theater at Versailles as well as the tiny theater in the Petit Trianon. Apparently she appeared in 20 performances at the Petit Trianon from 1780 to 1785 and participated in operetta until the Revolution.

Marie Antoinette was a peerless clothes horse; the wig made her tall, she shimmered, she wore rouge, and above all she was the epitome of scandal, promiscuity, and risqué to the French, as the news media of her day lampooned her for harlotry, incest and lesbianism. Writes Lynn Hunt in her essay "The Many Bodies of Marie Antoinette,"

> Public virtue required virility, which required in turn the violent rejection of aristocratic degeneracy and any intrusion of the feminine into the public. The many bodies of Marie Antoinette served as a kind of triangulating function in this vision of the new world. Through their rejection of her and what she stood for, republican men could reinforce their bonds to one another, she was the negative version of the female icon of republican liberty.[44]

The Queen, who had created hyperbolic styles, was a trendsetter for European royalty to simplify their attire and their hairstyles—and by a shift to plainness keep up with the French.

Regarding the repetitive appearance of the queen in the spectacular-type Parisian revues, Lynn Hunt says, "I think that Marie Antoinette is irresistible because of the combination of her reputation for interest in fashion, the way she was a subject of rumors about affairs with her brother-in-law, her ladies in waiting, and her male servants, and then to top it off that she was executed—the only case I know of a queen being executed who was never eligible to actually hold the throne."[45]

The Queen symbolized the beautiful, frivolous life and its perils. The lavish revues of the twentieth century would pluck her as arch-showgirl from the same costume wardrobe archives that delivered up other historical caricatures, including la comtesse du Barry, Lucrezia Borgia, Madame de Pompadour, Casanova, the Marquis de Sade, and Don Juan. The *ancien régime* balls were the sort of parties that gave the *fournisseurs* of Paris music-halls a model for opulent spectacle. Whether on the Parisian music-hall stage or in the Sofia Coppola movie, sumptuosity foreshadows the queen's gruesome finale. She has been the quintessential royal around whom to build a poignant glamour, used like a wedding cake in the center of a bake shop display.

When the Folies Bergère reopened after being refurbished in the early 1990s, the figure of Marie Antoinette appeared in white wig and roller skates and took a Charleston lesson from Josephine Baker, dressed in an outfit of pineapples. This was carrying parody of the queen to a desperate length, and the famous music-hall soon ceased staging showgirl extravaganzas.

Marie Antoinette was an antecedent to the showgirl, and the eighteenth-century court ladies of Versailles were generally an inspiration to the costumers of music-hall revues. This is why savvy 1920s showgirls the Dolly Sisters had the boudoir of the Marquise de Pompadour reproduced in their own chateau, or, in the midst of a very American story, a tulled Madame de Barry appears in the movie *George White's 1935 Scandals*. The richness of court dress would offer a challenge to costumers who tried to compete with its effect. Louis René Boquet's design for a costume of Mademoiselle Chevallier, preserved at the Metropolitan Museum of Art, has notes for copious decorations and an approximately 18 feet circumference. In the Jazz Era, such gowns would have to be dropped over showgirls' heads at the rear of the stage because nobody could walk down stairs in them.

Costumed for a Private Stage: Emma Hamilton

Lady Emma Hamilton (1765–1815) took to the stage (in Sir William Grenville's Neapolitan villa), choreographing and costuming the act all by herself.

Her costumes for the Attitudes she performed to great acclaim were inspired by the tunics and flowing robes of the Classical world. In a light chemise and using a shawl as an accessory she created poses of different characters and ushered in sensual tableaux vivants.

Born in poverty, her mother shortly widowed by her blacksmith husband, Emma went to work while still a girl. She lost her place as a lady's maid and took a job at an eatery frequented by a bohemian crowd of artists and musicians. Her bodice-ripping story continues with being a kept woman by a baronet (until she became pregnant and he spurned her), modeling for George Romney and Sir Joshua Reynolds, and being mistress to the Honorable Charles Grenville. He married for money and passed her to his widowed uncle, Sir William Grenville. Grenville, a diplomat, volcanologist, and connoisseur of antiquities when they were being excavated from Pompeii, was envoy to the royal court of Naples when, in 1786, he was persuaded to marry Emma (he was 61 and she 26). In 1798, with a ring on her finger, Emma began an adulterous and blatant relationship with the great Lord Horatio Nelson. They met when he sailed into Naples to gain the King's assent in the war against Napoléon. Together they would have a child (Emma has descendants today).

Early on, though, Emma and Sir William formed a perfect pair. She ingratiated herself with the Queen of Naples, and Emma's poses, which she called Attitudes, were a display case for the vases, urns, and statuary he was collecting. She was eager to become cultivated and put her old life behind her; he in turn delighted in her beauty and enjoyed showing her to society. To please Sir William, Emma took his passion for Classical myths and history and grafted on it her bold verve, creating pantomimes of legendary figures. The Attitudes began when Sir William objected to how a limb of a marble statue of Athena, located in the royal galleries of Naples, had been renovated. Emma took the same pose and Sir William marveled when she got it exactly right. When she started to imitate the figures in his collection, Sir William coached her.

She developed a show for her husband and then for the elite world. It involved moving from pose to pose in a range of what built to 200 different pantomimes. Thousands of tourists to Naples came to see her perform the artistic Attitudes, of Venus, Cleopatra, Helen of Troy, Niobe, Danae being showered with gold by Zeus, and more. She also performed male characters, such as a blinded Oedipus and Orestes sacrificing his sister, in a short tunic. For the female roles such as the Three Graces, the Baccantes, Hebe and Juno, Emma wore a light, loose muslin chemise copied from Sir William's Etruscan vases or ancient Greek images, swished shawls as props around her body, and wore flowers. She flipped through the Attitudes with only a pause between. The Attitudes, if often sexually charged, were acceptably high-brow, and received stellar praise from Goethe, Horace Walpole, and naturally Sir William. Walpole called Emma "Sir William's Gallery of Statues."[46]

A caricature by Thomas Rowlandson in 1791 shows a naked Lady Hamilton performing the Attitudes before a group of lusting men. The satire touched on the reaction this revolutionary performance provoked and on Emma's personal background. It is likely that in an early incarnation she was a mannequin in the "Temple of Health" which was run by a galvanist who treated people, mainly couples, for infertility. She may also have danced on the baronet's tables and seen the impersonations, called Attitudes, which were a stock in trade of brothels. Emma did her movements in Naples and then London not naked but scantily dressed. The first time she entertained Sir William's guests she was in a huge box, turned upright and painted black inside, and usually she performed by candlelight for greater effect.

Not only was Emma linked to Marie Antoinette through her play-acting but also Sir William presented Emma to the Queen while she was in the Bastille, shortly before she was beheaded. Emma was gratified to have touched the Queen and very moved. Emma made showing off the female body acceptable.

Daring Ballet Costumes at the Paris Opera

The owners, impresarios, and designers of music-halls invented a multi-sensory aesthetic where costumes strove for gorgeousness. Much was shaped on stylistic nostalgia for mythical joy and luxury. Yet as a new frontier the music-hall also borrowed "sideways" from living sources, the ballet, discussed in this section, and the circus, discussed later.

In the Renaissance, Venetian courtesans had revealing clothes and sometimes wore divided legs and were much admired. But a reaction in Europe set in during the Counter-Reformation, so that revealing clothes signaled a red-light district. Surprisingly the move to more exposure of the body was at the august Paris Opera and for practical reasons (shocking attire that allowed spritely dancing) as the art of dance developed. The French ballet became famous before the French Revolution for sexual allure and the most daring costumes in Europe.

Their mode was to tantalize. Showgirls in the music-hall and dancers and actresses at the Paris Opera shared a reputation for sexual independence; revealing costumes furnished their appropriate dress. The entertainers were not at the bottom of the social ladder, although it was not a healthy life, that is, Paris Opera dancers, skinny, chilled, and working long hours, suffered disproportionately from tuberculosis. Another commonality was that music-halls hired ballerinas and brought in balletic dancers from the beginning. Spectators that never would have attended the Paris Opera received a classy treat at the music-halls whenever a well-known dancer or tableau in the style of the ballet was appropriated. Moreover, a performer on the legitimate stage became more famous if she accepted a billet at one of the more prestigious music-halls.

Since ballet garments in all decades tended to the avant-garde, leading rather than responding to fashion trends, the music-hall had countless ideas to borrow from. Until the seventeenth century, ballet had been performed with masks and costumes that followed court fashion. The decorations and headdresses identified the role. *How to Compose a Successful Ballet* advised costumes with matching headdresses, and to simulate the real thing by candlelight, to use silver and gold colored tinsel. For the *Ballet des Fêtes de Bacchus* (1651), a noble portraying Autumn had headgear like an upturned broomstick to represent wheat sheaves and an overflowing cornucopia; and the River of Forgetfulness was strewn with artificial poppies and had plumes swishing from a high fur hat, representing waves.[47] Since the dancers were amateurs, courtiers who danced in the ballets as their aristocratic privilege, they surely needed all the technical coaxing a director could impose. Carol Lee, a historian of dance, points to what Saint-Hubert was formalizing, the means "to produce a continuously changing visual display."[48] How similar the aim of Saint-Hubert seems to that of the director of the showgirl spectacular three centuries later.

When a director sets a play and its costumes ahistorically, it wakes up the audience; moreover, the choice is usually not arbitrary. A third explanation is the simple fact that one cannot costume entirely to a period. Franco Zeffirelli filmed *Romeo and Juliet* in vaguely Italian Renaissance clothes that a half-century later look to me like the year I graduated from college and he made his movie, 1968. Costumes derive from what we wear partly in a way that cannot be perceived until later.

The seventeenth-century master of the art of theatrical dance championed invention and clarity (easy identification) for costumes. The really fabulous costumes that he championed, however, were for men. Women had roles in the elegant court dances but Saint-Hubert threw up his hands when it came to making their costumes exciting, as long dresses and an established silhouette left little room to transform female dancers into something other.

This might seem an intractable negative whereas it would have for the history of women on stage a positive consequence: the intermingling of women's fashion with the costumes they put on for court theatricals and dances effectively bound fashion and costume together. Feminine fashions encompassed feminine costumes all the way through the showgirl/music-hall period. A Parisian showgirl in the early music-hall period would wear a flamenco-like costume that suggested lightly a Spanish senorita, or garb herself as a polar bear, whereas a man's costume would tend to go the whole distance to mask and transform him.

Claude-François Ménestrier, a Jesuit choreographer, in his *Des Ballets anciens et modernes selon les règles du théâtre* (1682) devoted a chapter to "l'Appareil," sets and costumes. He asserted that fashionable attire was more of a problem than asset. It matters so much because in a ballet the clothes speak for the unspeaking actors.

Costumes should not be cumbersome (*embarrassant*) but leave the legs and body free to dance, though this applied just to men as the costumes worn by female dancers were the least suitable to dancing. Unlike most writing about the stage of that period, which tends to abstraction, Père Ménestrier declared just what he meant by à propos.[49]

Verisimilitude seemed his chief judgment of costumes, virtually all of which were allegorical. A religious figure could be in red, patterned with gold crosses; Night was black covered with stars and a crescent of the moon on his head; flame-colored hearts covered Love, dressed in pink; and Envy's yellow robe was decorated with open eyes. Feathers wafted on the heads of Winds, Spring wore a crown of roses while Fall wore vines. Rivers should be in wavy outfits but Père Ménestrier went further—the Tage River in the Iberian Peninsula for example required "paillettes d'or" because of its golden sand. Ménestrier embraced costumes as a dramatic opportunity—a colorful costume all of ribbons seen on an actor in Turin, a headdress, earrings, and hands and face painted black for a Moor, or big feather bouquets for Zephyrs, for example, and he seems to have looked to many nations for gorgeous prototypes. That said, women had to be dressed in the fashion of the day, accessorized and decorated to "speak" their roles.

The basic garment of female dancers was the same as the fashion for dresses for another century until the advent of story ballets or "ballets d'action." Jean-George Noverre, credited for putting ballets with dramatic plots onto the Paris Opera stage, in his *Lettres* of 1758–1760 tossed the old costume tradition aside. His theorizing was based on having created many ballets.

> Take off the enormous wigs and gigantic hairdos, that cause the head to lose its just proportions that it ought to have in relation to the body. Abandon the usage of the stiff and unnatural bustles that deprive the movement of its charms, disfigure the elegance of poses, and erase the beauty of the contours that the bust should have in its different positions.... I endorse reducing three-quarters of the ridiculous corsetry of our female dancers.[50]

He described specific combinations of sets and costumes to create a foil (*répoussoir*) for the action and make a ballet scintillate. A rich setting in Constantinople should have relatively simple costumes, a blue castle needs costumes of contrasting colors and design, the strongest colored costumes should be those in the background lest they recess, and so on.

Towards 1800 and in the first decade of the nineteenth century, neo-classical costumes changed dance, and dance costumes inspired fashion. Salvatore Viganò, a Neapolitan dancer, met Maria Medina in Spain and they married and became a dancing couple. Maria inspired shoe design and hairstyles, enthralled the emperor, and Beethoven composed a minuet "à la Viganò." Of her dance attire the Viennese writer Caroline Pichler wrote that the fluttering crepe skirts were like a *falabas* (wraparound in West African style) when they fluttered in the day, and that her whole body could be seen in the flesh colored *trikot*.[51] When she became pregnant, the ladies of Vienna arranged the draperies of their dresses to imitate her plump abdomen; the mode was called a *Viganobauch*.[52]

Now dancers at the opera had shorter costumes and a new freedom of movement, but the flowers and feathers on the heads of the women in their sheer costumes continued to be a means to identify and draw attention to characters. Sometimes it looks as though a dancer is tripping lightly despite wearing a palm tree or tower of sweetmeats on her head.

The ballerina Marie Camarago raised her hemline several inches, high enough to perform what hitherto had been done only by her male partners.[53] "La Camarago" is credited as the first woman to execute the *entrechat,* in which dancers crisscross their legs midair. The turmoil caused by exposing her calves was only resolved when she consented to wear "calecons de precaution" (briefs or under-drawers). She and Monsieur Maillot, *bonnetier fournisseur* of the opera in the 1820s, are credited with the invention of a tightly knitted garment covering the hips. This was pink or white, silk for the star and cotton for the corps de ballet. It was thick and pleated and known as the *maillotier*, similar to the French word for bathing suit today. Other dancers adopted the new shorter style of dress, which resulted in a police order requiring the briefs with it.

At the Paris Opera, costumes changed to lighter and shorter, and slippers and sandals replaced the high heels that inhibited, but identified the elite of the time. Pierre Gardel was the master of ballet at the opera from 1787, surviving the Terror, the First Empire and Restoration. His wife Marie played Psyche in a production of that name in 1788 and wore a dress that had an unboned handkerchief-like bodice with shoulder straps, which embroidered ribbons tied to the high waist. The dress dropped only to her knees, and at the hem, appliqued acanthus leaves and bands of color, like on a Roman fresco, drew attention to her legs.

In this period when neo-classicism pervaded the arts, there was a new attempt to match the drama of the ballet with costumes, usually classically inspired. Clothilde Chameroy, a star dancer, had different roles in *Télémaque*, which debuted in 1790, stayed in the repertory for 36 years, and played 408 times. She danced as Calypso in a draped blouson and skirt gathered and tied at the center waist, which ended mid-thigh. A series of ribbons decorated the border hem. Clothide also triumphed as Cupid, a role usually played by a man. Gender transgression was established, thus, in costume much before the variety acts and skits in fin de siècle music-halls.

When Swedish-born Charles-Louis Didelot produced and danced in ballets in Paris, St. Petersburg and London he had people flying on wires to represent mythological creatures. Dropping in from above had a long tradition, in the religious floats in Italian pageants and ballets at the court of Versailles. According to the authors of *Dance as a Theater Art*, in the Biblical episodes portrayed on the moving floats, the apparatus of wires and wood was hidden by cloth springing with stars.[54] But there was no pretense of sacred underpinnings in Didelot's shows. He danced the part of Zephyr, the West Wind, who falls in love with a nymph, his real-life wife Rose, in a spectacle that, with its illusion of weightlessness, must have been magical, but brought opprobrium in London in 1797. The dancers wore pink stockings, breasts were apparent through sheer fabric, and skirts were shorter than on Scottish highlanders. At the House of Lords a discussion was ongoing related to a divorce case on March 2, 1798, when the Bishop of Durham rose and railed against Didelot's female dancers: "The indecency of those appearances far out-shamed any thing of a similar nature that had ever been exhibited."[55]

The ballet was postponed and when it re-emerged the dancers had less revealing costumes as well as white stockings to replace the pink ones.

In 1800, the ballerina's costume tended to be white, Grecian-style and show her legs and thighs when she danced. Under this she had on flesh-colored (at least in Paris) tights of cotton or silk, and the silk leotard called a *maillot*, after the director of the Paris Opera. The costumer didn't have to go too far from contemporary dress to have skimpy costumes. An illustration of Mademoiselle Bigottini starring in *Le Carnaval de Venise* (1816) shows her with Grecian-style hair and sandals, wearing a wispy dress that is practically all skirt, as her shoulders and back are naked, and breasts barely covered. The tunic has fur trimmings and triangular cutouts tipped with little bells. The character she played was a countess who abducts a suitor to force him to prove his love for her.[56]

A close study of documents related to the 87 female dancers who appeared at the opera in the first quarter of the nineteenth century revealed that most had short careers (less than five years). Some had gallant adventures and others led model lives; whether minors or married, they were "emancipated ... from all parental or moral tutelage, and they lived as they pleased."[57] Two points that Natalie Lecomte uncovered suggest correlations with the belle époque showgirls.

First there is the instance of Mademoiselle Delisle (born around 1696). She was the mistress of the depraved Charles, Comte de Charolais, a Condé whose villainy has been considered a model for some of the Marquis de Sade's activities. In exchange for her favors he paid her dressmaker's bills; one spring she was seen on the Paris stage "dressed in a costume of pure silver that cost two thousand *écus* to dance a solo in the current opera [Philomèle]."[58]

Secondly, just as the music-hall showgirls portrayed frivolous, bubbly roles, so the dancers at the Paris Opera, from the time women first were allowed onto the stage in 1681, got the lightweight or positive parts: Venus, Diana and Flora and their corteges; nymphs, baccantes, dryads, nereids, mermaids, priestesses and huntresses, country girls and shepherdesses, the Hours but not the Arts, and so forth. "In general, roles associated with the destructive power of nature, such as winds, or those conjuring up the sulphurous infernal world, were male specialties. Of course, women could incarnate fairies (the female equivalent of enchanters, their usual companions), but there was no female elf or genie."[59] Men also got the roles of female witches and furies.

Within the parameters of the upbeat, the female dancers had access to colorful roles, which sound like a page out of the music-hall revues, as lady sailors and gondoliers in nautical fêtes or commedia dell'arte characters often reserved for men, in scenes of masked balls and carnivals.

A designer of ballets at the opera, Auguste Garneray, had a window of opportunity during the Bourbon Restoration to push the aesthetic envelope. Judith Chazin-Bennahum, in her study *The Lure of Perfection: Fashion and Ballet, 1780–1830*, describes what Garneray created for the ballet that went with the opera *Aladin* (1822):

> Bigottini wore a bustier molded in a skin-colored jersey, a kind of very short, transparent and peach-colored loin cloth, along with a white oriental scarf floating along her legs.... Mademoiselle Caroline's costumed role was even more shocking than Bigottini. She wore a white muslin, thigh-length tunic. Other dancers who played "bayaderes" also wore practically nothing—a little half-skirt, all of it transparent, with a pearl-decorated scarf over the shoulders and the hips. Here, Garneray created an oriental fantasy, the kind of hothouse setting that exploited the public's taste for fantasy and exoticism.[60]

Gradually, writes Chazin-Bennahum, the social status of the opera dancers went down in the course of the nineteenth century.[61] By the time the music-hall era began, ballerinas at the august opera were apparently recruited from the slums, depicted by Degas as trying to catch a rich patron in the notorious *foyer de la danse*. Then again, posing as a dancer or actress would have been a frequent ploy of prostitutes.

Giving the illusion of more nakedness than there is has constituted an inveterate trick, through to Léon Bakst's costumes for *Schéhérazade* of the Ballets Russes. Valerie Steele describes flesh-colored midriffs built into the costumes of dancing girls and concubines, "costumes with billowing pants, in colors such as bright green or hot pink, whose amplitude contrasted with form-fitting bodices which gave the effect of brassiere-like tops, exposing a belt of flesh."[62]

The diaphanous, filmy fabric and pastel shades of the ballerina costumes had an effect on the popular images of the feminine. Thus, when in the mid–nineteenth century Gaiety Girls became the rave on the burlesque stage in London, Captain Alfred Thompson, who had studied art in Paris, introduced light, lacy pastels with delicate detail, identified as a French style.[63] In the 1890s in America the Gibson Girls were fragile flowers in pale, sherbet-hued, lacy concoctions.

Trademark French Style and Gallic National Character

The spectators' expectancy of ooh-la-la completes the excitement of costumes. French culture has been associated by foreigners with sexiness first of all, and sexy entertainment furthermore, which has added the *je ne sais quoi*. After seeing women dance during an interlude of Italian opera, Abigail Adams wrote from Autueil to a friend in America,

> I felt my delicacy wounded, and I was ashamed to bee seen to look at them. Girls cloathed in the thinest Silk and Gauze, with their petticoats short. Springing two foot from the floor, poising themselves in the air, with their feet flying, and as perfectly shewing their Garters and draws as tho no peticoat had been worn, was a sight altogether new to me.[64]

It is a case of perception. The message is that French sexuality is steamy and naughty— as in "French kiss" or "French letter" (a condom). Whether at the 1900 world's fair, during the six months when officials of many nations met in Paris to sort out the new map of Europe at the close of World War I, or when American tourists came on Cook's Tours seeking titillation in the 1950s, foreigners found what they had fantasized, visible on the music-hall stage. The titillation was free of consequence, a mere surface sparkle of sensation.

From a lifetime of studies on the travels of Americans abroad, William Chew III has developed a theory of the origins and continuity of the cliché of randy French culture. Visitors of the first wave were Protestant merchants from the Eastern seaboard prior to the American Revolution. Mercy Warren warned her son Winslow, traveling to France in 1781, "France, the seat of dissipation, where luxury is refined upon, and enormities are fashionable that would put a savage to the blush."[65]

Along with censuring the French for perceived immorality was fascination with the Frenchwoman and her charming dress and manners. Washington Irving observed, "I have seen a pretty Grisette who had put on her short gown and petticoat—her red apron and her large cap in so piquante a manner as to attract the attention from a belle decorated in all the finery of the last fashion."[66] On the other hand, dancers at the Paris Opera who

The fitting of a made to measure costume by a dressmaker. Illustration by A. Vallée from *Paris Plaisirs* no. 28, June 1926 (Mary Evans/Everett Collection).

showed a bit of calf and had tightly fitted outfits with décolletage shocked American sensibilities as improprietous. Abigail Adams wrote, "There is not a lady in our country, who would have gone abroad to dine so little dressed."[67]

Apercus of French Sexuality

William L. Chew III[68]

Late twentieth-century apercus of French sexuality all indicated a stark stereotyping of French manners and mores by American observers. Such clichés are not only durable but in the making. Applying Fernand Braudel's concept of durée historique to the history mentalities—as Braudel himself did—then we must certainly search for the origins of these stereotypes in the longue durée or the durée moyenne. Cultural stereotypes are not formed on the level of history événementielle, where politics are played out, though political categories or developments (such as domestic or international tensions) can, however, influence or color already existing or inherited stereotypes. Thus a working hypothesis would lead us to reasonably expect the origin and prominence of the stereotype of French sensuality in periods in which heightened contact—as against first exposure—of Americans and the French made a significant enough impact on the formation of perceptions of national character to have a lasting effect. The first period of heightened contact was, of course, the revolutionary and Napoléonic era, a period in which the American national character was still in the making, and Americans were still very much English in their attitudes. Thus, cultural baggage and the contemporary diplomatic and political setting were to help determine the perception of American observers.

Thomas Perkins, in a journal entry of April 23, 1795, commented on the dress of actresses in a performance of *Telemachus* at the Paris Opera: "The nymphs, upwards of forty in number, were dressed with all the wantonness imaginable: their dancing, too, is to us Americans, indecent in the extreme."[69]

Similarly, William Lee, American envoy to Bordeaux, confided in his journal after going to the theater there in 1796:

> The dress of the actresses I do not like. Their arms are generally uncovered and one of their breasts. There were a number of elegant dancers, but their figures disgusted me ... their chemises ... though longer than their petticoats ... did not come below the knees. A silk net covered part of their arms, their breasts, and the lower part of their bodies, of a flesh color, so that at a distance I thought they were half naked; for this cobweb covering was drawn over them so tight that you could discover every muscle. Such indecent representations can never lead the mind to virtue. All the exhibitions I have been at appeared to me to be calculated only to inspire libidinous thoughts.[70]

The evidence mounts up. Washington Irving wrote a friend, Alexander Beebee, in September 1804 that American girls would hardly dare to look at such a "shameless exposure" through their fans[71] and in March 1815, Maria Bayard, a New York merchant's daughter, characterized ballet costumes as "shocking indelicate, the dress is made to fit their shapes as tight as possible."[72] Only two travelers glorified the physical display of female theater performers, one of whom, the American Wanderer, remarked that "a delicious exquisitely formed female" would exhibit herself in such a fashion as to "force a dying saint to recollect he was a man."[73]

To give Abigail Adams credit for broadmindedness, she was indeed shocked by the girls at the ballet "perfectly showing their garters as though no petticoat had been worn." But she grew accustomed to the French manners and came to enjoy the dances, confessing "that repeatedly seeing these dances has worn off that disgust, which I at first felt, and that I see them now with pleasant."[74]

In the final analysis, the image of the French as depicted in the travel accounts of Americans sojourning in France during 1775–1815 is remarkably similar to the modern stereotype, suggesting that the contemporary cliché built upon earlier, eighteenth-century perceptions.

The perception of sexy costumes preceded the actual costumes of female stage performers. The fin de siècle courtesans who did their stints on the music-hall stage had the effect because their sizzle carried over to their offstage personae. The line dancers at the Folies Bergère were a tease which the bolder spectator could carry forward by engaging the services of a tart that cruised the *promenoir*. The showgirl might be a chaste wife or ingénue but her costume provoked the naughty image that France held for foreigners back to the eighteenth century.

Le Bal des Quat'z Arts

Masked balls were important antecedents of the showgirl spectaculars because they combined the display of a patrician party with the opportunity for debauchery (or reputation for same). Masquerading only took a pause in Paris with the Revolution. Already under the Directory outdoor dances had a masquerade theme, as some Merveilleuses wore red necklaces to identify with the victims of the Terror. A concert hall from early in the century, the Elysées Montmartre at 80, Boulevard Rochechouart, was the most famous of numerous establishments to hold masked balls in the city. Sundays and Thursdays, all who came to the Elysées wore disguises. A bas-relief of a woman swirling in dance was brought from the old Bal Mabille; today it stands at the entrance of the entertainment hall called Le Trianon.

When Alva Erskine Smith, a socialite from Mobile, Alabama, attended boarding school in Paris in the 1860s she must have wished to attend such a masked ball. When she married William Vanderbilt, she and her husband built a chateau at 660 Fifth Avenue in New York which she christened with a costume party with French touches. Mrs. Vanderbilt's ball became legendary for reconciling the louche with the high-class. Mrs. Cornelius Vanderbilt II was literally lit up as "Electric Light," Miss Kate Strong had a taxidermied cat on her head, cat tails on her skirt, and a diamond crown, and Alva Vanderbilt herself was a Venetian princess in a fabulous dress whose cap was a jeweled peacock. Dozens of men were dressed as Louis XVI with powdered wigs, and dancers in matching all-white costumes danced an eighteenth-century quadrille. Professional photographs were taken of many of the guests, so we see not only over-the-top Gilded Age impressions of Bourbon attire, but costumes that could be a page from a music-hall program, like a woman dressed as a hornet with a headdress of diamonds. The ball was undoubtedly inspired by the French culture of masked balls and was the sort of party that gave the music-halls a model for opulent spectacle.

The female nude in France conjures up a marble Artemis in the bosk of a chateau, or Nereids splashing in a fountain in Paris. But nakedness in French culture has also been associated with parody, in political cartoons and in a medieval saturnalia called the *Fête des Fous* (Feast of Fools). This red-letter day fell on the Jour des Innocents, December 28, in many localities of rural France. Priests wore crazy masks, sang obscene songs, and did sacrilege like eating sausage on the altar and burning old shoes in the censers. The idea was the inversion of the social order and the central ceremony involved taking individuals, sometimes priests, naked from their beds to the church, where they were doused with water at the altar. The celebration was forbidden in the mid–fifteenth century,[75] but Victor Hugo casts Quasimodo as the "pope" of the *Fête des Fous*, paraded by revelers as the ugliest person in Paris, in his *Hunchback of Notre Dame*. The fête demonstrates how broad public nudity was in France until Parisian art students reinvented it as artistic spectacle.

Parisian carnivals were permitted after a hiatus, in the Second Republic. Celebrants masqueraded, played pranks, danced all night and paraded in bawdy company. The students of the branches of architecture, painting, sculpture, and engraving of the Ecole des Beaux Arts initiated the first Bal des Quat'z Arts in 1892. A joint ball (hence the "Quatre") was the idea of Henri Guillaume, professor of architecture, and the balls became a tradition. In the parade, artists' models posed in scantily clad costumes as part of tableaux vivants and floats, recreating academic paintings which depicted nude females. From 1900, the ball had a different historical motif each year, such as ancient Rome, the Vikings, Carthage, and Samurai; and prizes of champagne were awarded for the most artistic or daring hand-crafted costume. The second of these balls was at the Moulin Rouge. This was, according to Charles Castle, the origin of the striptease, when two girls on tables were judged for who had the prettiest legs, thighs, hips, breasts, buttocks and shoulders.[76] Several models at this second iteration of the Bal were arrested for nudity outside the Moulin Rouge, flashing to irritate passers-by. The Bal always ended with, writes Mel Gordon, "a drunken orgy of naked bodies and made sprints into the Seine by those still able to stand."[77] The second year, the Bal provoked a student riot and a young man sitting in a café was killed by police. Of a model named Marie-Florentine Roger who was arrested and may have committed suicide in connection with the goings-on, the poet and absinthe drinker Raoul Ponchon wrote, "O! Sarah Brown! Si l'on t'emprisonne, pauvre ange, Le dimanche, j'irai t'apporter des oranges" (Oh, Sarah Brown! If they take you off to prison, poor angel, On Sunday I'll come bringing you oranges).[78] A few rioters who were imprisoned were lightly fined and released, whereas the prefect of the Paris police was fired. Writes Castle, "in championing Mona, the first 'nude' in Parisian show business, the students had proved once again that the French capital had the democratic right to choose liberté—in any sense it wished."[79]

The combination of artiness and debauchery had a great appeal. Parisians vied for invitations and the accent remained on creative costumes. All who came had to be thoroughly costumed: the invitation read, "Le comité sera impitoyable pour tout costume qui ne serait pas de l'époque" (the committee will show no mercy to anyone whose costume isn't on the theme).[80]

Four years later, a separate tradition of a carnival parade was revived after having been forbidden (as a disturbance) after the armistice between France and Prussia in 1871. At the carnival "the 'sauvages' wore tall feathers and there was a masquerade of antique, medieval, and modern costumes, with druids, Olympians, allegorical figures, Turks, Chinese, horsemen and archers."[81]

These student happenings in France went back to carnival parades and also to the *Fête des Fous*. Interestingly, this popular tradition of costume ribaldry was definitely on the lighthearted side of masking, and a reversal of the status quo. At the saturnalia, no one was really scared nor were masks used it seems as an excuse for crime, and the Bals functioned as displays of creativity and energy of the artistic sector, and renewal of Gallic spirit. Crazy dress-up and let's pretend were to get public attention and demonstrate student solidarity. It was individualistic yet effectively communal. As C.G. Jung put it in 1928, "The persona is a complicated system of relations between individual consciousness and society, fittingly enough a kind of mask, designed on one hand to make a definite impression upon others, and on the other, to conceal the true nature of the individual."[82]

The music critic Michel Calvocoressi, a friend of Maurice Ravel's and the French adviser to Serge de Diaghilev, described the 1908 Bal des Quat'z Arts, which was held at

Neuilly so as to be outside the city limits: "There were many naked women, and men in a ceinture of bones that concealed nothing." He said that when he left at four in the morning he saw a naked woman calmly standing in the street, smoking a cigarette, and surrounded by a crowd.[83]

The music-hall built on the idea of nudity as theatrical divertissement or burlesque. It co-opted nudity which went from spontaneous celebration of the carnival and Bal des Quat'z Arts to an indoors, choreographed element with a new vocabulary for revealing clothes—*bustier, cache-tetons, bijoux de seins, le string, coiffure de plumes*. The costume of the showgirl left her face free and her expression neutral. Her sexual morals might be chaste but in phenomenal terms, she was like a whorehouse with its shutters closed, or a statue in movement, bedecked but unreal. The "free spirits" who attended the masked student balls of the Incohérents pushed imaginative costumes to the limit.

Shopping and the Stage: Fashion Reciprocity

While the seedy side of the showgirl life is often remarked, the brilliant Mel Gordon, who has studied the entertainment underworld, paints a contrasting picture. He theorized that the danceuses in the "nude" spectaculars could experience their métier as a glamorous and frivolous priviledged calling of the ideal Parisienne.

> In the French entertainment industry, women were given certain corners, like choreography, and gay men were the costumers. In France it matched perfectly because the culture was set up this way. As it was such a huge industry, tons of showgirls felt creative, had interesting lives, and embraced the work while others were merely showcased or exploited, and hated it. Overall, the expectation in America from corresponding periods was to look great, marry, and talk to your grandchildren about your life on stage, where revues offered a flexibility and mobility, and the nightclubs were a huge industry.[84]

Music-hall performers were admired as a distinct caste above prostitutes. Their "look," their costumes and how they wore them, caused spectators to toast their beauty from the fin de siècle through the Jazz Era. The costumes were inventions on a fashion knife-blade: They had to be acceptable to a largely bourgeois audience yet be a little shocking. To meet this demand there were mostly independent design workshops with their own "costumiers" and "premiéres" (head seamstresses), so, although couturiers have contributed to shows, beginning with Paul Poiret, the music-hall costumes ran parallel with fashion, with reciprocal glances. Moreover, with the advent of upscale department stores, the costumes needed to be distinctive from the flood of common clothing, hats and undergarments, fabrics and trimmings, shoes and makeup available to all to look at and some to buy in the stores.

The showgirl costume aesthetic spread in international entertainment as designers, mostly in Paris, imagined costumes to star in the fragile reality of the revue.

According to Michele Majer, the establishment in the 1850s and 1860s of a couture industry "intensified and underscored the existing reciprocal relationship between fashion and theater.... For the actress, a selection of eye-catching custom-made gowns was imperative in securing principal roles and in achieving and maintaining a fashionable position in the public eye."[85] A leading actress who wasn't wearing Worth, wrote a columnist named Pierre Véron for *Le Monde Illustré,* "runs the risk of remaining disdained and ignored among the cheap chorus girls."[86] Moreover, the theater magazines had advertisements for dressmakers and businesses, just as a twentieth-century French movie might credit this or that outfit as "habillé par." *Le Théâtre* offered readers a shopping service, literally. What women saw

DERNIÈRE MODE

"Dernière Mode," by Georges Mouton, a genre and portrait painter, showing a cancan dancer. Postcard, 1909.

on stage sparked consumption, which fashion and theater publications knit together.[87] Meanwhile its sexual charge stimulated virility; thus showgirls were patriotic citizens during World War I. What the showgirl costume took from the luxury clothes market was a high quality of craft and financial investment as well. Josephine Baker or Andrée Spinelly was not going to wear or be satisfied with ragbag costumes; moreover, after costumer Erté made her a silver lame dress, Spinelly told Erté, "I never pay for anything." Another means to dazzle at the turn-of-the-century was to have one's lovers buy one's stage clothes.[88] Public expectation was for the high quality of couture. The showgirl's stage costumes blended in the public mind with what she wore to Maxim's. But generally the costumes were a huge draw and edgy witness to the lofty accomplishments of the luxury trades. Thus when Le Crazy Horse partnered with a high-end underwear designer, Aubade, in 2016, the nightclub turned it into a promotional gambit, fashion becoming like a headlining star.

When the means of dissemination of commercial products on the European continent was the bazaar, the Duke of Burgundy himself would ride to Bruges or beyond for a fair to see what velvets and satins merchants were selling, and the latest style of border cutouts (such as daggings) for themselves and their horses. From the eighteenth century, Parisian chic magnetized the haves; before the French Revolution, fashion dolls were exported throughout Europe and to the United States, and illustrative plates in fashion magazines informed on what was in. In the mid–nineteenth century the bourgeoisie had exacting standards of attire that required a set of clothing for each activity, and women changed their outfits several times a day. Bourgeois culture was consumer culture, effectuated by the sheer proliferation of garments and trimmings produced once sewing machines were used in manufacturing. A remark of Ernest Hemingway's when he and his wife Hadley were in Paris in about 1922 testifies to the importance of a classy look, which stores and music-halls were fully aware of: "I saw my wife trying not to look at the strange, steerage clothes that Miss Stein wore."[89]

Michael B. Miller animates the eclectic extravagance of that new phenomenon the department store—the crush of consumers manipulated by displays, events and clever pricing, and tours for the awestruck of the store. When there was a white sale, it conjured up the frenzy of the cancan: "the entire store was adorned in white: white sheets, white towels, white curtains, white flowers, *ad infinitum*, all forming a single *blanc* motif that covered even stairways and balconies."[90]

Today we would not describe the experience of going to a department store as similar to seeing an extravaganza on stage or film. Yet an article in the contemporary press (*L'Orphé*) did just that on January 5, 1886: "all in the end shimmer, sound, and run together … and one remains dazzled, dazed for some time while trying to recover the necessary stability to arrive at some sort of judgment."[91]

The Universal Exhibitions in Paris in 1888 and 1900 declared to the world that Paris reigned over fashion as the grandest bazaar. The city was reclaiming tourism and cultural leadership after war with the Prussians. Millions of local people and tourists from elsewhere attended. A rolling electric raised sidewalk ran from the Champ de Mars to the Invalides, and the visitors pursued the classic French entertainment of people-watching. The 1900 world's fair was "devoted to the ephemeral and the fashionable," its focal point being a 16-foot high "effigy of a woman sporting the most up-to-date creations of Paris haute couture." Haute couturier Jeanne Paquin was tasked with designing the effigy's costume; admirers of the statue's dress could obtain patterns through the newspaper *La Mode Illustrée*. Colin Jones writes that "the show seemed to demonstrate that style—a rather feminine, decorative style at that—*was* the substance which made Paris so distinctive, so radiant, so up-to-date, so modern."[92] Madame Paquin was president of the fashion section of the Great Universal Exhibition of 1900, and a master of plumes and aigrettes.

It seems amazing from the present perspective how in league the music-hall and the fashion industry were. According to Sarah Gutsche-Miller, "By 1900, stylish Parisians could ill afford to miss Folies Bergère premieres, which were by then major society events. The halls had become fashion runways for the upper classes and premieres occasions for patrons to show off their latest purchases."[93] Dressmakers and milliners, says Gutsche-Miller, waited until the beginning of the Folies Bergère season to launch new collections. The stores had clothes in fabrics already cut to the length of the fashion. With it one bought a lithograph and sewing guide. The sewing machine was in general use and machine-made trimmings like lace, braid, fringe and ribbons were sold widely (lace was displayed at the first Paris world's fair in 1867).

Dressing elegantly was of more importance to the mistresses of the day than the wives. The more elegant toilettes were seen in the audience Tuesday through Saturday; at the music-halls, the other two days were typically attended by the common people.[94]

Actresses and music-hall performers also acted as models for fashion houses. Being seen at smart places in clothes from the newest collections had symbiotic benefit for the wearers and the dressmakers. That Cléo de Mérode was seen in the company of Leopold of Belgium, or Gaby Deslys with Crown Prince Wilhelm of Germany strongly endorsed their fashions. Gaby's hats came from Maison Lewis in London and inspired Cecil Beaton for those Audrey Hepburn wore in *My Fair Lady*. King Manual of Portugal saw Gaby in the production *Sans Rancune* in 1909 in white arctic fox and ropes of pearls which were then copied on chic clothes without the element of risqué. As display pieces, the wearers were like movie stars, fitting to a tee Andrea Stuart's observation of the showgirl as "a female icon whose power rests not on her virtue but on her moral ambiguity, an icon who has been able to carve out that territory between Madonna and whore that many of us dream of inhabiting."[95] These demimondaines were enviable erotic symbols for the very reason they could go from costume to fashion. They exhibited sexual availability in the risqué clothes on stage which they confirmed by a gossiped-about private life with adoring male company off stage.

Yet for all the impression on style made by female performers, the music-hall impresario had to self-monitor the taste of the costumes. Laurence Senelick notes that "the chorus girls were often untrained and hired from brothels or the streets."[96] Revues were "sexual showcases" that "euphemized the prostitutes in public places." If a showgirl dressed like a fine lady, this would offend the self-regard of the haute bourgeoisie. The showgirl costume had to be extravagant rather than reflect the most put-together fashion sense. For example, fuchsia and orange "said" showgirl costume, not elegant dress. This is supported by a remark in 1888 from a critic named Edmond Deschaumes, quoted by Professor Senelick:

> What really distinguishes the prostitute from the stage actress, someone who learns her trade from a pimp from a Conservatory student, is that the prostitute, who knows admirably how to undress before a rich and high-class man, is in complete ignorance of the art of dressing up to appear before the theater public.
>
> [Ce qui distingue en effet la prostituée de la comédienne, l'élève de la grand proxénité de l'élève du Conservatoire, c'est que la prostituée, qui sait admirablement se deshabiller devant un monsieur riche et de meilleur monde, ignore absolument l'art de vétir pour paraître devant des amateurs de théâtre.][97]

The music-hall stage existed in an elastic rapport with the fashion industry of Paris. They influenced, patronized, and displayed the fin de siècle and early twentieth century couture. Between the wars, Jacques-Charles of the Folies Bergère said the décor of the music-hall had come to look like a department store so that one looked for the signs for lingerie, house goods, and garden tools.

Napoléon Bonaparte had started a trend of the government encouraging women to buy and wear fine textiles made in France. Contrarily, there was an intense ideological movement in France in the decade before 1900 to limit the interests of middle-class women to the familial and reproductive, removed from the realms of fashion. They should decorate their homes and themselves; only *hommesses* wore plain clothes and rode bicycles. Having pretty lingerie, now, at department stores, more affordable, was a patriotic act by which a woman showed she was feminine and not that menace, a *nouvelle femme*. How it must have reassured men whose wives expressed a desire to aid their impoverished sisters, and gain some control over family finances, to go to the Moulin Rouge and bathe in women who were obviously not involved in any such departures from the status quo. The costumes were designed to seduce and the dancing (cancan, Spanish, etc.) practically mimed orgiastic sex. The vision of frivolous showgirls confirmed the bourgeois order every night. The ubiquitous man of letters Octave Uzanne belonged to the widespread aesthetic movement who raised up the delicacy of femininity of Madame de Pompadour and Marie Antoinette as models and railed against "androgynes." In work after work he advocated a return to the female adornment of pre–Revolutionary France. Writes Debora Silverman in her study of fin de siècle style and politics,

> Madame de Pompadour's exquisite costume represented her singularity; her bourgeois descendants could achieve an equivalent form of decorative distinction in their subtle and diaphanous undergarments. Uzanne envisioned the femme nouvelle replaced by the contemporary woman who created an exquisite "vision of a beneath," where her "delicate husband" could "lose himself in soft and evanescent delicacies of colors, groping for supremely sheer and sutble textures."[98]

The costuming of a revue took two decided aspects from the luxury clothes market: high quality of craft and sangfroid about expense. A showgirl like Josephine Baker was not going to be satisfied with quotidian costumes. We think of today's couture being over the top but, relatively, the bills for some Twenties costumes were hard to surpass. According to Angelo Luerti, authority on European costume art, the costume for Mistinguett to wear as the "Oiseau de Paris" at the Casino de Paris in the 1925 *Bonjour Paris* had an unsurpassed price tag. Florenz Ziegfeld in New York spared no expense as he was a costume perfectionist. His "magical touch"[99] was founded on attention to detail and educated by the dress designers who turned to doing risqué costumes for his shows: Alfred Edel and Erté from Paris, Lady Duff Gordon beginning in 1915 from England, and Ben Ali Haggin from the U.S. Ziegfeld followed Paris and mandated statuesque showgirls (at least 5'8"). Naked women could not move on stage so he glorified the female body in stationery poses. On the stage might be bevies of milkmaids, Fragonard-inspired girls on swings, clock faces and nymphs. For a salad number, the costumes were witty vegetables.

A spectator of a Ziegfeld show could go to a Fifth Avenue department store and purchase an evening gown she had admired on stage. A spectator at a Paris music-hall or someone who saw showgirls at Maxim's and wanted to emulate the dress might likewise find the dress goods pre-cut at the department store or go to the Faubourg Saint-Martin and find the same merchandise. And generally the costumes were a huge draw and a witness to the luxury trades.

It was because the world of fashion and decorative arts copied Paris that the city's music-halls worked so well as vitrines. People had made pilgrimages to the homes of French merchants in colonial New York City and Joseph Bonaparte's home in the

Delaware Valley personified elite French culture in the early 1800s. Even the State of Maine became appreciative of French decorative arts because of imports by sea, including the cargo of Marie Antoinette's furniture and belongings that a sea captain brought back from Le Havre to Maine's Midcoast, alas, not with the Queen as had been his plan. Despite the Civil War's devastation, American women wanted to know what was being worn in Paris. In the 1860s, a husband-and-wife team, Ellen and William Demorest, began to publish a "Mirror of Fashion," which took its place along *Godey's Ladies Book*. According to Gloria Groom, the prototype of the Parisienne by the 1860s and 1870s "occupied the center of a cultural wheel whose radiating spokes included the fashion industry and the avant-garde. As Arsène Houssaye, editor of *L'Artiste*, noted in 1869, there were only two ways to be a Parisienne—by birth or by dress."[100] Mrs. Demorest went to Paris every year to research style; by 1866, there were 300 branches of "Mme. Demorest's Magasin des Modes" in the U.S., Europe, Canada and Latin America.[101]

The nouveau riche in the U.S. yearned to rise permanently to an aristocratic status. They bought their way into titled families by giving their daughters irresistible dowries, and built houses in a grand style, e.g., in Newport, that they filled with opulent European furnishings. English landscape gardens and riding clothes, gems with European pedigrees, Italian silks and brocades, and marbles dug up from archaeological sites were necessary accoutrements to be upper class. For a French woman, dressing in the elegant merchandise created in her land was patriotic; for an American it was a dimension of striving for success in a fluid society.

Marine Costille in her analytic work on four music-halls describes the music-hall both as an "industrial sector" and "oligopole," and explains how the costumes for the most elaborate shows, at the Casino de Paris and the Folies Bergère, came from the department stores and the boutiques alike:

> Les grands magasins du Louvre sont un des fournissseurs récurrents. Mais ce sont le plus souvent des boutiques du quartier qui servent de fournisseurs: le chausseur Aaron rue de Châteaudun, le tailleur Joe-Jo boulevard Poissonnières, les chapeaux Léon rue Daunou ou encore le coiffeur Charles rue de Clichy. Les adresses de ces derniers figurant dans les programmes, ainsi que des publicités pour les commerces les plus importants les fourrures Weil, autre fournisseur important des revues, situé dans le même quartier, rue Saint Anne.[102]

> [The department stores around the Louvre are venerable suppliers but the small neighborhood boutiques are more frequently used: the shoemaker Aaron on Rue de Chateaudun, the tailor Joe-Jo on Boulevard Poissonnieres, the hat shop Leon, Rue Daunou, or the hairdresser's Charles, Rue de Clichy. The addresses of these last two appear in the programs, as well as publicity for that most important business, Weil, the furriers, another important supplier for revues, situated in the same *quartier* as the other shops, on Rue Saint Anne.]

As filmmaker Robert Bresson observed, "Money likes to know everything in advance. Producers, like distributors, are usually gamblers who avoid risk."[103]

Says Professor Miller,

> The one thing I keep coming back to is how properly dressed these fashionable men are in the Toulouse-Lautrec paintings, certainly in contrast to how men would dress for a comparable experience these days. This, of course, implies that fashion, or culture models, were still emanating from the top (and its codes of dress and comportment), rather than from the bottom up, as has been the case since the second half of the twentieth century. It also probably indicates that going to the Moulin Rouge or the like was a stop among others in more respectable surroundings, where one dress code fit all. In that sense, I don't know that one should be seeing a visit to a cabaret in competition for consumers' time with other venues rather than as one more option among these pleasures. The reverse, then, would

equally hold: that the purveyors of entertainment (the cabarets and music-halls) were, like the Bon Marche, selling consumption and pleasure, especially to tourists from abroad or from the provinces whom, I believe, they increasingly came to rely on for their clientele.[104]

Though published in 1883 during the Second Republic, Emile Zola's *Au Bonheur des Dames* (in English, *The Ladies' Paradise*) is set during the Second Empire, a time of extravagant consumption. Zola created a department store mogul named Octave Mouret and modeled the store after Le Bon Marché. The first ten episodes of the BBC series *The Paradise* were based on the novel.

Octave Mouret is a merchandising genius who uses people up and discards them like "empty wrapping paper." He built his temple of commerce to traffic on female desires but scorns the customer, who pays for her impulse purchases with drops of her blood. Luxurious clothes intoxicate her and she lives with the secret shame of her passion as if she were yielding to a tryst. The woman intoxicated by luxurious clothes lives with the secret shame as if she yielded to seduction in some seedy hotel.

A woman, bosom heaving, trailed by her husband, goes through several new departments of the fictive store, where luxury goods are arrayed. The displays of bonnets, flowers and feathers, and lingerie departments conjure up a cancan troupe. White silk mules are trimmed with swans down and shoes and boots of white satin have high Louis XV–style heels. The central gallery, lit from above, has expanses of artificial silk, velvet sprays of flowers, and the feathers of ostriches and colorful birds. Then, beyond what Zola calls the dull corsets begin the vast galleries of luxury deshabille. It is in the trousseau department where "all discretion was abandoned" and sales items are a melee strewn on counters.[105]

The original cancan dancers would not have had the pocketbooks for Le Bon Marché. If they went to the store they would have been in their element in a scene reminiscent of a cancan spectacle. Zola made the point that the commoner and rich woman both shopped in the trousseau department. "Frills and flounces escaped from boxes, rising like so much snow. White petticoats 'fell' of every length—petticoats tight across the knees, and petticoats with a train that swept to the ground, a rising tide. The trousseau department had plaitings and embroideries and Valenciennes lace, and depraved the senses as it overflowed in costly fantasies." The cancan was danced in a blizzard of a mostly white version of Nicole Kidman's exciting costumes in *Moulin Rouge*.

The Orientalist Mystique

The belly dancers who performed for men only, on the little stage inside the stucco elephant in the summer garden of the Moulin Rouge, which moved there from the same world's fair for which the Eiffel Tower was built, were not just any act but an act that captivated men for years. The belly dancers promised other sensual entertainment within the hall.

The belly dancers, odalisques and Salomés which pervaded the early music-halls passed from the general aesthetic of fin de siècle. Loie Fuller, a dancer who had a genius for publicity, when she performed at New York's Standard Theater in 1886 did Oriental numbers and called the evening "The Arabian Nights."[106]

Jean Renoir in his faithful cinematic reimagining of the Moulin Rouge began the movie with a belly dance scene. Oscar Wilde wrote his scandalous play *Salomé* at Torquay

Photograph of "Dasson." A famous showgirl was often known by just one name.

in 1891–1892 after seeing Gustave Moreau's decadent and sexy "Salomé" (first shown at the Salon in 1876). Salomé in American burlesque was barefoot and wore breast plates of ropes of pearls, a diaphanous skirt with pale briefs underneath; the vaudeville performer Eva Tanguay claimed she could carry her Salomé costume in one closed fist. Jean Lorrain, a journalist, published in *La Revue Blanche* in 1893 a description of a dancer whose movements evoked "those proud and subtle nudities, rustling with gemstone and flashing with light, which that master-sorcerer Gustave Moreau builds into his precious watercolors."[107] Bram Dijkstra cites that in the movements of the exotic dancer, Lorrain saw "those dancing Salomés, wrapped round with agates and sparks of electricity, those princesses of lewdness and unconscious cruelty who offer, with the swooning grace of monstrous flowers, the mystery of their sex and their smile to aging kings who have become children once more."[108]

Margot Dervilliers in partially sheer costuming. Cropped image from an undated postcard.

Oscar Wilde went to the Moulin Rouge with the Symbolist poet Stuart Merrill, who spearheaded a petition in America for Wilde's release from prison. Wilde and Merrill saw a Romanian acrobat dancing on her hands and Wilde had an idea to ask the acrobat to perform in his own version of Salomé.[109]

Eminent art historian Oleg Grabar has discussed the nineteenth-century Western fantasy image of the Middle Eastern woman:

> Whether recollections of beauty or evocations of evil, cultural myths and fantasies lend themselves to images—in order better to be publicized but also because they are in fact images (albeit initially only mental ones)—and are thus easy to transform into representations. Thus first the snake charmers and Middle Eastern dancer were seen in sideshows and in variety theaters and then the image became fixed in the imagination and it was only natural that the Moulin Rouge would open with belly dancers or Mata Hari would perform at the Folies Bergère the Eastern style dance she picked up when her husband was stationed in Djakarta. The image became impressed on the public mind. Theda Bara, aka Theodosia Goodman a blond smalltime actress from a middle class Cincinnati background could dye her hair black, outline her eyes with kohl, and rise to be the first cinema sex symbol. In 1915, promoting her first starring film the Fox Studio fabricated an "Oriental" background for her—that she was born "in the shadow of the Pyramids" of an Italian sculptor father and French concubine mother.[110]

The son of my prep school headmistress went on an aid program abroad in the mid–1960s, right after graduation from an Ivy League college. The young man sent his parents a photograph of himself with a shaggy beard. "Why do you relax your standards because you are over there?" his mother asked. "Do you suppose they don't care?"

The son shaved the whiskers off. Yet the beard had allowed him to ease up during an adventure, and experience the Edenic aspects of a foreign setting. And so the music-hall audiences regaled in "Oriental" costumes and acts.

Legendary fin de siècle dancers including Loie Fuller, Ruth St. Denis, and Anna Pavlova partook of the Orientalist craze, adopting movements and associated clothes from the Far East, Western Asia, Mediterranean and North African dance traditions. Ruth St. Denis, for example, dressed very simply but had two Indian headdresses plus a Mughal style one for a dance called "Legend of the Peacock." Naturally these famous dancers were not pretending to be from those regions. Sometimes the Mata Hari posed as from India. She brought Orientalism to its apex in the music-halls of the Folies Bergère, Olympia and Casino de Paris. Oriental dance styles were ways to flex the muscles and use the hips in ways that stage performers had not before, and to animate the popular *Thousand and One Nights.*

Mata Hari appeared first on stage as an Eastern temple dancer upstairs in the library at the August Musée Guimet in March 1905. She danced as a temptress of Lord Siva in front of a half-human-size sculpture of the god.

In 1909, Diaghilev was on the stage and the dramatic, swirling costumes of Léon Baskt influenced any performer who wanted to project exoticism. The Russian émigré dancers in Diaghilev's company who stayed in Paris and sought work in music-halls brought the influence of their folkloric styled costumes. According to textile and fashion curator Roger Leong, "Orientalism had been popular in nineteenth-century art and literature for over half a century, but not until Schéherazade in 1910 did it filter down into fashion and interior design."[111]

The Orientalist costumes amalgamated—Byzantine medallions on chains, filigree, ancient helmets, and shields positioned on breasts, looping necklaces and pearls, the sashes and architectural headdresses of India and Java and Romany coin jewelry. Mata

Madiah Surith, a belly dancer born in Russland, Saxony. Undated postcard.

C. Dalida on an undated postcard.

Hari would wear a snake (like a mythical princess) on the head. One of her costumes consisted of huge, glamorized pseudo fish scales; two big papier-mâché or pressed metal fish locking mouths right on her pelvis between her legs. Were these costumes perceived as authentic? They were theatrical excuses to have no corset and a skirt that wrapped and flowed and seemed to commence at the bottom of the hips, and the merest circular ornaments for a brassiere. Authenticity wasn't at issue. A similar costume was worn by Mlle. Djemile Fatme, purportedly Turkish, at the Folies Bergère in 1913. Her wrapped slit skirt looks Indonesian and is covered with corsages of flowers, as are her breasts. Her headgear is Assyrian. The sometimes funny results of raiding the Oriental theater trunk are counterbalanced by the look in the eyes of the models and dancers that appear caught up in the heady mix of the sex appeal of the Oriental costume.

Orientalism as a style motif had different tonalities. It could, as historian Edward Said theorized, be motivated by a Western impulse to dominate the Orient politically and aesthetically. But it also spelled a slower tempoed precinct of eroticism. Art scholar Holly Edwards noted that the World's Columbia Exhibition in Chicago in 1893 "transformed America's notion of the Orient, sexualizing it, and bringing it conveniently home … women in brightly colored outfits belly dancing (known as the hoochie coochie) at a 'street of Cairo' on the Midway was among the most popular attractions, with dance 'a formative means of liberation.'"[112]

Millions of people visited the world's fairs in Paris, which likewise brought the Orient as window dressing home. Long ago I was director of a sleepy branch library in Cambridge, Massachusetts. This was the 1970s and we decided to enliven it with a zoo. The Boston zoo and patrons lent snakes, turtles, fish, and gerbils. Then we heard of a belly dancer who couldn't keep her rabbit because it was nocturnal and so was her employ. Someone said she danced on the top of the multifamily unit and I pictured myself as the dancer in magenta and purple silks with sequined fringe and gold coins, holding hands with the big white rabbit, gyrating to the percussion of rabbit thumps. The library adopted the rabbit; it was very large and ranged comfortably around the large enclosure my husband made for it in the least used section of the library—heaven help anyone who wanted to look at reference or the Dewey two and three hundreds. I had already lived twice in the Middle East, and later went to Marrakesh, where a magazine put me up at the beautiful Mamounia Hotel, and the photographer and I were dazzled by the belly dancing show right at dinner, and in the Atlas Mountains we were allowed to hold huge snakes. But it's the fabulous imagined costumes that have stayed in my mind clearly, not the real performance or real snakes: this is the power of imagination and of a dream of otherness.

Because French royal stage entertainment operated under exacting regulations about who could sing, dance, and perform types of plays, pantomime became a popular type of Parisian street performance. Victor Hugo saw a tableau vivant from England in 1847 where women in transparent pink body stockings posed in various attitudes on a revolving wooden disk. That same year, his mistress, the former actress Juliette Drouet, described the bustle backstage at a Parisian theater, including seven women coming and going "avec l'air de la plus naïve tranquillité."[113]

By 1890, belly dancing went indoors, with other features of what had been sideshows and the carnival parade, into the costumes of performers at the circus and the music-halls. *1001 Nights* had become part of the narrative of entertainment from the time people threw rocks at the window of Antoine Galland, first translator of the great story corpus into a European language, to hear the rest of a tale. Soldiers brought souvenirs from the Crimean War.

The myth of the exotic realized on stage was immersive. Social codes of female behavior and dress could be transgressed and the faraway culture showed up the constraints of the society the audience lived in. The myth, writes historian of belly dance Andrea Deagon, has provided a persona for Western women "to express sexuality, desire,

Nearly naked woman, undated postcard.

authority, and transgression of social codes—all while conforming in some respects to traditional expectations of feminine behavior."[114] The woman in Claude Monet's "La Japonaise" (1876) revels in her long loose red kimono. Her blond hair is about to tumble from its pins.

Snake charmers are on the list of vanished entertainment but figured on the music-hall stage as stock exemplars of Eastern mystery. In the fin de siècle they, like the snap of a hypnotist's fingers, mesmerized an audience, removed them to their unconscious and an opportune interlude to look inside. Meanwhile the snake charmer wrestled with death every moment of her sensual act. Nala Damajanti, supposedly Hindu but eventually revealed as from Nantey, France, debuted at the Folies Bergère on February 18, 1887. She had already toured with P.T. Barnum's circus and may have been a partial inspiration for Henri Rousseau's haunting *Snake Charmer*. She was a former governess who married an acrobat, a ceiling walker, and wore sari-inspired costumes, and showed her leg and midriff. She could have seen belly dancers and snake charmers in many French localities on the street.[115] In Paris, where the earliest cafés were decorated to look Persian or Turkish, these female acts were on view in outdoor cafés on the big boulevards. And then there were the paintings, dressed rooms at the universal exhibition 1867, and *Le Corsaire* at the Paris Opera in the same year.

Nala Damajanti became her artistry. When her birth identity was exposed it did not make her a fraud—she still charmed snakes. As Oscar Wilde said when told he was confusing the two Salomés of the Bible in his dramatization of Salomé, the daughter of Herod and a dancer, "I prefer the other truth, my own, which is that of the dream. Between two truths, the falser is the truer."[116]

The music-hall's make-believe was the ideal venue for Orientalism, from slave girls to Cleopatras, and Salomés dancing with John the Baptist's head to adagio belly dancers holding candelabra. Both in terms of borrowing elements of costume and complete identification with a miasmic Eastern culture, the Orientalism billowed before it shrank. After Ziegfeld's evocation of Salomé in the Follies of 1907, the star Madame Dazie was busy giving women of New York two-hour classes each morning on the rooftop garden of the New York Theater.[117]

The fashion and music-hall designer Paul Poiret, known to contemporaries as the "King of Fashion," showed Orientalist designs from turbans to harem pants. Cecil Beaton, socialite photographer, said that to enter Poiret's salons in the Faubourg St. Honoré was to step into the world of the Arabian Nights. Poiret gave a costume party called "The Thousand and Second Night" a year after Sergei Diaghilev's *Schéhérazade* opened to acclaim in Paris. The couturier played a sultan, and his wife was the favorite in the harem. Guests and semi-naked dancers were provided with dress up clothes of furs, brocades and silks, jewelry, and aigrettes.[118] A few years later, in 1919, Poiret threw a party to mark the reopening of the House of Poiret and asked everyone to dress up as royalty.[119] Liane de Pougy and her husband, a Romanian prince, went as the king and queen of Albania. They wore fur-trimmed royal blue and apricot cloaks with Balkan embroidery, and fur toques with diamond aigrettes. They made an entrance with a "slave" that carried their Italian greyhound, and the dog wore a gold collar and lay on a velvet cushion. The scene must have looked like a design by Léon Bakst. Angelo Luerti points to Poiret for not only assimilating the splendor of the costumes of the Ballets Russes but leading a dual revolution in fashion and music-hall shows and their costumes.

The Orientalist fashions were often subtle in themselves, if probably shocking if they turned up at dinner parties. The style allowed an escape from heavy corseting before it was abandoned in the Jazz Era. It did not have to go with exposure of the body à la Mata Hari. A design for a music-hall revue by Gaston Noury (Houghton Library, Harvard University) had the brassiere with big medallions, veiling fringes, and big bracelets but the emphasis was on the hips. The overskirt wrapped tightly, creating an almost fishtail effect, and the dress, while sultry, covered the body more than many of the fashionable evening gowns of the pre–World War I years.

When flapper dresses came in, modernism replaced the fascination with the Orient. Yet the undress of beads and sparkles, jeweled brassiere and transparent wafting skirts, veils, and big arabesque jewelry, interpreted an exotic archetype. Broad-stroked Orientalism stayed a fixture of showgirl costumage always ready to be adopted from the closet of the past to inspire dancers and audiences. Toni Bentley writes pithily of the prototypes of the "veiled and beaded sexually aggressive Vamp (sexual vampire) of early twentieth century theater and film" which "highlight modern woman's power to reveal and to conceal to both create desire and to control her vulnerability."[120]

No society was immune from the music-hall's seizing costume and theme ideas from foreign places. An 1879 poster has Europeans dressed up between two natives of the Americas in colorful robes. Yet the reimagined harem served as one of the greatest inspirations on showgirl costumes. Ironically the look of colorful, midriff baring undress was forged from impressions of societies where women were in public modestly covered.

The Circus Influence

When I was young, my mother "counted the shrimp," my parents could not afford to send us on field trips. To have paper to draw on, I waited until the cereal box was empty, or my mother did a home perm and gave me the curler papers she did not use. But we did go to the circus and had good seats; it was my father's ritual. I remember in Norfolk, Virginia, being two (we moved every year so I can pinpoint my age) and watching my father watch the circus. I had never seen him so transported. He was in a trance, so much so that it embarrassed my mother.

The next year we went again to the Big Top and again my father went into a trance. This time my mother, who tried to help her overemotional family members avoid excess, put her foot down. No more gluing eyes to the female preternatural trapeze artists. The yearly outing was switched to an amusement park. When I read the memoir of music-hall producer Jacques-Charles, I think of my father's trance. Russell O. Merrill had fought in a world war and served in one or perhaps two ships that sank. He wanted to leave the Navy and go back to school but he had a family by his mid-twenties. The circus was where he allowed himself to experience pure female charm and enchantment. Jacques-Charles could not have made the connection between the showgirl spectaculars and circuses more vividly: "Indubitably, undeniably, the circus was the ancestor of the music-hall."[121]

Circus entertainment in European cities and towns, and posters promoting the arrival of a circus, spread the aesthetic of flamboyant skimpy female costumes. The wagons were fancy and so were the ladies performing. These were grand affairs: In 1889, Barnum came to London with 450 performers, 300 horses, 21 elephants and 35 wagons. The circus people were dressed as characters. In the acts they might be dressed by themes like the Chinese imperial court or fairyland.

Naturally, female circus performers set the style for showgirls on stage as everyone went to and marveled about the circus, the genre of entertainment that brought another world to audiences before cinema could. Along with traveling with tents, French circuses performed in permanent buildings, eight of which remain today. In 1889, an impressive and unusual building (designed by a pupil of Gustave Eiffel) was erected in Amiens, just outside the city center, for its municipal circus. Some doubted the roof would hold. Jules Verne, author of *Around the World in 80 Days,* and an attorney on the city council, lived nearby. Having championed the permanent circus building, he declared that as it withstood the loud clapping the day it was inaugurated, the building was sound.[122]

The Englishman who introduced the three-ring circus was "Lord" George Sanger.

Leona Dare on a cabinet card (1869–1874) by Jeremiah Gurney (1855–1922) (courtesy Minneapolis Institute of Art, 89.114.260).

In the parade for Sanger's Circus, four cream horses led a gilded carriage, and Mrs. Sanger, dressed as Britannica, rode on top, holding a shield and trident and wearing a Roman helmet.

Costumes for the traveling circuses accustomed the public eye to looking at the bodies of living women. Moreover, the performers who did the horse and trapeze tricks were not reputed for loose morals. The first human cannonball stunt was done by a teenage acrobat, Rosa Richter ("Zazel"), who was shot into the air by coiled springs attached to a foot platform. When she flew out of the barrel into a safety net, a gunpowder charge was set off. A photograph[123] recorded her cut satin teddy-style sweater, the bodice of which is like a low-cut ball gown with straps angling towards the shoulders. A corsage of artificial flowers covers each breast. Her tights end just above the ankles. She wears socks or a soft boot, designed to make her legs look naked. Dark lace trim on the shorts at the top of her thighs gives the appearance of garters. She toured with P.T. Barnum, and did her daredevil act in Europe and the U.S. Zazel nearly perished doing it in 1891.

It is clear that to do a circus act, whether trapeze, animal or equestrian, requires clothing that is sleek or close-fitting. Also, to have everyone experience with immediacy the acts, colorful outfits are a tradition. Some of the thrills of a circus are acts that inspire fear, so the clothing is often silly. Finally, trim like ruffles and edging serve a dual purpose of making the performer less muscled and more as though she is having fun. All of these colorations of the circus costume moved right into the music-hall revue, and given that circus acts continued to be part of many music-hall shows until the First World War, the shops and designers who did the circus costumes doubled working for the newer demand for showgirl costumes.

Human clothes are on occasion modeled after animals: children's bear and bunny suits and catsuits, for example, and the headgear people have put on horses was recast as a central feature of a showgirl costume.

Acrobats and acts with horses have been the most important circus traditions. "Dancing" horses seen on earthenware tomb figures dating from the Tang Dynasty (608–907 AD) indicated they entertained high-ranking Tang nobles and the emperor. The horses were specially trained to perform during festivals and special occasions.

Roman horses raced unmounted wearing nodding plumes or feathers on their heads. Slaves did gymnastics on them, like standing on their backs or reaching down to pick up coins thrown by the spectators. Horse racing in ancient Rome was a gambling sport but the unmounted races of beplumed horses were early theatrical circus acts.[124]

In the Victorian era, the horses on an

LEROY
(Folies-Bergère)

Cliché Walery   ★ *Paris*

Leroy at the Folies Bergère.

impressive *corbillard*, or funeral coach, were richly caparisoned and wore black or white (this could denote the deceased was young) plumes. In England the horses that carried mourners and the coffin wore plumes that told the world the deceased's financial status: two plumes bespoke modest means and seven a really rich person.[125] Its absence or replacement with another decoration is felt to be a stylistic departure from the norm; after looking at many posters with the showgirl icon, one is bound to have a tinge, despite the great variety of revue costumes, that something is missing when the costumage is plume-less.

Paul Bouissac states that the plume on a circus horse has been an "abundant iconography" back to the beginning of the nineteenth century.

> They are fixed onto the head, usually screwed on the top of a special halter, connected to the rest of the trapping. Also often on the horse's back … unless incompatible with the exercises performed, for instance, if equestrians are balancing on the horses' backs … plumes are a diacritical sign that distinguishes circus horses from farm or sporting horses. Also, as observed in circus posters, the be-plumed head of a horse symbolizes the circus itself. Let us note finally that, within the paradigm of the traditional circus, horses and feathers appear to be congruent in some respect; their conjunction has an effect of felicitous naturalness, usually summarized in journalistic accounts of circus performance, by the word "elegance," or other metaphorical expressions suggesting that a certain "truth" of the horse is set forth through this particular type of decorative association.[126]

Surely the key to costuming attractive women on stage who do not have to do gymnastic type athletics has to do with creating a sign of luxury, elegance and being the pride of the stable. The showgirl is dressed like a prized circus animal. Her beplumed head symbolizes the show, if it does not probably have quite the ritual impact of the plumes on horses and humans doing feats.

Regarding circus acts in the early Paris revues, the connection of the two forms of entertainment were considerable expressly because the performers of the acrobatics and horse acts wore what was safe and showed from a distance; the female circus performers had a reason to wear tights, body stockings, short sleeves or sleeveless and tight outfits.

The equestrian Ernest Molier opened a private circus in Paris in 1880 which attracted the elite. In this Cirque Molier or Cirque des Amateurs he initiated historical tableaux of fencing bouts and in a fashion all the spectators were part of the show. Men had to bring one beautiful rose in a competition. Another competition was of the ladies' hats. It seems that no one came to the circus except by invitation and it occurred as a semi-annual charity event, in a *hôtel* in Passy near the Bois de Boulogne furnished largely from a hippodrome that had closed. No one had made a circus so theatrical before and it required many and varied costumes for the acts, which included clowns, magic, Greek dances, "acrobaties égyptiennes," and especially trick riding and strong men. A weight-lifter carried a piano and pianist on his shoulders, while horses danced to Spanish music, jump-roped, and wrote letters on a board.

One poster for the Cirque Molier has a line of women in a diversity of costumes, from a black full riding costume with black top hat to the merest lingerie. Equitation was the most important skill of this sportive circus because it symbolized the superior skill of the French aristocrats and haute bourgeoisie. Another poster has Ernest's wife Blanche in a little orange outfit with puffed short sleeves and short bloomers. A metal band holds back her black curls and over her ears are big orange pompons. The circus continued until 1933.

The ring circus came to Paris from England in 1783 and was developed by the Franconi family. It had wild animals, contortionists, clowns, trick dogs and so forth. It was almost inevitable that the music-halls would take advantage of circus talent to include it in their potpourri. When the circus acts were reduced to small variety bits between the world wars, the showgirl costume got very feathery, having no competition from the circus professionals and presumably attracting many of the wealthy who dressed in their fine clothes and jewels to be seen at the Cirque Molier.

Circuses were a rage in Paris and Montmartre had two. The bourgeoisie patronized the circuses more than the cabarets before the turn of the century. To the circus, fashionable women wore bright dresses and hats piled with feathers, dresses with wasp waists, black stockings and décolletage. Circus performers, dancers and ladies of the night gathered in bars after hours.

A codicil to the link between circus and revue costumes is nomenclature. Chorus dancers in Broadway shows from the time of Ziegfeld on were called "ponies" to distinguish them from the taller "parade dancers." According to Doris Eaton Travis, the Ziegfeld Girl who danced from 1904 into the 21st century, the showgirls promenaded and if the show had topless showgirls, they promenaded that way. "The term 'pony' as I understand it came from the Englishman John Tiller, who had trained precision dancing chorus lines, and in one of them had the dancers imitate horses—hence ponies."[127] Dancers in Broadway shows are also called "hoofers," associated naturally with dancing feet, while "pony" conjures up an image of dignity and self-regard. The male imagination arguably becomes the rider.

The circus and music-hall histories in Paris were closely intertwined from the beginning, when Leon Sari, who became director of the Folies Bergère in 1871, hired a manager named Rosinsky who had worked for P.T. Barnum to book acts for his music-hall.[128] For the animal acts, a menagerie was built behind the stage and in 1877 part of the entrance was razed to bring a lion cage onto the stage. A pair of Algeria-born magicians, Emile and Vincent Isola, became directors of the Folies Bergère in 1901 and, engaging all kinds of fabulous variety shows, brought the Folies into glory. (The Isola brothers started out poor. But because they performed three solid days of magic shows for a dying child, and refused payment from the mother, she brought them into directorship of theaters to thank them.[129])

Furthermore, the Nouveau Cirque was opened by Joseph Oller, who had already founded a hippodrome and roller coaster and would create the Moulin Rouge. The Moulin Rouge was at the location where Franconi's circus had been. In some of the early shows in the 1880s, the arena transformed in minutes from horse acts to a huge pool where swimmers and clowns plunged and fought. (At the Folies Bergère, meanwhile, audiences enjoyed wrestling matches; championships were apparently fixed to put French wrestlers in the championship finals.[130]) Nautical pantomime and equestrian-nautical revues were on the program at the Moulin Rouge in the 1920s. Oller's slogan was "le droit à la joie" (joy for all) which was in itself revolutionary, given the crushing employments of the working class.

The metaphorical expression of "hoofers" for dancers in Broadway shows and "ponies" for showgirls in the chorus suggests that there is something equine about the showgirls' posture and decoration. The showgirl prances; the movement is "gambader," like the frisky spring of a jumping horse. She holds her head high and has superlative posture. The equine comparison does not disparage.

Headdresses have been weighty in revues since the 1920s when they sometimes weighed 15 pounds. There were six poufed dancers on stage at one time, each with a headdress four feet high, for the Folies Bergère's *Une Nuit à Versailles* (1926), which had flowing side swags and feathers, draped stoles, and jeweled corsages. Designers have created incredible headdresses the only limitation on which is they have to stay on the head. Sometimes they have fallen off but mostly they seem to defy gravity and stay in place by magic. For instance, Bill Campbell, for a Vegas show, tipped one great beribboned rose garden on a showgirl's head, matching another on her bustle; the cleverness was to adjust it so it wouldn't fall off.

Circus outfits are the popular costumes that led for sparkle. Says Pascal Jacob, circus authority,

Considering the human passion for light and embellishment, I am confident that people started to play with shiny materials in the same time they were creating painted shapes on the walls of their caverns. Paleontologists say that these first artists were using mica powder to enhance their work. The word used to describe the small fragments of mica is "paillettes," the same word used for the small shiny pieces used by fashion since the nineteenth-century and to cover the white face clowns' costumes since the beginning of the twentieth century.

The sequin (French or English) translates the old Italian word zecchino, which identifies a coin invented in Venice in the thirteenth century, but inspired by an example from the Middle East (more precisely Lebanon). It has been used notably by the Romany people on their costumes, a tradition of sewn coins on outfits shared by some Indian clothes as well as flamenco dancers.[131]

The leotard was invented to show off the muscles of a trapeze artist, Jules Léotard, born in 1838. It was hand knit and originally covered the legs and was called a *juste au corps* from 1886.[132] A sleek one-piece, it had cap or long sleeves or no sleeves. It helped Léotard develop a flying trapeze act at the Cirque Napoléon in 1859, where he had up to five trapezes in motion and he swung from one to the other. Léotard was the main aerialist at the Franconi Circus and performed in London. He was a heartthrob who in the late 1860s inspired a music-hall song sung by "Champagne Charlie" George Leybourne: "He'd fly through the air with the greatest of ease, the daring young man on the flying trapeze." Léotard died, possibly of smallpox, at age 28. For female dancers on stage, the leotard molded the body yet maintained modesty. Until 1918 or so it offered a way to call a show "nude," where the dancer or dancers were actually dressed. A tractable fabric such as a fine velvet was used for the leotard (or in French, since the nineteenth century, justa-corps).

States Jacob:

The main difference between circus costume and showgirls' costumes is practicality. Some headpieces are really heavy and the only thing the ladies can do is walk. They can dance a little bit but we don't talk about strong choreographies. For the circus people, the costume has to become another skin, so even if they are wearing a cape beautifully decorated for their entrance, they will leave it as soon as they have to start their act.

Staging Fairyland

Folk tale protagonists like Jack (of beanstalk fame), Red Riding Hood, and Hansel and Gretel dress humbly, according to their station. For the Miller's Son to impersonate a prince, the Booted Cat has him remove his peasant rags and stand naked in the river. In the 41 volumes of the *Cabinet des Fées*, most penned around 1700 by female and one male (Charles Perrault) aristocrats, the trimmings are from life at Versailles, diametrically opposed to the rural, natural life of peasants. The *conte de fées*, or fairy story, a word invented by the Countess d'Aulnoy in her 1797 collection, were spirited amalgams of what nurses told their high-born charges and the fantasy happy endings of the storytellers themselves. Naturally, the orphans and ensorcelled characters that move through the action and demonstrate their pluck, at the denouement are encrusted with jewels and shed their rags—or even metamorphosized animal bodies—for magnificent clothes and jewels.

Two centuries after most of these stories were greatly in vogue, when a French producer was creating a revue he looked at subject matter that afforded an opportunity for fantasy and gorgeousness. The fairy tales did just this and were the epitome of French gaiety and frivolity as well. A fairy tale setting was like a common language for producers and costume designers: the art of the rococo—soft, fluffy eroticism, feathery arabesques, silvery, pale blue pink and pastel hues, pearlesque skin tones, sensuous poses on swings and in boudoirs, and the artifice of the long-gone court merging with the fairy stories. Madame de Maintenon herself had said that Versailles would be remembered as a fairy tale.

In brief, the French fairy tale bespoke a lot of flowers and flesh, décolletage and garlands, which would figure as essentials of the showgirl costume.

There were more than a hundred stories studded with bling that became familiar in the French nursery. Look at the presents a monkey princess receives in *Babiole* by the Countess d'Aulnoy: "There was a dress spun of spider web, embroidered with little fireflies, ornaments in an eggshell, cherry balls, all the lingerie was covered with paper lace; and besides that a basket of all sorts of shells, some for earrings, others for bodkins, which shone like diamonds."[133] In *The White Cat*, not the metamorphosed (to a feline) princess but the lost stranger who comes to her castle is the one costumed. As soon as he steps inside, bodiless hands push him forward and undress and adorn him in a dressing gown frosted with gold and embroidered with the cat's monograms done in small emeralds. After the prince is served a magical repast, the cat fêtes him in a hall where a dozen each cats and monkeys perform a ballet. The prince sleeps in a bedroom with floor to ceiling mirrors (mirrors not yet being quite that large when the tale was composed), butterflies whose colors form myriad flowers, rare bird feathers of a sort never seen except in that place, and a bed covered with gauze fashioned by a thousand knotted ribbons.

The French predilection to festoon stories with material elegance crossed over literarily to England. The eclectic European fairyland was a stock setting for the elaborate British Christmas pantomimes, a genre of their own, with stage sets, original music and lyrics, and line dancers with special appeal to adults. The playwright J.M. Barrie was slumming when he created Peter Pan, and seized on putting a showgirl on the stage of his story. In "Peter and Wendy," his 1911 novelization of his 1906 play, the first sound of Never Neverland is the golden bells of fairy language. Tinkerbell has appeared at the Darlings' nursery in the chapter "Come away, come away!"

> There was another light in the room now, a thousand times brighter than the night-lights, and in the time we have taken to say this, it has been in all the drawers in the nursery, looking for Peter's shadow, rummaged the wardrobe and turned every pocket inside out. It was not really a light; it made this light by flashing about so quickly, but when it came to rest for a second you saw it was a fairy, no longer than your hand, but still glowing. It was a girl called Tinker Bell exquisitely gowned in a skeleton leaf, cut low and square, through which her figure could be seen to the best advantage. She was slightly inclined to *embonpoint*.[134]

Mlle. Delacroix on a postcard postmarked 1906.

The play also ended with countless fairies represented by bell and stage lights, but Tinkerbell stands out; she has an inherent quality of glamour that Wendy can never have. Tinkerbell, a star showgirl, is a complex persona flickering with insubstantiality and tinkling with vibrant sexuality, as well as, naturally, possessiveness towards Peter. Tink was looking for Peter's shadow self. He, courageous and inclined to heroic exploits, while also thoughtless and boyish, only partly formed. The shadow was blatantly his anima, a feminine side which Tink was trying to find for him but certainly not intending that a human girl would sew it on "her Peter."

The evanescence of the showgirl comes from her preternatural identity, betokened in the feathers, sequins and fixed smile (a show of teeth indicates one can keep the headdress aloft). All fairyland nineteenth century theater has an undeniable antecedent in the romantic, literary (as opposed to folk, cynical funny and earthy) authored French fairy tales of the late rococo. The circle of women authors in the final years of the Sun King's court garlanded their tales with not treasure chests but opulent clothes which made further transpositions into the music-hall stage's costumes. Fairyland provided a recurring theme of showgirl revues in the twentieth century. It was historically inclusive, so a revue costume was as likely to be a tall medieval hennin with a filmy veil over a *ceinture de chastité* as a topless bustled gown with lace collar and high hairdo. Costumes had to complement the sets and pantomimes but they could be plucked from any (especially France's) eras for the theatrical illusion.

The 1890s' dominant style of art nouveau interlaced with revues and their glamorous costumes. The gossamer fairyland dresses so often appearing in art nouveau illustrations, the mise-en-scène of tendrilly, twisted flowers and vegetation, the flying figures, elongated kinetic women, sumptuous colors, insects and flowers that become women and vice versa, and a mood of sexual arousal—all the familiar and beautiful typography—typified the music-hall sets and costumes of the period as much as book illustration, architectural decoration, jewelry, and so forth. The peak of art nouveau, from 1890 to 1910, matched with the creation of the showgirl revue, and conjured up the *féerique* on stage—indeed the showgirl costumes, revealing and celebrating the body, embodied the art nouveau ideal.

A salient example of the influence of art nouveau on bringing fairyland to the music-hall stage is the trope of beautiful girls emerging from a device such as giant seashell, fish, or egg, etc. The first was Molière's partner in forming his theatrical company and favorite for soubrette roles, Madeleine Béjart, who appeared from a shell as a naiad, performing at Vaux-le-Vicomte, in Molière's *Les Fâcheux* (1661).[135] In delicately framed scenes of nudes in 1920s Parisian shows, this is a stock theme, women encapsulated but not imprisoned, and "born" on stage. In a fascinating study comparing the coming of age of art nouveau with cinema, Lucy Fischer describes the work of a Spanish filmmaker working for Pathé in Paris, Segundo de Chomón, who used the revue spectacular type of fairyland tricks to great effect. Chomón's movies were often hand-colored and he invoked the fantastical moth/butterfly dances of one of the most famous showgirls of the era, Loie Fuller: "He invokes the whiplash curve in producing his own version of Fulleresque choreography in *Creation of the Serpentine* (1908), which presents a magician conjuring a fabric-draped woman who multiplies into numerous dancers—Loie Fuller squared, as it were."[136]

In Chomón's film *Easter Eggs* (1907), starring his wife Julienne Mathieu, she produces from an intricately designed curving bower giant eggs that materialize into showgirls, ballerinas and butterfly ladies. In *The Magic Mirror* (1908), "A female magician opens a jewelry box and removes a series of trinkets (a belt and two tiaras), then conjures women from inside them." Fischer observes that the woman not only is a pivotal figure in Chomón's films but is frequently cast as "a powerful magician, a role usually reserved for the male.... Some female wizards even triumph over their male counterparts, as in *The Red Spectre* (1907) and *The Golden Beetle*."[137]

The wizards are, in the lineage of the French fairy tale, powerful females like the White Cat. There are revues with plots where women are caused suffering or humiliation but the prevailing joie de vie seems to have required them to get free and/or triumph. Beauty in fairy tales always wins.

The knight in the tradition of French fairy tale was traditionally told not to stay too much in the women's realm lest he become stupid, lose his sense of enterprise and spiritual development. This is how Samson lost his masculinity. This psychic desire of men to gird their masculinity must have been particularly important after the First World War, when the French did not want to be caught unprepared: A knight must not "verliegen," he loses by lying too long, as psychoanalyst Marie von Franz writes, and as in the courtly romance *Erèc et Enide*, Erèc told his wife after their prolonged honeymoon.

TWO

The Scene Is Set

"Ma femme aux hanches de nacelle / Aux hanches de lustre et de pennes de flèche / Et de tiges de plumes de paon blanc / De balance insensible." [You with hips like a small boat / Like a chandelier, arrow feathers / and stalks of white peacock plumes / of imperceptible balance.]—André Breton, "Ma Femme à la Chevelure de Feu de Bois"

Material Moment

It was at the bottom (la Butte) of Paris's tallest hill, along a boulevard of Montmartre, that showgirl costumes began and evolved in a time of glitter, opulence, and theatricality. A woman showed her social status by the silks, velvets and feathers of her clothing. As a Parisienne watered plants on her balcony, her fine gown trailed behind her, and she went to the market with gloves to match. The opulence of the era's bourgeoisie dress was so endemic that when fashion was pared down in the Jazz Era, the aesthetic of the show-girl costume remained a gaudy and often nostalgic dream. The iconic costume was born not in central Paris but Montmartre, which had a distinct identity and only became part of Paris in 1860 when city limits were extended outward. Popular mass entertainment had consisted of sideshows as well as people-watching in the parks and on the boulevards, and during festivals and parades. In the mid–nineteenth century came cafés-concerts. Now there were more interior places for nighttime entertainment. Writes Colin Jones, "The appearance in the 1890s of the striptease and nude dancing added to the appeal of the city's entertainment industry for a strong current of sex tourism."[1]

The male figures in Toulouse-Lautrec's lithograph poster of La Goulue contrast to the frilliness of the dancer. They are figures all in black, like shadow puppets.[2] Bourgeois standards were exacting and a gulf separated the men in their top hats from the lower classes. Yet there they were, for the sensuality that had magnetized tourists since the eighteenth century, and Paris was eager to recoup its tourism and cultural hegemony of Europe after war with the Prussians. Yet pure white neckcloths distinguished a gentleman and a coquettish dancer showing off layers of petticoats with machine lace trimming was boasting that in the oasis of the music-hall she had "pure white" status too.[3]

An actor can declaim a speech, or a theatrical troupe put on a scene, outside the theater. But to a large extent a showgirl, and to total extent what she has on, are woven inextricably in the locus of a revue—a music-hall, nightclub or casino show. Scholars including Charles Rearick, Dennis Cate, Susanna Barrows, and Dominique Kalifa have traced the progression to the revue from prior types of entertainment in Paris—cabarets, café-concerts, public fêtes and student balls, the Universal Exhibitions of 1889 and 1900, and arty Montmartre cabarets. The music-halls themselves started offering a potpourri and then worked out the formula of the spectacular. It was all like making champagne and when the cork was off the showgirl emerged from the bottle. The old café-concerts where entrance was free and a man could drop by, have a smoke and a drink, unconcerned about whether he had mud on his shoes, had morphed into high-style emporiums with lavish set pieces. Laurence Senelick sums up the trend: "The narrative of Western theater in the nineteenth century may be read as its progress from disreputable diversion to an agent of cultural enlightenment."[4]

Before that "pop," there had to be public drinking. Alcohol consumption tripled between 1840 and 1870 and, with the grape harvest blighted by phylloxera in the late 1870s, those who drank turned more to cider and beer, absinthe and aperitifs. There were different types of drinking establishments, from elite to working class and almost all offered clients boules, billiards, card-playing and music; couples could dance. After the Commune, during the 1870s, cafés were repressed to curb political opposition, raucous behavior, and immorality. In 1877 it was forbidden to read political opinions in newspapers aloud. The police, however, liked the cafés; they could eavesdrop on the masses, especially during Napoléon's rule. Napoléon as a young man played chess in the Café Franconi but, once in power, he posted spies in the cafés, and three years after becoming emperor, outlawed cafés, which only reopened under Louis-Philippe. The lifting of restrictions on cafés in 1880 meant more cafés and more competition, which caused

Postcard: "Le Sacre Coeur."

proprietors to paint their facades, and install appurtenances like fancy counters and gaslight fixtures—the café "du coin" and deluxe cafés.

By the turn of the century pretty young women replaced waiters in what were called the "brasseries à femme." They were dressed in flesh-colored tights or overall costumes—for example, at the Devil's Angels, hems were raised above the ankles, Tyrolean hats were donned, and heart-shaped blouse fronts exposed their arms. The *serveuses* were new indeed. Some cafés had women dressed in Scottish kilts or sailor suits: "the most popular guises were those drawn from France's colonial empire from Algeria, Tonkin, or Morocco … the clothes of the empire."[5] Raids on the establishments to uncover décolletage or scurrilous décor were common, to whit the Auberge Saint-Denis was found to entice customers with obscene murals on the ground floor of cats making love.[6]

The precedent of women in costume circulating among the male customers was established. When Thomas Jefferson or Aaron Burr visited Paris they saw a female cashier at a café; she was depicted in drawings by Englishmen but she was an anomaly. Now women as objects to gawk at were in. When the Folies Bergère opened in 1869, Paris had over 200 cafés.

The *café-concert* (or *café chantant*) was the pre–music-hall song saloon. Mostly along the Champs-Elysées, some installed scenic elements in front of the tables and a columned promenade. This made the café-concert more a place to go and mix socially. Until the taxonomic rules about which purlieus could have what portion of the entertainment pie were abolished during the Second Republic, the performers had to wear ordinary clothes with no accessories or wigs and only a painted backdrop for décor. The traditional design of an ensemble of young women sitting in a semi-circle, *la corbeille*, continued as if they were a basket of flowers lifted from the past. As the laws began to loosen, pantomimes were permitted as part of the show from 1867 so that the Folies Bergère opened with an accent on sketches and singing.

When the Opéra-Comique burned in 1887, the café-concerts turned into theaters with stages and *promenoirs*. Castle writes that after the Prussian War the secretary to Alexandre Dumas took over the management of the Folies Bergère and Léon Sari inaugurated a corps of dancing girls which presented a less classical display than the ballerinas at the opera but were not openly outrageous.[7]

With some exceptions, writes Dominique Kalifa,

> The café-concert stayed an illegitimate theater, with liberal hours and identities, where the public could be seen and fool around. From the place often emanated a racket and noisy hilarity, marked by bursts of Gallic laughter. The triviality of attractions was denounced: bearded women, *petomanes* and fire swallowers. The erotization of the spectacles progressed equally, which exhibited the female body. [Le café-concert reste donc un théâtre illégitime, ou horaires et tenues sont libres, ou le public s'exhibe et vient faire du "potin." De la salle émane souvent un boucan et une joie bruyante, marques d'éclats de rires gaulois. On dénonce la trivialité des attractions: femmes à barbe, pétomanes et cracheurs de feu. L'érotisation du spectacle progresse également, qui exhibe les corps feminins.][8]

The sexy contingent was the corps of dancing girls and the public might shout out remarks. Often the "dancing girls" are ascribed to have made an appearance at the café-concert theaters not until the turn of the century, but theater historian Laurence Senelick in a series of pivotal studies including "Eroticism in 19th-century photography," in *Theater History Studies*, demonstrates that risqué female attire came earlier than the advent of music-halls, as women from brothels infiltrated the chorus line in the 1860s. These were popular skits in fancy pantomimes, revues, and vaudevilles, known as the *pièces à femmes*.

Professor Senelick adds: "Of these 'exhibitions of living flesh,' Arthur Pougin said in his *belle époque* theater dictionary, 'they closely resembled that of certain savage tribes exempt from all prejudice in the matter of clothing.'"[9]

The shifting identity of the proto-music-hall, geared to assaying the public taste, is exhibited by a period at the Folies Bergère for a while in 1881 when Léon Sari fired his staff and invited composers to consult on a program of orchestral music. The group was incredibly select: Gounod, Massenet, Saint-Saens and Delibes. From the unpopularity and failure of this trial highbrow offering came the first big spectaculars of the music-hall. After Sari's death and new ownership by Monsieur and Madame Allemand, Edouard Marchand, who had married the Allemands' niece, brought chorus girls into the show. They were Danish born and from New York City, where they were advertised as "The Wickedest Girls in the World." They dressed alike in baby doll clothes, wore blond wigs, black stockings, and frilly, beribboned underwear. The Barrison Sisters did synchronic movements with kicks and smoked in public to show how exceptional they were.

The proletariat began to have some free time. The work day for women and adolescents in industry was limited to 11 hours a day in 1892; the work day for men was 12 hours until 1904 but they got a day off each week in 1906.

The three world's fairs of 1878, 1889, and 1900 focused on products and industry and the value of work itself. The cabaret culture by contrast stood for, as Paul Lafargue the Marxist put it, "Le Droit à La Paresse" [the right to be idle]. Lafargue,

Café Concert des Incohérences by José Roy, 1888. Color lithograph, 217 × 75 cm (85 7/16 × 29½ in.) (Collection Zimmerli Art Museum at Rutgers University, class of 1937 Art Purchase Fund, 1993.0034; photograph by Jack Abraham).

Undated postcard of a be-sequined and be-feathered showgirl.

son-in-law of Karl Marx, said it was the proletariat's duty to enjoy itself, and that everyone should be able to work a three-hour day, and laze around and carouse the rest of the day and night. There was a new inclination for leisure for commoners and the entry fees and a price of a drink at the cabarets and music-halls would sift out the poorer people. When "le peuple" went out it was to drink and dance in merry company and when they did so they had as is so very French an idea to bolster them, of Rabelaisian sensuality and opposition to religious and governmental pieties.[10]

By 1900, prostitutes were no longer allowed to solicit in the *promenoir*, and all the sexual vibrations were between audience and performance in stage shows incorporating semi-nude review at the Folies Bergère, Olympia, Ambassadeurs, etc.

> From 1894 on, Victorian-style striptease acts, involving more display of petticoat and chemise than nudity, became part of the music-hall repertory, bringing new outcries of disgust and condemnation. Dancers like Violette entered the stage to calls of "Take your panties off" and "higher, show it." A lascivious taint derived also from reports that some directors forced women performers to make themselves available after the show—for the directors themselves or for select clients. Spectacles such as women's wrestling (borrowed from the fairs) and sometimes fatal daredevil stunts brought further reproach— and eager crowds—to the flourishing establishments.[11]

There is no evidence that the ethos of the music-hall was denigrating of showgirls. Arguably they were it girls in the capital of fashion. Balancing the undoubted seamy side of the music-halls was the chance to dance, possibly marry up, and take home a paycheck, show off one's looks and stage talents—something to aspire to without the kind of undertow it had in America.

Mel Gordon contributes the insight that it was long tradition for a girl to come to the metropolis to make something of herself, and to be on stage was not shameful, but a far preferable alternative to prostitution or drudgery as a dressmaker or modist.[12] This dovetails with a comment of producer Paul Derval, written in the early 1950s with a long backward glance: "The girls are bold at the Folies Bergère; it is a tradition which perhaps expresses best that piquancy and slight provocativeness which distinguishes the 'Parisienne.'"[13]

Defining the Showgirl Face: Cora Pearl

Music-hall stars endorsed skin care products—Billy Burke, Florenz Ziegfeld's wife, endorsed Crème Nerol and Pond's cold and vanishing creams to maintain natural beauty.[14] The first star to suggest that by use of makeup, women could be as comely and alluring as she, was Cora Pearl (1835–1886), born Emma Crouch, the courtesan who said memorably, "My independence was all my fortune."[15]

In France, makeup had not been for middle-class women. There was a prohibition against women outside the court wearing rouge during the royal dynasty, when makeup generally was identified with prostitutes past their prime. According to biographer Katie Hickman, Cora was one of the first Parisians to wear couture (she was an early patron of Frederick Worth) and fancy lingerie.

Cora was the daughter of a cellist, pop song composer and singer in Plymouth, England, who remarried after her husband ran off. Cora was sent to boarding school in France for eight years, learning French. Back living with her grandmother in England, one day she was seduced on the way to church and decided not to return home; she ran off with the five pounds the seducer gave her to make her way in the world. She was 19 and came under the protection of a dance hall owner who took her to Paris where they saw the sights. He left but she stayed and became the rare chorus girl that made it. Cora never had one single lover but rather a set of men who extended their wealth and attention. She entertained on a lavish scale which confirmed her status as a *grande horizontale* and kept an account book with columns for her clients, the date of their *séjour* with her, what they paid, and her observation. She had a detached attitude which she called a "rancure" or scorn for the swains who made a fetish of worshipping her.

At the zenith of her career, Cora was living in a mansion that Prince Napoléon had purchased for her, and her jewels alone, given her by what she dubbed her "golden chain of lovers" were worth a million francs. Instead of a bed of leaves at a banquet, oysters were laid on a bed of violets. Once she warned her guests that she would give them meat that none would dare to cut. She won the bet when she had herself brought in on a silver salver borne by four men, sprinkled with sprigs of parsley.[16] Above all, the demimondaines dressed sumptuously on stage and off.

In 1866, Cora appeared as Eve at a fancy-dress ball at the Restaurant des Trois Frères Provencaux, dressed only in her diamonds, for 12 nights. The next year she appeared at the Théâtre des Bouffes-Parisiens as Cupid in Offenbach's *Orphée aux Enfers*. The entire membership of the elite Jockey Club attended. The Duc de Grammant-Caderousse quipped that "if the Frères Provencaux served diamond omelets, Cora would go and dine there every evening." Cora was outstanding but also loopy. She and another courtesan dueled in 1863 in the Bois de Boulogne with riding whips over a prince from Serbia or Armenia.[17]

She had a theatrical sense of fashion. "She was known for changing the color of her hair, her carriage, and her servants' livery as the mood struck her."[18] Her red hair might be made pink, and she dyed her dog blue to match a dress. She inspired a mode in Paris for a drink called "Tears of Cora Pearl" and as Gustave Claudin would recall in "Mes Souvenirs," she introduced modern makeup to France. She tinted her eyelashes and used face powder tinted with silver and pearl. Her bottles of toilet water and powders were sent from London.[19] Jean-Philippe Worth said once of her appearance that it was "shockingly overdone" and her hair was the identical lemon yellow of the satin in her carriage.[20]

Kitty Traney, equestrian, on a 1905 postcard.

She reintroduced wigs that had been left behind with the French Revolution and used coils of false hair. Seeing that some performers retained their stage makeup during the late evening, with the result their faces looked pink or orange, she applied a much lighter paint for going out on the town.

She was a reigning beauty who spent a fortune on her jewels, clothes, parties, stables, rare books and art objects. When a lover sent her a thousand pounds sterling of orchids, she had them strewn across the floor and danced a hornpipe on top of them. Keeping up one's reputation for gorgeousness and luxury usually resulted in penury for a woman of a certain age. The gambling vice often went with the territory. One rainy night an English gentleman crossed the garden of the casino at Monte Carlo and saw a woman sitting on the curb. She had been turned out of her lodging and her belongings had been seized, she told him. Astonished on learning that she was Cora Pearl, he took her to the villa he shared with two friends. Everyone treated her courteously. They dined, she revived, and she told stories of the Second Empire. When her host escorted her to the best bedroom he left her with his dressing gown. He retired to his library and soon Cora reappeared, wearing the dressing gown which she let drop to her feet, leaving her naked. "I could not sleep, she said, until I had shown you that, if Cora Pearl has lost everything else, she still retains a form of beauty which made her famous."[21]

Emile Zola's fictional showgirl Nana had carmine lips and eyes ringed with kohl, and admirers gathered in her dressing room to watch her prepare for a show. But Cora Pearl used makeup not to be subtle but to bring excitement to her offstage look. Writes M.R. Kessler, "Pearl set her face up as a canvas on which she could 'paint' using various colors."[22] Some women even followed her lead when she tanned her skin.

When France was defeated in the Franco-Prussian War, many blamed the debilitating influence of courtesans like Pearl, who exiled herself temporarily from the land. A fake memoir of Pearl, written by the English journalist Derek Parker, came out from William Blatchford in 1982. The claim was that the book was by a friend of hers, a count and former army officer, and was a relic discovered only in the twentieth century. Her purported self-description at an 1866 ball of the French "Minister of the Marine" as wearing only a girdle of tulle and jewels "carefully disposed"[23] sounds made up, yet Cora Pearl cultivated her bad girl image and would have relished it.

The Cabaret

Twirling cancan dancers unsettled and removed men's hats with their toes. Mistinguett, a showgirl who over a long career was the *ne plus ultra* for versatility, tweaked social pretensions. She did this by her choice of costume, swift changes from urchin to glamour girl, cheeky proletarian to pampered beau monde. Audiences loved it. The music-hall revue would develop early in the twentieth century by presenting a box of petit fours, dancers in artful flourishes of spangles and feathers, yet the Parisian revues have always been defined by an edge of mockery of the status quo. This attitude derives from the nature of another feature of nightlife, a precursor to the revue spectacular by a few decades, the cabaret.

First on the cabaret scene came the Bon Bock dinner, named after a portrait (which can be seen at the Philadelphia Museum of Art) of a jolly old boy smoking a pipe before a stein of Strasbourg ale, by none other than Edouard Manet, already a hallowed figure.

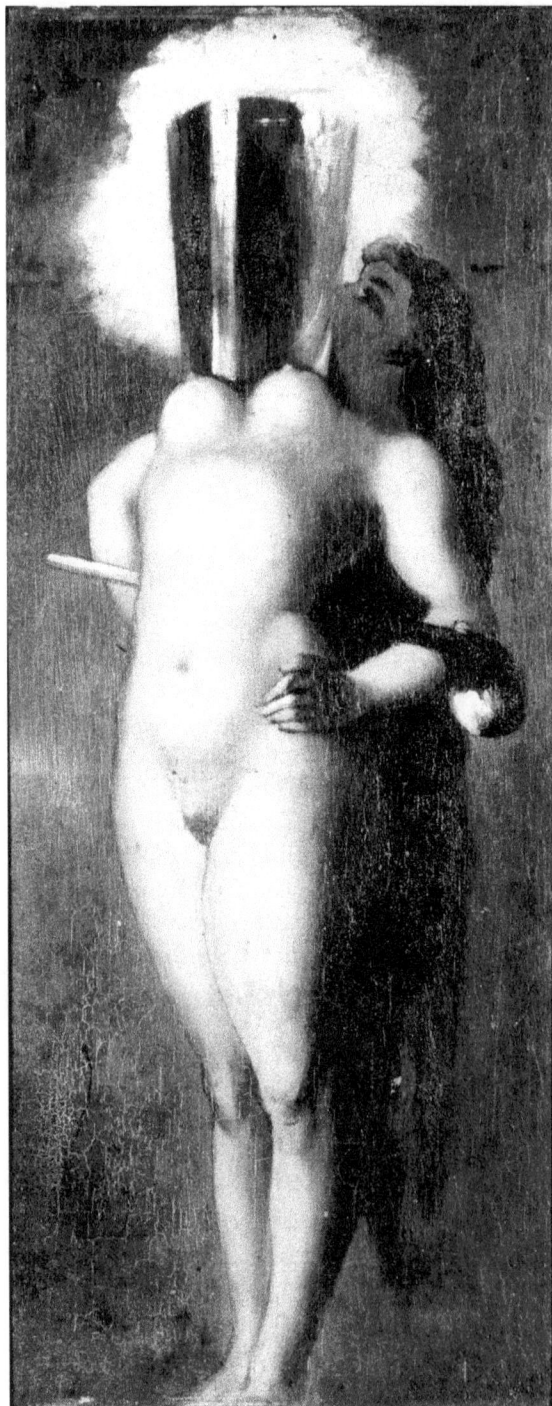

La Femme au Bock (1883), after André Gill. Oil on panel, 55.5 × 24 cm (21⅞ × 9⁷⁄₁₆ in.) (Collection Zimmerli Art Museum at Rutgers University, Class of 1937 Art Purchase Fund, 1993.0034; photograph by Jack Abraham).

In about 1880, a dispute had arisen between the fans of French beer and German beer. In 1885, Edouard Manet depicted an engraver named Belloc hosting a jolly all-male meal out for chums who were bright and funny like him. The occasions became a regular thing and the members published a humorous paper, "Le Bon Bock," where early on, Belloc defended the superiority of French beer over the German. The "Bon Bock dinners" moved around to various brasseries of Montmartre. Belloc referred to the Moulin de la Galette (an actual windmill and landmark) as their "lady of Notre Dame." The cabaret now replaced the theater and café proper as the gathering place for intellectual and artistic chic, in a patriotic if anti-authoritarian vein—*l'esprit gaulois*. Emile Reynaud made the film *Un Bon Bock* in 1892 using hand colored film, one of the very first animated movies. He unfortunately threw it into the Seine after screening it at the Théâtre Optique, but it does attest to the trendiness of the retro Louis XIII/ Three Musketeers mood.

Capitalizing on the arty intellectualism of a group of men, the Brasserie le Bon Bock was founded in 1879 in the neighborhood of Pigalle. A painting of a naked woman called "La Femme au Bock" (Beer Woman) hung on the wall. She holds a long pipe behind her back and a glass of beer on her head. The artist was the caricaturist André Gill, who had in 1875 created another totemic cabaret picture, of a rabbit jumping out of a saucepan. This was a sign for the notorious Cabaret des Assassins, which people began to call the "Lapin a Gill," evolving into Le Lapin Agile, which Picasso and Utrillo frequented and painted.

Gill often drew big heads on undersized bodies. By the time he painted the "Femme" he was mentally ill and would die soon after, in his forties. The Zimmerli Museum of Rutgers University has a painting which is a copy made in 1883. At the cabaret it replaced Gill's original artwork, sold to pay for his hospital costs.[24] What the peculiar mascot balances on her breasts are "d'estaminet," meaning either "belonging the tavern" or "regulars"—and it is respectful regulars who make a café: I recall Tito Gerassi, a biographer of Fidel Castro and Jean-Paul Sartre, making cafés in Greenwich Village and Paris his offices.

A clubby Bohemian watering hole, the Chat Noir was founded on playful cerebrality, and a lifestyle called *fumisme*. The fumistes of course were men only. The only women around were those who served the beer, in itself an innovation, and prostitution was kept at bay. Witness to the mood of the cabaret scene is a spoof perpetrated by a fake "Excessive" art movement, where patrons of a cabaret called Le Lapin Agile attached a paintbrush to the tail of the proprietor's pet donkey and exhibited the resulting canvas as a "sunset" at an art show.

A cabaret had an ambience contrasting with the elegant period cafés with their tall mirrors, gilt furnishings and zinc bars. The cabarets were themselves spectacles, dark inside, with retro decors based on France's past of the Communards, or Henry IV, or Chinoiserie. In 1887, Vincent Van Gogh decorated Le Tambourin, which had tambourines everywhere and serving girls who wore Italian peasant costumes. Van Gogh was enamored of "La Segatori," the Italian woman manager, and did the decorating for free.[25]

Le Chat Noir, where the *montmartrois* spirit coalesced, was furnished in a merry, masculine jumble of medieval and Renaissance paraphenalia—copper and pewter pans, church pews, old weapons, coats of arms, and oak paneling. Even in the author's childhood, such objects were ubiquitous and very inexpensive in the Marché aux Puces:

> The waiters were dressed in the uniforms of members of the Académie Française, and [Rodophe] Salis himself usually appeared attired as a préfet, addressing his clientele in such terms of archaic dignity as "Monsigneur" or "Your Exalted Highness." So famous did the Chat Noir become that such honorifics might not always have been misplaced; amongst the visitors there during the first ten years of its existence were the kings of Greece and Serbia, the Prince of Wales, Renan, Pasteur and General Boulanger.[26]

The ideal called upon the sensuality of the writings of François Rabelais and, in these early years of the Third Republic, Frenchness was defined in cultural more than political terms, as an ancient way of life under the *tricolore*. The Chat Noir was during the decade and a half of its existence, 1881 to 1895, the Parisian cabaret with the most mystique. The founder, Rodolphe Salis, set out to uphold republican freedom and masculine swashbuckle in contravention of bourgeois blandness—or as his friend journalist Emile Goudeau termed it—"our sugar-coated society [nos moeurs édulcorées]."[27] Ironically, going to Le Chat Noir to be amused by bright song, humorous poetry, and shadow puppetry paved the way for enjoying the varied and sugary entertainment of the music-halls.

Of the cabarets in Montmartre, Le Chat Noir in particular inspired "the cabaret mania that swept across turn-of-the-century Europe as well as Paris itself."[28] That its proprietor died only six years after it opened made him comparable to James Dean, a romantic figure. A loose association of young men calling themselves the Hydropathes (a joke predicated on a shared scorn for H_2O, many preferring absinthe) led others to Le Chat Noir. Their most known legacy is Charles Cros's delicious poem "Le Hareng Saur" (Salted Herring), quite surreal, funny, and often read to children.[29]

Fast following on this circle was another called the Hirsutes, stubble suggesting the male bonding. Some gained great fame—Willette, Steinlen, and Paul Signac among the artists, Alphonse Allais and Charles Cros of the writers, and August Strindberg of the

New Year's greeting postcard, French.

playwrights. Erik Satie, the genius composer who wrote the first cabaret music, played at the Chat Noir's piano from 1888 to 1891. One feature of the segregation by law of types of entertainment in Paris was that cafés could not have pianos but Montmartre, even after it became the 18th arrondissement mid-century, was outside central Paris, and the law against pianos was relaxed for Rodolphe Salis.[30] The Montmartre cabarets, which were very Republican French in their recitations and songs, did not feel the pressure of the censor as the café-concerts or even the Left Bank cafés frequented by students did. "Hence," writes Steven Moore Whiting, "l'esprit montmartrois could develop its satirical, irreverent voice without serious interference from the police."[31] Similar tolerance would be displayed towards political mockery in skits and female nudity in the music-hall revues.

When passersby looked through the window and saw the long-haired bohemians they sometimes thought them females—plus ça change, plus la même chose![32] The habitués of Le Chat Noir were self-aware about making cultural history—a periodical called "L'Hydropathe" had on every one of its 32 covers the portrait of one of its Hydropathie clan.

Le Chat Noir was a smash success, if surpassed by the music-halls a decade later: "la gaîté ne s'arretait plus, et les poètes debout sur les tables, disaient leurs vers avec de grandes geste fou." [The gaity never stopped and poets standing on the tables declaimed their verses with big crazy gestures.] Emile Goudeau compared an evening at Le Chat Noir to a fine bouillabaisse, with a range of customers from some who eschewed laughter to "idiots who mistook the gathering for a café-concert and demanded funkiness" [des insensés qui, prenant la réunion pour un café-concert, exigaient des flonflons].[33] When he came to Paris for the Universal Exhibition of 1900, Pablo Picasso was disappointed that Le Chat Noir had closed soon after Salis's death. The mood at the turn of century was changing from clubby and male to showy and female, the camaraderie of Montmartre cabarets to the sexy spectacle of the music-hall, where women were part of the audience and powered up the show.

A Geographical Sketch of La Butte[34]

In a conversation with this author, historian Charles Rearick situates Montmartre and its attractions in relation to other parts of Paris.

C.R.: For about ten years, a month or two every year I rented an apartment that was one block from the Moulin Rouge. I could see the faux-windmill from one window of my apartment. I often walked up the Butte—on the steep Rue Lepic that winds up the hill Montmartre.

J.M.: Is la Butte, which literally refers to a hill, just a different name for Montmartre?

C.R.: Parisians have ideas in their heads that are vague and subjective regarding topographical borders (most subjective of all: their *quartiers*). Short answer: yes, the Butte is Montmartre … but some parts of the Butte are, more than others, what people think of as Montmartre.

Some sides of the Butte—the lower areas to the north and east—are *not* the Montmartre that has played a historic role in art and entertainment. The north side (which I would call the backside) borders the present suburbs (*banlieues*) Saint-Ouen and Clignancourt. The eastern side—toward the Rue Rochechouart and the Goutte d'Or—are poor immigrant areas that have never had entertainments or celebrities like those of the famous "Montmartre" scene.

Essentially, most of that historic Montmartre of "pleasures" is at the foot of the Butte and around an old village center on its summit. The top of the Butte is now a place of touristy restaurants and the painter-filled square, the Place du Tertre and, nearby, the basilica Sacré Coeur. A short distance down on the outer side (nearer the city limits) are the Lapin Agile and La Maison Rose, the pink café made famous by Utrillo (his mother, the painter Suzanne Valendon, met there with Degas, Renoir and Toulouse-Lautrec). At the bottom of the Butte, along the "boulevards extérieurs," were the cabarets such as Le Chat Noir, the former dance hall (now a music-hall) the Moulin Rouge, and the theme cabarets L'Enfer, le Ciel, and Le Néant, among others. All that is the famous "Montmartre." The still-thriving Moulin Rouge is on the Place Blanche on the boulevard de Clichy, which runs along the bottom of the Butte.

In sum, the main entertainment zone of 1890 to 1930 was on the southern side of the Butte, closest to the city center (toward the Seine and the Opera, etc.), along the Boulevard de Clichy and on small streets just off that Boulevard and the Boulevard de Rochechouart. The original Chat Noir was on that latter boulevard. When Rodolphe Salis moved it, he chose a smaller street (now the Rue Victor Massé) one block south of the boulevard.

The official designation for whole area dominated by the Butte is the eighteenth *arrondissement*, which includes much territory beyond the Butte to the east—extending all the way to the other side of the railroad tracks serving the Gare de l'Est.

Here's some background for the messiness of these geographical terms: before the annexation of Montmartre into the city of Paris (in 1860), it was a "commune," an independent suburban town just outside the city limit, which ran along the "exterior boulevard." After 1860, the term Montmartre has lived on as a vague (*not official*) popular designation, bringing to mind above all the notable parts of the Butte mentioned above.

The most famous and successful music-halls of Paris (except for the Moulin Rouge) were down in the central districts of the city. Many were near a stretch of "interior" boulevards called "les Grands Boulevards" (built much earlier than the outer boulevards near the Butte Montmartre) and on the Boulevard de Strasbourg nearby. The Grands Boulevards run from Madeleine and the Boulevard des Capucines to the Boulevard des Italiens (just off the Place de l'Opéra) and continue on to République (their names change every few blocks).

Yet Le Chat Noir was what brought spectacle to the Butte. When Salis expanded the tiny premises to take over the space of the clockmaker next door, the artist Willette did a large painting of a procession descending from Montmartre's Moulin de la Galette to the Seine, towards a hole where sirens wait for their prey; the café habitués rise in a casket decorated by a white cross to a starry heaven.

Besides drinking, recitation and singing, the minor theater genre of shadow puppetry was done brilliantly at Le Chat Noir. If I could turn back the clock to the fin de siècle, I would be looking through the window to see plays acted out there, behind a backlit screen in silhouette, to live instrumental accompaniment. The owner, Salis, took it all over France. The cutouts were paper on zinc. Forty shadow shows were produced and many other "théâtres d'ombres" cropped up in Paris; Erik Satie composed for a Christmas show, and Miguel Utrillo, father of Maurice Utrillo, designed the puppets and stage décor.[35] Recalled now mostly in the black shadow figures in Toulouse-Lautrec's paintings, these were major productions of a minor genre. "L'Epopée" at the Chat Noir was an epic with 50 tableaux of the military glory of Napoléon Bonaparte.[36] Italian Futurist Gino Severini created highly movemented paintings of showgirls that are both saturated with color, with figures prismatically broken up yet richly costumed, and exhibiting grace and emotional turmoil. In one of Severini's music-hall dance series he identified the performer as dancing "the chahut," which was the early cancan with male and female dancers. The vision of speed and jerky movement connects with cabaret shadow puppetry: *Danseuse Articulée* (1915) is a breathtakingly complex assemblage of cardboard shapes that can be put into motion by a system of tiny ropes. That painting is in a private Italian collection but Harvard Art Museums has Severini's luminous *Yellow Dancers*, also evoking puppet figurines.

Thus artists and writers gathered in Montmartre, which became a showplace of the world's picture of Paris. The imagery drew more avant-garde young artists, such as Pablo Picasso. From being avant-garde and Bohemian, Montmartre became center stage for a performance of Gay Paree, with, routinely on the weekend, costumed parades of models and artists billed as special evenings. Rearick reveals that some of the Bohemians were hired, as were policeman "kept visible to show that the authorities were concerned about keeping order, and at the dance halls, Baedeker guides warned, some of the fun-loving girls were 'decoys.'"[37]

The Folies Bergère opened in 1869 and the Moulin Rouge twenty years later, but they did not spawn the showgirl revues until a large body of entertainment venues formed in Montmartre. The cabaret crowd looked at the music-halls and the crowds they brought as interlopers. In 1885, Rodolphe Salis moved his club to a bigger and finely furnished location a few blocks from the original one but some resisted change. Goudeau wrote in 1900:

> Having sufficiently disdained wealth, it [Montmartre] turned to the Golden Calf and offered it ironic, licentious, and waggish excuses.... The cabarets saw at their formerly modest doors the throng of emblazoned carriages and the wealthiest bankers contributing their subsidy to this former Golgotha transformed into Gotha of the silly songs.[38]

Thus light, pretty, and effectively feminized entertainment in Montmartre was criticized for commercialism from the beginning.

Assets in Petticoats

Coexisting with the cabarets were indoor and outdoor dance spots as well as indoor sites with outdoor gardens. Luc Sante quotes a contemporary flâneur on how ubiquitous dance halls became: "Before 1848, you couldn't walk down any street in Paris without noticing, above a wine shop, a pitifully flickering lantern on which was written Bal."[39]

In the 25 years between 1879 and 1913, the population of Paris doubled, and the amount spent on entertainment tripled. The dance hall provided cohesion for Parisians and a place for everybody to stretch their legs. I worked in Paris in the 1970s at the Institut Atlantique. From the basement of the magnificent old building the institute's publication went out. Monsieur Delvaux, *chef de diffusion*, was 80. He knew everything about the institute, probably including that it was CIA funded. He laughed and joked and really had twinkling blue eyes. Monsieur Delvaux had a deft way of folding wrapping paper and tying knots on packages that mesmerized me, as did the memories he shared. "We lived to dance," he would tell me, returning to a favorite topic of how he met his wife under electric lights at a popular dance spot.

> We dressed nicely and combed our hair, and got in to a dance hall for a pittance. A fellow had to go to a different dance hall—they were all over the city—if he got unruly. But it wasn't a raucous pache scene. We made our reputation as young men at the dance halls. We were poor and had no money in our pockets but we demonstrated our politeness by how we danced.

This was, he would stress, the nightlife of the little people, sheer revelry, that would carry over to the music-hall stage.

The essence of the first revue costume was no gorgeous raiment seen coming down a curving staircase on a grand stage but a raffish show of panties on a crowded dance floor. That Monsieur Delvaux repeated so much the "politesse" of the dancing spots also indicated it was a bit of an issue to keep rowdiness at bay. The dance scene was as sexual as incandescent. The last stanza of a popular song by Aristide Bruant, brags that,

Paris Qui Danse postcard, no date.

Le riche a ses titres en caisse,
Nous avons nos valeurs en jupon,
Et malgre la hausse ou la baisse,
Chaque jour on touche un coupon.[40]

[The rich keep their securities in a vault,
While we have our assets in petticoats,
And whether the market is up or down,
Each night you can touch the fluff."]

Usually, Aristide Bruant was more acerbic. Bruant was *compère* (master of ceremonies) at Le Chat Noir, famous for Toulouse-Lautrec's depictions in a black felt hat, red scarf, and black cape. The elite flocked to hear him chew them out. He was the presenter as well for the first revue at the Folies Bergère, *Place aux Jeunes* (1886).

The fin de siècle was a period of political upheaval. The government had been shaken up and a new generation including socialists, syndicalists and anarchists was, in the absence of newspaper censorship, heard. Athleticism came into favor, cycling, tennis, games and workout, and the first modern Olympic Games were held in Athens in 1896. In 1889, workers in 60 towns of France marched for an eight-hour work day, there were miners' strikes from 1890 to 1893, and the first May Day was celebrated in 1890. Men were also drinking and smoking more, including the alcohols drunk only in taverns and cabarets like absinthe and aperitifs. According to Eugen Weber, it was a fine time to throw care to the winds: "While goods and services became cheaper, those citizens who could consume them without having to produce them found unusual opportunities to do what they did best: nothing in particular." He continued, "The spice of life lay in the showing off."[41]

The cancan developed from the last figure of the quadrille (crossed, some say, with a polka).

Postcard with raised printed surface on the petticoats, c. 1890.

At the Moulin Rouge, La Goulue (the Thirsty One) and Jane Avril perfected the splits and the "porte d'armes," high kicks where the dancer catches her ankle and holds it there while spinning on the toes of the other foot. La Goulue began her career by dressing up in borrowed fancy dress from the laundry where her mother worked and parading off to dance halls in them. She is credited with the proto-feminist gesture of lifting off men's top hats with her toe at the end of the *galop*. Jean Renoir's *Le Moulin Rouge* is romantic yet accurate. It shows the rehearsals which were important for the demanding dance. At the Moulin Rouge the orchestra played for an extra half-hour when customers had left, so the quadrille dancers could rehearse. This was apparently when Toulouse-Lautrec sketched.[42]

Baron Haussman instrumented Napoléon III's order to demolish Paris's medieval streets and replace them with grand boulevards and the undertaking continued. Yet in Montmartre, up the steep steps past gardens and medieval houses were still vineyards and working windmills. The hill of the Butte was outside the city limits until 1860. Here, outside city gates, tolls had not been imposed, and taverns where drinks were cheaper had cropped up. Also, during the Paris Commune, insurrectionists hid in Montmartre, which gave it flavor.[43] Scholar Richard Thompson aptly calls Montmartre of the Third Republic "a porous frontier where there was seepage between the smarter classes of central Paris and the proletariat of the outer suburbs, where the two might meet in the commerce of leisure and prostitution."[44]

The boisterous Bal Chicard, where the cancan was born, was just off the Rue Jean-Jacques Rousseau, near Les Halles. The dance hall was an uninhibited scene and the dances hardly basic—polkas, mazurkas, and dances with names embodying their foreignness like the *hongroise* and the *sicilienne orientale*. The Chicard was noted for "outlandish costumes and wildly stylized attitude."[45]

The artist Gavrani went every week to the Bal Chicard and did an album, *Souvenirs du Bal Chicard* that evidences the crazy dress-up that identified the dance hall. Monsieur Levasque, nicknamed Père Chicard, was a leather merchant whom all Paris admired for his dancing. His getup was Louis XIII bandito—flowing fabric belt, trousers tucked into high boots, gloves, and a comical plumed helmet. In an illustration that was also a cover on a song called "La Quadrille Chicard," popularized at the famous Eldorado, Chicard's dancing partner looks like the cancan girls of the Moulin Rouge a half-century later. A journalist contemporary to Gavrani said that Chicard's wife was dressed like a secondhand clothes dealer ("une revendeuse à la toilette"). This suggests circumstantially that the cancan dancers at the Moulin Rouge at the turn of century wore used garments, whether borrowed from the laundries of Montmartre or bought secondhand. A petticoat could have lace that saw several lives.

The plumed helmet of Père Chicard provides a proud and jocular touch similar to the headdress on a showgirl costume. Chicard, along with the fancy getup, had a brazenly bare chest; it was understood that Chicard and his wife were godlike, and nudity was indispensable to gods and goddesses. Chicard's plumes stayed on even if they danced up a storm, and the headgear was light enough not to interfere with his movement. Luc Sante's *The Other Paris* includes the drawing "The Chahut" by Constantin Guys, dated from the 1850s, that shows a crowd of men in top hats looking on as two couples dance. One woman is in a strapped low-cut top, trimmed, possibly with fur, and a full ruffled white skirt fluttering so high it looks detached from her body; she holds her right leg almost straight up in the air. The other woman, who lifts up her skirts to her thighs, is costumed more as a Bourbon, with a high wig and big jewelry. Her skirt is trained and

"Extra Dry"—Danse Nouvelle by Mlles. Luciana & Raymondine, Théâtre Marigny. Undated post-card.

extends from a bustier that descends to a V. Both wear the fancy tight boots that cover most of the calf, just what Moulin Rouge cancan dancers would wear in the 1890s. The two women appear to be competing. Sante says that 50,000 people attended the popular balls every Sunday in around 1835, and that at the Bal Chicard, "outlandish costumes and wildly stylized attitudes predominate. Its dances were said to be especially unbridled"; the orchestra comprised ten pistols (shot off during the chahut), four bass drums, three cymbals, 12 cornets, six violins and a bell.[46]

The Moulin de la Galette was a dance hall where La Goulue and other cancan favorites like Grille d'égout (Street Drain) first danced. The windmill of the Moulin Rouge did not grind wheat, and the red sails were of wood, but artifice had always been part of French diversions. The Moulin Rouge was a noisy newcomer in 1893 so that Picasso, Modigliani and Utrillo often chose quiet conversation at the Lapin Agile.[47] Yet Picasso painted the people of Montmartre including sketches of young women doing the cancan and the acrobats of La Cirque Fernando.

A model of an elephant was brought to the Moulin Rouge from a Fairyland amusement in the Avenue Rapp near the Eiffel Tower. Soon belly dancers performed on a small stage inside it. The cancan was a highlight of the quadrille danced in the garden, lit by thousands of lamps in summertime.

The Moulin Rouge had masked costume balls on chosen themes. They were called *redoutes.* Occurring five times a year from 1894 to 1897, the *redoutes* were discontinued after being rained out in 1898.[48] The balls were associated with exuberant freedom from constraints and, like masques generally, flirtation. Invitations went out and attendance kept costumage a hopping matter. La Goulue, according to *Figaro* journalist Jacques Passis and theater director and historian Jacques Crépineau, co-authors of *Le Moulin Rouge,* "had the effrontery to be nude at gala nights and procession her breasts outside her bodice" and arrive in her own coach with her pet goat.[49]

The cancan dancer showed, in the frantic movement, a glimpse of her usually unseen body. As much as the exposure, what signified was her knowing manner. The dance said "bring it on" to the men in the audience. In her memoir, Jane Avril described the gallop of the dance that lasted exactly eight minutes, whose music was typically *La Belle Hélène* from Jacques Offenbach's *Orpheus in the Underworld.* The quadrille consisted of several partner and group moves except the last one, in which each dancer gave expression to her fancy, and selected a spectator, ending her dance with a nimble and skillful kick to send his hat flying. The dancer's petticoats, as much as 12 yards in circumference, had lacy inserts and lace bands; the pantaloons were lace trimmed as well and worn usually over black stockings.[50]

Lest one picture a sea of foam, the Moulin Rouge dancers were very colorful. An 1890s edition of the *Guide des Plaisirs à Paris* describes the entr'actes where men and women

> like in a debarcadara mix, graze, and swirl with all the tumult of women's plumed hats and chapeaux melons mixed with top hats, soft hats, and even helmets. The bodices of cherry red satin, green, yellow, white, blue, and the multicolored skirts are of a gaiety that delights the eyes and fills the observer with joy. At left at little tables the "petites dames" who are always thirsty either offer or wait to be offered drinks. When they say thank you they propose right away their heart to love—on condition you meet their price.[51]

Photographs and accounts by people who danced at the Moulin Rouge do support the fabled inches of bare thigh—which the *Guide* references jocularly to tempt the tourist: pale or rosy flesh seen through the pantaloons or the transparent silk stockings—"samplings of these pretty merchants of caresses" [échantillon de ces jolies marchandes de calineries et d'amour].[52]

In this period women would face the hems of their skirts with stiff material like cambric or wire to give the skirt more body. Yvette Guilbert, café-concert diva, recalled La Goulue's attire of black silk stockings, sky-blue satin bodice, and 60-odd yards of black lace petticoat, and a heart embroidered on the back of her knickers.[53] The assertive nature of La Goulue is evident in what she declared about cancan clothes:

> One must have pretty knickers. They're indispensable. Without nice knickers, no Cancan. Me, I prefer white knickers, long petticoats with fine lace, and pantaloons furnished with lots of ruffles. It is possible to wear colored knickers, but they should be pale. Tights must be black, the better to stand out against the white.... When you're dressed like this you can raise your legs without any worry. I must nonetheless add that I never dance without first attaching the bottom edge of my pantaloons to my stockings with pins. Women who show their flesh, that's disgusting.[54]

The dancers who performed the cancan knew they were fabulous. It is likely that they didn't want people to giggle about their indecency. And yet it became a fable. In Noel Coward's *Easy Virtue* (1926), a girl of the gentry shows herself naked under her skirts because she thought the dance required it. "Nelly No Knickers," her older brother teases her (the excellent British movie version came out in 2008).

According to Shazia Boucher of the Musée de Beaux Arts et de la Dentelle in Calais, the back-lacing corset worn by the cancan dancer was likely slightly more comfortable that that worn everyday by bourgeois women. She added that "pettycoats added frills when the leg went up, but crucial was the *pantalon femme*, which was still reserved for young girls, and prostitutes."

By 1879 every type of handmade lace could be copied by machine lace. Naturally, this reduced the price of lace and made it less of a social distinction. Yet the availability of lace in Paris was surely heady to female shoppers; by contrast, fabric remained graded so that quality velvet was dear.

Zola and the artists of Montmartre give us the eyes to see what was before a woman who dreamed she was a cancan dancer: petticoats like churning sea foam, feathers as hair ornaments, lacy drawers. To dance at the Moulin Rouge one had to have the frou-frou; economies were possible by buying just trimmings, or everything secondhand. In photographs, the lace tends to be a rim of an inch or so, on pantaloons or petticoats.

Even when the cancan became just an element of a spectacular, its attire, representing "Gay Paree," did not stay entirely fixed. As Jonathan Conlin observes, "The cancan costume did not get stuck. The *cartes de visite* show that it evolved over time."[55]

In the year 1889, at the second Universal Exhibition in Paris, from which dates the Eiffel Tower, corsetière Marguerite Cadolle launched her underwear invention for the modern woman. The lower part cinched in the waist and the upper part held the breasts up by shoulder straps. By 1905, the upper half was being sold separately as a "soutien gorge," "gorge" being an old French word for breast, the name by which bras are known in France today. It was viewed as flattering for the modern, less bosomy figure. Mata Hari, photographed in a jewel studded bra, was among Cadolle's customers, and *Vogue* mentioned brassieres a few years before they were widely advertised as a French innovation around 1910.[56] Progressive variations made of silk handkerchiefs without the whalebone and bandeaux for the slender flapper look followed. The detached bra, which still allowed a waist-cincher, would be repeated in the showgirl costume.

Revue-type shows, including *Place aux Jeunes* at the Folies Bergère and *Circassiens et Circassiennes* at the Moulin Rouge (an Orientalist reference since it was believed the Ottomans sultans prized concubines from the region of Circassia), filled in the entertainment gap after the world's fairs. The cancan wasn't a big enough drawing card after the Exposition closed in 1900 and took away the tourists, and one innovation at the Moulin Rouge was "genuinely nude" women in "poses plastiques" (like sculptures) featured in the foyer. Soon more spectacular revues were presented, in competition with the trend of other Parisian music-halls. The costumes became more elaborate at the turn of the century, perhaps none in illustration exceeded by what Caroline Otéro wore starring in *L'Impératrice* at the Olympia (1900), all over embroidered on green lined with white fur, high jeweled color and crown; over the top for the look of Theodora, who rose from dancer of ill repute to empress.

The razzle-dazzle came in like thunder. *Tu marches?*, which opened in March 1903, had circus acts from England and a revue with 150 performers and ten sets, including the castle wall at Elsinore for a Hamlet theme, 100 maidens at the kingdom of Saxony, and a chariot race. Costumes were opulent. Alain Weill writes, "Plots were often tenuous, becoming a pretext for an ever-growing display of petticoats."[57]

All dances had their day on stage and Liane de Pougy and Caroline Otéro joined in on the cake-walk. Audiences had loved the cake-walk since they saw it at the Nouveau Cirque the year before (or at the 1889 world's fair). Having these paragons of glamour perform a complex, athletic African-American dance from pre–Civil War, invented by slaves on plantations, and part of minstrel shows, spoofed the attitudes of the French bourgeois audiences. Yet it may have been the earliest democratization of showgirl costumes, which Mistinguett for one of her stage personas, the waif, would embrace. A show called *La Belle de New York* opened in 1893, and the U.S. ambassador attended the premiere; this was revived in 1911 with 200 new costumes by the House of Landolff, a renowned husband-and-wife couture team. "Sylvia" had—in the days when, as Cole Porter's "Anything Goes" recalled, "a glimpse of stocking was looked on as something shocking"—a slit in her brocaded long skirt cut up to her waist. The hats were bizarre beyond words, presumably because hats of fashion were so extravagant that those for the stage had to outdo them.

A huge fire on February 27, 1915, destroyed the auditorium and lobby of the Moulin Rouge. Three weeks before, *La Revue Tricolore* had opened with elaborate sets and costumes. A slender story set in fairyland and Chinese palaces, and showcasing the Cocktail Sisters, *La Revue Tricolore* exemplified the elaborateness of the revues. More was more, and Pessis and Crépineau observe that "as for the exquisite Cocktail Sisters, who flit about amid shafts of gilded light, fairy scenery and Chinese palaces, they play the only French girls in a show where all the characters are English."[58] This despite one of its numerous patriotic scenes portraying French soldiers in the trenches. The applause was deafening at the appearance of Maréchal "Papa" Joffre, hero of the battle at the Marne the previous fall.

Stage-Door Johnny

Insight into the ethos of men of fashion who flirted with decadence and would have been in the audience comes from published diaries of a man about Europe: Benjamin Frank Wedekind (1864–1918). Prototype of the decadent, bleary-eyed but priapic

Postcard, postmarked 1907: Le Cake-Walk. Danse au Nouveau Cirque. Les Soeurs Pérès.

bohemian, Wedekind was in Paris from 1892 to 1894 and described what paramours wore for private belly dances, and how one had a rope attached to two bedposts so a showgirl could practice her high kicks. Wedekind takes us very close to the plucky, marginalized showgirl of the early music-hall. Wedekind's other legacy is he wrote edgy plays, above all *The Lulu Plays*. Utilizing the character of the murderous sociopath who leaves no trace, Alban Berg created the terrifying decadent opera *Lulu*. John Simon in the *New York Times* recalled him as the greatest turn of the century American playwright,[59] which was tongue in cheek as Wedekind had a Swiss mother and a German father, was conceived in San Francisco and was born in Hanover, Germany. Doubtless, Wedekind had worldly sophistication. He immersed himself in the life of an urban sensualist, when young, before intensely devoting himself to marriage. He wrote plays about the crazed and doomed which inspired not only Alban Berg's *Lulu* but also my favorite rock band Metallica. Posturing as a wolfish roué in his diary in his late twenties, he recorded social interactions and brief encounters in Berlin, Munich, Paris and London. Many years later, his daughter released this diary, which was translated to English.

"Search fearlessly for every sin, for out of sin comes joy"—in his formative youth Wedekind lived by his mandate.[60] Paris had so many diversions, or *distractions,* for the determined decadent. The locales had names like Bullier's, Maison Fara, and Casino de Paris and were located around the Champs Elysées and in Montmartre. They were by now very posh. *The New York Times* noted when the Casino de Paris opened in November 1880 that it had grooms to get carriages, buttonhole bouquets, and service of ice water and even ice for other drinks! It would become Paris's third largest music-hall. Mel Gordon states that of the three it "attracted the greatest number of Frenchmen, and imported many Broadway and Harlem offerings from the Cotton Club and elsewhere. It was to be sure, America's most glamorous showbiz outpost in interwar Montmartre."[61] There were unadvertised night spots for more determined sinners. The options for frolicking with friends, relieving boredom, and pursuing willing girls filled Wedekind's nights. Typically he was shagging someone while looking over her shoulder at someone else. Most were prostitutes but many young women in the city were in flight from elsewhere or with dreams, feigning carelessness.

Wedekind averaged for a week in the spring of 1892 two entertainment spots a night. On May 23 he spent the evening at the Cirque d'Été. On May 24 he went from the Hotel St. George to the Moulin Rouge, with a lover. Another paramour was there, however, and the girlfriend he was with "carried on," engendering a skirmish that enlivened his night. He dined at the Golden Pheasant on the 25th. The following evening, after going to the Hotel St. George to meet female acquaintances, he ended up at the Concert Ambassadeur on the Champs Elyées. Two days later he went to the St. George to take the libertarian pair to the Hippodrome but instead spent the evening at the Théatre de Renaissance, seeing *Femme de Narcisse.* He was generally unsure who was a prostitute so he approached the matter skillfully. He discovered track marks on the arms of a woman dancing barefoot in a crimson-lined black velvet gown. He went home with her from a café and she was a morphine addict ready to sell her favors. On May 29 he went to the Jardin de Paris with male friends and wrote: "Very sophisticated variety show. Brilliant danseuse. Extremely elegant audience. We sit in a café behind the Opera until three o'clock. In the end, a superbly handsome creature in dressing-gown and overcoat appears and I procure her for Weinhoppel at the cost of a few kisses. Weinhoppel takes the bait somewhat reluctantly."[62]

Paris s'amuse au Moulin Rouge, showing the practice of a dancer high-kicking and knocking a man's top hat off his head, by Xavier Sager, c. 1890.

The Moulin Rouge was a hot spot but Wedekind made a point that the cancan dancers were lower class and most indifferent dancers, amateurs. Condescension was part of the sport, as it was in a more viral way for white customers of the all-black cast at the Cotton Club in New York a few decades later. Yet le Moulin Rouge was fun and the dancing was fun and distracted the fashionably decadent. It was a cynosure. He dreamed all of a week in June, he says, about the body of a dancer there; he shaved before going, and admired a dancer in a seaside costume who had the bruises of yesterday's lovemaking on her neck. The next day someone he recognized from the Jardin de Paris, an indifferent dancer but alluring, with "Eastern" features, had him and his *copain* up to her room where she and a cancan dancer did a belly-dance (the companion in floor-length diaphanous black lace).

On the night of July 3, Wedekind and his friend Weinhoppel went to the Jardin de Paris. They lunched late at a fine restaurant and strolled down the Champs Elysées to the cabaret:

Extreme feathered headdress on the cover *L'Assiette au Beurre*, January 28, 1909. The illustration is titled "Tante Lily" and signed Crésus.

We watch the first half of the variety show, and since there is no dance and the audience is distinctly plebian, we take a cab to the Moulin Rouge at ten o'clock. We've scarcely entered the hall when I spot Kadudja and give her a wide berth ... she asks me to dance with her. I decline, but when I notice that Weinhoppel's brow is urging me to agree, I hand him my umbrella. I dance as if inspired by some superior power, I get into the swing of it so smoothly, and don't stop until she's exhausted. I'm on the point of collapse as well.[63]

Kadudja shrugged off Wedekind's advances at the door. She dropped into an armchair, lifted her skirts and let Weinhoppel fan her body. Fired up, Wedekind had sex with her in the closet. Then she showed them the progress she had made in the cancan. Over the head of her bed Kadudja had fixed a pulley with a rope running over it.

At the same time in

Copyright. 1910. by C. Hobson.

A 1910 C. Hobson postcard: "If they do that dance in Heaven/ shoot me hon' to-night at seven."

America, a poster confirms the subtext of the young woman wanting to work on her can-can while aiming at proficiency in another "sport," cycling. A modern young woman wanted to flirt and, being a bold outsider, titillate, but she wasn't a man's toy. The poster, at the Library of Congress, is *Bon Ton Burlesquers 365 Days Ahead of Them All*, where stereotypical men could be Wedekind and his pals, held by the dancer's strings.

A Son Façon

The showgirl costume has always been a bold look. The showgirl struts like a goddess on earth, not a mincing miss. This is where the cancan had a great import in creating the icon.

The Nostalgic Cancan
VANESSA R. SCHWARTZ[64]

France has served since colonial times as the favored destination of privileged American travelers. With the expansion of tourism generally in the mid–twentieth century, France became the primary stop for Americans crossing the Atlantic for the first time. Moreover, since a comparably small number of immigrants came from France to the United States, France avoided association with the poor huddled masses, and remained a fantasy-land of culture, civilization, and oo-la-la.

Whereas elite French culture has made its impressive contribution to international arts and letters for centuries, it was the late nineteenth century that the French, especially Parisians, innovated in the popular sphere of culture, with lithographed posters, photography and movies disseminating to the world. Then, a vibrant back and forth between America and France evolved as the countries' film industries evolved, which created a lasting impact. It began from the earliest days: Thomas Edison visited Paris for the world's fair in 1889 and saw Etienne-Jules Marey's "chronophotographe," which helped him develop the Kinetoscope that led the Lumière brothers to create the Cinématographe that they exhibited in Paris in 1895. Hollywood and Paris joined to dance a duet in the progressively global business and art of the cinema, resulting in the extravagant Frenchness of 1950s movies, and their stars from Brigitte Bardot and Leslie Caron to Maurice Chevalier and Yves Montand.

The favorite setting was the belle époque, the nostalgic use of the post–World War I mythology of the turn of the century Paris as an innocent and joyous time, sidestepping the reality of the Vichy regime and Americans positioning themselves as the liberators of France. Old clichés were repeated to guarantee that Paris of the movies would please the senses. Paris was wicked, wonderful and artistic, while Montmartre became the touchstone for representing Paris in 1900.

An American in Paris (1951, not filmed in Paris) began the wave of films that used dancing Paris to interpret what was a new visual culture in the French capital in the 1890s. That Paris in the 1950s had neighborhoods that retained the appearance of the belle époque and Montmartre and Cancan dancers made the use of filming on location more credible. Some of the Hollywood films that celebrated Paris's music-halls and dance ambience were *Silk Stockings* (1957), *Les Girls* (1957), *Gigi* (1958), and the slightly later *Cancan* (1961) and *Black Tights* (1961), where the homely scenes of cabaret dancers is paired with Cyd Charisse and the cast in balletic choreography.

From its origin in the 1830s and forward, the Cancan provoked the forces of moral rectitude to object to its performance; eventually the dance turned into a charged symbol of French sexuality. It traveled to London and around the United States; its fame spread around the world. In the early years, the dancers were drumming up business of a sexual nature, and the association of the dance with solicitation contributed to its eventual integration into the saloon culture of the American West. By the 1890s, the dance became the crowning moment of the evening at numerous Parisian entertainment venues, launching such bright if fleeting careers as that of La Goulue and Jane Avril at the Moulin Rouge. The Cancan dance included the lifting of the leg not only in kicks that revealed the bare upper thigh and the dancer's undergarments, but also the slow lift of one leg in a circular motion that highlighted an exposed and moving buttocks. But it was later in the dance's 1890s revival that introduced greater fetishistic allure as dancers emphasized the actions of the skirt and petticoat that they manipulated with their hands and with their kicks.

The Cancan and the moeurs of belle époque entertainment in Montmartre eventually codified the old saw of Rabelaisian France … through the emergence of the entertainment industry that manufactured "la gaîté française."

The cancan's ancestor was performed during Napoléon Bonaparte's campaigns as a solo by one of the soldiers, and became part of the *quadrille des lanciers*. The dance's military drive is palpable, an automatic dimension of gestures that would be the basis for music-hall line dances. Journalist David Turecamo underlines the military nature of the choreography: "There is the chase, like a charge, the cavalry (right shoulder arms!), like

Postcard photograph of showgirls, by Henri Manuel.

the military carrying a rifle (it's the *port d'armes*). And then there is the *battement*, which means beating—think of a line of marching drummers."[65]

Both an energized and gymnastic polka and the cancan brought fame to the Bal Mabile, an upscale open-air dance hall that opened in 1831 (it closed in 1875) on the Avenue Montaigne. The Bal Mabile appeared in literature in the works of Honoré de Balzac and Hans Christian Andersen. Posters for shows in Chicago and Cincinnati feature "French Cancan" dancers doing their energized steps. A poster at the Library of Congress (1890) advertises the first time in America of the troupe from the "Jardine Mabile," and the dancers look straight out of the Moulin Rouge, in their plumed bonnets, low tight bodices, many petticoats and striped or black knee-highs with high heels. But the posters date from 1881, eight years before the Moulin Rouge opened. The Bal Mabile from a lithograph dated 1850–1860, preserved in the New York Public Library, looks like a heavenly refuge in the city of Paris, with lawns, trees and shrubs, sand paths, a grotto, and even a merry-go-round, lit by 2,000 gas lamps; no wonder the cancan got a fashionable start there.

The ante kept being raised so that cancan dancing was on the police radar. Thus the French Finette on a London engagement gained fame because of a police report that alleged indecency not for her boyish costume, which covered her body, but for her furious kicks.[66]

An Englishwoman, Kate Vaughan, brought her "skirt dancing" to Paris in 1876. Whatever the figure she danced she clutched her long skirt and moved it in time to the music. Her typical attire was lace-fringed petticoats, gold-spangled black tights, long black gloves and leather ankle boots. She showed her lace petticoats on stage first on Christmas Eve 1880. "Audiences were hooked not because she was lifting up her skirt, but because she seemed to be struggling unsuccessfully to keep her skirt down."[67]

The "French cancan," as the dance became known, took its ultimate form (and costume) at the Moulin Rouge, danced to galloping compositions by various musicians including Offenbach and Hervé, a founder of French operetta, and friend and rival of Offenbach's.[68]

A poster by Willette of 1901 is a close-up of the leg of a *cancaneuse*. She has a cotton black stocking seamed at the back which extends halfway up her thigh and is tied with a wide ribbon done up in a bow. In the 1890s nicknames like Peau de Satin ("Skin like Satin") or Nini La Belle en Cuisse ("Pretty Thighed Nini") became common for the most popular dancers. Observes Colin,

> The focus had changed from personal habits or facial features to parts of the body newly rendered visible by ever higher kicks. For all we or her contemporaries knew, Nini Bels Dents might have had pretty thighs as well. But nobody would have seen them when she was dancing back in the 1860s. As Cancan dancers revealed more of themselves, they lost their identity, becoming just elements in a line-up of what twentieth-century Parisian audiences simply called 'les girls.'"[69]

As time went on, the style of the costumes for the frenzied dance became more and more teasing, shorter and more open.

A big colorful poster adorned the entrance to the Moulin Rouge which showed a great deal of leg. It depicted Louise Weber, "La Goulue," a typical poor working girl who gained fame at the Moulin Rouge, rose and fell, and for a time was the toast of Paris. She showed up at fancy parties with her she-goat on a leash and her parrot on her shoulder.[70] La Goulue did not succeed on her own when she left the Moulin Rouge; eventually indigent, but brazen still, she returned to Montmartre and sold shoelaces and candies from a box around her neck.

Postcard of Arlette Dorgère.

Jane Avril replaced La Goulue when the latter left the Moulin Rouge to strike out on her own. Avril had been treated for hysteria, the Victorian Age putative female disease, in the Salpêtrière mental hospital. She danced with such concentration that her neurologist thought she was able to live in the outside world, and she danced first in nightclubs on the Left Bank and then in Montmartre. She said she was indifferent to material things and only interested in love. This departure from the demimondaine model struck a chord; the cancaneuse was admired for her devil-may-care attitude yet was associated with epileptic movements of exotic peoples. Writes Rae Beth Gordon, "Notice how the cancan dancer has come to symbolize la Parisienne for other European countries, while for the French she represents the hysteric and the savage." Journalists of around 1890 commented, however, on a possible benefit of the obscene dance: "The sexual desire that surges forth from ogling the movements of the cancan might possibly serve the patriotic cause of increasing the birth rate."[71]

By 1925 the cancan was choreographed (as opposed to maniacal), with dancers in matching petticoats and silk stockings. The first time I took the metro and emerged to see the red sails at the Place Blanche, I turned back; at that time, in the mid–1970s, it was infested with sex shops. Between 1889 and 1902 it had not only the "bal" or dance-hall indoors but, behind it, a large, attractive pleasure garden with small enclosures for dalliance. The poster for its opening is by Cheret, one of the trifecta of poster artists of music-halls, with Toulouse-Lautrec and Willette, and my favorite for the kinetic line and unforced verve; it has the working class girls, exposed to the thighs, and living it up and riding the donkeys that were a feature of the Moulin Rouge's garden. Photographs of the period show risqué costumes with some unity but also variety of the performers. Laurence Senelick informs on how to read these old photograph portraits: "Suggestive hints were conveyed by attitude, attire or some other visual clue to be interpreted by the knowing viewer."[72] This would include dresses in shiny fabric, décolletage, a slip as outerwear, naked arms, and high plumes attached to jaunty caps so that the hairdo showed to the maximum. Black and white stockings were worn with heeled shoes or dainty boots. Lacy undergarments were on display unless one was wearing the slip as outerwear.

But change was in the wind and the costumes, instead of being thrown together haphazardly, were designed by costumers. The movies made people expect more of costumes. The Casino de Paris, once Paris's "Pole Nord," a gaslight-lit skating rink, had revues mingled with American movies from 1896. In late November 1902, the Moulin Rouge was changed to a variety theater; no more dancing by nonprofessionals. With a new plush decor and keeping up with the trend of other Parisian music-halls to compete with and sometimes screen cinema there were now choreographed dazzle and fast revues: "if cinema astonishes people, the music-hall cannot do less" ["le cinema les étonne, le music-hall doit y parvenir également"], remarked journalist Jean Prasteau.[73] The Barrison Sisters were a rave for their bawdy synchronized dance. They had international success with one act where they did their kicks with kittens under the flouncy dresses, then raised their skirts over their knees and asked, "Would you like to see my pussy?"

Light

High heels, red lips, feathered headdress, spangles, and semi-nudity, features which constitute the iconic showgirl costume, come to life under lights. Showgirl costumes

Angélina of the Casino de Paris.

from the dawn of Argand theater lamps and electricity looked better on stage than off, now matter how fine the material and the construction.

Fire was a risk when gaslights lit the stage. The muslin dresses that ballerinas wore were highly flammable. A dancer could soak her dress in alum, which made the costume uncomfortable, or risk a tragic end brushing the gaslights. The English star Clara Webster

De Moralis on an undated postcard.

was playing a royal slave who was sprinkling her attendants with water from her bath when her filmy costume caught fire; she died a few days later (March 1855). Theater directors and audiences were aware of the danger to the dancers, which may have added to the tittilation.[74]

Charles Cros, as a "fumiste," or turn-of-the-century French hippie, thought that trains and planes, gas and electricity, mechanized labor and assembly lines were here to stay, and had to be worked into one's art. His poem "A les amants" encouraged lovers to make love in the here and now, in a woodland setting, but, second best, "if you please go into the theaters, to the best seats, under the gaslights." Music-hall audiences were seeing in their nightlife a degree of illumination they would not have in their homes.

When Victor Hugo heralded Paris as "the city of light" he meant in terms of intellectual enlightenment. In tourist literature and newspaper reportage related to the Exposition Universelle of 1900 the expression "Ville Lumière" was more literal. While most of the city was still lit by gaslights, the fair had electric lights illuminating the Eiffel Tower, other monuments, and boulevards.[75]

When the *Place aux Jeunes* opened in November 1886, the Folies Bergère already had five electricians; "they were known as 'projectionists' and worked with oxygen lamps. The auditorium was lit with compressed gas and every night, about midnight, a 'gas cart' drew up outside the Folies to refuel the theater for the following day's performance."[76] By the 1950s of the 340 support people there were 18 electricians.

Liane De Vries at the Folies Bergère.

Paule Delys at the Alcazar d'Été on a 1904 postcard.

Actresses and showgirls wanted to exhibit glitter to the maximum. They exteriorized their femininity, making it easy to impersonate them in plays of the time and later. Thus Cécile Sorel invited Oscar Wilde to her marvelous Paris townhouse. When Wilde was coming to dinner, she greeted him with panache—lackeys who lined the steps of the great stone staircase and servants in white jackets and stockings. She was wearing a diadem, a full complement of her necklaces, bracelets and rings, and a tight-fitting gold

Arlette Dorgère on a postcard postmarked 1906.

dress. She shone in the light of, as she recalled, a "forest of lights." Wilde responded to the quintessential display, according to Sorel, that she was the woman he had often dreamed of, the image of the woman he created in his imaginings: "Vous seule auriez pu me sauver…. Je vous connaissais mieux par ma Salomé que par la Comédie-Française. Pour moi, vous étiez toutes les déesses, tous les êtres, tous les sexes et toutes les âmes."

[You might have saved me. I knew you better for my Salomé than the Comédie-Française. To me you were all the goddesses, all the beings, all the sexes and all the souls.][77] Light and costume created the effect where the individual was effaced and the glamour was something separate, lifting off.

The Croqueueses de Diamants

The revues had the stars whose costumes outdid the bourgeoisie's. They usually dressed as dancers in the photographic portraits—especially Spanish dance, which had been popular in French theater since the compositions of Jean-Baptiste Lully at the French court. Dancing was the alluring art that required lighter than ordinary clothes. When the music-halls started, lingerie, corsets, bustiers and brassieres suddenly were in evidence on stage. They were markers of the showgirls and could be incredibly fancy. Wearing undergarments as outer garments was a great innovation. Even the lacing of a bustier was part of the costume. These articles of lingerie had to be dramatic because the fact was they covered body stockings, a foundation not dispensed with until the late 1910s.

In general, the fin de siècle sirens played up the trope of the woman voracious for money and sex. A glimpse of a few of the women who participated in the image follows.

Liane de Pougy

At the Folies, Liane de Pougy, who was famous for beauty rather than talent, had an act where she wore a diamond pasty on each nipple (we recall that showing leg was more titillating than showing bosom). She may have been the first of the lineage of this style of undress on stage, but "firsts" related to music-hall nudity are so disputed as to be only of interest as approximations of what came first where. There are very few images and descriptions by contemporary viewers, and reviewers tend to exaggerate levels of undress. It is sure, nevertheless, that de Pougy's costumes were designed to shock. In a sketch written by a gossip columnist, her friend Jean Lorrain, said that the costume of *L'Araignée d'Or* (The Golden Spider) consisted of merely "a few tatters of gold lace, in which she posed at the center of a vast, shimmering wire web, in which were trapped several helpless male victims, all elegantly attired in full evening dress."[78]

Maxim's was quite new and served as the watering hole of rich decadents; here Liane de Pougy, Caroline Otéro, and others outdid one another with their finery. They fought one spring evening in 1896. Liane entered Maxim's squired by a trio of elegant gentlemen, bedecked with a glittering array of pearls, emeralds, and sapphires, plus a diamond tiara. The next night, at Maxim's peak hour, Caroline made an entrance up the red-carpeted stairs, wearing a long sleek black gown and no jewelry. Behind her was her housemaid wearing the dress Pougy had worn, loaded with gems. Yet Pougy gave a journalist this opinion of two demimondaines, Lina Cavalieri and Otéro, in 1919: "It's like this. When Cavalieri wears real jewels they look false, and when Otéro wears false jewels, they look real."[79] In fact, since Lina Cavalieri was very lovely, this quip may have been more intended to insult Cavalieri than compliment Otéro.

The lust for froufrou, baubles, and temporary freedom from inhibitions filtered down to ordinary men and women who may not even have seen a photograph of the likes of the showgirl courtesans. Mary Louise Roberts points out how they projected a societal

Dora Parnès, the Moulin Rouge singer known as "La Belle Napolitaine."

id: "Because in the popular imagination women were thought to lack a rational, autonomous self to begin with, they served as a convenient symbol for the newly recognized powers of irrational drives."[80] In Guy de Maupassant's short story "La Parure," Mathilde, a charming girl from a working class family, loses the necklace she had borrowed from a rich friend in order to attend a ball, and works to the bone over the next ten years to pay off the debt she incurred to replace it, only to find out that it was paste. Rachel Mesch, in her study of the fin de siècle through the lens of women's magazines, calls such texts, of which Gustave Flaubert's is the most famous, "Cinderella-stories gone awry; women longing to be lifted out of their mundane existences in order to become princesses, but denied happy endings." The authors responded to the lifestyle of the most materially successful performers on stage by writing cautionary tales about women's unbridled ambition "bred of consumerist lust and the desire to imitate those more fortunate."[81]

LOIE FULLER

Loie Fuller (1862–1928) enchanted Paris with her butterfly-like dances, lit by colored electrical lights. Born in 1862 in Fullersburg, Illinois, she started off in vaudeville and circuses, and developed a special dance of Salomé. One evening she was accidentally caught in the multicolored beam of a light projection, a happenstance that inspired a lifetime of experiment on the interaction of dance and light. With fans billowing the folds of her gigantic silk veils, hit by colored lights, she did dances like none that had gone before and became a personification of Art Nouveau.

She first did her Serpentine Dance in February 1892 in New York. She appeared at the Folies Bergère that November. This time she performed her Fire Dance, in which she danced on a sheet of glass, and a red light, coming up through a trap door, made it look as though the fire engulfed her. "She held long baton-like wands of aluminum or bamboo and swirled the translucent silk fast and furiously. The movement came from her core as she twisted her torso, keeping the batons suspended during her performance."[82] This was set to Wagner; later she would dance to other avant-garde composers of her time.

She was unhappy with being billed after Caroline Otéro and the five cutie-pie Barrison Sisters from the U.S., who sang and danced as a small chorus line. After the 1893–1894 season, she left the Folies Bergère and went elsewhere in Europe where she had continuing success. She varied her personae from one manifestation of Salome to the other: the destroyer of men's souls, in daring dark satin slinky dresses wrapped round her, to the chaste unattainable beauty, having a garden of flowers on her body and in her hair. For her repertory of five dances—Night, White, Firmament, Fire and Lily, the costumes involved vast amounts of silk robes and scarves in dramatic colors, sometimes medleys of hues or iridescence, spangles, and décolleté bodice but modest tights. For her shortest dance, Lily, she wore a costume that contained 500 yards of thin silk, which when in motion extended ten feet from her body in every direction. To keep the material under control she had to run about the stage while quickly waving extra-long wands that were attached to her dress. This created what looked like an enormous calla lily.[83] The performance lasted a half-hour.

Fuller had at different times diverging explanations for her type costume—that an Indian officer gave her a sari that blew round her when she performed (of muslin or silk, she varied that). Or that she and her mother were starving in a London garret, and when she had an opportunity to dance she had nothing to wear so she and her mother looked in some old trunks and came upon yards and yards of cheese-cloth, which they arranged on her body with their few pins; she discovered the garb created an effect when she lifted and raised her arms, twisting and swaying.[84]

When Fuller returned to Paris from America in 1897 she reappeared at the Folies

Paule Morley on a postcard postmarked 1902.

Bergère as a star, due to her numbers utilizing electrical light. She created her avant-garde dance at a transitional period between gas and electrical stage lighting. Gas lights could be centrally controlled so as to light up the stage when the audience area darkened. Limelight (obtained by heating a cylinder of lime) was a means to have a single light glow intensely. By 1849 at the Paris Opera a third type of stage lighting, an early form of electrical illumination called arc lamps, was used. Then, consequent to Thomas Edison's invention of incandescent bulbs, theaters had a less glaring, safer, and cooler light source. Sometimes theaters possessed their own generators, supplemented by the gas and limelights for special effects.

The Currents in their biography detail the effects that Fuller devised for the Serpentine Dance:

> Her "limelight" consisted of an arc light in a box with an opening and a lens, in front of which was a rotatable disk with colored gelatin circles around the edge. This arrangement was common enough; what she contributed were her private formulas for tinting the gelatin and her refined techniques for blending and dissolving the colors when they were projected on her swirling draperies. "How this is done by limelight is my secret," she boasted.
>
> She had a slide projector, arc-lit, for which she made the slides herself. To make it more flexible she used a double projector, called a stereopticon, to superimpose one image on another, for a fluid transition or a shimmer. She relied on secrecy for her gelatins and slides although she patented some of her stage mechanisms, the many (34 for her Salomé dance) lamps and her hand-held projectors.[85]

Subsequently, dancing to lights became popular on music-hall stages in Europe. Marie Leyton, "The Electrical Serpentine Dancer," floated with blue gauze over a blue jacket and appeared to catch fire as colored beams struck her. Leyton claimed that she and Loie both got their inspiration from London's Gaiety Theater, where a costumer had made a dress for the dancers that had a very high waist and full gauzy skirt, presumably looking magical when lit by colored lights.

Fuller designed her costumes and worked out the colored gels and chemical salts for luminescent lighting. She achieved a sort of phosphorescence like what is seen in some Art Nouveau glass. The Lumière Brothers filmed her Serpentine Dance in color in 1896. Dance historian Angenette Spalink captures the effect in words:

> The motion of the dance and the movement of the fabric along with the play of light and shadow cause Fuller's body to be both visible and invisible, both absent and present. When her body is not present it appears as though there is a whirling colorful "other" on stage.... Eventually, her body will briefly come into view again and thus remind the spectator there is indeed a human body performing onstage. However, then the body will evanesce and all the eye will perceive is the whoosh of colorful perpetual motion as the body disappears, reappears, and disappears.[86]

A dance that Fuller choreographed in 1898 was fundamentally the first go-go dance: she performed inside a glass box and saw herself in mirrors.

Many artists found Fuller intriguing and represented her in painting, sculpture and the decorative arts. The veils flash with color against black in Jule Cheret's poster for the Folies Bergère, while Toulouse-Lautrec depicted her in a series of pictures of a ghostly metamorphosis.

The glaring lights gravely damaged Fuller's sight and then she became fatally ill from the chemicals used for stage effects. She died poor like many of the women on the stage of the era, not from living too high or addiction but, according to Jacques-Charles, from devotion to her art, overspending on research in lighting for the dances.

CAROLINE OTÉRO

Interpreting Spanish and South American dances was an art in itself, most realized on the Paris stage by Caroline Otéro (1868–1965).

The brassieres Otéro wore were of the same ilk as what an undergarment designer for Victoria's Secret told me were called in-house the one-minute bras. Made with lace, embroidery, veiling, metallic threads and rhinestones, the one-minute bras are intended to allure but be quickly removed during sex. Showgirls in Las Vegas, and the daring stars of the music-halls of Paris in 1900, had gems welded on their brassieres, for glamour, longevity and safety.

La Belle Otéro showed a leg to reveal a garter belt made of jewels designed by Boucheron, the jeweler where royalty purchased their bijoux. Writes Griffin, "Born illegitimate and poor in a small village in Spain, were it not for her cheekiness Otéro would never have set foot in Boucheron. Thus, the image of the garter belt is doubly insolent, sparking effrontery, audacity mingled luxuriantly with seduction."[87]

Loie Fuller, lithograph by Henri de Toulouse-Lautrec (courtesy Henri de Toulouse-Lautrec Collection, Boston Public Library).

The courtesans of the latter part of the nineteenth century capitalized on male bravura. To make a conquest of a courtesan added to a man's importance because "le monde" knew who she was and how demanding, materially and one could presume sexually. Appearing in music-hall shows and displaying her charisma put Caroline Otéro in front of wealthy men about town. She had a fabulous lifestyle that she fought to maintain. She got the richest men and royalty because of men's insecurity. Thus the courtesans did not gain fame by strutting on the boulevard or parading through the Bois de Boulogne. Thousands of people in the audience saw them on stage and of course, like Sarah Bernhardt, they dressed as riotously offstage as on. Another expression for these early showgirls is "le haut de pavé," or "the upper class of the pavement," from the fact that people in fine clothes would walk at the edge of the street that was a little higher.

Due to the slow speed of early photography, and the advantage of studio lighting, the abundant photographs of courtesans are "stagey" and only complement what is known of their lives. Liane de Pougy, Emilienne d'Alençon and Caroline Otéro were known as

Left: An undated French postcard. *Right:* Caroline Otéro on a postcard postmarked 1902.

the Three Graces of the Folies Bergère, humorously also known as the "grandes horizontales." Pougy was famous for being famous. She took some acting lessons from Sarah Bernhardt who advised her to display her beauty but when she got on stage "you had better keep your pretty mouth shut." When Pougy was appearing at the Folies Bergère, she sent the Prince of Wales (the future Edward VII) an invitation to the show. He accepted, and her star rose. Emilienne d'Alençon was her friend but also her rival. They had a battle of fashion. One night both women were invited to the same dinner party. D'Alençon let on to Pougy that she was wearing a casual skirt and blouse. Pougy agreed to dress down as well. But, arriving second, d'Alençon made her entrance wearing white and gold brocade embroidered with pearls, diamonds and rubies. "Pougy never trusted her again," wrote Ian Graham in *Scarlet Women*.[88]

No one appeared on the music-hall stage more bedecked in jewelry and dramatic costumes than La Belle Otéro. Among the demimondaines who tweaked the rules of society she also had the most brazen reputation. The papers tallied her high-profile swains and receipts of deeds and jewels, as well as praising her dancing and singing. Her mother had four sons and two daughters, and no husband. She bought castanets for the daughter who danced with natural elan. One day, as the girl walked in the woods, the village shoemaker raped and nearly murdered her. After that, villagers shunned her. In her memoirs, she recalled a sweet existence that when she was eleven went up in flames. Six months later, she took the name of her dead sister, Caroline, and with the help of impresarios who would be among her lovers, she made her way in the world of stage.

She eventually came to Paris and became featured at the Folies Bergère, known for her Spanish dance and the clothes she conjured up. Often they were eccentric and evidenced her taste for the voluptuous. She might appear Orientalized, as a Byzantine princess or belly dancer, in layers of skirts with a Romany flair; or play the soldier, amazon, or Pierette. The dresses accentuated her bosom and sculpted her figure. The costumes look cumbersome in still photographs yet must have allowed for her energized performance. (Like other demimondaines she licensed postcards whose distribution extended her fame, and took her costumes and gestures with her from the theater to the studio.[89])

During the years Colette spent on the stage after her divorce from Willy, she and Caroline became friends. Colette saw that nothing counted more to Caroline than making a fashion statement. Colette wrote in *Mes Apprentissages* that Madame Otéro "was pure ornament": "'You look out of sorts, my little one,' she once said to me. 'Remember that there is always a moment in a man's life, even if he's a miser, when he opens his hand wide.' 'The moment of passion?' 'No. The moment when you twist his wrist.'"[90]

In Paris and New York, Caroline's style of dance impressed audiences with its fury and energy, like an exorcism of her childhood trauma. She wrote in her memoir that childhood troubles "penetrate deepest … their hurt is most complete and hopeless."

She was also famous for her male conquests. One such story is that one night a male confidant came to the door of her dressing room to say that an Englishman in the audience was eager to meet her, and that he was enormously rich. La Belle Otéro had many royal lovers so one would not suppose she was interested, but, famously avaricious, she was, and arranged to meet the admirer for lunch. But she got up sooner from the table than he would have liked, apologizing that she had an urgent appointment.

With whom, he asked? Surely not an engagement more important than with himself.

It was very important, she told him. It was to collect an advance of 40,000 francs with which she needed to pay a dressmaker's bill.

If all she needed was 40,000 francs he would give them to her, he said, on condition she go to London.

She agreed but said if she missed a night at the Folies Bergère she would have to pay an expensive fine. He did not mind taking care of the fine; she excused herself to telephone her dressmaker. "You know I owe nothing but I want you to make out a bill for 40,000 francs and I shall come round and pay it. But the money is mine, you understand." She next called the manager of the Folies and said she was ill and couldn't perform for a week and was paying her forfeit but wished it back.

Brassieres of filigree, jewels and pearls were a trademark. No one hitherto had accentuated the breasts with what looked like jeweled armor: it was a look out of Valhalla and belly dancing—only one bejeweled cup on the bra for her Amazon costume. The cancan dancers embellished and showed the garter of their stockings but none equaled hers, with dozens of jewels attached to the very fine silk knit. Her breasts are supposed to have inspired the architect Charles Dames to design the cupolas of the Hotel Carlton in Nice.

It was de rigueur for a cocotte to perform internationally and she performed Spanish dance in New York in 1890, at age 21, making her American debut at the Eden Musée, a combined wax museum and performance hall at 55 West 23rd Street. She created a sensation; the crowd was posh and of both genders; women came to evaluate her clothes. Perhaps that night they would see the necklace of Empress Eugénie or the Empress of Austria.

Andreys—another single-named showgirl—on a 1905 postcard.

To be a demimondaine (or cocotte) as a career alternative ended with the First World War, when big spenders lost their fortunes and aristocrats their levity and largesse. When Otéro died in 1965 in Nice, a life of gambling at the casinos had consumed her wealth—she had only trinkets left—which fit the trope of the showgirl's life of excess and became a morality tale.

A huge advantage of the courtesans was their being able to commission their own costumes for the music-halls. The music-halls were competing and more society ladies were in the audience ogling the historical and contemporary designs. Costuming varied from one hall to the next and the photographs taken by studio photographers probably exaggerate how revealing the costumes were. Attention paid to costumes grew so major, writes Sarah Gutsche-Miller, that "it took on almost comic proportions in the 1900s. Programs from the 1880s and 1890s already included the names of all costume designers and makers. After 1900, they also detailed the provenance of every costume, hat, accessory, wig, and shoes." Gutsche-Miller points to a 1908 show at the Casino de Paris whose program listed the names of costume and set designers, Maison Bor for shoemakers, Maison Baudet the wigmakers, and Maison Plimsaults the jewelers, yet omitted the choreographer.[91]

Among Caroline Otéro's lovers were Prince Albert of Monaco, King Leopold II of Belgium, Prince Nicholas I of Montenegro, Grand Duke Nikolai of Russia, and the Prince of Wales before he succeeded Queen Victoria as King Edward VII. Otéro referred publicly to their relative virility and vaunted her sexual encounters like sports matches. She told a laundress who worked for her, "Je fornique utile, et quand c'est possible en y prenant du plaisir" [I find sex useful, and when possible, take pleasure in it].[92]

Vague about her life, she had total recall of her jewel collection, and reeled off chapter and verse the gifts men bestowed on her. She was another example of a Marie Antoinette fantasy, as she ordered a reinterpretation of Marie Antoinette's necklace from Cartier's. She also created her own legend, and her offstage life, it is said, included doing a striptease at the Grand-Véfour of the Palais Royal at a private party, and being served naked on a tray to a table of guests of an aristocratic host in Russia.

An impression comes from the Swiss artist Paul Klee of her "orgiastic" Spanish dance:

> Now at last the real Otéro! She stands there, her eyes searching and challenging, every inch a woman, frightening as in the enjoyment of tragedy. After the first part of the dance she rests. And then mysteriously, as it were autonomously, a leg appears clothed in a whole new world of colors. An unsurpassedly perfect leg.[93]

How men could slavishly devote themselves to the demimondaines is hard to grasp. The men clearly needed to be kicked, if not literally, as the pursuit of the femme fatale was epidemic among high-status men. Likely also, in contrast to the ideal of domestic wife the brazen hussy excited them. A cocotte like Caroline was cool-headed about the act of love. She revealed to Colette that she liked the grand politician Aristide Briand, then President du Conseil, because "huit ou dix fois par nuit, il remet le couvert. Ça c'est un male, un vrai!" [He gets it up eight or ten times a night. That's a true man!][94] For the music-halls, the reciprocity was great. During the years 1880–1900, when the cocottes reigned, their fame as sex bombs obviated the need for major talents (who, like Mistinguett, followed them in the next generation). One can only imagine the brio of the Spanish dancer sweeping on stage in a diamond corselet fashioned for her statuesque self by Cartier himself, two armed guards surveilling from the wings.

GABY DESLYS

Showgirls descend curving staircases. It shows they are insouciant of headdress and high heels. Gaby Deslys (Marie-Elise Gabrielle Caire), born in 1881, was the star who first descended the celebrated staircase of the Folies Bergère, with her partner, New Yorker Harry Pilcher. She did so in a burst of feathers, her trademark that ushered in the astonishing elaborate feathered costumes later used in music-hall revues.

Cecil Beaton called her "a key transitional figure and successor to the grand Parisian cocottes of the nineties on the one hand and, since she was a theatrical figure, the precursor of a whole school of glamour that was to be exemplified 20 years later by Marlene Dietrich." To Erté she was the greatest star of music-hall (he wrote this in a foreword to James Gardiner's biography of Deslys).[95] Erté designed her costumes for the reopening of the Femina Theater after World War I, a revue called *La Marche à l'Etoile*. The costumes were credited to the important costumer Madame Rasimi but the ermine skirt with two high trains, one on each side, have the stylistic imprint of Erté, who liked to multiply trains, thereby sometimes dressing several people in a single costume.

By 1905 Gaby was singing and dancing in a revue that included a short movie. She was hired for the Gaiety Theater in London as a glamorous accessory with a three-month contract starting September 1906 which promised her superb costumes. She burst out of a basket of silk roses in a low-cut dress, ruffled petticoats, beribboned garters and high-button boots, just like what she had worn at the Olympia in Paris. Her costumes were known for suggestive glamour, such as the sea-motif outfit with starfish centered on her breasts, straps that left a shoulder bare, and a whisper of a sleeve on the upper arm. She did a modified striptease, in the category now referred to as Victorian striptease, at the Alhambra in London in the winter of 1907. She played a spinning diabolo top, wore a tight sheath from neck to ankle, and during the act the sheath unwound to a low-fitting bathing dress. In 1910 she changed her sweetheart image to a siren and appeared at the Alhambra in a tutu with a leotard top, whose thin straps and beaded fabric shaded darker over the nipples.

Gaby met her dream partner when she was performing in New York City. She was the diva and Harry Pilcher was one of the "boys" holding the train on her dress and forming the line around her entrance. A tailor's son, he had danced at age nine on the stage with Fred Astaire. When Gaby returned to France she took Pilcher with her, along with 64 suitcases and 22 hat boxes, two dogs, a monkey and a maid "bent over by the weight of the jewelry box."[96] Together they popularized ragtime dancing in Paris.

Their dancing in the 1910s was seen as racy. Harry and Gaby gave a dance competition in July 1912 and the kaleidoscope of the guests' costumes was inspired by Léon Bakst's designs of 1909 for Serge Diaghilev's Ballets Russes. She introduced the jazz band to Paris, writes Damase, and, "smothered in plumes and feathers, bejeweled like a queen," she performed dances "of an almost insane ferocity."[97]

Her two flops both occurred in New Haven during American engagements. Gaby was already famous. Americans were doing spectacular revues when the Shubert Brothers brought her to the U.S. in 1911. Before opening in New York, she had the worst night of her career at New Haven's Hyperion Theater on November 19. Yale had lost to their arch rival Princeton, ticket prices were raised, and the show lasted over 2½ hours, with Gaby's entrance delayed until after the intermission. When she finally appeared, she was booed and an apple core hit her in the leg; students rioted, ripping up seats. Gaby had to fulfill her Shubert contract and when she opened in New Haven the Yale students forced her off the stage again (in early 1914).

For *A La Carte* she wore harem pants topped by a lampshade skirt, and danced up and down a staircase, which would become a feature of revues. In one scene she powdered her legs (which were clad in stockings), an ultimate tease about naked legs before music-halls actually bared them. Backstage in her dressing room at the Palace banked by lilies and wearing a blue chiffon peignoir with white marabou, she gave an interview to a reporter. People, she said, thought her dressed improperly but she was a religious person and a well-behaved girl. As Gaby spoke, her marmoset monkey clambered up, and fell into a large pot of rouge.

By now early conservationists had introduced a bill (U.S. and Canadian, 1916) banning the importation of the many species of rare birds being slaughtered for ladies' hats and clothing, but Gaby returned to Europe and was mocked at times for her feathers but not censured.

For *Marcher à l'Etoile,* April 1919, the reopening of the Femina, Gaby dolls were made up for sale by Madame Rasimi, available in the foyer. She flew in a plane with Harry over Paris, scattering gold paper coins with their names and profiles. In the show Gaby wore a huge headdress: "One critic contrasting the smallness of the auditorium with the vastness of Gaby's headdress said that his seat was so close to the stage that, at one point, he was afraid that if Gaby's feathered monster was not firmly anchored to her head, he would end up wearing it."[98]

Decorative artifice is distinctly Parisian. Fake pearls were invented in Paris, the making of silk flowers was a great secret, and feathers for hats, headdresses, boas and so forth developed to unequaled art. This has been true all the way to the Vegas shows, when feathers were brought in with a multimillion dollar bond, and feathered costumes had to be returned to France or destroyed. The story of showgirls and feathers is a story of boggling excess. In the 1920s, Mistinguett's favorite stage costume had a 25-yard-long train of ostrich feathers, yet it was Gaby who is properly identified with the principle that more feathers is more.

Like many other showgirls, Gaby had a symmetrical, plain face on which various emotions could be writ. Her eyebrows arched so that they were highest at the bridge of her nose and framed her eyes exactly. Her upper lip turned up kissably and as though she was always happy. The variety of the feathers seen in photographs is remarkable. They are attached to lacy caps, crocheted cloches, crowns, and bands. White feathers make her look swanlike. Dark feathers curve in a double arabesque and are laced with strands of pearls. At the end of a stiff three-foot "pole" a plume shakes in the air. Not all the feather decorations are swishing and soft. On a helmet the feathers are stiff as boar's brush and they stick out every which way on another headdress that looks like an open milkweed pod.

When Gaby died of a recurring throat malady at 38, she willed use of her considerable fortune to her sisters and mother, with the totality of her goods and jewels to go later to the poor of Marseille, and for her villa to become a hospital.[99]

Leona Dare

Until the 1910s, women's swimsuits had high necks and sleeves and legs were covered to the knee. They were functional and plain. What must women have thought when they saw Leona Dare (1854–1922), or her picture, in her exciting designs, with low necklines,

Aragon, undated postcard.

and showing arms and thighs. In photographs, Leona Dare looks as pretty as a bandbox on the Fourth of July.

Leona Dare learned acrobatics from the Hall brothers in New Orleans and married Thomas Hall. They had a stunt where she was suspended under a hot-air balloon and lifted Thomas off the ground holding him by his waistband in her teeth. Leona's own brother was a one-armed circus acrobat who performed in Europe.

She became a premier female circus performer in America and Europe, fêted as the "Queen of the Antilles" and the "Pride of Madrid" (she had dark hair and eyes) and went back and forth performing in Europe and America. At the Folies Bergère she would hang from her metal mouth guard and descend from the dome. However, she had ups and downs with her partners. She and her husband had a disagreement and when she performed at Oxford she asked that he not be hired and not be a spectator when she performed. When she was back in Chicago, Thomas Hall claimed she had abandoned him; moreover he sued her for the apparatuses she used which he said he invented during the four years they lived together, and which because he used "fourth grown hickory" (the wood in its fourth growing season) he could not reproduce.[100] Thomas lost because Leona Dare had got a quick divorce. *The Times* commented: "Mr. Hall does not seem to have been favored with much of the society of his brilliant consort, but that, perhaps, is the general lot of those who are united to women of European reputation."

Dare was married to her second husband, a Viennese from a banking family, Ernest Theodore Grunebaum, when she dropped her aerial partner, who died of the injury. The year the Moulin Rouge was founded she was performing in Paris and went up in a hot air balloon with the Swiss balloonist Edouard Spelterini who took amazing photographs from his balloon. He took Dare very high, perhaps rising to 5,000 feet while she did acrobatics. Then he left for Egypt for more romantic adventures.

In 1890, Dare broke her leg in Paris during another balloon demonstration and in 1894, at 50, she stopped performing. She lived on the West Coast of the U.S. for the rest of her life.

Posters and photographs record the stunning costumes Dare wore for her aerial acrobatics. Her waist was always cinched in with a corset. She favored fancy boots, sometimes with high heels, lacing, or a decoration like (at the Folies Bergère) little wings. She had a lavish bush of frizzy hair which she wore in a variety of styles, usually knotted high at the back and flying behind her, ornamented with a hairband across her forehead or a crown. By applying dainty appliqués to her costumes she concocted bright color combinations, and in every guise looks svelte and self-possessed. The typical cap sleeves are trimmed with fringe or little swags, which, by intention or not, played down her muscles. The deep square neckline and shortest tight pantaloons she wears in a cabinet card by photographer Jeremiah Gurney are typically daring, the pantaloons being cut to show thigh. Presumably she always wore white stockings but whether she had on a bodysuit mitigating the bare look of her shoulders and gorge is hard to judge. She brought the display of a muscular yet feminine body to the music-hall, as well as a certain outrageousness in her clothing.

SIMONE D'HERLYS

Simone D'Herlys (1881–1920) reveled in little nothings as no one before. A star in the U.S. and Paris, whom the London "Tatler" called the "most sensational dancer in

Paris," Dherlys, as she was known, performed at many music-halls, is documented as the first to perform nude in one, and later became Madame Jacques-Charles, wife of the legendary director of the Folies Bergère grand spectacles until 1918. The police determined that at the Moulin Rouge "la belle Dracy" was performing shocking immoral exhibitions in a tableau of the show *Cache ton nu*. The government might slap a hand but the charges were not severe, and in any case it was July 1914 and there were more serious matters to attend to.

Dherlys starred at the Theatre de Paris and the Casino de Paris from 1913 for eight years, also filling in the interstices with roles in Ziegfeld musicals in New York from 1916 to 1919. In postcards she wears pearls and feathers, or pearls and rhinestones, tastefully undressed and at ease. Ropes of pearls drip from her neck or waist—she preferred them to gemstones. She wears a Deco diadem or other minimal hair ornament, and as covering brief shorts, a skirtlet tied around her waist or a decoration on her mons. Her gestures suggest that a robe or stole is incidental, in the photographs. Her hair is short and fluffy as if she modeled the New Woman as well as the femme fatale.

In November 1915 she was expelled from England for immorality on stage. Nude revues were still embryonic and her graceful nudity was remarkable. She appeared as Venus at the Théâtre de Champs-Elysées with barely a stitch on and in the more prurient duet with a male partner who had her wrists tied in bondage in *Paris qui Jazz* with costumes by Paul Poiret. The same year, 1920, she played a "vision" at the Théâtre de Paris.

In turn-of-the-century society, a conventional man wanted an old-fashioned girl, not a New Woman. A suffragist and fiction writer, Sarah Grand (born in Ireland in 1854), has been credited with coining the phrase New Woman. She put in the thoughts of an artist, a male narrator in her fiction, the current female ideal. When he sees a new model under electric lights he thinks:

> They were the mocking eyes of that creature most abhorrent to the soul of man, a woman who claims to rule and does not care to please; eyes out of which an imperious spirit shone independently, not looking up, but meeting mine on the same level. Now, a really attractive, womanly woman looks up, clings, depends, so that a man can never forget his own superiority in her presence.[101]

The "Nue" and Female Consciousness

LELA F. KERLEY[102]

Originating in the 1890s, the term "New Woman" represented a crucial transitional female figure who challenged the patriarchal order in her attempts to achieve social, economic, and political power. A large part of this self-realization had to do with women rediscovering their corporeal selves as a source of identity, self-pleasure, and empowerment. One way in which women contributed to the creation of new body culture during France's Third Republic was through an engagement with the Nude as artist-models, writers, and performers. I argue that demands for greater sexual freedom and individual self-expression were most visibly manifest in "la femme nue's" disavowal of clothing within the "bal public" and popular theater. By making public spectacles of themselves, the models of the Bal des Quat'z-Arts and "les femmes nues" of the music-hall defied the traditional boundaries of normative bourgeois femininity represented by separate spheres, physical modesty, and self-abnegation.

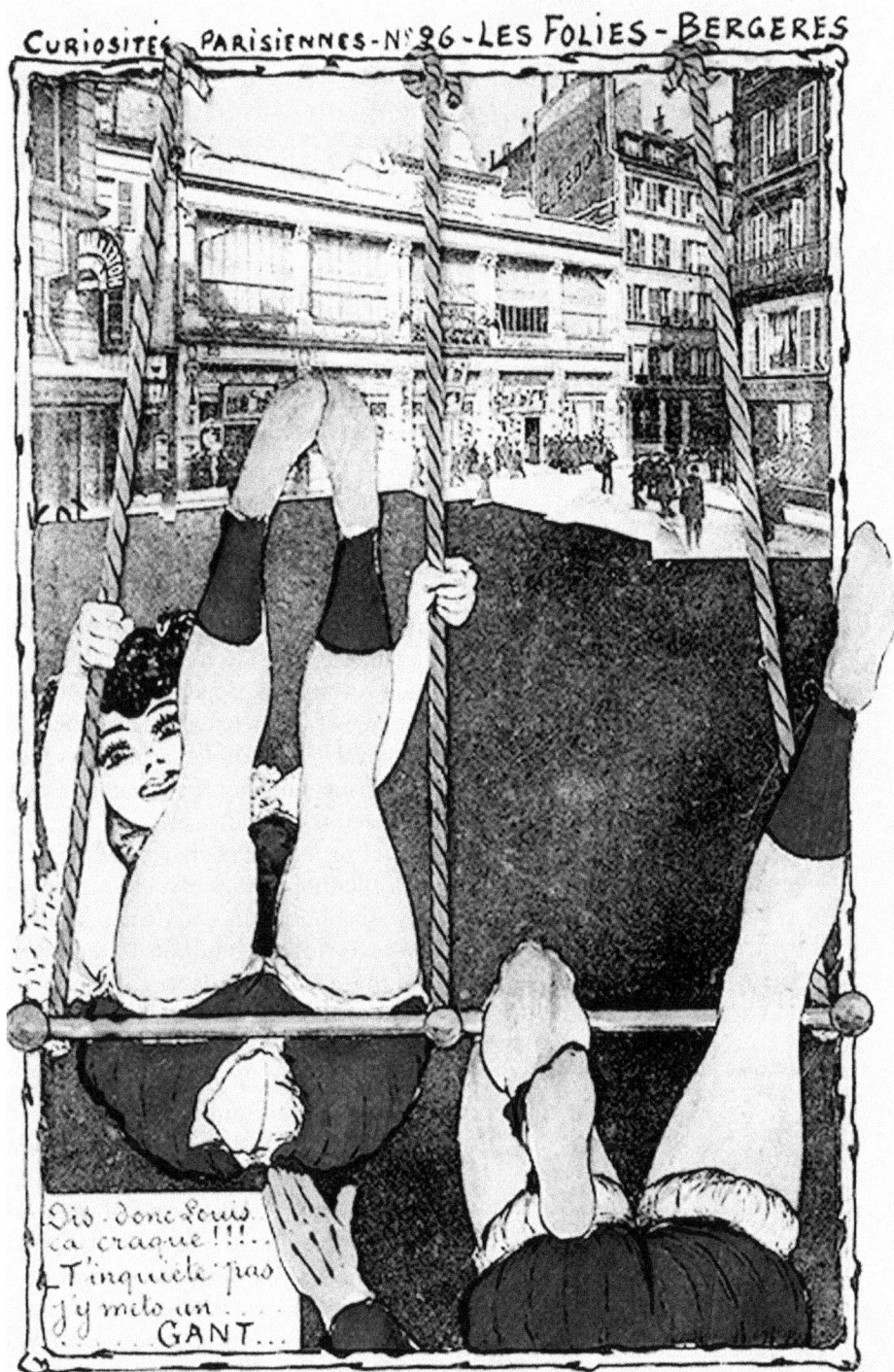

Postcard: "Curiosités Parisiennes no. 96—Les Folies Bergères." The amusing verse at the bottom references not worrying about a "crack"—there is a "glove."

The performative female nude coincided with and contributed to the formation of an alternative femininity embodied by the New Woman. Her experimentation with nudity and themes of undressing was indicative of what Mary Louise Roberts calls "feminine aesthetics," that is to say, "a public image that was transgressive yet culturally agreeable."[103]

While initially provocative and at odds with contemporary mores, a reimagining of the body as free of religious dictates, physical restraints, and cultural surveillance occurred at the fin de siècle that would eventually give rise to a new body culture, one in which women like Colette could promote the exposed, sexualized body as a new feminine ideal.

Naturally, in order to normalize such a radically different conception of French women in relation to their bodies, a system of physical dependency evinced by women's fashion had to be overcome. The removal of rigid undergarments by female performers during the Naughty Nineties violated what many saw as "a moral requisite for correct behavior." Considered "a titillating gesture of naughty, provocative promise," the public appearance of women without outer or undergarments on the stages of Paris was of special concern to those most apprehensive about a decline in morality and a blurring of gender.[104]

It is important to note that the real "femme nue" did not see her actions as part of a collective project or feminist in nature, but rather in terms of interiority, self-improvement, and mobility. Writing in her memoirs, Colette reflected on the days when, as a music-hall performer, she exposed her breasts and performed without a bodysuit. "It has seemed to me that

Top: Armande Cassive, belle époque actress. *Bottom*: Arlette Dorgère at the Variétés on a postcard postmarked 1906.

Postcard showing De Gab, apparently in a question mark.

Postcard: "Curiosités Parisiennes no. 14—La Tour Eiffel" by "Fox." Text reads: "Le Censeur" (the censor) and "Monsieur Veut Monter?" (Mister wants to go up?).

Suzanne Marley, undated postcard.

I was exercising my body in the way that those prisoners who aren't concretely planning a breakout still braid a sheet, sew gold pieces into a lining, and hide chocolate under their mattresses."[105] Colette, like her fellow "femmes nues," believed that progress in terms of women's roles, French body culture, and morality would have to happen one performance at a time.

Undated postcard of a "nude."

Undated postcard of Mlle. Daisy at the Théâtre de la Cigale.

The Role of Plumage

Plumage in medieval times meant "appearance" as well as "feathers." Some women today do not feel ready to go out into the world unless we have on earrings. Many showgirls over the history of music-halls and spectaculars must have felt similarly about their plumage. The explanation of the role of feathers in making the icon lies in French royal and military history.

Charlemagne had peacocks in his garden and Crusaders carried heron feathers back to Europe as spoils of war. They were worn on knights' helmets and later set in jeweled clasps of the brooches of court ladies' headdresses. The profession of *plumassier* (originally called *paonniers* or peacock merchants) was introduced to France from Italy in the thirteenth century and formed into a corporation by Henry III in the sixteenth.[106]

Masquerades at feast days and carnival time were occasions for medieval nobility to put on plumage, literally. A tragic dress ball took place on January 28, 1393, and became known as the Bal des Ardents. Charles VI and five of the gentlemen at court appeared at a fancy dress ball as savages, covered which feathers that were glued on with tar and wax. The ball was held to distract the king, who had suffered his first attack of insanity the summer before. Charles's brother, the Duc d'Orléans, came too close with a torch in his hand to figure out who wore the disguises. The costumes were highly inflammable and four of the men burned to death. The king's aunt, the Duchesse du Berry, saved his life by smothering the flames with the train of her gown. This tragic accident has imprinted on Parisian history a terrifying warning about feathers and fun.[107]

The greatest of Balthasar Beaujoyeulx's spectacles for Catherine de Medici was the *Ballet Comique de la Reine Louise* (1581), created for the betrothal of the queen's sister. It has been considered the first ballet. In terms of costumes it had also the importance that it was the first published libretto, which circulated to the courts of Europe. Generally decorations on garments and masks created the effects of the supernatural but there is a row of damsels who wore stars on their gowns and rays made of feathers on their heads. Headdresses were all the more important because the performers wore masks in all the dances that evolved into the royal ballets de cours, so fanciful headdresses relieved the sameness and identified characters.

The battle cry of Henry IV of France, "Raillez-vous à mon panache blanc" [follow my white plume], shows how focally symbolic the feathers were. "Panache" came from the Latin *pinna* (feathers) by way of middle French *pennache* (plume or tuft of feather). In the military, where the word was first in common use, the panache was fixed on the top of a helmet, while the plume was placed behind, in front, or on the side. At the time the music-halls were picking up steam, the biggest high in legitimate theater was Edmund Rostand's *Cyrano de Bergerac* (1890). Rostand's figurative use of panache in Cyrano's dying speech brought it to mean swagger but also dressy display, as Cyrano is a man of many parts: "There is something still that will always be mine—something I'll take uncreased, unstained out of this world—my panache."[108]

The Comte de Buffon wrote in *The Natural History of Birds* (1771) of these "aigrettes" that had once decorated the sultan's turban and the warrior's helmet that "at present, they serve for a gentler use; they deck the heads of our beauties, and raise their stature: the flexibility, the softness, and the lightness of these feathers, bestow grace on their motions."[109]

Henry VIII of England on one occasion was reported wearing feathers of "some Indian bird" each of which was four and a half feet long, and costly. Plumes were, however, not worn but carried during the Renaissance by fine ladies. The 1604 friendship album of a man from Nuremberg traveling in Italy shows an elegant lady with towering collar and blond curls, holding at her side a huge ostrich feather fan. An album design is nine black feathers symmetrically arranged in a fancy metal holder.[110]

Plumed headdresses had borne witness to French nationhood since the 1600s. The Sun King, Louis XIV, purposely domesticated nobles, and men and women at Versailles wore huge plumed hats or headdresses. A patriotic headdress might be two feet high with boats representing the French navy sailing in its curls. Just when women's gowns had reached four feet across and a lady had to go into a door sideways, the French Revolution simplified fashion to the radical chemise dress, the "wet look" that was so transparent and little corseted that the wearer could look nearly nude. Naturally, fancier dress crept back in as Napoléon created his own order of nobility, and wives and daughters of the new elite, as well as the old aristocrats invited back to the country, needed to demonstrate their social status by their clothes. The ladies of Napoléon's court kept the basic form of high-waist dress with little bodice and puffed or long tight sleeves but they followed the fashion models of his wives Josephine and Marie-Louise, which entailed high plumes on their bonnets and tiaras.

Just as Roman legionnaires wore brushes or plumes of horsehair, the French had plumed helmets. Keeping his metal polished and his plumes spruced kept a soldier occupied between battles. Just as wearing a tall crest bespoke prowess, the plumed headdresses of dancers in revues have symbolized their pride as entertainers.

Marie Antoinette is credited with bringing peacock and ostrich feathers into female fashion when she stuck them into her updo and received a compliment from Louis. Her *marchande de modes*, literally "fashion merchant," Rose Bertin, piled hairstyles with stuffed birds and feathers along with bibelots. "Rose was more like a modern day stylist," comments Cassidy Zachary. "She would literally decorate the Queen's dresses and hats with additions of embroideries, laces, ribbons, and so forth."

The Romantic style took over in dresses after Napoléon's downfall but plumes still expressed royal dignity. Marie-Amélie de Bourbon, who became queen in 1830 when her husband acceded to the

Top: J. De Lafère on a postcard postmarked 1903. *Bottom:* Unknown woman on an undated postcard.

throne as Louis-Philippe I until the Revolution of 1848, was a sensible and family-oriented person who looks regal but a bit lost in the headdress she wore at 49 to sit for Louis Hersent: five ostrich plumes dripping like branches of white lilacs over a velvet and diamond crown that rides on a smaller crown.

The military look in women's attire returned during the Second Empire. Napoléon III, grand-nephew of Napoléon Bonaparte, met his wife, Eugénie, in the Bois de Boulogne, where she was riding in a fine plumed costume. He was an accomplished engineer with overconfidence in his ability to strategize conquests. The soldiers of the Second Empire carried out their military exploits dressed in a dazzling mix of uniforms and paraphernalia. Besides the plumes of the uniforms modeled after the first Napoléon, there were regiments of Zouaves (native French) wearing green turbans and Algerian "Turkos" in white and blue turbans. Fashionable women wore plumes to Napoléon III's court as with their splendid riding costumes. The Second Empire ended after the defeat by the Prussians in 1870, but the circus and choreographed cabaret dances of the Third Republic retained the plumes with their military flavor.

A showgirl prances; sometimes her movement is *gambader*, like the frisky spring of a jumping horse. She holds her head high and has superlative posture. Her beplumed head symbolizes the show. Its absence or replacement with a top hat or other type of decoration is felt to be, as Paul Boussiac says of circus plumes on horses, "stylistic transgression of a norm." Nothing is more traditional in the iconic showgirl costume than the headdress waving with feathers.

THREE

New York

"Well," I said, "Paris is old, is many centuries. You feel, in Paris, all the time gone by. That isn't what you feel in New York—"
He was smiling. I stopped. "What do you feel in New York?" he asked.
"Perhaps you feel," I told him, "all the time to come."
—James Baldwin, *Giovanni's Room*

The Risqué Hits Broadway

The sense of the "better burlesque" in music-halls and showgirl spectaculars needed a new word to define their borderline nature of sexy but not depraved. The word settled on was *risqué*, and the reason it's perfect for the costumes discussed in this book is that, in English, it originated on the boards of the stage, for a wicked song, in the 1860s. Over the next decades it passed from song to literature.

Authorities on the Broadway musical see what Robert G. Allen calls "feminized spectacle"[1] arising in the 1860s. What female performers wore is the pith of the story of what Peter Leslie has called the first equestrian melodrama,[2] when Adah Isaacs Menken rode onto the stage on the back of a real horse, dressed in "fleshlings," skin-colored body stocking and long shorts, called in the business a "tights play." From a 21st-century perspective it seems easy to have become notorious. Menken became the mistress of both Alexandre Dumas and A.C. Swinburne. Lydia Thompson brought the suggestive Victorian burlesque with her troupe of British Blondes in a show called *Ixion* in 1868. A photograph of her as Ixion has her in a short toga with Greek Key and polka dotted sheer fabric, a frill at the bodice, a flower crown and black shiny leather lace up booties. The corsetry cinching in her waist and the neck to ankle bodysuit are a style hard to see with the eyes of her time, as Menken looks both skimpily dressed and as though she can hardly breathe.[3] *The Daily Telegraph* (London) raved about the British Blondes in a vehicle produced by James Robert Planché in Covent Gardens in 1872:

> Such a glitter of gold, such burnished armour, such tossing plumes and jeweled headdresses, such tunics of brown and blue, and black and scarlet, such lavish wealth, such fringes of bullion ... such comely faces, and such superb specimens of womanhood, have never surely yet been combined with such scenes.[4]

Popular ballet in New York was another polite vehicle for under-dressed women in fancy costumes. The costumage of the melodramatic Broadway mélange, *The Black Crook,*

"New York Showgirl," a drawing by Maud Stumm (1870-1935).

was fundamentally French. When the venue for a French ballet burned down a few weeks before a run was to begin, William Wheatley, the manager of Niblo's Garden, a 3,200-seat theater at the corner of Broadway and Prince Street, bought the sets, costumes and dancers' contracts and transformed the melodrama into the first Broadway hit musical. It opened in September 1866 and was performed 474 times over the next two years. *The*

Black Crook was a daunting show built on a prosaic fairy tale romance, where a sorcerer uses black magic to separate lovers and get the girl, but is foiled by a heavenly white dove. The costume designer, David Costa, who had a dual career as comic actor and costumer, put the 100 dancing girls in semi–Classical dress. In flesh colored tights they pranced around a moonlit grotto singing "The March of the Amazons."

The Black Crook

DOUG RESIDE[5]

Often considered the first big Broadway musical, *The Black Crook* came in pieces from Europe right after the Civil War. Two producers, Harry Palmer and Henry C. Jarrett, decided what New York City needed was an extravaganza, and they sailed to Europe to put one together. If they went with *Ondine*, as it was in the public domain, there would soon be a half-dozen other theaters mounting the same show, so the promoters went to France and engaged a ballet company to do *La Biche au Bois*, a fairy tale in which an evil stepmother transforms a girl into a woodland deer. To make a splash, they got a set from Covent Garden in London, which had a giant waterfall and spectacular fairyland scenes; it could be used for either *Ondine* or *La Biche*.

In April 1866 the partners arrived in New York, intending a typical ballet at the Academy of Music on the southeast side of Union Square. When the theater burned down a few weeks before the run was to begin they had to improvise. Jarrett, a manager of middlebrow shows during the Civil War, was supposed to present Edwin Booth in *Hamlet* in Boston the night President Lincoln was assassinated. All things considered, Jarrett decided, it was best to cancel that show. Now he went to the current Niblo's manager, William Wheatley, and they discussed the *Biche* and concluded a new work was better as it could be copyrighted. The playwright whose work they chose, Charles Barras, was not well known. It's said that when Barras read Wheatley his play, Wheatley fell asleep, then woke up confused and said, "We'll take it." He gave it to the treasurer and they agreed that while the story was poor, a derivative of Faust from German opera, the title was good: *The Black Crook* was engaged.

Quickly the theater was redesigned and outfitted with trap doors, and *The Black Crook* was a giant, like the *Spider Man* of its time. It ran over five hours the first night and reviews were that merely the dancing was interesting. Barras thought the production cheapened his art and the show's future was uncertain.

Meanwhile, P.T. Barnum and the *New York Herald* had fought and *The Herald* was unwilling to promote any theater associated with Barnum. But the publisher of the newspaper liked Wheatley and while he couldn't review the play could report on the religious speakers who thought that the costumes were creating a scandal of the most corrupting sort. The dancers wore pink-colored stockings and the full form of the females could be discerned through the gauze. *The Herald* reported on the reformers' condemnations and, effectively, how immoral and scandalous the show was. And now everyone wanted to see it!

Indications of how this first Broadway mega-hit appealed are that reports mentioned the times when certain things happened so a man could see the scandalous parts and return home. Also the ladies could go, in a man's company and veiled.

In *The French Spy*, a dramatization of Lord Byron's *Mazzepa*, the celebrated Adah Isaacs Menken showed her body stockings up to her hip. By 1866 she was performing the role in Paris.

If nothing was particularly groundbreaking about the ballet tutus on many dancers of *The Black Crook*, the large number of dancers kicking their legs made them a kind of Rockettes of their day. In a number called "Pas de Demons" (the Devil's Dance), the controversial costumage was close-fitting pantaloons of gauzy material over tights.

Titillation was designed with a close eye to convention. Allen writes on theater costumes, by extension showgirl costumes, the importance of this dialectic:

> Like all transgressive forms that remain within the boundaries of bourgeois culture, *The Black Crook* represented a dialectic of transgression and containment, excess and recuperation. The lavish, "almost painful," spectacle of sight, sound, motion, color, and displayed feminine physicality was yoked to a romantic, melodramatic plot."[6]

Moreover, the plot of *The Black Crook* was moralistic, where the hellish wizard lost his magical powers.

In the Billy Rose Library are photographs from *The Black Crook* and, particularly, photographs where actresses convey voluptuousness by their exposed arms and shoulders. As for the historic show's lead dancer, Maria Bonfanti, she married a 17-year-old scion of a patrician Fifth Avenue family, journeyed to San Francisco to perform in the hit musical, and eventually opened a ballet school in New York.

Queen of Hats and Late Suppers

At the same time that dancers whipped off men's top hats at the Moulin Rouge, an ad, now at the Library of Congress, for the Bon-Ton Burlesquers in New York showed a shapely blond with plumes in her big hat, and full skirt with tight ruffled bodice and white gloves, holding five ribbons that "pulled the strings" of five inebriated men in evening attire. They are of a size where several could fit into her hat. If from a 21st century perspective we can see the joke of men controlled by their mistress, it's sexy because it's daft, along the lines of Susan Sontag's statement about what makes camp—"It's good because it's awful." No wonder people longed to see undress when the plumed hats, like the murderous corsetry, were so ungainly.

The scale of showgirl headgear owes its grandiosity to Lillian Russell, born Helen Louise Leonard in Iowa in 1860, who made her first appearance as a chorus girl in Chicago, long before Ziegfeld's spectaculars. She came to New York City in 1878 to become an opera star, and became a comedienne and singer at a vaudeville theater instead. Her career was launched at the Union Square music-hall. She was famous for her irrepressible sensuality and public affair with "Diamond" Jim Brady that lasted through her four marriages in the 1880s and 1890s. Brady gave her a bicycle with monogrammed handlebars encrusted with diamonds and emeralds which she rode around on in Manhattan. Another admirer, Alexander Graham Bell, made hers the first voice to travel over the Atlantic by phone in 1891.

Lillian Russell set the style; in the Gay Nineties women wore padded clothes to look like her. She would have loved the hats that Pete Menefee designed for *Jubilee!* at Bally's

Casino. She might have considered Cecil Beaton's hats for the movie *My Fair Lady* elegant but plain. She wore hats that sat on her head at a tilt so that tresses of her hair showed. They were feather fireworks. She might wear a single high feather of a rare bird sticking up from a small arrangement of fabric on her head. To accessorize a hat she might hold by her side an ostrich fan like what was used in ancient Persia. The hats demonstrated her luxurious and fun lifestyle to her public. The Darwinian rage to identify and stuff rare birds had its effect on ladies' fashions and Russell set out to go one more. While the revues were testing the public's taste for nudity, she tested the public's toleration for quite ghastly feathered hats.

In New York by 1911, writes Lewis A. Erenberg in his authoritative study of cabaret in New York, cabaret-style entertainment flourished. Now forgotten opulent "lobster palaces" followed by other dinner and dance nightspots might include a risqué show:

> The theater-restaurants were a concept from Paris: It is clear that wealthy men and women had been visiting such places in Europe in the 1890s, as the Parisian haunts themselves began to attract tourists.... It was also true that one of the first major acts in a New York cabaret was the apache dance, taken from the slums of Paris and performed in Louis Martin's in 1911.[7]

Postcard, postmarked 1905: "This is a picture of stage life as it is written but not as it is. Pauline."

The French apache dance was danced by Mistinguett in the rags of a street gang moll in the same revues where she wore jewels and feathers.

The first music-hall in New York was patterned after those in Europe and was opened by two vaudeville entertainers. It had a champagne bar, a balcony promenade, and served dinner. There were naughty French songs and on view were the legs of girls in bathing suits. This took the name of the original Folies Bergère and was decorated along a French theme. Advertisements explained how the word was "pronounced cabaray" and boasted that the new music-hall was more Parisian than Paris. The model of restaurant and entertainment is realized in the movie version of *Hello Dolly!* wonderfully.

The American developers wanted to emulate more than a name from France. A building west of Times Square was built to house the short-lived Folies Bergère; it would eventually become the Helen Hayes Theater, be demolished in the 1980s, and have 150-foot pieces of its glazed polychrome terracotta murals sold at public auction in 2011. The mural showed vaudeville figures marching to the music-hall in a throne. The artist, William de Leftwich Dodge, had already won a competition to do a mural for the Library of Congress, for which he chose the theme "Ambition" and depicted people at the top, still reaching up for more. While Dodge won that competition he was in Paris. He had sat at a café with his friend William MacMonnies, who would design one of the bronze doors for the Library of Congress, exhibited first at the Paris Salon of 1896.

> When do you think of all these ideas? asked Mac. I see you at l'Ely's or Bal Bulliers almost every night.
>   Well, I'm not wasting my time with the girls now. When I get my last payment of the $8,000 allotted for the Library job, I'll have enough to marry Fan.[8]

Thus Dodge was Paris-trained and had been to the music-halls a lot in Paris.

New Yorkers would have dinner and a show in an ambience decorated in representations of Louis XIII and Louis XIV style (or imperial Rome or Cleopatra's Egypt).

> Offering French atmosphere, French names, and often French food, the cafés were able to slough off their disreputable associations and provide an image of cosmopolitan European fun. They also offered tinges of unconventional bohemianism together with respectability and success.... *Variety* wrote that the easiest way to be posh "was to borrow cabaret" ... that Folies Bergère had adopted for its $1.50 midnight novelty performance.[9]

The Gilded Age saw the development of enthusiastic restaurant-going by New Yorkers and lobster, caviar and Baked Alaska, synonymous with elegance, were on the menu with, often in the late hours, the show.

The first troupe of pretty young things to perform to acclaim in New York was Lydia Thompson's British Blondes (1869). According to Erenberg, they started out playing drag roles in a Classical spoof, wearing revealing, close-fitting tunics, and by 1873 were performing in a chorus line. Soon a dozen such troupes performed in the city, "specializing in scanty skirts, male impersonation, and living statuary." The essential was, as a theater critic put it, to look like "frosting on life's cake."[10] The burlesque image of saucy and sinful vamp would change to the fresh sweet young thing from the late 1890s through the 1910s, Erenberg explains, until Ziegfeld inaugurated his spectaculars with a show called *Just Girls* in 1915, the subtext of which was that New York was the place for girls from the sticks to make it and find true love.

Dancing Girls and Dining
Henry Voigt[11]

The lobster palaces began in the entertainment district of New York City around 1900 and were in full swing by 1910. They provided music, but no dancing girls. The tango and other dances arrived via Paris in 1912 and by 1914 the lobster palaces had installed dance floors. In about 1915, some of the lobster palaces had evolved into cabarets, a forerunner of the nightclub. Cabarets such as Reisenweber's (Columbus Circle) and Rector's (Times Square) brought in the Jazz Age in the late teens.

The first food service connected with dancing girls (that I know of) appeared in about 1915, when Zeigfeld staged his Midnight Frolics on the rooftop of the New Amster-

Marion Martin in *George White's Scandals*, Apollo Theater, New York, 1928-1929 (Everett Collection).

dam Theater. The glitzy show called "Nothing but Girls" featured a glass runway on which chorus girls paraded in ankle-length bloomers over the audience. They mostly posed … don't know whether they actually danced. However, the dance craze was still going strong—the audience tangoed and turkey-trotted before and after these performances and during the intermission.

A menu from a late-night supper at the New Amsterdam Theater, catered by Reisenweber's of Columbus Circle for "Nothing but Girls" goes from a bevy of appetizers including caviar to six lobster entrees and five crab, squab, woodcock and so forth. It emphasizes cold dishes, with a sprinkling named for Ziegfeld—"Fruit Salad, Follies," "Crabmeat Ziefeld," and "Spaghetti à la Ziegfeld"—and notes that service was before and after performances and during intermission. A second menu, attached to the first and reflecting the nature of the late-night crowd, has only chop suey and chow mein specials "Cooked by Lee Wung Ho, Late Chef of the Emperor of China."

The showgirls were fun girls; this projection went all the way from the mid–nineteenth century to the Jazz Era. A rare business card in Henry Voigt's collection from the Motter House in York, Pennsylvania (circa 1888), has a device like a locket or watch case inside of which is a photograph of four showgirls from the "Ziegfeld Danse de Follies." They are posed as a unit. One wears a kepi and zouave trousers, two are draped in Hellinistic garb, and the fourth, sitting in the foreground, wears a dress with a tutu skirt, a bodice that displays her shoulders, and a conical wizard's cap, with four stiff horizontal projections like mountain goat horns. On display, naturally, are curves, the rationale of the costumes, of which the headdress is the most curious feature. The headdress identifies the young ladies as from the scandalous world of theater.

The "Glorifier"

Florenz Ziegfeld was an American success story yet his inspiration came from seeing music-hall shows in Paris during the First World War. When in 1919 the line of seven Girls dressed as gemstones spelled out "DEAREST," that was a necklace for sale at Cartier's. Dolores in his *Midnight Frolic* in 1920 epitomized Paris meets Broadway. She was presented as a "white peacock," a fan of sheer white embroidery with paillettes and sequins designed by Pascaud of Paris. The late-night show took place on the rooftop of the New Amsterdam Theater on a hot night of July 1915 and men were encouraged to burst the balloons on the Girls' minimal costumes.

Ziegfeld's Vision of Tinsel, Spangles and Light

MICHAEL LASSER[12]

Florenz Ziegfeld was the greatest impresario in the history of the Broadway musical, yet his reputation rests primarily on the Ziegfeld Follies, the extravagant theatrical revues he supervised, shaped, and staged each year between 1907 and his death in 1932. More than anyone of his time, Florenz Ziegfeld shaped the American perception of female beauty, showing the world that no one could be as magnificent as a Follies Girl. Regardless of what else he might do, there was always the gleaming staircase down which stepped his glorified showgirls in perfect step, alternately dressed in mink, satin, chinchilla, and lace.

No one ever revives a revue because they are, by definition, topical and occasional. In 1909, six years after the Wright Brothers' flight, Ziegfeld's featured star, the beautiful Lillian Lorraine, circled up and over the audience in a miniature airplane hanging from the ceiling, scattering roses while she sang a long-forgotten trifle entitled "Up, Up, Up in My Airship." In the same Follies, Ziegfeld dressed his showgirls as taxicabs and outfitted them with battery packs. At a suitable moment, on an otherwise darkened stage, they turned on their headlights.

It was his first wife, Anna Held, a soprano he wooed on a European trip in 1896, who suggested that her husband open (in the summer, when most Broadway shows closed) a smart revue based on the satiric cabaret shows then popular in France. Ziegfeld named it the Follies to evoke the Folies Bergère. He understood that he needed to set a sophisticated continental tone to appeal to a well-heeled audience looking for something to while away New York's oppressive heat and humidity. Instead of a chorus line, he would have 120 glamorously dressed "mannequins."

The production numbers soon became a riot of inventiveness. In 1909, the girls wore miniature battleships on their heads in a tribute to the 48 states. When the stage lights darkened, the ships lit up against a background of Manhattan's tallest buildings. Ten years later, Ziegfeld began the Follies with one of his most remarkable spectacles, "The Follies Salad," in which the girls paraded as Lettuce, Spice, Oil, Paprika, Chicken, Vinegar, Salt, and Pepper. The Ziegfeld Follies was, among other things, beyond parody.

The most famous of all the mannequins was known only as Dolores, a statuesque blond with a patrician manner, and for a while every girl in America wanted to look like her. Ziegfeld paid her $650 a week, more money than any other mannequin at the time ever earned, and also used her in the smaller nightclub revues he ran on the roof of the New Amsterdam Theater. Dressed in a pearl-trimmed white satin sheath, she walked in a pin spot across a dark stage. As always, her walk was haughty and proud. Her arms outstretched, she paraded in glittering blue-green and pink spangles and bugle beads embroidered to resemble a peacock's feathers on white satin. She wore a white satin cap tied under her chin, and peacock feathers hung from a satin band around her forehead. Her shoulders and arms were bare. She wore a fan that towered over her and surrounded her, so large it seemed to lift her into the air. It is said that the audience gasped before it began to cheer.

Consumerism merged seamlessly with over-the-top revue style in both New York City and Paris.

The Designer Body and the Ziegfeld Girl

LINDA MIZEJEWSKI[13]

Long before the Kardashians and Ivanka Trump, brand-name figures such as the 1890s Gibson Girl embodied fashion and feminine ideals. In the first decades of the twentieth century, as the Victorian era faded and images of "the modern girl" appeared, the Broadway chorus girl or showgirl captured the popular imagination—the Weber and Fields Girl, the Casino Girl, the Shubert Girl, the Dillingham Girl. The most prestigious and highly publicized was the trademarked Ziegfeld Girl, the invention of Florenz Ziegfeld, Jr. (1868–1932), who produced twenty-two acclaimed Follies and Frolics shows between 1907 and 1931. Like other Broadway revues, the Ziegfeld extravaganzas included comedy skits, musical numbers, and circus acts, but they were best known for their over-the-top production numbers featuring the Ziegfeld Girl who, in her elaborate headdress and sumptuous evening gown, was more fashion mannequin than chorus girl. Naming his Follies after the Parisian Folies Bergère, Ziegfeld set out to produce a classy, upscale show, and showgirl.

As early as 1910, the Ziegfeld shows got attention for outstanding costumes, and in 1915 Ziegfeld made a bold move by hiring renowned fashion designer Lady Duff Gordon, known as the couturier Lucile, in order to showcase a clothes-model showgirl. Traditionally, revue chorus girls functioned as décor or background, twirling their parasols or swaying to music, with a small team of talented dancers brought forward for special numbers. But in the production numbers developed by Ziegfeld's dance director Ned Wayburn, the women were divided by height, body proportion, and type of dance they could perform. The tall, clothes-model showgirls—the "A-team"—were the highlight of these spectacles, in which the smaller chorines, the "ponies" or "chickens," performed dances entailing soft shoe, acrobatics, and tap, while the A-team paraded slowly down staircases or across the stage. Ziegfeld's costuming was famous for being provocative but artistic. For the A-team gowns, the use of sheer fabrics such as chiffon often produced an illusion of nudity, a "special effect" that kept the revues carefully balanced between the racy and the respectable.

The Ziegfeld public relations office regularly announced the high cost and authenticity of the jewels, fabrics, and furs onstage, even in apparel not seen by the audience—Irish linen petticoats and silk bloomers. A 1919 publicity piece proclaims that "only in shoddy chorus girl shows would girls be forced to wear cotton tights and $2 shoes." The identification of the Ziegfeld Girl as upscale fashion model was so prevalent that, ten years after the Follies folded, John Robert Powers of the well-known modeling agency felt the need to distinguish his brand-name model from the Ziegfeld Girl in his book *The Powers Girl*. In fact, the use of professional models on runways had originated in department store events early in the twentieth century, a staging Ziegfeld tapped for his first Frolics show, when the runway was made of illuminated glass and fitted with blowers to lift the girls' skirts, cleverly merging fashion show and girlie show for popular entertainment. This sensationalized showgirl gimmick soon gave way to more strategy; the runways were replaced by steep onstage staircases, requiring the showgirls to use an unusually artificial thrust of hip and shoulder to keep balanced. Perfectly coifed and choreographed, the Ziegfeld Girl embodied a traditional ideal of femininity in the face of the looser behavior and clothing popularized in the Jazz Age. But more than classy fashions and ladylike behavior were at stake.

Only certain bodies, the tall A-team women, were suitable for this choreography and costume, and the whiteness of those bodies was pointedly emphasized in the Ziegfeld publicity machines. The Ziegfeld Girl is more than a theatrical footnote precisely because she was not just a fashion icon but icon of a fashionable body. In the age of accelerated immigration, she spoke to anxieties and uncertainties about what an American looked like. As early as 1914, the Follies girls were being described by Ziegfeld's publicists as "strictly American," claiming for them an authenticity of nationality to match the authenticity of the silks and pearls onstage. By 1922, the Ziegfeld Girl was officially dubbed the Glorified American Girl, celebrated as "glorious specimens of American womanhood," as the publicity boasted. Within the revue lineup, skits featuring Jewish, ethnic minority, and African American comedy, including blackface, functioned as a defining contrast to the Glorified American Girl, most famously in the clowning parodies performed by Jewish comedienne Fanny Brice. In countless interviews, Ziegfeld explained that his Follies girls were "native" Americans whose grandparents and great-grandparents had been born in this country. The point of this outrageous fabrication was that the Glorified American Girls were not supposed to be immigrants from southern and eastern Europe, dark-skinned, or Jewish. When sun-tanning became popular in the 1920s, Ziegfeld paid bonuses to the showgirls whose skin stayed white.

The Glorified American Girl as a white ideal appeared at a time when the idea of an "American race" was popular. The pseudoscience of eugenics, with its aims of breeding a superior race, was widely popular in the United States as well as Europe early in the twentieth century. Best-selling books such as Madison Grant's *The Passing of the Great Race* (1916) and Clinton Stoddard Burr's *America's Race Heritage* (1922) deplored the "mongrelization" of America through immigration from eastern Europe and the Mediterranean. Eugenics declined in popularity only after its goals were brutally carried out by Nazi Germany in its genocide programs. Meanwhile, in the United States, racial tensions increased in the 1920s as African Americans migrated from the south to northern cities, which saw a resurgence of the Ku Klux Klan. Countering these multiple new populations, pop-culture versions of an American Girl demonstrated the need to impose a singular

Marion Benda (center) in the "Feather Number" from a stage production of *The Ziegfeld Follies of 1925* (Billy Rose Theatre Division, New York Public Library).

model of what an American looked like. Local and national beauty contests became popular at this time, and a model of blondeness and fairness associated with northern Europe was eventually claimed by eugenicists as typical of the "American race." White women played a crucial role in the rhetoric of the eugenicists and nativists given the importance of the reproduction of racially pure bodies. So as the Ziegfeld stage developed into a showroom, the Glorified American Girl modeled not just chic fashions and authentic jewels but glamour itself as white and painstakingly in step to a conservative choreography.

The provocative costumes of the Ziegfeld Girls were never as nude as what was a norm in the Parisian showgirls by the Jazz Era. The designer Ben Ali Haggin persuaded Ziegfeld to introduce the first nudes to his shows—undraped but representing famous paintings, but the most daring revues were at Earl Carroll's theater. Writes Rachel Shteir,

> Even more than Ziegfeld or Minsky, Carroll, influenced by the Folies Bergère—which he had seen in France during the war—filled the stage with bubbles, marble statues, rainbow lights, mosaic glasses, friezes of metal, bars of gold, revolving flowers, subterranean fog, feathers, chandeliers, and bejeweled ruffles. Carroll also used clear plastic—which led people to call his showgirls "virgins wrapped in cellophane."[14]

Earl Carroll himself was arrested when one of his shows featured a girl who was bathing in champagne in 1926, although Carroll claimed it to have been ginger ale. Carroll was arrested because champagne violated Prohibition; the girl's nudity was not an issue.

The consumer man of the theater was George White, whose "Scandals" did not compete with the lavishness of the Ziegfeld sets or huge casts but lived up to the wow factor in terms of eye-popping costumes. The "Scandals" appeared annually between 1919 and 1926, and other editions in the 1930s were filmed. The edition of 1934 became a movie and launched the movie career of Alice Faye. Ann Miller danced in the "Scandals" as well, and George Gershwin wrote five of the scores.

FOUR

Between the Wars

Costumes Skyrocket

Between the wars the various art movements were unified by an ambition to make beautiful things from the broken pieces of the past. The shows at the music-halls indulged the senses; with dreams come true and zany humor they offered brief oblivion. Jacques-Charles, the producer commissioned to write a revue while still recovering in a hospital from a war injury, makes the connection clearly in a memoir, linking the music of Ragtime with the spread of spectacular revues while the First World War still raged. Soldiers on leave wanted to see the big star Gaby Deslys dancing with Harry Pilcher and be able to return to the Front with her song in their hearts and pumped up by the hot-stepping dancing.[1]

The costumes of the tableaux, which were more or less pantomime, came across as ideational, if metaphors quickly understood, droll, and avant-garde. The audience could see what was being referenced and analogued, and for a sophisticated audience this is flattering. The viewers, faced with breakneck-speed mutating costumes, moved from some aspect of the body to adornment and back. In that movement was the charm and frisson, like the form of the hummingbird realized in its flight. For the viewers, the reflections of their world were present in a discontinuous show, a brilliant eclecticism escaping definition and passing by skepticism or despair, as they registered the breakdown to parts of the undress—feathers, spangles, high heels, costume jewelry and theatrical design effects. Designers borrowed from Giuseppe Arcimboldo's vegetables, fruit and fish arranged into people, to Larmesson's seventeenth century *Fancy Trade Costumes* series (*Les Costumes Grotesques et les métiers*), where 70 artisans are dressed in the materials of their occupation, to how Surrealists like Paul Delvaux played with desire by delving into the subconscious.

The stakes were raised with the popularity of cinema. Audiences expected more glamour and more thrills. Silent black-and-white movies in the 1910s and 1920s were a-sparkle. They incorporated showgirl acts, even a regular scene of nobs having cocktails had some spectacular hats, necklaces and gowns similar to what might be worn for a nightclub or music-hall act, like "real" clothes but punched up. Music-halls screened movies and brought in more sensational and elaborate costumes, such as polar bears dressed as humans, scenes involving sailing vessels, and gladiatorial combats. In 1933 in a tableau of *Folies en Folie*, the star Jenny Gilder made her entrance by bursting out from a movie screen. The factors of technology, the avant-garde, and the new venues collided like tectonic plates. Angelo Luerti writes:

> The Moulin Rouge, the Folies-Bergère and the Casino de Paris became symbols of the cosmopolitan climate in Paris…. Expressionists, futurists, Dadaists, constructivists, artists of the Dutch group De Stijl, cubists and French surrealists all broke radically with the nineteenth century bourgeois artistic tradition, formulating new images, and experimenting with new materials, techniques and methods.[2]

Together, makers of revues and makers of costumes maximized the glitz and minimized the coverage of the body's natural symmetry from, it is generally agreed, the end of World War I through the mid–1930s. Joie de vivre was a secular balm applied to the spirits of a devastated Europe. The movies made in the United States before the implementation of the Hays Code were a reciprocal source too. Pascal Jacob points to Edward Marchand, the artistic director of the Folies Bergère, originating the "revue à grand spectacle" as early as 1886 but Michel Gyarmathy at the Folies Bergère played the "carte du faste avec un gout pour la démesure" [winning card with a taste for immoderation]. This was the heart of the story of costumes between the wars. Jacob continues: "Bien sur, les Folies Bergère n'ont pas inventé les plumes ni les stras [artificial diamonds], mais la richesse des productions est un marqueur du temps, un témoinage de cette frénésie brutale, de cette course à l'abyme dans laquelle s'est lancé l'Humanité tout entière." [Of course, the Folies Bergère did not invent the feathers or the rhinestones, but the richness of the productions is a marker of the time, a witness of this brutal frenzy, of this race to the bottom to which all of humanity is launched.][3]

In this period, the one-time village of Montmartre transformed into a virtual amusement park. Local protests against rampant development saved a green space for a vineyard but mostly the tourists extrapolated from postcards showing Utrillo paintings. The youthful expression of laundresses, shop girls and their "mecs" on precious hours off became one choreographed act in the music-hall revue's evocation of Gay Paree. In competition with movies, the settings became blockbuster, and showgirl costumes became more colorful and sexy, and the world of fantasy lay right

AU TEMPS DES CERISES

Postcard illustration by H. Did, c. 1920: "Au Temps des Cerises" (in the time of cherries).

at the other side of the foot-lights, with none of which the cinema could compete. A number of Paris revues featured glass tank swimming pools, for instance, for next-to-nude water ballet numbers.[4] Not long before, Oscar Wilde said that nothing succeeds like excess. The music-halls aimed to prove him right and the costume designers jumped on board. The writer Alison Lurie has suggested that "people done up in shiny colored wrappings and bows affect us just as a birthday present does: we're curious…; we want to undo the package."[5] Such was the appeal mined by the geniuses of the music-hall costumes in Paris between the world wars.

To picture the costumes it is not enough to browse through images; one has to imagine an aesthetic revolution vis-à-vis all prior entertainment, with every luxury fabric and decoration known at that time available to work with to build the show. Erté spoke of the beautiful fabrics before synthetics: "There was a velvet you could draw through a ring on the finger, and it draped beautifully."[6]

Undated photograph by J. Mandel.

Claiming he could not sew on a button, Erté also gave Charles Castle insight into his method:

> There is nothing more difficult than creating costumes for so-called naked dancers. Generally speaking, I was always guided by two principles. The first was to find one detail (hairstyle, jewellery or some other accessory) which was sufficiently interesting or striking to suggest the idea for a costume. The second was to build a costume by extending the lines of the naked body into decorative arabesques.[7]

The music-hall costumes belonged to a flood of avant-garde—incarnated by the androgyny of the Ballet Russes but evident in every aspect of theatrical design. A female performer

Mlle. Maryse of the Folies Bergère, *Paris Plaisirs*, **no. 56, February 1927 (Mary Evans/Everett Collection).**

could for instance be wrapped in cellophane, the new material picked up for sets of the operetta *Four Saints in Three Acts* by Gertrude Stein and Virgil Thompson in 1934.

Peter Leslie called the music-hall period from the end of the First World War through the 1920s the "age of superlatives":

music-hall revues were remarkable visually; they did use vast amounts of costly materials; they were indeed extremely expensive to produce; and the end product certainly gleamed, scintillated, coruscated—or glittered. Nor was that glitter a tinsel effect. This was the period when chorines at the Folies sported G-strings covered in genuine diamonds, with the mime Ida Rubinstein spending 30,000 francs in gold each month on sets of silk underclothes destined to be worn only once, when the rough sketches for Erté's costume designs were executed in flakes of silver and real gold leaf.[8]

Describing the most daring revue yet, *Paris qui Danse* at the Casino, Luerti writes of

> splendid female figures "dressed" as Manon, Carmen, Aphrodite and other female heroines of opera comique [coming] slowly out of an enormous piano magique surrounded by a luminous halo.... Not to be outdone the Folies Bergère, in the same season, presented a blonde girl on a flowery float wearing only a miniscule triangle. Such audacity marked the beginning of displays of constantly diminishing chastity and modesty on Parisian stages. There followed a series of scandals for indecent behavior ... all skillfully exploited by the theatre directors for publicity.[9]

The cache-sexe was a small triangle of fabric glued on for modesty; patches were sometimes also affixed to the nipples. When, from the 1920s, for many years Paul Derval of the Folies Bergère took his company outside Paris and to other countries, he had to heed more prurient etiquette about undress:

> So the Folies travelled with a set of little stars carefully tailored for the breast of each showgirl or dancer. Every night, a star one size smaller than that of the previous night would be fixed by spirit gum. After fifteen weeks in Buenos Aires, the stars would be no notable impediment to the visual pleasure of the keenest connoisseur in the audience, and this method also helped to keep the show packed until the end of the longest run.[10]

The costumes were created as theatrical costumes had always been. The director communicated the themes to the designers who sketched and colored drawings (often with gouache and sometimes decorated with silver or gold). These were presented to the director who selected the designs and the colors and/or fabrics to be used. In this period, as in decades later when Bob Mackie or Jerry Jackson designed for Las Vegas spectaculars, the designs had notes, sometimes details and back views, and swatches. The hundreds of costume designs required for the tableaux of a revue's thousand or more costumes for a single revue went to the battalion of technical people and leading costumers.

At the Casino de Paris, Antoinette Hostalier reigned with a staff of 50 that she increased by a hundred leading up to a premiere. They went from simple sketches to finished products in house. Some shows came already costumed from Broadway and Harlem.

Bénédicte Rasimi, the wife of the director of the Casino de Lyons, created for London, the Casino de Paris, and the Folies Bergère. Luerti notes that she was popular with Maurice Chevalier, Mistinguett and Josephine Baker, that her taste was impeccable and the perfection of her costume art unequaled. She was known as the queen of elegance and good taste.

And then Max Weldy became the hottest costumer for the epoch between the wars. His workshop of dressmakers, tailors, hatters, shoemakers, and wigmakers supplied for his biggest client, the Folies Bergère, tens of thousands of costumes, on themes from Cleopatra's Egypt to desert harem to cowboys from 1919 to 1938. His final career stage was in Sarasota, where he designed production numbers for the Ringling Brothers.

A thousand costumes, a dozen costumes for each member of the company, took thousands of yards of cloth and millions of sequins. The contract of a music-hall star was a document she read not only to see her salary but also her allotment for costumes. Mistinguett, to thank Léon Volterra for having done her a big favor in London (he found her an apartment when she was going to be thrown out of her hotel because she was sick

Monica Bannister in *The Great Ziegfeld* (1936), directed by Robert Z. Leonard (MGM/Photofest).

and declared contagious), later as a big gesture paid for her own and the "girls'" and her dance partner Harry Pilcher's costumes for a show at the Casino de Paris. For a Moulin Rouge show called *Ça c'est Paris* (1926), whose music included Jacques-Charles's abiding words, "Paris c'est une blonde qui plaît à tout le monde," Mistinguett's demands amounted to 2,500 costumes.

An original drawing by Jenny Carré: "Le Cancan. Les Menostero" (MS Thr 113426-28, courtesy Houghton Library, Harvard University).

Praising the finale, the author of a biography of Mistinguett writes,

Golden rain, a golden stage, golden cloth and lamé, golden florins, taler, pounds, marks, pesos, dollars; golden decoration all spread out at the top of the stairs and at the foot of the large platform; and in the middle of an avalanche of golden coins, a small woman electrifies the entire room.[11]

Mistinguett's costumes were brilliant and had a flapper flavor but the mythos created around her meant that the greatest attention was to her legs. She wore two or three pairs of silk stockings, one over the other. This gave her legs sheen, writes Castle, and a single line without showing muscle so her knees did not seem to exist. Being proud of her legs, she wore short skirts and took poses to display them. One can't help having an image of striated and lumpy stockings, given the multiple layers, but then, producers of silk stockings had evolved them over three or four hundred years, well before Shakespeare parodied them.

The glamour emerged from the individual and inimitable drawings of Jazz Age artists from many countries exercising their métier in Paris. These designers created posters, costumes for movies and the circus, and fashions, and experimented with all the innovative art styles of the day, including cubism, futurism, and expressionism. Precisely the same years when the showgirl icon was coalescing and appearing in myriad costumes that dazzled and teased, the art of fashion illustration also developed. In 1908 Poiret commissioned the printmaker Paul Iribe to illustrate his clothing designs for a promotional publication and the French edition of *Vogue* in 1920 brought with it a profusion of drawings for advertisements by the talented music-hall costumers.

One can visualize a designer deliberating how to use a hoop skirt (for a topless design) as a platform for the kind of little scene that went on hats of the court ladies at Versailles; figuring out how to get the most out of a requisition for a bubble gum–theme costume; Alec Shanks transforming a woman into the Tower Bridge of London by strapping towers on her shoulders, and giving her tiny bikini a wide train rippling with waters in graduated hues of blue and green; Jean Le Seyeux exploring where to use the motif of bells—putting a performer in a flattened cowbell painted with edelweiss and hanging 30 bells from her arms; or Gesmar looping three performers together with the middle figure's train.

The sizzle came too from the sparkle of the individual showgirls (as would be true of the shows in Las Vegas as the showgirl's status rose). Performers now came in twos, like the Dodge Twins and the Dolly Sisters and troupes such as the Jacksons, Hoffman Girls, and Tiller Girls. The replication factor played up what a pair wore, on stage and off; for example, Jean Patou dressed the Dolly Sisters for their first appearances in Paris, at the Casino de Paris, while their clothes at the house parties at their chateau or walking their little dog at Deauville or Cannes were instant news. The second category of multiples involved athletic routines that required wearable outfits for precision high kicks. The dancers who dreamed of and beat their way to Paris had to live on small salaries but costumes for "les girls" were provided.

John Tiller opened a boarding school to train dancers for the popular theater and sent troupes to perform abroad. He devised the dance routine where girls kicked with their arms around each other's waists. Jacques-Charles, who put on shows in New York and South America as well as Paris, wrote a revue called *New York–Montmartre* when he was in the hospital recovering from war wounds. When he recovered, he went to New York to negotiate with the Dolly Sisters and the Hoffman Girls, the latter of whom debuted on the Paris stage in 1924 at the Moulin Rouge. Mrs. Hoffman was a German-American from San Francisco, often appearing as Salomé in the U.S., and had been several times arrested by the police for going too far with suggestive dance. Her troupe was as athletic as the Cirque du Soleil and did their acts to fast jazz numbers. They were athletes and did acts on ropes, fencing scenes, and somersaults, cartwheels, and synchronized movement like the mechanistic routines of Busby Berkeley, with many jazzy costumes. The versatile Hoffman Girls performed distinctly more athletic routines than the synchronized parade of showgirls in tulle, feathers and evening gowns typifying the showgirl revues.[13] They would throw their dresses to one side to appear in neat gymnasts costumes, and, suspended by tackles, launch into the air. Amidst their acrobatics they would reappear in all red costumes, the action continuing so in a spiraling flow.

The appearance of the Hoffman Girls at the Moulin Rouge was a typical Paris–U.S. connection. The two dozen Hoffman Girls kept in shape on a transatlantic voyage on the S.S. *Hamburg* by shuffleboard, fencing, and boxing, for their debut at the Moulin Rouge in 1924. They appeared for the first time in *New York–Montmartre* with some of the costumes by Zamora.

In French newspapers, reviewers gave primary attention to costuming. Also, the standard of costumes had to be high if a revue was going to travel out of Paris to elsewhere in Europe or the Americas. Costumes had to last, satisfy expectations, and not press the "undress" too hard.

Paul Poiret, who was after Frederick Worth the second real star couturier, was described by Jacques-Charles as a great showman, from his "abracadabrantes" clothes to his luxurious mansion with its fine garden in the middle of Paris. Jacques-Charles produced a show with a 1001 Nights theme and years later recollected costuming a tableau called *The Indiscreet Moon or the Jealous Sultan*. From his recollection emerges a rare glimpse of the creative flurry of costuming a show as well as the power structure where the designers had a living and had expression but knew their place. Poiret had asked the producer to come and help put together the costumes for the tableau:

> I found him, when I arrived, at ten in the morning, sitting in a place of honor, like a nabab, on piles of sumptuous fabrics, while his slaves, pardon, his mannequins, waited in silence upon the wishes of their master. As soon as I got there he began to drape the textiles on the bodies, to measure, cut, trim, wreck, and waste. All that was mere spectacle, "du chiqué" intended to expose me to the full view of the goings-on. He pretended to improvise his costumes directly on the bodies, as a sculptor would, with fabrics. But I knew that secretly, hidden away in a little office, a young Spanish designer, José de Zamora, drew my sketches, because, having misplaced his list, he had not dared admit it to Poiret and had come asking me for it.
>
> By noon the studio was littered with expensive fabrics, wasted in vain, because the master had found nothing to his satisfaction. As I left him manifesting my regret at this useless slaughter ["hécatombe"]: "What do you want, my dear man, my spontaneity should not be hampered by the least consideration pecuniary or otherwise." And that was the final word of his little comedy.[14]

The Hoffman Girls' acts were a calibrated assortment inspired by cinema. Their hair and makeup were as carefully individual as though for the silver screen. They also had a theatrical fencing act and a number called "Webbing": 18 dancers in white rhinestone-encrusted leotards did gymnastics suspended by their wrists, feet, and teeth, from long white cords.

Most of the many "girl" troupes (nearly always homogenous performers) were not lauded like the Hoffman Girls but they traveled internationally, and dressing them required finesse so they would look pleasing not boringly repetitive. Among the numerous girl troupes, the Tiller Girls were the beginning of "fancy dancing," or precision dancing, and the Hoffman Girls brought a more dynamic type dance and fast formula of tableaux. Mistinguett wanted this formula of rapid scenes one after the other. Jacques-Charles recalled that there was no time to clap and called the Hoffman Girls "une folie collective" (collective madness). The Parisian revues were at the apex of entertainment. In the movie *Gold Diggers of Broadway* (1929) the chorines sang, "If you are a dough boy you saw the Folies Bergère and the dollies there. This is how it's done in the USA."

The Piollet Collection

From 1918, Paul Derval brought spectacular sets, dazzling costumes, and nudity to the Folies Bergère. The Moulin Rouge had closed in 1915 for ten years after a fire, which gave other music-halls an edge. The stages grew and the revues gave dozens of European designers a livelihood and a showcase: a single show could require a thousand costumes for a bevy of dancers. No more (as of 1918) were prostitutes issued fortnightly renewable cards at the Folies to solicit in the *promenoir*. If the whole gorgeous theater including louche goings-on had been the tableau, now the tableau was located on the stage.

The costumes were fanciful, daring and often exotically themed. The formulation was a phoenix-like return of divertissements after the Great War—fashion plates, and boyish bobbed hair and short shorts, contrasting with the languorous and feathery. The English novelist J.B. Priestly, a young adult at the time, wrote of "the revenge of the starved senses." An American example of the frisson this created can be seen on YouTube in scenes from *Gold Diggers of Broadway*, the performers costumed first in evening gowns, next nostalgic-looking Paris showgirls with the backdrop of Notre Dame and the Arc de Triomphe, and then the snappy singing, dancing kickers.

Ambition was the leitmotif. One famous revue, *Coeurs en Folie* (1924), had costumes of the Directory and First Empire period but also included Spanish and Egyptian dances. The fast-changing scenes were intricate and presented a challenge to the costumers. The tableaux included a midnight party at the Tivoli Gardens, the ascent of a hot-air balloon, a Roman chariot race, a showcase where young women represented rings, bracelets, earrings, and necklace pendants, and a several-story-high monster coughing smoke who dissolved into a dance troupe.[15]

An enormous anthology of talent, masters of technique infused with the energy of the Deco, created the burst of fabulous costumes for the music-halls in the 1920s. They worked for a costumer, first of all Maison Pascaud's and later Max Weldy. The costumers had authority. When Jacques-Charles was producing revues during the Jazz Era, the costumers were, writes Charles Castle, "affronted when he insisted on accompanying them to choose materials."[16] The costumer's stamp is often on the designs. The University of Georgia has the largest collection of 1920 to 1940 designs (6,000

A "fruit girl" design by Brunelleschi Rizzi (courtesy Angelo Luerti).

music-hall costume drawings in the Hargrett Library). Parisian music-hall costume draw-ings are dispersed elsewhere in the U.S.: Harvard University houses a small (59 drawings) but notable collection, as does the New York Public Library (including those of Ladislas Czettel). When one thinks how fragile the drawings are, on board or sometimes just trac-ing paper, it is clear someone preserved them because they are beautiful.

An imposing private collection is the Piollet Collection to which belongs a flowering of thousands of the designs that were worn by showgirls in the revues in Paris. It derives mostly from the workshop of the costume-maker Max Weldy. Weldy replaced the Maison Pascaud as the main costume designer on the Parisian stage and designed mainly for the Folies Bergère from 1919 to 1937, but also for Broadway productions, movies and theaters worldwide. He founded his company at 18, rue Saunier near the Folies Bergère in 1918, and its output was huge. On behalf of the designers of his workshop, he originated obtaining

"Maison Hollandaise," a costume design by Hugh Willoughby (courtesy Piollet Collection).

copyright to reproduce several costumes from a single design. He introduced Erté, who had previously worked for Paul Poiret, to the Folies Bergère and also to Broadway. Weldy left Paris at the brink of the Second World War and opened a workshop (in 1939) in America where he worked for Ringling Brothers Circus.

The costumer's skill is differentiated from the dressmaker's by the greater degree of imagination that is called for. The dressmaker may have a problem to solve of where to bustle or pin a train, but the costumier takes an artistic concept drawn on paper and renders a finished costume, including its back, which is usually not rendered in the drawing. It took expertise to translate the detail of a sketch into an element that would register from a distance, and skill to construct a costume that would survive the action on stage. The costumier decided between painting, stenciling on decorations, appliqué, and embroidery. If embroidery, the choices were silk or cotton floss, beads, metal studs, or flocking (bits of fabric put on with adhesive); and possibly to paint, dye or stencil to execute decorative elements. No fewer than 300 dressmakers, states Sabine Piollet, worked in the atelier of Max Weldy, the costumer of the Folies Bergère, sewing thousands of roses on dresses, deftly applying rhinestones, pearls, feathers, and other decorations.

The most famous designers who emerged were Erté and Charles Gesmar, and then Georges Barbier and Umberto Brunelleschi. But there were many others, with a significant proportion immigrants to France, and many also designing for shows in America and Hollywood movies. A designer who arrived in Paris from Hungary in the mid-thirties, Michel Gyarmathy, had an uninterrupted career of 58 years. He made a poster in 1927 for Josephine Baker (it was not the first of her European posters; those were done in 1925 and 1926 by Paul Colin). Gyarmathy has a special place in the constellation of designers because he became the only designer for the Folies Bergère from 1936 and its director in 1946. Evocations of some important designers (by no means a complete list) evidence the international identity and versatility of these men and women.[17]

Georges Barbier, famous for his Art Deco style and engendering the haughty female figures, illustrated two albums to celebrate the Ballets Russes and went on to illustrate the creations of famous courturiers including Worth, Lanvin and Poiret, and designed costumes for Parisian theaters and music-halls. He was inspired for the costumes by Etruscan paintings, ancient Greek vases, and Renaissance carnivals. He also collaborated with Erté on American film projects including *Monsieur Beaucaire* (1924) starring Rudolph Valentino. Finesse and elegance that he pushed to the point of improbability made him a reference point for Deco illustration.

Umberto Brunelleschi, Italian, had a distinguished career in book (including erotica) and magazine illustrations in a flamboyant style, as well as his sets and costumes for Folies Bergère (1923–1926), the Scala in Milan, and the Roxy Theater in New York. Decorations could be baroque, in unexpected colors and transforming a dancer into a butterfly, a queen or a pasha: his style was opulent yet humorous and light. He worked in various iconographies and was renowned for his fairy tale, eighteenth-century Venetian, Indian and Persian, and Chinese designs, always done with clear-cut, calligraphic lines and refined coloring.

Jenny Carré had a spectacular 25-year career designing for the Casino de Paris, the Palace, the Mogador, and the Concert Mayol as well as theaters (her father was director and theater manager at the Opéra-Comique). She did the set for an Opéra-Comique play by her father and for Mistinguett. She dressed the showgirls with swank and swishy luxury that emphasized the natural lines of the body.

Vigne Vierge by José de Zamora (courtesy Piollet Collection).

Ladislas Czettel, a Hungarian, after studies in Munich and Vienna, worked for the celebrated designer Pierre Poiret in Paris. He was Leon Bakst's disciple and designed for music-halls in Vienna, Berlin and Paris, especially the Folies Bergère. Czettel learned an impressive technique from Poiret of creating a costume on the model's body in three minutes, using a few yards of cloth and pins. After designing for the music-halls, he did opera productions in the U.S., designs for MGM and the Barnum and Bailey's circus, and couture fashions for Henri Bendel.

Erté brought Slavic art and Persian miniature art to design. His costumes seem to me akin to signatures on an Ottoman *firman* and he had a career of six decades in art, as well as working for fashion magazines, especially *Harper's Bazaar*, and for Ziegfeld Follies, the Folies Bergère, and George White's "Scandals."

The dancer Mlle. Spinelly discovered Charles Gesmar. He was very sensitive. Devastated when once she criticized him, he tried to shoot himself. But the bullet went into the cistern of the lavatory and flooded the house, ending their relationship. Gesmar worked for various music-halls, did 12,000 costumes, and died before his twenty-eighth birthday.

Jean Le Seyeux had a genius for using motifs from the past. After working in Paris in 1920 he did whole shows from 1937 for Earl Carroll's "Vanities" on Broadway. He, along with Gesmar and Gyarmathy, was one of the artists to have created whole revues. The costumes could go down the runway as dresses today; as well as having the element of surprise Combining volume with the skin-tight he was a master of almost hypnotic sexiness. They look so wearable.

Michel Gyarmathy began designing for the Folies Bergère in 1934, became the sole set and costume designer two years later, and from 1946 the artistic director. He made strides in stage design and did costume designs with an emphasis on the light and airy.

Many of Edouard Halouze's designs were derived aesthetically from Cubism. They also reference Persianate art and Russian enamels. He designed for all the music-halls and the exclusive fashion periodicals.

Marco Montedoro, from Milan, worked first in Paris and then from 1913 was the art director of the Metropole in Berlin. During World War I he designed posters for theater and cinema in Italy. Returning to Paris in 1923, he designed costumes for revues staged at the Palace, Les Ambassadeurs, the Moulin Rouge and Folies Bergère but also worked in Poland, London, St. Petersburg, and in New York from the early 1930s for the Schuberts, where he did *La Vie Parisienne* in two versions, 1941 and 1942, and Radio City music-hall designs, 1930 to 1939, like *Alice in Wonderland*. His inventiveness and craft were extraordinary: a 1920s music-hall example is his Chinese-princess motif costume in yellows, green and brown that has patterned tights, fur-trimmed high-low hemline, and an otherworldly green headdress dripping with jade pendants. The virtually topless robe had a "cold shoulder" design that attached at four points: a crisscrossing crystal necklace met the dress at the nipple, and three more points down the arms and at the wrist, the result being a complex robe gracefully "falling off" the elegant princess.

René Ranson was one of the founders of the artistic community in Montmartre, and participated in the Bal des Quat'z Arts. He designed for the music-halls and American and French cinema. He joined the Resistance during the Second World War and illustrated some of its publications. Ranson's costume drawings are extraordinarily original. He might clothe the lower leg but leave the thigh bare, or suspend most of the costume so it is barely worn, and he could do things with cuffs, bustles and headdresses that are vaguely Byzantine but thoroughly modern. His historical costumes are so subtle they would make others look clumsy by comparison.

The prolific English Art Deco artist Alec Shanks designed for the Moulin Rouge in 1926, collaborated with Erté, and worked freelance for Max Weldy, creating lavish Folies Bergère costumes from 1929 to 1932 (and being known for running over budget). He opened his own theatrical costume house towards the end of the decade, employing artists including Erté. During the Second World War he did hundreds of designs for Resistance press. His signature was a glorious opulence that integrated Art Nouveau into Deco; why put a few big artificial flowers on a costume when you could suspend dozens from wire stems emerging from the base of the nude's spine? If two feet of crystals looked smashing extending from the dancer's chandelier earrings, why not attach the same design but bigger and longer to her wrists? The practicality for movement does not seem to have been a primary concern.

Dolly Tree designed for revues in Europe in London, Madrid, Rome and Brussels, worked for the Folies Bergère from 1919 to 1929, and later in Hollywood, creating gowns for Jean Harlow, Judy Garland, and Lana Turner. (See Gary Chapman's précis, below.)

Hugh Willoughby was sent to the front in the British army during the First World War and was a prisoner of war for two years. From 1920 to 1925 he designed for Paris revues such as *Piff Paff* at the Marigny (1920) and *Un Soir de Folie* at the Folies Bergère. In the late 1930s he emigrated to the United States and created a theatrical costume house in New York. His costume drawings are precise and meticulous feats of fashion engineering.

Freddy Wittop was Dutch and learned to design costumes at the age of 13 as an apprentice at the Brussels Opera. He went to Paris in 1930 and designed hundreds of costumes for the Folies Bergère, the Théâtre de Chatelet and the Folies at the Alhambra from 1931 to 1936, for the showgirls and the stars Mistinguett and Josephine Baker. He then settled in New York, acquired American citizenship in 1942, and enlisted in the Army. He became a famed designer for Broadway, Ice Capades and musicals, and won a Tony for *Hello, Dolly!* He is said to have sketched around 50,000 costumes. His shows animated equally the French past (*Le Décolleté sous Louis XVI* and *Le Décolleté à la Renaissance*) and modern theater works, like Jean Girardoux's play *Judith* in London. Wittop also became a professional Spanish dancer under the name Federico Rey.

Doing something new with a common motif was a Deco specialty. In a José de Zamora design, the dancer as a black butterfly appears to be bitten by half a dozen smaller butterflies. He specialized in the art of undress—dressing the female nudes. The Spanish Civil War took him back to Spain in the 1930s.

Alexandre Zinoview ("Zino") was a Russian painter who designed for all the music-halls of Paris from 1919 to 1925. His fine-spun line and jewel-like colors seem close to the book illustrations that Kay Nielsen did for classic books.

Dolly Tree
GARY CHAPMAN[18]

A long-lost artistic genius of the Jazz Age, Dolly Tree (1899–1962) had an international reputation as a costume designer in the glamorous 1920s and 1930s. A prime example of

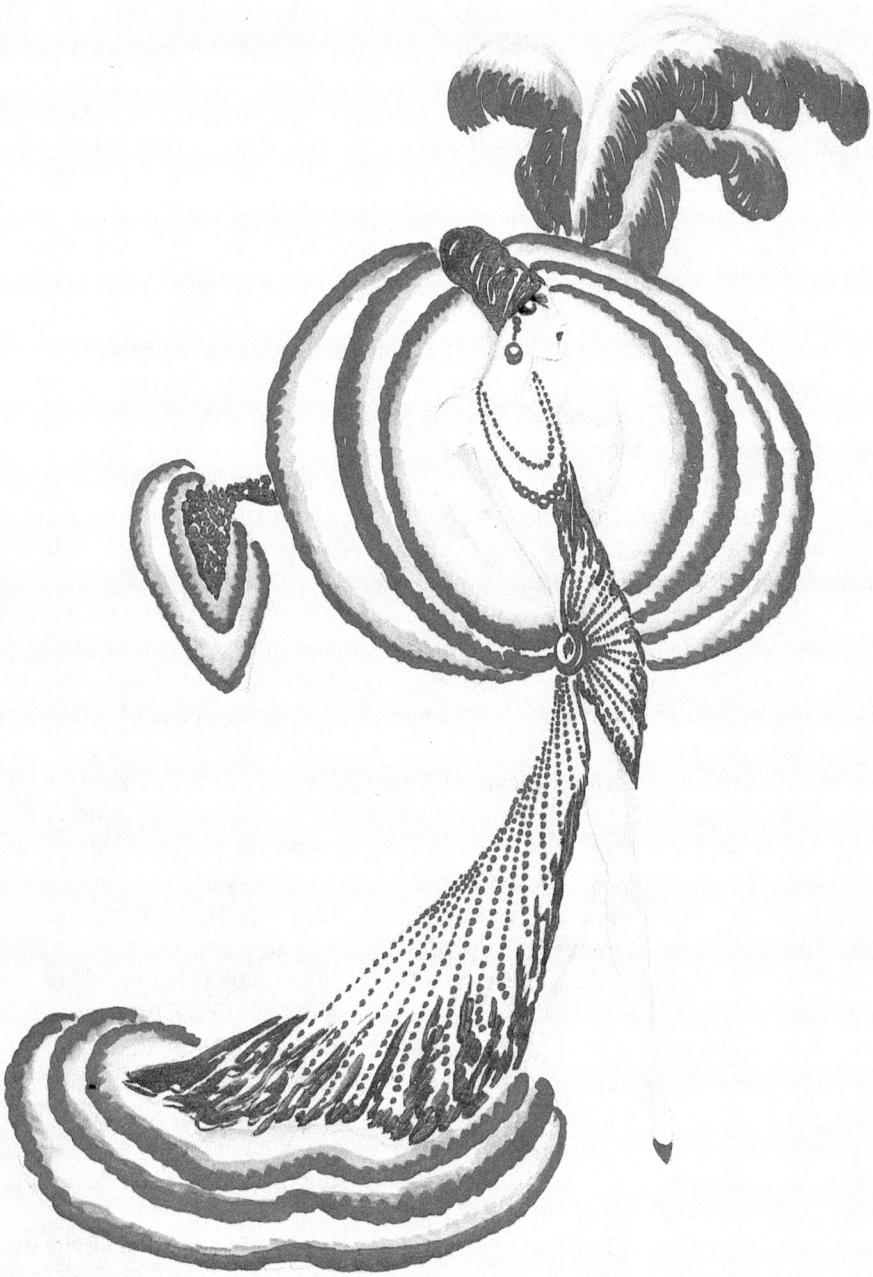

Red and gold costume design by José de Zamora, 1920s (Mary Evans/Jazz Age Club/Everett Collection).

the New Woman, she was England's leading stage designer during the 1920s and also made a big impact in Paris, where she became the first English person and the first woman to design for the Folies Bergère. In New York in the late 1920s she created the quintessential 1890s look for Mae West in *Diamond Lil* (1928) that became West's enduring image. Finally, she became one of Hollywood's major screen designers, working for MGM

Design by Dolly Tree (courtesy Piollet Collection).

during the 1930s, and creating elegant gowns for such stars as Myrna Loy, Jean Harlow, Judy Garland, Rosalind Russell, Virginia Bruce and many more.

She was unique in the breadth and scale of her productivity by working in London, Paris, New York and Hollywood and having several distinctive careers designing for the legitimate stage, cabaret, couture and film. Very few of her contemporaries could match her myriad achievements. Dolly Tree's creativity had a profound impact on fashion and her modern approach to dress designing with its chic air of simplicity has given her creations a timeless quality that can still be glimpsed in modern couture.

Dolly Tree was a truly European designer with a firm foothold in both London and Paris. Although she became the chief designer to the London theatrical producer Julian Wylie in 1919, her emphasis was not just the British stage but also the Parisian music-hall. Immediately after the Great War, during the period 1919–1920, she spent some time in Paris and elsewhere studying. She must have given presentations to the major costumiers such as Maison Pascaud and Max Weldy on the basis of commissioning them to execute some of her designs for British shows, which they both did from 1921. These meetings would also have had a benefit, opening the door for her to the Paris music-hall. The role of the costume designer in Paris was quite different from the designer's role in London. Unlike the London theater directors, the Parisian directors did not on the whole secure favored designers. Rather, the costume maker and the costume houses played a pivotal role. Unlike in London where the designer selected the costumier, in Paris, the costumier selected the designer.

Although uncredited, her first work in Paris appeared at the Folies Bergère in 1920, followed by credits for the 1922, 1923, 1928 and 1929 shows. This was matched by contributions to two shows at the Concert Mayol in 1921 and 1922. Her work also appeared at the Palace Theatre in 1923 and later, she began work with Edmond Sayag and costumed his summer show at the Kursall, Ostend in 1926 and designed his spectacular shows at the Ambassadeurs Theatre in Paris in 1926, 1927, 1928 and 1929. She also contributed to many more shows across Europe in cities such as Marseille, Barcelona, Madrid, Brussels and Berlin. It is clear that Dolly Tree was as busy in Paris and the rest of Europe as she was in London but unlike London, it is difficult to verify her exact activities and it is likely that she worked on a great many more shows but for whatever reason was denied credit.

During the eight-year period from 1919 to her departure for New York in late 1926 she provided designs for a minimum of sixty-two productions in the UK. Of these at least one third were staged in a London theatre, eighteen were pantomimes staged in London and other major cities and twenty-four were regional shows.

The costumes of the Jazz Era stood for the show and the show for a robust, sexy, gallant, civilized and "well-blocked" society of France, observes Sabine Piollet. Many of the motifs were national, purely French references to the Three Musketeers, the Bourbons, Pierette, Perrault's fairy tales, or the French colonies. Music-hall owners and directors set up a competition organized around a theme, such as "French Revolution," "Jewels," "The Garden of Metals," and "The Seven Deadly Sins." The tableaux were created as vehicles for the famous singers and the line dances and variety acts filled in. Each costume represented a character or an object, animal, plant, building, sport, food or other topic that went with the annual theme.

The populace longed to be amused after the desolation of war. There were no fewer than 77 revues in Paris during the Twenties and in other cities of France as well. So many claims are made for the first nude on stage, and the definition of nude was so vague, that when and where a nude was first part of a revue is virtually unknowable. Furthermore, their entry was probably subtle, as caryatids on the periphery. One can put pins in the timeline, however, for where sources make their claims. I would judge that it was probably either at the Casino de Paris or the Concert Mayol in 1910, or the Folies Bergère two years later. The potential of showmanship of nudity belonged to Josephine Baker when she wore regally a skirt of a string of artificial bananas (the idea of her friend Jean Cocteau). In a troupe with jazz man Sidney Bechet she brought her great verve to Paris in 1925, dancing a pas de deux with her partner Joe Alex at the Théâtre des Champs Elysées. In fact, the introduction of nudity in revues was not announced with fanfare, it was low-key. That helped keep stiff-necked officials at bay, but also nudity was "used by the avant-garde, determined to bring theater out of conformity" ("elle est aussi utilisée par l'avant garde, décidée à sortir le theater du conformisme").[19]

The revues mixed comic sketches, song, circus numbers, and various kinds of dance—acrobatic, humorous, exotic, and "fantaisiste" like Loie Fuller and her veils. The "revue des femmes" was part of the revue and was directed to combine taste and fantasy. Humor reasserts so the revues were jolly not sedative, and the predominantly male audience would be stimulated, not driven to physical distraction or dissolution.

A design by Dolly Tree (courtesy Gary Chapman).

The writer Maurice Verne studied the music-halls in 1929 and relayed statistics about the costumes at the Folies Bergère: 2,000 meters of velvet and silk fabrics, 380 kilometers of ribbons, 400,000 *strasses* (artificial pearls), a thousand jeweled hair ornaments (*mèches de perles*), all of which added up to the equivalent of millions of euros. To create the beauty and illusion took over 2,000 persons. Each of the three major music-halls, the Folies Bergère (Paul Derval, director for 48 years from 1918), the Moulin Rouge (Jacques-Charles) and the Casino de Paris (Léon Volterra, later the mayor of St. Tropez) had 50 tableaux over the course of three hours, one every four minutes.

Yet the genius of these Jazz Age costumes is that look of inevitability. Designing was a mental process before the artist put paintbrush or chalk to the paper. For *Nuits de Folies* (1932), Alec Shanks, for example, did a billowing pale blue gown drawn with silver sequin

A design by Endré, 1920s (Everett Collection).

stars, in a design that had a mountainous headdress of blue-dyed ostrich feathers. But the costume had an overarching idea in silver: tassel jewel earrings over a foot long matched by bracelets with similar tassels and a tassel as a cache-sexe. Like so many others it was an "it" dress.

The shows were exported with variations. The finale in Paris might have five nude women, Berlin only four, and New York only one, compelled to stay immobile. With Prohibition in America, nudity was out; a similar interdiction came with Mussolini in Italy. Sometimes when a show arrived the performers were by intention more covered than after they had their success for a few nights. Still, if a show could satisfy a critical audience in Paris it was sure to be a hit abroad. As Jacques-Charles wrote, "Le public français est le plus exigeant et le plus difficile … en France on va au théâter avec le parti pris de critique." [The French audiences are the most demanding and difficult…. The French go to the theater with their minds made up to criticize.][20] This attitude goes a distance to explaining the perfection of music-hall costumes beginning in the Golden Age. Meanwhile, the world beat a path to the doors of the Paris music-halls. The showgirl costumes emanated from its ateliers and surely raised the bar of costumes at revues everywhere and in Hollywood productions. *The Gold Diggers of Broadway*, the big hit movie musical of 1929, starred Winnie Lightner, who had performed in George White's "Scandals," and other New York showgirls. All the line dancers had sparkling flapper costumes, all different, that contrasted beautifully with the men in top hats and tails when the cast tap-danced and somersaulted and sang saucy songs like "Tiptoe through the Tulips."

The Golden Age of Costumiers

SABINE PIOLLET[21]

All told, close to 80 Parisian theaters produced revues during their golden age between the wars. Naturally not all revues had 50 tableaux like at the biggest music-halls, but even the small theaters could put on a revue of ten tableaux. Little theaters made their own costumes or engaged a lesser-known, and therefore less expensive, costumier. Some costumes, though, were made by the Galeries Lafayette, and accessories came from specialty stores such as Vuitton. *C'est de la Folie* of the Folies Bergère in March 1921 consisted of two acts and 35 tableaux, for which there were 200 performers and 800 costumes.

In the 1920s, the music-hall costumiers numbered about 40, of which certain ones (comparable to Christian Lacroix or Jean-Paul Gaultier today) were major couturiers like Paul Poiret, Madame Rasimi, and Zel, and, of greatest pertinence for the Piollet Collection, Max Weldy.

Max Weldy became active at the end of the First World War. Music-halls quickly recognized his talent and hired him. He became the designated costumier at the Folies. It was reported widely that he furnished one and a half million costumes for a sole year there. That seems exaggerated, yet the number, taking all the costumes reproduced for tableaux and revues that were exported, was phenomenal. For example, young Florenz Ziegfeld after seeing *Paris qui tourne* at the Moulin Rouge, contracted with Jacques-Charles to adapt tableaux for a revue on Broadway.

To create all these outfits, Weldy sought out the best artists, known as *dessinateurs*.

As a consequence, he hired the stellar talent Erté, considered the father of Art Deco, and other artists of the top rank each of whom brought unique style, such as René Ransom's or Umberto Brunellischi's glittering enchantresses or Alexander Zinoview's fey confections. Fifteen artists might be involved in one revue; in our collection we have sketches by 70 different artists yet the collection does not represent the *dessinateurs* exhaustively.

Weldy initiated a fair formula to remunerate them: he obtained the rights to reproduce numerous costumes from the same design, so that artists received royalties from all over the world for their drawings. The principle was to keep the original at the atelier and make reproductions that were sent to theaters abroad, the sketches being used from Buenos Aires to Shanghai to Oslo. To create costumes from the drawings, Weldy had an army of almost 300 seamstresses on three floors. Weldy's trove of boxes contained as many as 10,000 sketches for each artist. For the 26 years of her career, Jenny Carré did 32,000 costume sketches; Freddy Wittop, who began in Paris in 1930 and ended in the U.S. in the 1990s created at least 50,000 costume sketches.

This was a world apart, full of effervescence, creativity, and imagination. When the costumes were worn on stage, all the artists were naturally anonymous, although many of them had significant accomplishments in graphic and fine arts; some showed in prestigious shows like the Salon des Independents. But Weldy demanded not only artistry but glamour. He would say, "Yes I see a nice quality of imagination for a poet but what poet ever sang a music-hall costume?"

Often, artists collaborated and sometimes they also had more control of a revue, as Gesmar and Jean le Seyeux did, or they weighed in with ideas for new stage sets, as Michel Gyamarthy did. The sketches from which the outfits were made moved around as the revue was being put together, so the original creations could serve as a model when there were retouches to do. The costumier confectioned a base that was shaped to the body of a real person, and over that base the definitive costume was made. A large number of costumes seen in Paris were done over or dyed before leaving as rentals for exportation. Often they were quite damaged but the fairy fingers of the seamstresses performed miracles!

All this not only dressed women up in sexy undress but permitted the transformation of women into objects, like pompoms, flowers, fans, and so forth. There were superstars like Mistinguett and Josephine Baker but also the troupe, mostly female, called "girls" and fewer men, called "boys." It was a hard life; you could say that the troupe for all practical purposes lived in the purgatory of the factory of desire.

Opinion reigned that without naked women a revue could not exist. Except for the rare Venus, the costume and how it was worn could accentuate physical assets. Max Weldy explained that the costume depended on the woman who wore it. Thus the American girls would have a low-dipping décolletage because they tended to have breasts lower than the English girls, and their fannies were more toned. A German or Scandinavian could not wear an Italian or French girl's costume because it didn't cover the hips correctly. Weldy had fixed ideas, so to him a Brazilian was skinny and the girls from the U.S. had the ideal figure for a revue.

The girls often had another job (salesgirl, typist, maid). When they first put on the skimpy costumes they were nervous but no one paid attention to them, and after hours of shows or rehearsals they hurried off so to not miss the last metro. Their life was running from one job to another, eating poorly and little. The tableaux rolled out at such a fast pace, often every two minutes, that the rapid costume changes stressed them. Except for the stars, the work of the showgirl was a redundancy of long months. Now this is even more so—as to introduce new revues like those at the Lido often takes four years—while between the world wars a revue was innovated every six to twelve months in the big music-halls.

By the 1930s, the phonograph, radio and television and the cinema contributed to the decline of the music-hall. New techniques of sound and light replaced the scenic effects, costume and accessories that had come before. The Casino de Paris and the Folies Bergère reduced their costs to a minimum and the *grande salle* of the Moulin Rouge became a cinema, the fate of many other music-halls.

FIVE

High-Style Undress

"Adornment, what a science!"—Coco Chanel

The Nude in the Early Music-Hall

Nudity advanced like a striptease in slow motion in Paris, whereas in New York it bounded ahead recklessly in the shows of Ziegfeld and Earl Carroll. First the audience glimpsed a thigh between stockings and pantaloon lace, then a full leg from slit of skirt. Then the contours of a complete, corseted woman, shrouded in a body stocking. Then brassieres and shorts, like circus acrobats, rather looking like feminine armor drew attention. Deft costumers by 1920 were studding artificial silks with rhinestones and replacing fabric with sequins (on chains or molded wire). The growth of the fashion industry and proliferation of theatrical *fournisseurs* in Paris arguably drove the progress of glamorous undress. The titillation was designed to be as respectable as a stroll through the Louvre.

In the gradualness of using nudity in the revues lay its strength as it emerged from tradition. When nudity was introduced to the music-halls around 1910, costume elements existed to give it grace. The tight-loose draping, décolletage was combined with a lavish train, the post–Revolutionary "wet look," use of shawls to wrap and unwrap the body, the concept of transformation, where the female body mimed something in nature (butterfly, seashell, flower, deer, etc.), and the ability of lighting to make the contours of a lightly clad body truly visible were already in place. The demimondaines exploited draping, slits (especially to show off a leg), and semi-nudity of breasts and hips combined with opulent brassieres and belts.

With modernity came asymmetrical and twisting forms so that a costume could shock by having one shoulder, leg or breast covered and the other naked. There were other new ideas: covering what is usually uncovered and vice versa, so a nearly nude dancer might wear long gloves, high boots, headgear, and a cache-sexe, period; monokinis or skimpy sports-style outfits either for athletic movement or to demonstrate the New Woman; having more nudity by means of more women (multiplication of breasts, thighs, etc., in a troupe), and, finally costuming "off the body."

Costume designers ran with this last idea. Whether the productions carried it to the limit that the artists did is a question. Nevertheless, looking at the costume drawings of the 1920s, the rendering of thematic transformation of the body where the costume actually lifts off the dancer takes one's breath away. The artist became an extraordinary magician, creating many fabulous costumes that left the female body virtually unclothed. The enigma was worthy of Heraclitus, dress and undress being a pair of opposites that are, if understood, one. The trick was over and over to invent a hot fudge sundae. The dress could mostly be in the train, or built up and out from the shoulders, or down from an umbrella-like structure on the dancer's head; or she could be wearing just a bit of a dress shared with another dancer. Like a capital and period on a sentence, the icon continued to have headdress and high heels, but the endlessly inventive ways to maximize effect with minimized coverage is what makes it the Golden Age.

Just as Henri de Toulouse-Lautrec wasn't the ugly gnome he was reputed to be, the fin de siècle music-hall revues were less provocative than billed. Tableaux vivants in the 1890s imitated paintings by great artists that showed beautiful nudes, such as W.-A. Bouguereau's windswept *Aurora* sniffing a calla lily and draped only on one hand and at her feet, but the stage representations were tame. The Folies Bergère in 1894 advertised Aurora unclothed, but audiences saw her in a bodysuit.[1] The limit of showgirl audacity was a display of shoulders and midriff, or a glimpse of legs. Then again, she was Spanish and made a point of dancing with unbridled passion.

Cléo de Mérode, the most admired fin de siècle beauty, as an elite ballerina crossed over to the Folies Bergère where she herself created dances. But when Auguste Rodin's friend Alexandre Falguière did a naked sculpture of her, scandal followed and he had to say she posed only for the head. Even in 1910 the Ballets Russes were garbed in body stockings, sometimes painted. Shocking nudity on the music-hall bills in the 1890s and until World War I often was a feint. Writes Lenard Berlanstein, "The theater business over the course of the nineteenth century became, if anything, ever more dependent on the sexualized body of the actress as the industry grew more competitive, more market oriented. Beautiful bodies, leggy chorus girls, and skin-colored tights were indisputable aspects of the theater industry costumes."[2] The music-halls had different costumers and identities but, gradually, and without much ado, a shedding of attire resulted in the iconic showgirl costume in this period. After all, this was Paris, where vulgarity was the absence of style.

During the early 1890s, striptease, that is, showing petticoats and chemise became part of the music-hall repertory. How the owner of the Divan Japonais, a popular night spot at 75, rue de Martyrs, for which Toulouse-Lautrec painted posters, billed the shows there gives a vivid sense of what risqué meant; a female troupe who sang "chansons sensuelles" were in "maillot complet," or "nue."

A famous act that put its toe into undress was the 1894 pantomime *Le Coucher d'Yvette* (Yvette at Bedtime), in which a woman strips off the layers of her clothing and climbs into bed. Blanche Cavelli, whose stage name was Yvette, did this ancestor of the striptease at Le Concert Lisbonne (the owner was Maxime Lisbonne), formerly the Divan Japonais. The décor was bamboo and red lacquer. This pantomime had the charming term *effeuillage,* taking the leaves from a tree, and Blanche took off her jacket, corset and stockings bit by bit, without suggestive gestures or postures. If part of the performance was behind a screen, showing just her *ombre chinois,* and she had a flesh-colored teddy from neck to feet, she nevertheless titillated by her dramatic tempo and the way she threw her boa, hat and skirt onto a chair, seemingly oblivious to being watched.

> The bodice with standing collar and leg-of-mutton sleeves, embroidered with a Byzantine motif goes flying.... Many corpulent spectators in orchestra seats wipe their foreheads....
> Blanche stays in the light, always remote from the situation, letting her percale tunic.... The big

Costume design by Edouard Halouze (courtesy Hargrett Rare Book and Manuscript Library, University of Georgia).

innocent eyes don't blink…. The mood of the public is at its height, but she ignores it, dressed only in her Zouave pantaloons, in pink batiste with black trim, tight over the knees, stockings, corset and a blouse that billows around her breasts.

A moment passes. Then, lazily, Blanche drops an ample nightdress over her head and jumps on the bed while the curtain closes.[3]

Cavelli chose not to repeat the success in theaters in Lyon or on the Champs-Elysées. The author of the pantomime accordingly sued her. Attesting to the importance of the costume to the act, Blanche had to return her costumes to a Monsieur Verdelet. A short film, lost, was made for Gaumont in 1897 of the *Coucher d'Yvette*. In 1905 Blanche married the lithographer Louis Huvey and was able to settle down after her notoriety.

The concept was picked up by others—nobody really undressed to the skin for now. The music-halls counted on invention for their copycat sketches, with titles such as *Le Bain de Maid* (The Maid Takes a Bath), *Suzanne et la Grande Chaleur* (Suzanne in a Heat Wave), *Liane chez le Médecin* (Liane at the Doctors), and, comically, *La Puce* (The Flea) at the Casino de Paris, in which the performer checked out her entire body to determine the source of an itch. Angèle Hérard went on a tour of Europe with *La Puce* where her act had to conform to diverging laws of decency: "In Berlin she was allowed to remove her stays, but was obliged to keep them on in Vienna. Munich permitted her to scratch her knee; Budapest forbade it."[4] Over and again in the history of showgirl entertainment, the person looking for obscenity is not just looking but staring.

These voyeuristic stripteases in the theater were undeniably arty. A woman getting into bed alone, or into a bathtub, was as pure an act as the common pantomime of a woman drawing water from a well. She was as unconscious of prying eyes as a Renaissance nude. On the other hand, the shapely form in the bodysuit apparently drove men wild. Actresses in Paris were expected to be *femmes fatales*, were generally admired, and could not be indecent, only alluring seraphim, while plying their trade. The showgirl was explicitly come-hither. In vampish costumes or dressed as dollies, cute bits of fluff, showgirls mesmerized with a message of frivolity—and safety. A man could go on to his mistress or his wife and stay clear of the brothel. The costumage was in tune with how the "petites femmes de Paris," the city's fantasy women, were marketed to tourists. Writes Rearick, "Guidebooks for men, erotic postcards and photographs, and magazines such as *La Vie Parisienne* depicted young Parisian women as a type—sexy, light-hearted, and ever ready for amorous adventures."[5] Arletty, star of Michel Carné's movie *Enfants du Paradis*, refused as a character (Garance) in the film to be a nude sideshow. The mime, played by Jean-Louis Barrault, sees her purity on the brink of indecency and responds to it as a cry for help. The fantasy of the courtesan with proud bearing in a bathtub was staged with speed and meticulous Romantic-era costuming. The staging, credited to Antoine Mayo, makes her reality all the more credible. (Jeanne Lanvin provided the materials, scarce during the 1943–1944 filming, and Mayo executed the designs for Alexander Trauner, a Jewish member of Carné's team.)

Arletty, whose music-hall career began by 1920 and preceded her movie career, once acted in a show called *Azor* where she appeared in a bathtub showing naked shoulders and limbs. This was at the Théâtre des Bouffes du Nord. It was at les Bouffes that Arletty first displayed the erotic trance, mirroring the desire in men's eyes, so effective when she played Garance in *Les Enfants du Paradis*.

A costume typically makes the figure more naked. Titian's *Venus d'Urbino* lounges in the foreground while her maid takes her employer's clothes from a fancy wooden chest (a *cassone*) in the background. Clearly fin de siècle nudity was a feature of revues that did not equate with total undress; in fact it was an opportunity to display dress. And a costume required sparkle to show off ritzy assets. The vocabulary of costume centered on fine textiles, glitter, and glamorous surprise. The brassieres that looked made for Valkyries and the ghostly look of white body stockings were, for instance, retired early in the new century. Costumers became au fait with making the showgirl look luxurious without weighing her down with the sumptuous. This contrasted markedly with the pinup portraits of early photography in which women were often wrapped in a fold of a heavy curtain at the photographer's studio. According to Pascal Jacob:

> Each music-hall outbid the other. The inspiration came from the salons and the street performers. The dressmaker Frederic Worth from 1858 and above all Paul Poiret from 1903 integrated spangles and sequins into their finery, as much to dress up their daytime clothes as to enrich and raise the impact of their evening gowns. Between 1900 and 1914, many tens of manufacturers of paillettes, these miniscule fragments of metal and jet, then plastic, created, inspired, and took over by entire bushels the ateliers and the couture houses. These fragile tiny ornaments overwhelmed the furs and evening capes, made the textiles iridescent, multiplied the effects and reflections, illuminated the fabrics, and above all gave a precious identity to their creations. Very soon, the music-hall became infatuated in its turn with this easy luxury: from London to New York, the lines of the garments disappeared until troves of sewn paillettes and plumes, as if posting on the body a desire for sex, which reveals itself as an irresistible philter for many of the spectators. A glaze of rhinestones, fur and lamé transcended the luster of the body.[6]

Walking through the music-hall costumes from the *fin de siècle*, the "peau nue" became another stylistic device, kept in check by self-censorship. Trial and error indicated what would pass with eagle-eyed officials. Notable was Senator René Beranger, whose soubriquet was "Père le Pudeur" (Father Prude), and his League of Decency. The senator obsessed over the external proprieties. He got a law passed that dogs could not urinate on the street, on the grounds not of sanitation, but that it was indecent exposure. In the literature pertaining to the music-hall, only two bans are notable: Colette's kissing Missy in their skit at the Moulin Rouge and *Paris qui tourne*, where the police banned the end of a long scene about the Countess Du Barry which ended at the guillotine.[7]

Presenting a sexy stage show has always involved sensing what the public is ready for. The artist John Vanderlyn did the first American painting of a nude which won a prize and Napoléon Bonaparte's praise, but back in America he did not venture to repeat his success. Thus, printed erotic photographs used poses where "half undressed women either crossed their legs or held them slightly parted."[8] On the stage, being public, titillation had to be carefully gauged. Frances Trollope, the novelist's mother, toured America in 1836. She made a point of going to an off-color theatrical performance which was so sensual that women did not attend, "gentlemen muttered under their breath, and turned their heads aside when the subject was mentioned," and clergy castigated it from the pulpit. In the course of a mythological tableau, two scantily clothed "figurantes" caused a sensation. Mrs. Trollope wrote in her travelogue that they probably came from Paris, and she observed that this was what the Americans must want: "When I was asked if I had ever seen anything so dreadful before, I was embarrassed how to answer; for the young women had been exceedingly careful, both in their dress and in their dancing, to meet the tastes of the people."[9]

Partial and full nudity on the stage popped up sometime before World War I. It was a hallmark of Parisian shows by 1910 and became prevalent during the war; a patriotic desire to please soldiers on leave is said to have had to do with it. In the U.S., Ziegfeld placed nudes like statues and not part of the choreographed dance after being in Paris during the war. Naked women were, in early twentieth century music-halls, allowed to move a bit; most everybody was dancing to some extent, less if one carried a great deal of feathers. In Paris, bare breasts were accepted in shows, and "total nudity" (always the cache-sexe) arrived in Casino de Paris's *Paris qui Danse* (1919), thematically the story of fashionable dances from the quadrille naturelle to the tango. Animated tableaux of nude figures became the practice in the Parisian revues in the numerous music-halls directed by Leon Volterra. On-stage swimming pools were a rationale for nudity.

It speaks for the difference between nudity as something "cheap" in America, despite the ascension of Ziegfeld's Follies, and an artistic posing in French civilization. The display of bare breasts was initiated by none other than a future grand officer of the Legion of Honor, Colette, so honored by the French in 1953 for her frankness in life and letters. How the commerce in nude display caught on in the upscale music-halls is noted by historian Felter-Kerley, who enumerates "enticing revues intitled *Nude in Paris, Paris All Nude, Hide Your Nude ... and But Don't Walk Around All Nude!*," and declares that the showgirl nude

> stood at the center of public debates on morality, censorship, the nature of public versus private, and the appropriate roles for women. Like the prostitute and the hysteric before her, she captured both the attention and imagination of writers, critics, moralists, politicians, and journalists as a desirable yet dangerous, transcendental yet transgressive, pretty yet perverse physiognomic type.[10]

The costumes, the sultry and the cute, testify to the duality of the showgirl persona. Lela Felter-Kerley asserts that the nudity evoked "fears of unregulated female sexual desire on public display." To have the sizzle a costume showed the female body that would normally be seen only by a lover. But the costuming itself regulated the sizzle. The devices of costuming with soft materials and using humor or metaphor, or presenting outlandish distance between the crazy exhibitionism on the stage and the proper people, most of the audience, to not drive the bourgeois to distraction and anxiety, the costume was cute, often preposterous and insisted on the performer's vulnerability or passivity—whatever she wears, a showgirl is in an erotic trance.

The dancing girls provided the whipped cream to the revues. When the *revue à grand spectacle* emerged at the Casino de Paris, it opened with a show by Jacques-Charles and starring Gaby Deslys called *Laissez-les Tomber* and with a multiplication of dancing girls. First at the Casino they became a visual force. With its horses that could do a Roman number with showgirls parading as Roman slaves or harem girls—the sets were multipurpose—costuming had vastly more potential. No man in the audience needed to fear it was about these pretty girls dropping him; on the stage they lived for him—any dominating women were off stage.

Academic nineteenth-century painters could titillate a respectable public with depictions of women being chased, or violated or sold. So long as the artist kept to mythological themes, ancient history and remote places in the world, the public was not riled. Perhaps seeing the Rape of the Sabines or an ancient examining a slave's teeth reinforced the male view's self-righteousness. The submissive odalisque with her blank look compares to the showgirl stare that looks only inward, as she carries off her appointed degree of nudity with sangfroid. There is the visual risk she will look like a captive female which would slash through the lighthearted tone of the revue. The shimmer came from the oscillation between the doll-like passive female and the dominating woman that rivals her.

Before nudity was part of the shows it was a feature of art and advertising. It was a hop, skip and jump from an illustration of a nude rising from a wine glass, as if from a man's thoughts, for the derisive counter–Salon art movement Les Incohérents, advertising their costume ball of 1893, to a woman playing that part on stage, especially as the art students and female models recreated at the annual student balls popular academic paintings that depicted nudes. In the 1890s, some waitresses at the Moulin Rouge were bare-breasted and a spicy revue called *Fin de sex* opened in 1905 at the Alcazar. Topless came in at the big trilogy, the Folies Bergère and its rivals the Olympia and Casino de Paris, at the turn of century, in their tableaux vivants, a fixture by 1918. To bring alive a scene provided the rationale for nudity, for example, a scene at the Maliere music-hall, preserved in a photograph of about 1900, of hell as a ravishing place to be. On a small lower stage, three girls in white loincloths cavort, while two male devils all in black with black skull-caps and mustaches stand duty with pitchforks. On an upper level of the stage, a third girl, held aloft by another devil, looks eager to be cast into the melée.[11] The women are all topless and gracefully swathed.

The music-halls veered to more lavish, and, paradoxically, more risqué and more middle class–pleasing revues. By World War I Casino de Paris, Folies Bergère, Moulin-Rouge, Olympia and the Ambassadeurs were the most prominent and, says Kalifa, the eroticization of the spectacle progressed, the mise en scène—costume, décor, lights and choreography—being what distinguished these spectacles from the café-concerts, and the female performers were "veritable décor vivant."[12] In America, Ziegfeld, from about 1918, rationalized the stationary nudes tucked into his fantastical sets as bringing masterpiece artworks to life, and his rival Earl Carroll used mythology as an excuse for costumes no more concealing than a few lengths of Saran Wrap. In Paris, where nudes abounded on public fountains and the stonework of buildings, audiences didn't need to excuse the animated tableaux when the "revue à grand spectacle" format with total nudity arrived at the Folies in 1918 and at the Casino de Paris in 1919. The critic Gustave Fréjaville, after seeing the revue *L'Amour en Folie* at the Folies Bergère, remarked, "Mais enfin, jusqu'on pretend-on aller dans cette voie? Une revue sans femmes nues aurait maintenant au moins une chance de paraître originale."[13]

Gallic naughtiness was in itself a stage set built by a series of those producers and directors who put their money on dancing girls. They included Edouard Marchand, who founded the "girl-centric" revue when he brought the Barrison Sisters to the Folies in 1890; Jacques-Charles, who set the frantic and demanding pace of the tableaux; and Louis Lemarchand, who excelled at sumptuous trappings and brought in the first lines of synchronized dance to the Folies. Paul Derval began as a comedian and for 48 years, beginning in 1918 at the Folies, created the animated musical postcards with seminude women parading amid glittering spectacle. These and other pivotal impresarios and directors "acted as catalysts. They all had one thing in common: as impresarios, they gathered around them the most brilliant designers, costumiers, choreographers, lyricists and composers of light music that Paris could offer."[14]

Those who performed the skits, songs, dances and jokes wore all kinds of trappings in the period around 1900. Take for instance the Folies Bergère's most outstanding hit of the era, *Chand d'habits* (The Clothes Merchant), first staged when the Barrison Sisters appeared, and revived in 1905. Pierrot murders a clothes merchant in order to dress up and go with his girl Musidora to a party. But the clothes merchant disguises himself as Pluto, haunts Pierrot, takes Musidora's place in the bed where Pierrot expected to find her, and carries Pierrot off to hell. The costume opportunities were many and diverse; likely most of the actors improvised.

With electrical lighting in place, the scene for the golden age of revues and costumes was now set. By the Twenties the costuming had been reduced to the skimpiest and the casts were big. At the Folies Bergère the troupe numbered several dozen showgirls and those who figured in nude tableaux "moved" (Paul Derval auditioned dancers at various dancing schools).

It is possible to see through the eyes of an American tourist who went to a revue at the Alcazar d'Été in 1902 or 1903. It had three acts, a "musical pudding" launched with a Cinderella story, where the newlyweds in the third act watch the revue:

> A hodgepodge of burlesques upon the topics of the day, ballets representing flowers and perfumes and the history of fashion, and choruses representing the different journals, the arts, inventions, and manufactures. The costumes are superb and the massing of color exquisite. The finale, "an apotheosis of gorgeous color," closes the spectacle with a "stageful of kicking, giggling, romping gaity."[15]

Staging and costume came to govern the revues. Even a star like Cléo de Mérode soon functioned as a satellite to the dazzle, or as a "center of gravity that kept the diverse elements of the show from flying off into incoherence and kept the house full."[16]

Mata Hari

While Mata Hari flirted with spying for both sides in World War I, her (possibly fictive)[17] statement "a whore maybe but a traitor never" has turned out true; she has been vindicated of having been an agent for the Germans. Her execution, for which she presented, in defiance, dressed as a fine lady, was a political (French) mistake.

There is no doubt, though, that she was inclined to spin stories about her past. She deprecated the snake charmers and said her dance was authentic since she was born and bred in Java: False, she was from Holland. Her costumes, like her story, were flamboyant make-believe while her vaguely Javanese inspiration was real.

Margaretha Zella came to Paris to be a fashion model in 1903 after splitting from her faithless husband. She was beautiful and sensual and started to perform in private homes voluptuous dances, claiming them sacred. She got away with showing her body because of the cachet that these were sacred dances.

Her first public performance was at the Musée Guimet, a new museum of Oriental art in Paris, in March 1904, and photographs as well as newspaper accounts give a picture of what she wore. An English correspondent for a society magazine, in a long praising article about the dancer's private performance the month before, wrote:

> Her olive skin blended with the curious jewels in the dead gold setting. A casque of worked gold upon her dark hair—an authentic Eastern head-dress; a breastplate of similar workmanship beneath the arms. Above a transparent white robe, a quaint clasp held a scarf around the hips, the ends falling to the feet in front. She was enshrouded in various veils of delicate hues, symbolizing beauty, youth, love, chastity, voluptuousness and passion.[18]

Her eyes shone, her movements intensified to a frenzy, and, one by one, she flung off the veils. At the end she unclasped her belt and appeared to fall to a swoon at the feet of Siva, Hindu god of creation and destruction.

The exotic Oriental dance was a raging success. When Mata Hari appeared in Vienna the next year it was called later "the war of tights." Her biographer, the anthropologist

Pat Shipman, writes that Mata Hari was seen in competition with two other dancers who wore scanty costumes, Isadora Duncan who wore loosely draped toga-like garments and danced corset-less, and Maud Allan, who did a seductive Salomé dance and "wore breast-plates, jewelry, and a headdress not unlike the one worn by Mata Hari, who regarded her as little more than a cheap imitator."[19]

The outfit was gracefully minimal, and when the Université des Annales in Paris invited her to illustrate a lecture by a music critic, she was at the last moment draped with a piece of red flannel on her hips.[20]

Off stage, Mata Hari was a fashion plate, in fine plumed, corseted gowns, and pearls. She understood the French idea of the perfectly turned out woman who was a torrid, indomitable mistress. In her modes there was always that little difference, like a dress cut lower than the fashion.

The prison of Saint-Lazarre where she ended her days in her early forties was dreadful and humiliating but she had lived an amazing love life and stage life. Her clear-eyed relationship to her success has particular appeal. She told G.H. Priem, a Dutch man of letters, after she had gained fame,

> I was pretty—why may I not say it now also one time?—and the people, the men, they love a pretty woman. They like to see much of a pretty woman until the border of the indiscreet. I have never been afraid to catch a cold, remember my décolletés, which my husband tried to forbid. Well then, I started to use décolletés, and to use décolletés more and more. With every veil I threw off, my success rose. Pretending to consider my dances very artistic and full of character, thus praising my art, they came to see nudity, and that is still the case.[21]

According to Priem, she said, "The artistic cachet to which I connect everything, that protects me against banality."[22]

Postcard illustration of a dancing girl.

Mata Hari danced at the lesbian garden parties of Colette's friend Natalie Barney in Neuilly, once making an entrance as Lady Godiva naked on a white horse. Colette commented, "She did not actually dance, but with graceful movements shed her clothes" and disappeared, "enveloped in her veils."[23]

The dances were admired and were it seems inspired by Javanese court dances, and the costumes were lovely. Her signature type of costume which she wore at the Guimet had a gold jeweled headdress, a beaded metallic bra, see-through veils wrapped around her hips, and Indian-style armlets, dangling earrings, and a necklace with what look like amulet pendants. She was barefoot and the most naked person that had appeared on a stage to that time. At the start of the dance she had a coiling belt but by the end her only cover appears to have been from breastplates up.

That her first public performance was at the fine museum, where she danced in the domed library and was introduced by the great collector of Asian art, Monsieur Guimet himself, established her bona fides.

Mati Hari was a hit across Europe and her interpretation was understood as such. *Parisian Life* reported about her as "Lady MacLeod, that is to say Mata Hari, the Indian dancer," describing what she wore as "the costume of the *bayadère*, as much simplified as possible, and toward the end, she simplifies it even a little more."[24]

She was frank about being highly sexed. This was refreshing to the Dutch journalist who recorded her remarks. Mata Hari said she was sexually excited by beautiful men, especially military men, from a young age,

1920s French postcard with Orientalist snakeskin touch.

loved men, and should never have married.[25] From her debut at the Guimet in 1905 until her tragic death, she burned brightly. If her grandmother was not descended from a Javanese princess, she wore her fantasy costumes of the East as no other music-hall star did. The draping, the cut, everything looked stunning on this vibrant, fearless performer.

Colette

Sidonie-Gabrielle Colette (1873–1954) thought she might be an actress before she settled in as an author. Her personal tumults gave her material for writing and the costumes she chose to wear on stage paved the way for the music-hall poster girls like Andrée Spinelly. As an intellectual who lived in her head, Colette played with exteriorizing her showgirl persona. Colette slept around to win her spurs until, one day, she decided she had aged beyond sexual relations and closed her bedroom door.

Once Colette's husband, the author and publisher known as Willy, let her out of their apartment where she ghostwrote his material, she rebelliously sought and thrived in the public eye. The theater drew her special ambitions and she began to act. Then the big scandal whipped up when she performed in her Cleopatra head piece and jeweled bra with "Missy," the Marquise de Morny, in *Rêve d'Egypte*. It is notable that it was Missy's relatives who asked the prefect of police to close the show down. Instead it reopened as *Songe d'Orient* and the new archaeologist was male.

In November of that year, Colette staked out new theatrical territory when she unveiled her breast (no concealing maillot) at the Apollo music-hall in *La Chair*, the play in which the writer reinvented herself as an actress. The celebration of physical beauty as well as prowess was in tune with the times. Writes Patricia Tilburg, "In the first decade of the twentieth century, shows involving sport or gymnastic displays began staging dazzling vaudeville revues that incorporated athletic events."[26] Bouts of the Great World Wrestling Championship concluded the evening at the Apollo and when *La Chair* played in Lyons the program included a troupe of Japanese tightrope walkers. Tilburg notes Colette dispensed with the flesh-colored maillot, the "nu académique" body-stocking in the music-hall as Isadora Duncan and Ruth St. Denis had in their modern dance.[27]

She had the role in *La Chair* of a peasant whose smuggler lover finds her in the arms of a soldier and almost murders her. The lover tears off the girl's clothes in the struggle, which is how Colette happened to tour for four years in France, Belgium and Switzerland, performing in her controversial costume. Colette was a New Woman, the opposite of the domestic angel of the bourgeois model and she repeatedly justified exhibiting her body as a work of art. Tilburg observes that the music-halls were presenting "corps fabuleux" where gymnasts, contortionists, boxers, and clowns represented the moral imperative of fitness and physical health as the basis for moral soundness.

In a photograph of her performance, Colette is *en profil* in her torn slip with left breast exposed. Her right arm is raised and her left foot pointed as she looks heavenward like a Hellinistic sculpture. Her left arm, though, she crooked against her waist where her hand is fisted defiantly.

> The belle époque music-hall was an especially inventive cultural site in which a modern aesthetic of the fit body was articulated and disseminated, perhaps even more widely than in the gymnase or on the athletic field. Music-hall professionals prided themselves on physical agility, and they exercised often as a part of their training. It was now respected to be a female music-hall performer: For indeed,

One of a music-hall postcard series: "A Travers les Coulisses" (in the wings).

the physically fit women of the music-hall were received by audiences not at all as masculinized amazons, but as the epitome of modern grace and, most interestingly, moral rectitude.[28]

As women became admired for athleticism in the new century, the ideal of beauty changed from the wasp-waisted bosomy mien of the courtesans to a new lissomness. Young women turned to cycling, tennis, boating, and so on to sculpt their figures and some, like Colette, took up boxing. Art critic Léon Werth wrote about Colette's appearance in *Le Chair* in a 1911 review of paintings by J-A-D Ingres and Albert Marquet. Whereas the male painters expressed their own fantasy in the women they painted, Colette realized "on the stage of a low-class neighborhood music-hall the dream of artists who would like to paint landscapes inhabited by beautiful nudes who are not mythological." The art critic contrasted Colette with fashionable ladies who "when [such women] have taken off their clothes, display their bodies with the embarrassment of a child who hides his eyes behind his arm and dares not look."[29]

Colette described the tattered garb of performers on tour in sketches she wrote based on her own experience on tour. The young women traveling on the train were like honeyless bees and wore "misery-hiding cloaks" and slept in their "crumpled bonnets." Only the "grande coquette" was differentiated by her pompous head gear "stuck on top of a dusty black velvet tray—three funereal ostrich plumes"—Colette compared her to a "discouraged beetle."

Several chorus girls in a dressing room are limned in Colette's *The Vagabond*. Brilliantine gets on the hands and greasy makeup "spells death to velvet and feathers." A chorus girl named Garcin wears only "a pair of trellised tights, all gold and pearls, with two openwork metal disks, stuck over her non-existent breasts. The rough edges of her jeweled ornaments, the coarsely punched copper pendants, the clinking chain-armor." During their break the chorus girls make repairs, permitting themselves the "candid illusion of being cloistered young women who sew." The makeup table has black and red cosmetic pencils, rouge jar, eyebrow pencil and woolen powder puff. Most of the dancers are fair-haired, slender and wore false blond curls, with mauve eye shadow and "such a heavy application of mascara on their lashes" that the color of their pupils could not be distinguished.[30]

Colette's arty semi-nudity and passionate kiss with another woman were brazen and self-consciously modern. Like another flamboyant writer, Anaïs Nin, in writing Colette achieved a more nuanced humanity. Without condemning or melodrama, only the fiction of Colette brings alive the music-hall backstage including the dressing up and undress. One of her music-hall sketches is structured as an interview with an accompanist, 26, a single mother whose five-year-old son is allowed to stay in the studio after his daycare. Her only complaint of her job is that sitting on a piano stool all day makes her sore.

The accompanist (who seems all the nearer for having no name) has been offered by her boss, Madame Barucchi, to go on stage as a showgirl—a nude dancer so as not to tire herself out by dancing. The piano player didn't wish to, she had replied, and not just from modesty:

> A dancer in the nude, as the saying goes, displays no more than any of the others. A dancer in the nude always means something in the Egyptian style, and that entails a good ten pounds' weight of beaten-metal straps and belts and ornaments, beaded lattice-work on the legs, necklaces from here to there, and no end of veils. No, it wasn't merely the question of decency that made me decline. It's my nature to stay in my corner and watch the others.... Bright lights, spangles, costumes, painted faces, smiles, that spectacular sort of life is not for me. I see nothing but careers, sweat, skins that are yellow by the light of day, and despondency.[31]

This wonderful description of iconic showgirl undress is also interesting for its lack of mention of feathers. Great plumes would characterize the music-hall reviews only gradually in the Jazz Era. Liane de Pougy describes in her diary how she was wearing a little hat trimmed with white lace and two women with huge hats adorned with ostrich feathers called her a tart. Liane's husband, Prince Georges Ghika, riposted to look back at themselves before they insulted others. A fracas followed, hurting his jaw and involving every-one's being taken to the police station.[32] Until after World War I, feathers were an appur-tenance of middle-class ladies whereas the showgirl costumes were distinguished by shiny ornament and sheer fabrics, more Orientalist than Versailles court.

Andrée Spinelly

Andrée Spinelly, noted star of all the main music-halls of Paris, made her debut at 14, and in addition to continual appearances in Paris had tours in London and New York including the Ziegfeld Follies. What differentiates her from earlier stars of music-hall was how she incarnated the Deco. She was also in the film *Spinelly cherche un mari* (1917) and is considered one of the first stars of the new art form, cinema. She became a flower as depicted on a poster with a full skirt in fanciful flounces of spinach green, carmine, yellow and black (1919, by Gesmar). The skirt rests on her hip. Her upper body is dressed in a white triangle of a bikini top with flower centers, and a green bracelet with red flow-ers on her wrists. The figure floats upward in slow motion with head thrust back in mental absorption. In another poster she holds a monkey that reaches out to pluck a shiny cherry from one of her dangling earbobs (1922, by Gesmar). Her backless dress is clementine orange, jade beads encircle her arms, and green eye shadow carries out the color scheme for feline chic.

Spinelly was resplendent in classy costumes. Andre Parugi, a shoemaker of Italian family in Nice whose shoes are in museums, handmade the shoes she wore on stage. From 1908 until World War I she relied on Paul Poiret for her costumes and gowns. She was the star of the Paris music-halls who made the greatest leap from belle époque to Jazz Age costumes, from corseted evening gowns to lilting Deco fancy, so that photographs of her trace the evolution of Paris fashions. What she wore on and off stage was news. The magazine *Les Modes* showed her wearing a trained elegant dress in 1908; by 1920, she had an exotic embroidered full skirt with a narrow beaded bandeau on her torso.

She met Charles Gesmar through Paul Poiret. (From 1917 until his death in 1928 Gesmar became Mistinguett's exclusive costume designer.) A costume for *Oiseau de Paris* (1925) by Gesmar (for Mistinguett in *Bonjour Paris!*—November 1924) looks like a mass of feathers from the top of her head to the tip of her "tail" yet with a focus on her legs in high heels with a lattice of cross-straps. Like Erté, the uniqueness of Gesmar was reach-ing for and bringing off extremes. A tight lacy jumpsuit continued up to frame Madame's face in silver, with the merest decorations of cherry blossoms on her cuffs and down her ankles. She has a silver cane with the head of Maurice Chevalier in top hat as its pommel. Then her designer was Juliette Courtisien, then for a few years it was Paul Poiret who came back from the war, then creations were by Louise Boulanger. In 1926 Spinelly was photographed for *L'Officiel de la Mode* in a dress of gold lamé with pearl arabesques radi-ating from her pelvis and low-cut V top. The line was slinky in the 1920s, sometimes simple but with fabulous fur, transparent fabrics, and spangles and tulle. Together with Charles Gesmar, Spinelly exploited Art Deco. Gesmar died tragically young and Erté lived to design objects and costumes in his nineties. No costumer has ever done more stunning drawings for the revues than these two.

The feathers on headdresses were attached, deftly and with invention, to a form like a motorcyclist's headgear or a circlet of jewels. A single garment could costume two or even

Yvonne de Balzac of the Folies Bergère. The skirt extends horizontally without evident support, yurt-like, as if a room with triangular passageways.

three dancers, and somehow the contours of the body were winsomely exposed while the Deco costumes were so creative, and often in such peculiar if graceful shapes, one almost wonders if the designers sat at a café sipping absinthe, the "Green Devil," as they drew.

Charles Gesmar
ANGELO LUERTI[33]

Gesmar was a precocious genius. At just 15 he was designing the costumes for Andrée Spinelly, one of the most famous actresses and dancers of those years, and at 16 he began working for Mistinguett, known as the "Queen of the music-hall."

A design by Charles Gesmar, c. 1924 (courtesy Angelo Luerti).

From his debut, the young talent was seduced by the charm of vivid colors, the sequins that sparkled under the beam of spotlight. He loved the beauty and luxury, sought the exuberant atmosphere, the effects of gorgeous feathers and silks, the glamour and pride of performance bursting with light. All were ingredients that Gesmar was able to harmonize effectively in his creations, enriched by a profusion of feathers, beads, jewelry, flowers, and veils. His costumes, sometimes slight and delicate, designed to enhance the plasticity of the bodies of women, expressed an uncommon grace that earned for the artist the admiration of a great public. No less sensational are the roughly sixty Gesmar posters for Mistinguett, Barbette, Maurice Chevalier, Dolly Sisters, Gilda Gray, Earl Leslie, Jane Marnac and Mitty and Tillio, to name but a few. From this point of view Gesmar can be considered a link between the artist Toulouse-Lautrec and the peerless twentieth-century fashion illustrator for couturiers and fashion magazines, René Gruau. In the 1920s, at the height of the success of the music-hall, Gesmar designs were imitated by many of his colleagues, most especially by Zig who, after Gesmar's death, designed Mistinguett costumes.

His first work for Mistinguett was the costuming of the *Grande Revue* at the Folies Bergère (March 1917). He then worked on several of Mme. Rasimi's shows starring Mistinguett, at the Ba-ta-Clan. He also designed costumes for a string of shows at the Casino de Paris starting from *Laisse-les Tomber* (1917) up to *Paris en Fête* (1925). Gesmar was also busy working for the Moulin Rouge from *New York–Montmartre* (1924) up to *Paris qui Tourne* (1928). He also worked for Théâtre Michel (1918–1925), the Palace Theater (1923–1927), the Théâtre de Paris (1923–1924), the Concert Mayol (1923–1927), music-hall des Champs-Elysées (1925–1926), Théâtre Daunou (1925–1927), and in Berlin and Vienna (1925–1928).

Mistinguett

An actress of stage or screen dresses for the part. The movies *Camelot* and *Taming of the Shrew* were period pieces (medieval and Renaissance England), nevertheless, Vanessa Redgrave and Elizabeth Taylor look 1960s. The costumes of showgirl revues are less tied to fashion generally. Photographs of Mistinguett, the darling (and eventually the highest paid performer) of the Paris music-halls during their Golden Age, show a progression in the nature of costumes as well as the personal panache of a great star.

Mistinguett's biographer, Martin Pénet, has said that she "invented the music-hall."[34] Her luster came from an inner light and a terrific costume sense. She used her magnetism and nearly always shows a lot of shoulder and leg and a beaming smile (her best features). Because her stage career was long, from 1895 until the beginning of the 1950s, photographs of her can be lined up to constitute a historical sort of album of paper dolls. The backup or line dancers could not outshine her but she had to fit in with their look. From the abundant photographs of Mistinguett, one can effectively cut out the images to see how notions of glamour changed.

Mistinguett had an on-stage wardrobe of endless glitz. Yet she often went back to the look of layers of petticoats (she debuted in the café-concerts in 1893 wearing a floppy hat, a dress with high neck and puffed sleeves, and about eight layers of petticoats). She also sang about petticoats in 1916 in a song by Emile Doloire, who directed the Folies Bergère orchestra:

Quand elles passent en crinolines,
Les mutines, l'oeil fripon,
Aussitot qu'elles se dandinent
On devine l'pantalon
En verite quell' mod'charmante,
Excitante, c'est tentant
On s'promet au premier coup de vent
Un p'tit coup d'oeil charmant.
[When they go by in their crinolines
The mischief-makers with their flirting eyes,
When they sally around
You can see their pantaloons.
Truly what a charming,
exciting, tempting outfit,
That makes a person promise at the first puff of wind
To take a pretty glimpse.]

A critic noted, "L'excellente Mistinguett porte la crinoline avec une désinvolture, un espièglerie, une grâce tout à fait amusant." [The excellent Mistinguett carries off the crinoline with a casual playfulness, a great deal of grace.][35]

She had to find and define her style. In 1903, at the pre–World War I café-concert on the Champs-Elysées, Alcazar d'Eté, she wore what can be considered an imitation of the costumes of Caroline Otéro. The show of her body is her shoulders and top of her bust. The dress is straight across the chest just above the breasts, giving a strapless effect, and big full dropped sleeves only attach to cords to the gown's straps, about six inches below her shoulders, then balloon. Mistinguett liked to wear Spanish and South American–inspired dance costumes and over this 1903 dress, a fishnet with pompoms twists around her

Gumball girl by René Ranson (courtesy Angelo Luerti).

hips. A characteristic Otéro-like element is a sash encrusted with jewels descending her front. Mistinguett's trademark of mirthful cheek is in evidence, as with this costume she wore an insignificant porkpie hat.

In 1905 Jean Cocteau did a sketch of Mistinguett singing and dancing the matchiche, a Brazilian tango. Her poncho was covered with blossoms and her two-piece dress left her midriff bare, was form-fitting at the hips, and fell above the knees. Cocteau put her legs surreally akimbo in the array of petticoats. Here too the hat, like a gaucho's, was a touch of humor. The future great writer, artist and filmmaker was 16 and signed it "Jean."[36]

In 1908 for a revue at the Bouffes-Parisien called *Aux Bouffes, on Pouffe*, Mistinguett invented her "funny girl" which she called "la Moche." She would throughout her career alternate in one revue number where she was dressed opulently with another where she dressed like a waif, or "pauvre gosse du chemin." With dance partner Max Dearly she evolved this look into the sexy moll whose body presses against and merges with her partners. At the Moulin Rouge they did the *Valse Chaloupée* dressed in black. Dearly had a black Turkish-style cap and a red scarf and she wore an unadorned slinky dress, with cute strappy heels. In a photograph that appears to have been taken on stage (there are strings of stage lighting in evidence), behind Mistinguett and Dearly are a troupe of about a dozen in a wonderful variety of clown and *pantin* costumes, contrasting with the dancing couple, and which harks back to marionette theater.

Punctilious about costumes—herself a costume director in the 1920s—Mistinguett exploited contrasts like black and white, dark and light, gritty and sultry, and girlish and elegant. In 1916 she performed in a pale lacy lingerie top, long black skirt, and a men's top hat. She always maintained a graceful posture (and lectured her long-time lover Maurice Chevalier to spruce up his mien too).

In December 1922, the Casino de Paris reopened, renovated after a fire, with a new swimming pool that inspired many numbers. The cast in the finale could make safer dives than in the small pool at the old Folies Bergère. Mistinguett, who headlined the show, had a jaunty seaside look in a tableau called "Transparent Skirts." The costume could nearly have passed in the season at Deauville—long draped silky skirt, dark tunic with white collar (only the tunic from waist down was see through) and bordered with sequins, suggesting underwear as outerwear. On her head she wore a two-foot bunch of ostrich feathers set into a little cap. While the ultra-feminine Gaby Deslys had been, as it were, drowning in plumes for some years, Mistinguett was just beginning to wear them. The comedienne powered up with full glamour in the 1920s, when the art of wearing a great deal and next to nothing at all soared.

In 1922, the top fashion designer of the times, Paul Poiret, working with the young talent the Spaniard José de Zamora, did the costumes for a tableau called *Les Armes de la Femme*, where Mistinguett represented a rose covered with petals, and a troupe of "girls" represented cosmetics bottles, everybody poised as a gigantic coiffeuse. Dancer Harry Pilcher came up and picked the finest blossom, Mistinguett. This was hailed as more than a revue, an artistic vision. Couturiers including the Houses of Doeullet, Lanvin, Jenny, Poiret and Worth provided dresses. Poiret provided for *Paris qui Jazz* (1920) the rose confection for Mistinguett but she rejected it:

> Wanting to innovate, he came up with a concept of a dress with petals from tones going from fresh pink to faded pink. This choice of colors provoked Mistinguett's fury:
>
> "I want nothing to do with a faded rose. I want the freshest pink, and with dewdrops and diamonds. I totally reject this old rose!"[37]

In his memoirs Poiret noted that a couturier who replaced him (not Gesmar as he was doing military service) made the new rose petal dress on the model of the one he had done.

"La Baker"

Not only was Josephine Baker (1906–1975) a peerless performer, humanitarian, and electrifying dancer but she also wore her jewelry and costumes with inimitable style and became the Folies Bergère's most celebrated dancer after Mistinguett. She was the first to wink at the audience in costumes that instead of being outrageously opulent were outrageously sexualized and comic. She used motifs of her African heritage, using a jungle setting, tapping into colonial stereotypes by leaping from a relief map of the West Indies wearing a girdle of silver spikes, but also freeing birds from cages in the movie *Zou Zou* (1934). She appeared in jagged hemlines, accessorized with deco jewelry and her costumes were often no more than a macramé pattern of feathers and glass or wooden beads. Naturally she capitalized on her command of the new jazz dances like the shimmy, and was a hit from her first performance in Paris in *La Revue Negre* in 1925 in the Music-Hall des Champs-Elysées. She wrote that in the mid–1920s,

> A striking poster had been designed by Paul Colin to promote the show. I appeared all over Paris emerging from a cloud of green feathers, nude except for ropes of pearls reaching below my loins, bracelets twisting from wrist to shoulders, sparkling shoe buckles and dangling earrings. Chiquita [her pet cheetah], seated on his haunches, a bow around his supple neck, was offering me an enormous bunch of flowers.
> In spite of its charm and humor, the poster was, of course, exaggerated. Chiquita was not one to offer posies, although I had supplied him with a collar to match each of my outfits.[38]

Baker led the revue *En Super Folies* in 1926. She would become a French citizen, personifying the Franco-American showgirl spectacular connection. Her dances tapped into the stage tradition of the noble savage,[39] which had moved from adventure stories to ballets at the opera of the Incas of Peru and Captain Cook in Tahiti. She entered the stage hopping like a mythic jungle creature, her body shaking with jerky movements, and did deep knee bends and wiggled. Her provocative pose, semi-naked and girdled with upturned bananas, thrilled and amused. As she danced the bananas swayed around her hips with each movement of her wild steps.

"Five A.M." in the second act of *En Super Folies* revealed her in a clinging gown of silver sequins accented with a plum-colored ostrich cape of sweeping length, which she dragged casually down the steps and across the stage to the sofa where the pantomime started.

This was one of hundreds of between the wars revues requiring costumes galore but it was what Baker wore and how she moved that people never forgot. *En Super Folies* had 50 tableaux, many designed by Gyarmathy and many with Baker. The production made her the queen of snow, enthroned on a fur sled pulled by eight Husky dogs, and a subcontinental Indian princess riding an elephant. She transformed into an ice cream vendor, a gamine in her hometown of Pittsburgh, a dancer doing the paso doblo at a bullfight, and so on.[40]

In *Un Vent de Folie* (1927) the dancers who backed her up wore costumes designed by Barbier and Erté. Baker opened her own nightclubs in Paris and New York. When she was brought back to the Folies Bergère in 1936, Gyarmathy, who had made the poster for her first European tour, designed a poster with an image of Baker semi-naked with red feathers around her ankles and waist, and on her breasts. The favorite scene of Baker in the show presented her in a gown of silver lamé, carried onto the stage in a feather trimmed litter which rested on the back of an elephant. Baker insisted the elephant's trunk be pointed upward, as Maurice Chevalier had elephants in his act, and he believed that dangling trunks were bad luck.

In a solo act at the Folies Bergère, *La Folie du Jour* (1926) she appeared to wear just a patch of pink flamingo feathers between her legs—but she had on "an early-day satin bikini," and feathers covered a large portion of her body. As so often has been the case, nakedness on stage has often been in the eyes of the beholder. Alicja Sowinska has traced the banana skirt from its invention in 1926 through the final performance in 1936. She shows how the costume became more covering in America, and how the persona of the superstar became commodified:

> Dolls dressed in banana skirts were sold across Europe by the thousands. Stickers publicizing Baker's movie, *Zou Zou*, were distributed among fruit vendors in Paris (to be placed on bananas they sold). Baker advised women to make moisturizers from bananas in order to fight wrinkles. She also advertised Le Bakerfix, a pomade to slick down hair, which brought her more revenue than all the other endeavors (except for her stage appearances).[41]

The banana skirt, argues Sowinska persuasively, became a means of mutual exploitation.

The next year, 1937, Baker became a French citizen. During World War II she was a Red Cross nurse and entertained the troops in various lands.

Barbette

A young boy in Texas saw a circus and told his mother he wanted to run away and become a circus performer. She said he should wait until after high school, which he did, graduating at 14. So Vander Clyde (1898–1973), who would perform as Barbette, picked cotton as an afterschool job as a teenager. His is an amazing story. He became the toast of Paris, a female impersonator who in a trice went from delicate blond beauty (doing a striptease followed by acrobatics) to throwing off the wig and female garments and displaying as a rippling male. Man Ray and Jean Cocteau praised "Barbette" and he was a spectacular success in the 1920s, until a fall caused him to give up performing, return to America, and become a teacher of acrobatics.

The costumes were exceptional and he wore them well. His star rose about 70 years before *The Adventures of Priscilla, Queen of the Desert* yet he too was able to have sophisticated fun with his act. Once a journalist asked Barbette his thoughts while he did his complex gymnastics. "Mes plumes," he said, explaining that his feathers could be damaged as he was on the trapeze, so he had the expense to consider. The contribution of cross-dressers to the development of the showgirl costume may be guessed at as the very exaggeration of the features of costume. Barbette demonstrated that the man as woman could be ineluctable and beautiful.

Cocteau's article, entitled "Le Numéro Barbette" and appearing in the July 1926 issue of the *Revue Française*, is interesting in itself as a commentary on how costume can convey or mime the essence of femininity. Barbette had to suppress all movements that would identify him as a man in the female portion of his act, when wearing a brief costume.

The Ballets Russes' risqué is taken a step further in the 1920s photograph.

Cocteau maintained that the sleight of hand where Barbette performed as a woman within the performance of trapezist raised his act to great theater—"trompe-l'âme" and "trompe-les-sens."

In a study of Cocteau's aesthetic, Lydia Crowson notes that being in a more intimate setting than a big circus meant that Barbette didn't have to travel great distances on a trapeze, movements where his being a man would be more evident. She writes of Barbette that

> in the final analysis he embodied Beauty which itself has a kind of surnatural sexuality. Although under close scrutiny "Barbette" dressed in his woman's costume and wig does not look completely like a woman, it is doubtful that someone who did not know his sex would guess it. What is striking about the pictures remaining of him is the refinement which characterizes his wig, make-up and every other accessory. Nothing is garish or exaggerated and, as Cocteau reports in describing steps of the actor's "metamorphosis" before the show, even the smallest features (which would have been judged insignificant by a lesser artist) were attended to.[42]

In photographs, Barbette has the look of a lean, preternatural cat. He has the tightly curled platinum wig, lots of eye makeup, oodles of feathers in some type of skirt or minimal sequined one-and two-piece outfits. His nudity seems like an extreme version of a costume for the Ballets Russes. By his "machine-like perfection,"[43] he achieved a strange androgyny as opposed to a predictable parody.

SIX

Accoutrements

"To my mind, a picture should be something pleasant, cheerful, and pretty, yes pretty! There are too many unpleasant things in life as it is without creating still more of them."—
Jean Renoir

Perspective on Plumes

In June 2012, after nearly 40 years as director of the Folies Bergère, Helen Martini sold her collection of 6,000 costumes and accessories, the equivalent of 20 truckloads. The sale, called the *Ventes de Folie*, took place at the former Bourse, now the Palais Brongniart. Some of the costumes were displayed like museum pieces; news photos show dazzling and wild ensembles, like an all satin panther five-piece with a fuchsia-lined panther cape, a "Pineapple Dress" with a sequined and feathered pineapple at the back, and a bumblebee-hued crinoline painted with arabesques with a wire-cage headdress attached at the waist, designed to surround but not touch a dancer's head. But amidst all this legendary froufrou it was the feathers that starred. Feathers of all colors, from tufts to long arcing plumes, were rising out of the trunks and floating magically in the air. Visually they dominated the sale, which seems poetic justice considering the importance of plumage to the music-hall revues.

We return to the part feathers play in the showgirl costume icon. At the end of the eighteenth century, Paris had 25 master *plumassiers*. After Marie Antoinette's execution, the tall (as high as two or three feet) feathered hats went out of fashion until the rococo style found favor among haute bourgeoisie of Paris, New York, and other large cities. In the fin de siècle, hundreds of *plumassiers* worked in Paris, for fashion and the stage. According to the scholar of ornamental plumage and feather trade, Robin W. Doughty, that meant that, to meet customer demand, nineteenth-century milliners used scores of species of birds for their colorful, strangely shaped, or patterned feathers; the rarer the bird, the more prized and costly the plumage. French officers were still wearing aigrettes when Queen Victoria confirmed an order for the discontinuance of the aigrettes (that were called "osprey plumes") in 1899, replacing them with ostrich.[1] The environmentalist movement, beginning in 1896, which championed bird protection spread fast from Boston to the rest of the U.S. and England; within five years style-setting Queen Alexandra shunned wearing plumes.

The French called all the feathers of birds other than ostrich "plumes fantaisies"

L. D'Horvilly on an undated postcard.

which speaks for the incredible uses made of the hundreds of thousands of feathers exported yearly from colonial governments from 1900 to World War II. Pascal Jacob tells the story of the craze of showing off showgirls' undress by contrasting it with feathers.

The Introduction of Feathers

PASCAL JACOB[2]

The use of feathers belonged initially to the battlefield. The "father" of the circus, Philip Astley, was a soldier. The feathers on top of the helmets, as well as the epaulettes on the shoulders, helped to emphasize the silhouette of the warriors, and also were a nice ornamental element for the classic military pageant.

With feathers on top of his shako, the soldier seemed to be bigger; it gave him superiority and a measure of elegance. So, because Astley was a military man, as soon as he started to present horsemanship exercises in a circus ring, he added feathers to his costume. His wife, Patty Jones, as an equestrian rider herself, was also creating and sewing the costumes, and she was playing with feathers, to give them a more significant allure.

It's interesting that the plumes were also a distinctive element for ropedancers from the beginning of the eighteenth century. Madame Saqui wore a brocaded dress, trimmed with fringe, just over the knees, with pantaloons. Most remarkable was the headpiece of an impressive feather bouquet attached to a helmet with stiff standing points. Moreover, there are many illustrations of performers wearing feathers even before the beginning of the circus in 1768. For athletic acts around 1800, the feathered headdresses (or turbans, like Josephine Bernharnais's) took primacy, complementing the simplicity of man's *maillot* and the chemise dress of the women. Feathers were decorative and gave an exotic feeling to the people wearing them. The equestrian star Andrew Ducrow created in the first half of the nineteenth century spectacular acts like riding two horses at once, for which he might wear a Roman-style outfit, strapped high sandals and a feathered crown. The use of feathers was quite necessary for his Indian hunter act, but I have no doubt it provided inspiration to many performers of the time. Antonio Franconi, the father of the French circus, is an example. He wore reddish, blue and white plumes and a red cockade on his big fur hat.

In these early days of the circus, men as well as women were beplumed. Later it is another story. Feathers turned into more of a feminine symbol, and men used them less and less. Muscles and partial nudity became more effective to identify a male circus performer and feathers were relegated to the souvenir box for this category of artists. Even if the equestrian ladies, dressed, say, as Hungarian soldiers, still wore some feathers on the side of their hats, this served more as detail than as real effect.

This was the first piece of the story. The second one starts with the creation of the famous Diaghilev Ballets Russes (1909–1929). Painters and designers created amazing silhouettes for the dancers, and the extravagance of the costumes, covered with sequins, feathers and gemstones, built with heavy silk and luxurious velvet, was and continues to be a revelation for the whole show business world. With it began the incredibly rich costumes for music-hall revues, literally inspired by this "Russian style" carried out by such designers as Léon Bakst, Alexandre Benois, and Natalia Goncharova. Based on this global fascination, circus performers started again to add feathers and sequins to their costumes.

A new era began for the circus, when women wore extravagant outfits with colorful materials, jewels, and feathers. For instance, a poster of Rogana, the impressive lady known as "the Baroness of Balance," shows her with a medley of head feathers along with a long boa, adding a luxurious dimension to the trim, tight and minimal costume.

Ringling Bros. and Barnum & Bailey used a lot of feathers, especially during the era of Don Foote (1969–85) the prolific designer for circus and ice shows. When, however, I designed the costumes for three shows between 1995 and 2000, I didn't use feathers so much.

In 2014, as a member of Dragone, a Belgian company and working notably as a talent scout, I participated in the creation of the new Lido revue, staged by Franco Dragone. In this "feathered temple" the costume designer Nicola Vaudelet tried to reinvent the use of this incredibly flexible element; and he worked with a young creator, Serkan Cura, who did an amazing job.

Costumers have in the past been backed up by craftspeople in independent workshops and merchants in shops. Today there are fewer and fewer workshops able to respond to the more and more elaborate requests of the creators. I worked with one of the last shops specializing in music-hall costumes, Fougerolle, formerly Marinette et Aumond. This shop worked for famous designers like Christian Lacroix as well as Michel Gyarmathy, the Folies Bergère production designer for several decades, and the Russian designer Roman Petrov de Tyrtov, known as Erté. Until the end of the 1970s, the big theaters, the Lido, the Moulin Rouge, the Folies Bergère, and the Casino de Paris created a totally new revue every four years. As a consequence, many shops were able to maintain their activity without any problem. Today the Moulin Rouge is presenting the same show for a much longer time. So, at the end of the 1980s, the work started to disappear and the shops closed one by one. Paris still has a few shops but they work for fashion as well as for dance, circus, or theater.

When I worked for Ringling Bros. and Barnum & Bailey between 1995 and 1999, I spent a few months in many New York costume shops. Michael John Parson and Mears, Eaves and Brooks, Pen and Fletcher (for the elephant blankets), and maybe the best, Barbara Matera. Some are closed now but the talent there was deeply impressive. The Moulin Rouge bought the last feather shop, Fevrier, a house dedicated almost exclusively to music-hall including, years ago, Las Vegas and New York shows. But there is a new generation of feather designers that have their own shops but work more for fashion than anything else. When Franco Dragone worked on the Lido revue "Paris Merveille," the creative team did amazing work, if quite far from the traditional taste and vision.

Through the nineteenth century, acrobatic and equestrian acts were the most developed and sophisticated entertainment in the sideshows of Europe. Then when the ringed circuses were born, circus stars wore fabulous, and skimpy, costumes. It was natural that impresarios looked to their costumage for how to dress the dancers on the stages of their music-halls. An indication of how much attention the public paid to female circus stars relates to Madame Saqui, who had a long career on the high wire, and performed for both Napoléon's wedding to Marie-Louise, and at the camps of his troops. The aerialist wore a very large headdress of many colors of ostrich feathers. In Paris so many women wanted to have a hat like it that the supply of feathers ran out and milliners could not fill their orders. Naturally it was not only in the circus one saw the features. Hats in the

1880s favored feathers and even complete birds, evening hairdos had plumes and aigrettes, and when the big hats went out of style the feathers shifted to the music-hall. At the premiere of the *Rite of Spring* in May 1913, every woman wore a headdress: dazzling tiara, embroidered bandeaux, or turbans with aigrettes and birds-of-paradise. On showgirl costumes or ladies' fashions, trimming of bird parts like swallow's wings or grebe skins added to the finery. The extremity of feather fashion was in the 1890s just when the look of the revues was coalescing; the American Ornithological Union estimated five million feathers were being imported each year. The *plumassiers* were a huge commercial interest. The feathers were graded—several grades of ostrich feathers, from five-ply to as high as 20-ply. Spotted feathers and feathers from rarer birds were more prized. It was desirable that the feathers not molt on stage, which was a problem with turkey boas. One technique was ombré, where the dyed feathers had to be woven in. Feathers could be cleverly glued to fan struts or a small head covering. The *plumassiers* used their skill to pull the end of the feathers and create a curlicue.

The Audubon Society and other bird protection societies worked to restrict feather imports and sales, and gradually the feather industry in the U.S. was curtailed. In France conservation efforts went to using farm-raised birds; ostriches and peacocks could be raised this way but most of the birds with the desired plumage could not. Today in the U.S. no feather can be taken from a bird that will kill or distress it, and costumes with exotic real feathers have gone the way of ivory piano keys, leopard coats, and many other abuses of animals.

A novel by Jacques-Charles (which seems semi-autobiographical) has a 50-year-old seamstress and her 17-year-old son run away from the stepfather who has tried to rape the son. The seamstress recalls that an old school chum has become a music-hall star, and the mother and son, half starving, go to an audition for backup girls to intercept the star. The school tie works and the star reminds her costumer that she is the director of the costume shop and her word goes (the poor seamstress has to start out repairing unwashed cache-sexes). The star and costumer have an exchange that reinforces that the star rules:

> "Et ma robe de plume, vous l'avez réparée?"
> "Oui, mademoiselle."
> "Vous avez remis les plumes?"
> "Deux douzaines."
> "Deux douzaines," glapit Dizzy en bondissant, "il m'en faut au moins trois, et si elles n'y sont pas ce soir, je n'entrerai pas en scène. Je ne veux pas avoir l'air d'une pouilleuse." Et rouvrant la porte par laquelle, tremblante, la costumière venait d'éclipser: "Quatre douzaines, j'en veux," hurla Dizzy, dans la couloir, "quatre douzaines."
>
> ["And my feather dress, did you repair it?" "Yes, Mademoiselle." "And have you put the feathers back on?" "Two dozen." "Two dozen," Dizzy yelped, jumping up. "I don't want to have the appearance of a fleabag." And opening the door again by which the costumer had just fled, "Four dozen, that's what I want," Dizzy yelled into the corridor, "four dozen."][3]

Feathers can reveal or conceal the body. Feathers stir up the female backsliding to the nature of a primitive, yet also angels that confer blessings.

The nearly nude dancer might have feathers on her head, her stole, and her train, while the only feathers covering her body were a fan that concealed the fact she was clothed. Tradition had the girls hold the feathers over their cache-sexes and use the feathers as accessories, in general stoles and headgear, while another idea was for the feathers to caress the body, as opposed to concealing it. The most memorable showgirl to play with feathers in her act was the irrepressible Renée "Zizi" Jeanmaire. Big ostrich feather fans (waved by two or three men) made trembling, teasing patterns around her body while she sang "Truc en plumes" [My Feather Boa"]: "Mon truc en plumes, ça fait rêver mais c'est sacré, faut pas toucher!" [My feather thing, it causes dreams but it's sacred—mustn't touch!][4] Sally Rand became the first legendary bubble dancer, striking sexy poses in a see-through tunic with a translucent balloon of about eight feet circumference. She was also famous for a fan dance, which played on concealing and revealing. She used white fans, whereas Zizi Jeanmaire, the French star, always had pink fans.

Feathers, however, did not merely furnish elegance; they also bespoke frivolity. Automatons wore them and the celebrated Spanish clown Géronimo Madrano (1849–1912) wore a feather on his nose. A mess of ostrich feathers swaying on a tall wrapped turban is a hilarious visual joke in a February 21, 1955, episode of *I Love Lucy*. Ricky is working on a movie in Hollywood and gets Lucy a bit part in a nightclub sequence in a movie. Everything the showgirls and she wear is unmitigated peppermint pink. Lucy keeps trying to balance the giant headdress, but it sways, shifts, and nearly pulls her tumbling down the staircase.

A staff of up to 18 people took meticulous care to keep the *Jubilee!* costumes in shape. Some lasted perfectly for 30 years. The feathery costumes were kept in muslin bags and a heavy costume was put in a drawer, not hung. Silk thread and nylon thread had different purposes. The feathers had different usages—ostrich, burnt ostrich, coque, egret, birds of paradise, turkey, pheasant, and the longer Chinese pheasant plumes. How each was dyed was different and in the Vegas revues the sources were plume stores in Paris.

Costuming in the U.S. has different challenges that resemble those of architecture. Pete Menefee has spoken of the hair and hats he designed for the *Jubilee!* (2011) and how 3½ feet of feathers changes the balance: "Everything is very precarious. We try to figure out how the attachments are going to fit."[5] The *Jubilee!* headdresses, constructed on a steel frame, weighed 30 pounds. They were made of feathers including ostrich, pheasant, and types of spotted or polka dot, many from South Africa; up to 5,000 feathers in one costume. Each feather was wrapped with wire and sewn onto a branch and then sewn onto a steel form and then fabric covered it and then any application, such as Swarovski crystals.

The delicate-looking hats for the Titanic scene of *Jubilee!* were polyester mounted on steel wire frames and the bows had the same stiffening used in industrial water purifiers.

The costumes from the Folies Bergère show at the Tropicana Hotel are now an 8,000-piece collection housed in a climatized level of the Nevada State Museum in Las Vegas. An asymmetrical, iridescent headdress on display once got the girl who wore it fired for her inability to balance the creation. The costumes had to be durable and had elaborate foundations—some of the embroidered and bejeweled brassieres lasted decades. There were budget cuts so that the crown of one headdress is rare crystal, augmented by a cap sewn with tiny mirrors, whereas a headdress from later years could be formed by wrapping embossed polyester around a cut-off soda bottle and attaching the plumes with a ponytail.[6]

Feathers have always been a medium for panache. As a young man, Grant Philipo, a model for Bill Blass and a dancer on the Strip, was inspired to make a better bird costume for a Vegas show. His creation, with a headdress of turkey and other feathers held together by Elmer's glue, worked, the audience applauded when the "white bird" came on stage and Philipo was hired to costume a show in Puerto Rico. "I was not going back to Iowa," Philipo recalled. "I had set my sights on Paris and Puerto Rico seemed halfway." He got the materials in California, learned in Puerto Rico how to operate a sewing machine, and completed the work—despite an uncertain moment when the Elmer's appeared to be melting in the island's humidity.[7] On display in Philipo's non-profit museum in Las Vegas will be costumes from his 20,000-item collection that he built as a sidelight to his show business career.

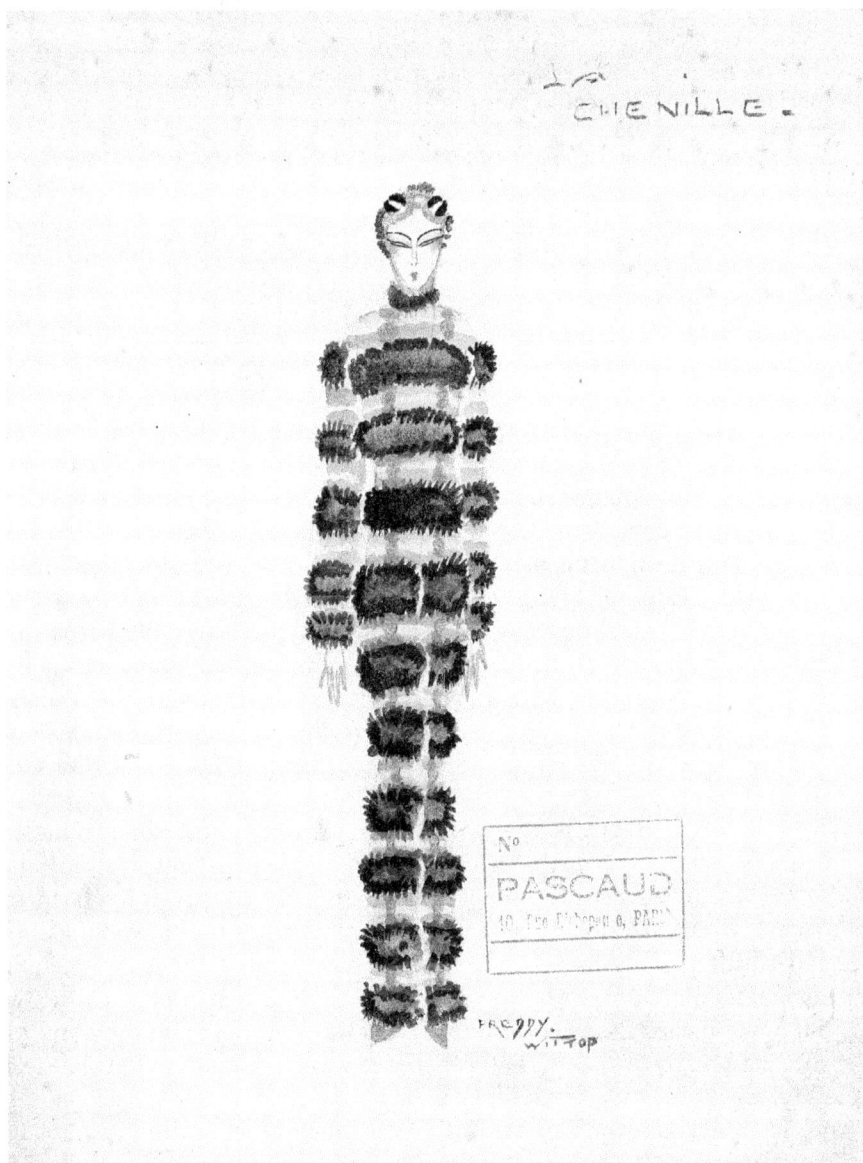

La Chenille, a drawing by Freddy Wittop (MS Thr 113426-28, courtesy Houghton Library, Harvard University).

The affairs of the feathers were nearly as exotic as the plumes themselves. A feathered costume item—parasol, shoes, headdresses, fans and so forth—arrived in a bond that would total over a million dollars. Pages of descriptions came with each costume, and after a few months of use the feathered costume had to be taken back to Paris or destroyed.

Fashion has been fickle with feathers, which went from fans and circus plumes to hats to the stage. There being now so few showgirl shows, the couture industry is reevaluating the use of feathers. Zoe Kravitz wore a rainbow feathered dress (looking 100 percent feathers) at the 2017 Emmy Awards. The dress was Dior Haute Couture and Kravitz said it made her feel she was in a fairy tale.

Today, as Burkhard Bilger writes in a *The New Yorker* profile of Eric Charles-Donatien:

> The world is full of birds, but the loveliest ones are off limits to plumassiers, protected by international conventions against the trade in exotics. Even antique feathers can be used only in the occasional, one-of-a-kind piece, and then only if the client agrees never to take it out of the country. All other feathers now come from farmed animals—goose, duck, chicken, turkey, pheasant, and ostrich. A plumassier is like a goldsmith who can afford to work only in bronze, or a jeweler who makes do with rhinestones.[8]

The aim of feather fashion/art, however, remains, "to try to make people as beautiful as birds."[9]

Feather Work

Eric Charles-Donatien[10]

In feather work for couture and accessories or for the stage there are not so many techniques. The techniques that allow someone to work with feathers are limited. It is the way you combine them that makes you creative; the way you master them that makes what you do quality. Thinking of the big picture I learned first to recognize the feathers, prepare them and sort them. Preparing means cleaning and cutting—like preparing oneself for a party and having a little haircut, then dying, shaping and learning to apply then by sewing or gluing, depending on the application. We treat or wave the feathers. We modernize old processes. Sometimes we burn the feathers or damage them to look different. Basically the techniques are no different now than in 1900 or 1920. We still glue, still burn, and still sew.

It is the way we eventually handle or color the feathers or push some of these techniques to another level that is distinct. Sometimes we feel we invent something and end up discovering that it was already done. Feathercraft is like any art. It has been around so long that everything has already been done, so you transform a bit, you update if you want, but inventing is complicated. In 20 years, I have created one technique that was not preexisting. It's more a case of an evolution: I did not invent sewing or even sewing feathers but how I turned the sewing on the fabric was very new, and the result as well.

For sure in the early twentieth century the idea was for feathers to look like feathers, and technique was at the very first level of having the feather look like itself—fluffy, colorful, light, feminine, and sophisticated in that manner. Most of the time, one feather was used at a time. What I developed was to mix feathers with fabric, leather and metal. Metal has been a favorite as can be seen in Chimera, the alcove ceiling that I designed for the Hotel de Crillon. I believe when we now think about featherwork we're not thinking of having exactly a feather look, and that's very different from thinking about this material during the early twentieth century.

Compared with now, a context where money seduces, when the first showgirls were costumed, it was a culture where it was the females that seduced. We want our objects of seduction to be as beautiful as possible, and when we want to seduce, feathers will be involved on couture or accessories and be as close to the body as possible. That is where in nature they belong.

Today there are many new laws protecting animals as well as us when we use chemicals. Apart from that, it is problematic to imagine hurting an animal to do beautiful things with it. It doesn't matter if we have to wait two seasons to get the quantity of feathers for what a designer or costumer wants. We respect nature and ourselves too much to put money over the art. We never kill any bird.

It also can be a fight to do featherwork for quality reasons. The animals no longer eat the right nutrition as formerly, and the feathers tend to derive from the food business. The diet has an effect and feathers are more fragile, the feather's opacity is now only 80 percent opaque. We do the best with what we have. We never hurt birds to maintain beauty in our shows. Featherwork for showgirls is a special vision; it remains quite similar through the ages. For me a showgirl is a kind of human bird, an angel in the natural environment. Images appearing in the showgirl spectacle center around birds and angels.

The music-hall has never been without the feathers. I'm glad that it seems the entertainment will last for a long time and yes it's a good platform for featherwork.

Perspective on Sequins, Spangles ... and Shoes

Showgirl costumes were not static. More dancing in revues, for example, required costumes be calibrated to the movement of a showgirl's body. Yet the signature of this other world remains—feathers, rhinestones, fake eyelashes, spangled makeup, and everything big enough to be exciting at a distance, whether for parade or pose. The play of light on sequins and spangles, beads and pearls is even more paradigmatic than feathers. Despite all the liquid, laser and LED lights of the electronic world, it is fashion news when actress Jessica Biel wears a Ralph & Russo party dress having 1.2 million Swarovski crystals.

A corsage of artificial flowers, a lace collar or silk scarf, or new trimming for a hat were not trivial matters for my mother, who had to dress for many parties and teas on very little money when my family moved to Paris in 1958. She dyed a white silk gown a fiery orange and matched it with a bracelet with a big crystal under which she taped a silk ribbon in bright yellow to match. For me, sequins were the little jewels of finery I liked best. To me they were as scintillating as the illumination of the Eiffel Tower. No wonder director Jacques-Charles described the backstage of a music-hall as "derrière les paillettes," or "behind the glitter."[11] In 1980 the pre-production costumer staff at the Folies Bergère included not only 15 milliners, 22 embroiderers, 80 dressmakers, and so on, but 30 pailleteuses who applied the beads and sequins.[12] The French had a word for it!

Bread, artichokes, or a cauliflower was a quick purchase at Saint Germaine en Laye's outdoor market but my mother lingered over some commodities like cheeses, and I would slip off to other stalls. The small round plastic containers of glittering sequins at the notions seller's caught my eye. Paris in the late 1950s was mostly gray (buildings and Citroens), and blue (working people's clothes and school uniforms). I used my allowance for a tiny container of the most brilliant green sequins, sequins that decorated many sewing projects for years.

One New Year's Eve when my best friend and I were 18, her boyfriend took us both to Greenwich Village. He was an artist who was sculpting sandals for a living. Little was open in the Village which had scant restaurants then but he took us to a secondhand clothing store he knew we'd like, and bought us flapper dresses. They were authentic. Mayra's was embroidered with chocolate and silver sequins and bugle beads, and had a pointy hem. Mine was peach silk with big patterns of red flowers, also loaded with paillettes and sequins. We tried the dresses on and decided to keep them on as we roamed the Village. By midnight we were very giddy and dancing in a dark coffee house that had rock music. We danced like crazy and when we came out into the cold air the dresses had virtually melted. All those years someone had taken care of the delicate sequined party frocks but now many sequins were shattered and the thread that held them to the cotton underdresses broken in many spots.

Two cocktail dresses sufficed for dating in 1965, but by 1968 their Peck & Peck style identified a preppy. A classmate and I made the long trip by bus and MBTA to Filene's Basement in Boston, where I bought an astonishing red-gold, all-over sequined mini that had a Texas label. We had never seen anything like it; too bad, like with the flapper dresses, I didn't save it for the Costume Institute. Even the straps were all-sequins and while it only reached to mid-thigh it had weight and good design so it didn't hike up when I wore it. No surprise to my daughters that at the next mixer I gleamed in the red-gold sequined mini dress that was hardly appropriate for college dances.

The terminology of the theaters that showgirls have inhabited can be compared in vagueness to the sequins-spangles muddle. Sequins were used in ancient Egypt on clothes in King Tutenkamen's tomb (the tomb's discovery made sequins even more popular), and something covered with flat shiny decorations is spangled; then what is the difference between sequins and spangles? Fashion and textile historian Leimomi Oakes, makes this distinction between the two words:

> Spangle was the English word for decorative metal disks in the 16th–early 19th centuries … almost always made by taking a very thin gold (or other metal) wire, and twisting it around a narrow rod to form a very tight spiral coil. The spiral is then snipped in a line all the way up, so that it falls apart in dozens of C shapes or jump rings, which are hammered flat, with only the tiniest gap at the opening of the C.[13]

By her differentiation, a spangle is a "seamed disk," whereas the decorative disk called sequins is formed by punching shapes out of a metal sheet and poking holes in the center—no seam. While "sequin" is also a word "regularly used as a generic term for a decorative flat metal disk," Oakes asserts that embroiderers stick to the "spangles-are-coiled, sequins-are-punched distinction," and that "paillettes" are properly larger sequins.[14]

What about the little shiny things that are not round, but flower or bugle shaped, for example? To me they are spangles but there is room in the spangle/sequin distinction for individuality.

The Venetian coin the *zecchino* (from the Arabic), in circulation from the thirteenth century until Napoléon conquered Venice in 1797, passed into French as *sequin*. Antoine Galland when he translated the *1001 Nights* into French has characters paid in sequins, or Venetian coin.

Postcard showing the quintessential showgirl costume.

The early music-hall costumes were decorated as handsomely as the fashions of the day, with sequins, spangles, embroidery, beading, and lace. Metal sequins, some patterned, were particularly used on the gowns of the Callot Soeurs, a French house of couture that opened in 1895 whose gowns la Belle Otéro wore.[15] These were likely metal but around the turn of the century, sequins made of electroplated gelatin were invented and mass produced. This tidbit appeared in *La Mode Illustrée* of March 25, 1894: "Sequins are newer than paillettes and are literally all the rage. They are made of gelatin, consequently very light, and come in all colors with iridescence [réflets changeants]."[16]

Incredibly, real fish scales have been part of traditional supplies for embroidery. They had to have been fragile, but then, doing sewing that is impractical has always been a sign that one's pastime is elite. In *The Subversive Stitch: Embroidery and the Making of the Feminine,* Rozsika Parker enumerates, as the materials needed for fancy work, "ribbons, spangles, silk, metal cords, feathers, beetle-wings, fish scales and aerophione (brightly-colored silk gauze)."[17]

The gelatin sequins melted as well as shimmered. Presumably the stage lights of the music-halls were not too bright. One theater costume that for sure had gelatin sequins was for the third ballet with an Oriental theme that Léon Bakst costumed for Diaghilev, *Le Dieu Blue* (The Blue God) in 1912: "Nijinsky's costume, photographed, was a brilliant tunic of printed silk, jewel-coloured satins and watermarked faille with embroidered silk and golden threads, coloured glass beads and gelatin discs imitating mother-of-pearl."[18] The headdress looks like icicles or flames, the tunic is form fitting and low-cut in the upper half and has a stiff flaring skirt, with complex designs that must have lit up as Nijinsky moved.

Langlois-Martin, founded in 1919, has been an outstanding manufacturer of sequins for stage and couture for three generations. They have produced sequins of all types. In their centenary year the company moved from Paris to Normandy, Domaine du Buat 6100 Saint Ouen sur Ton, close to the city of L'Aigle. Here, besides the workshops, Langlois-Martin are locating a museum of sequins. The following is based on an interview with the company's director.

The Craft of Sparkle and Flash

J.B. DRACHOVITCH[19]

Very few details remain from the old sequin manufacturers. For example, all paper archives from the Rech company, which was the larger one, with Langlois-Martin, smaller in the 1970s, disappeared when we bought them in 1974 when they closed. The problem is the same with famous embroidery workshops from the 1950s which have closed, the sample archives and designs spread all over the world. We have nevertheless, since 1974, bought little by little the fancy sequin handwork tools, so as to have the most complete collection of them, in addition to most of the tools used by sequin manufacturers since the beginning of the twentieth century.

The making of sequins for the music-halls is the same work as for couture. The costumes used the same kind of materials as well as the standard items, flat or cup sequins of all sizes and colors and fancy shapes according to the costumers' designs.

The production of sequins involves the cutting and stamping of different kinds of

The deco effect is created by the metallic fabric that goes between the breasts and over the shoulders into a train, and by the sequined ribbons that form the skirt.

materials which have changed with the years. It started with metal, then animal gelatin was used, then the early thermal plastic Rhodoid, then cellulose acetate. New plastic materials appeared in the 1950s with PVC followed by polyester. We keep using cellulose acetate for many kinds of our sequins, because the effect is the most beautiful, but we have to use metallicized PVC for the glistening look of silver, gold and so forth (viz. our metallic colors cards 2000–2500, as the metallicized cellulose acetate disappeared in the Eighties).

We don't work with polyester as this material is very tough and doesn't allow good shaping. For example, you see today cup sequins which are very low-curved compared to the "French cut" we do which is very curved. Moreover, polyester is unsuitable for old tools and high-end items as it doesn't mold well. Our standard at Langlois-Martin is to have kept the old techniques of production. We keep dying our raw material according to our color cards which are the most extensive charts extant, more than 1,400 colors, or creating any color to pattern on customized requests. Other manufacturers require two or three thousand meters per color to pattern whereas we can do 1.5 or 100 meters or more. Similarly in the production of items, all is handmade (stringing, bunching, modeling, etc.) except for some automatic machines to make the standard flat/cup for cutting. The fancy sequins catalogs we have collected from sequin manufacturers have 5,000 different shapes and more than 1,400 colors, adding up to something like seven million different possible items—not counting the specific stamped material since as Guilloché, Martellé, Tubé, or Perlé. As such specific stamping can be done on any colors for any items, it heightens the possibilities by six or seven times.

All the embroidery work was and is still done by hand on a tambour-frame. The technique of sewing with the Luneville hook is quite old and already existed at least in the 1910–1920 decade; an embroidery needle is used if combined with other sorts of embellishment. So, a costume today will look like an old costume except for the aging of the material.

If for the stage you want a modern material to look old, there are various possible techniques but you can't always reproduce the effects of time. Gelatin, for example, gets a yellowish tone which can't be reproduced—you can add yellow in the color bath but it won't arrive at the same effect and there is more or less the same problem with old metallicized acetate or even PVC from 30 years ago.

Sometimes the sequins are glued directly on a base. Cup and flat sequins as well as *paillettes soleils* ("bikewheels") are sewn through the center; there are also border hole sequins, fantasy sequins, and dit sequins (often used for theater curtains). Langlois-Martin has the world's largest collection of cutting tools for fantasy sequins back for a hundred years, the tools representing almost 5,000 different patterns, each one having been used at least once in an embroidery creation.

The durability of sequins depends on the material used and the kind of cleaning. Gelatin material didn't like water of course. Neither do metal materials which can get oxidation from different solvents. The new materials like cellulose acetate, polyvinyl or polyester require some care. Dry cleaning treatments are the most common, the specifics depending on the country, but it is still a matter of use and care of the cleaner: too much solvent, too high temperature, or too much iron heat or steam can damage the sequins and work. Simple hand washing in water tempered with soft soap remains the easiest and safest way. For the music-hall the cleaning is done professionally with the costumes if needed. Our sequins keep being used for twirling, synchronized swimming and they hand wash without problem. We don't know for sure the origin of the sequins used for the new music-hall shows—probably from China or India, or maybe they keep going through the embroiderers. We maintain relations with the Moulin Rouge, Cirque du Soleil, and French Disney.

Traditionally the music-halls ordered through the embroidery workshops, like Lesage, but then the work went to cheaper shops. The last one in France is likely the atelier of Caroline Valentin (18, rue Notre Dame de Lorette, Paris VI), which bought the former ones. She keeps working for the circus and other music-hall companies from time to time. On our side, all three last French sequins manufacturers (before we became the last one in 2001) used to work directly with the main embroidery workshops. Since the 1990s, fashion brands also come to us directly to buy the materials and have the work done outside. But we keep constantly working with the main French embroidery workshops like Lesage, Hurel, Montex, of which six remain in Paris, as well as some large ones in Italy and even India.

In the mid–twentieth century, Herbert Lieberman developed acetate sequins from the acetate he had been using in his work at Eastman Kodak. They were still flimsy and he eventually protected them with Mylar so they were washable and wouldn't melt, say, while the wearer was dancing or under stage lights.[20] Metal sequins are still sold for the discriminating seamstress because they mirror light in a way the vinyl plastic ones cannot.

From the earliest showgirl outfits before 1900, it was a popular style to dress performers in what looked like 100 percent threaded rhinestones (in general over body stockings). The showgirl looked like a human chandelier. Subsequently the designs became more sophisticated, with costume jewelry used that had to withstand all the movement and hard use. On stage, to lose an earring can be treacherous. So the earring had to be sewn on the head, or clipped to the headdress. From the early twentieth century, undress was created by different sorts of costumes but the iconic remained those made of almost all rhinestones or pearls. Bead workers knew how to do a pinstripe so the beads all lined up. Many of the rhinestones and fabrics came from International Silks and Woolens, which even today is a big source for TV's *Dancing with the Stars*. Beaders hung their keys up on a board when they went in to work because they would get lost in the fabric.

A costume with sequins galore, detailed in the photographs of brassiere and headdress, was created by Jerry Jackson for the 2001 edition of the American *Folies Bergère* and remained in use onstage through the production's final curtain in 2009. This glamorous item is now found at the Nevada State Museum, Las Vegas, in the institution's *Folies Bergère* archive. The traditional embellishments of rhinestones and sequins continued to be employed in cabaret costume design in Las Vegas, and served to enhance the overall impact of the costumes, choreography, and stage lighting.

An active tradition of luxury trades is requisite to the artisanship of costume accessories. In Paris one aspect of costuming a revue, boots and high heels, continues at a specialty boutique/workshop, the Maison Clairvoy, located near the Moulin Rouge on the rue Pierre Fontaine. The Moulin Rouge bought the Maison Clairvoy in 2006 to ensure that the *cancaneuses* would have shoes to dance their numbers in. Edouard Adabachian, who founded the shop in 1945, was known as the *peintre bottier,* as he painted and hung his art on the walls of his shop. By the 1960s, Maison Clairvoy supplied shoes to the the-

Original gouache by movie costume designer Mary Ann Nyberg (1923–1979).

atrical world. Today the company makes about 400 pairs for the Moulin Rouge, Lido and Crazy Horse, and also shoes for dance, circuses, movies, opera, theater, and private clients wishing "le sur mésure." Lucky Luke in his live-action movie had special footwear from Clairvoy to make his legs bow, Asterix and Obelix had, in theirs, Clairvoy shoes in an ancient Gallic style, and each new revue requires about 800 pairs of footwear.[21] For a nearly nude dancer to be comfortable in hip-high leather boots requires great skill on the part of the shoemaker.

In the workshop are the wooden forms for all the dancers. To fashion a shoe, the form is traced on paper, then the leather is cut, assembled, and sewn. The sole is slid into the shoe's upper and handstitched. Counting the piercing of the sole, fixing the heel, and finishing touches, a single pair has about 250 steps in production and takes five shoemakers 40–60 hours to make.[22]

The Moulin Rouge's lapis blue-and-red mini-boots are used for two or three performances of the cancan. Their heels may not exceed five centimeters and the zippers are placed on the outside to allow for rapid changes and also to prevent injury to the dancers from the zipper when their legs thump on the stage during the grand *écart*. Decorations like lacy metallic leather or ornamental lacing down a boot are designed to lengthen the appearance of the leg.[23]

SEVEN

The Berlin Revues

"The Cabaret posed a direct challenge to the cult of domesticity."—Lewis A. Erenberg,
in Steppin' Out: New York Nightlife and the Transformation of American Culture

In the mid–1920s, the erotic revue supplanted cabaret in the roster of Berlin's night life. Mel Gordon writes that although originating in Paris and New York,

> the erotic revue blossomed in sensation-hungry Berlin. It was mammoth, hectically-paced, thoroughly cosmopolitan, and oozed Girl-Culture sex. Berliners flocked to the revue-palaces, bought the Tin-Pan Alleyish recordings, marveled at the chorus girls' legs (which became iconic images in the pictorial monthlies). Revues were a testament to Berlin sophistication—what other city had its own Gesamtkunstwerk erotica? But the revue structure also spoke, in a subterranean way, to the Germanic need to control desire through objectification and derision.[1]

Dance troupes were imported with well-known starlets, but according to Gordon their routines had to be fit into the plot of the production, created by a single Berliner team. In photographs the costuming appears to have a tendency to have less finesse than the Parisian, as well as, like a Bauhaus building, few frills. Without blossoming within the music-hall tradition, the dancers come across harshly, like tarts. The revue palaces though were impressive. Naturally, inveterate traveler Frank Wedekind found entertainment in Berlin.

Das hat die Welt noch nicht gesehn was the title of a 1924 Berlin revue directed by impresario James Klein. To think about Berlin revues visually is to think big. To think of their true effect one has to imagine the haunting tunes and the scale of the shows—Eric Charell typically filled a 5,000-seat theater (the Grosses Schauspielhaus) with his spectacles.[2]

Before electric lighting, cities prided themselves on gas lighting, especially in the longer nights of the year. Besides keeping crime down, this allowed for a lit-up night life. In the nascent years of the film industry, cinema competed with the music-halls. Movies won out for close up but music-halls put on the bigger spectacles. It is interesting to see how differently the iconic elements of showgirl spectaculars, sparkling, revealing and often feathery outfits on semi-nude women were interpreted in Continental Europe's other entertainment capital, Berlin, in the 1920s. Here the songs and music counted for more, the tableaux likewise overwhelmed with fast-moving action and plenty of glamour, only some might consider the costumes more racy than refined.

Display of the body came with a good report card. Subsequent to Germany's defeat in the First World War, the body beautiful—sculpted and sportive—emerged as a powerful ideal. Girls infused with the righteous joy of physical culture gamboled across the lawn and did gymnastics on the beach, and, *pari passu,* girl troupes became ubiquitous in the lit-up nightlife of Berlin. Eric D. Weitz writes:

> We can find almost any kind of popular amusement somewhere between Potsdamer Platz and Kurfurstendamm. We can listen and watch sharp-tongued political cabaret…. We can watch the "living theaters" of nude women, unless they happen to have been shut down by the police that evening for violating public standards of morality and decency.[3]

Yet the same Weimar social theorists who concurred with body emancipation decried the mechanistic movements, manic speed, and *en masse* performance of imported troupes like the Tiller Girls and Jackson Girls, and their native equivalents. Freewheeling sexy entertainment, albeit elaborately costumed and choreographed, was not art. The spectacles offended the sensibilities of the reactionaries on the right while the on-stage vision of Prussian militarism and the American assembly line disturbed those on the left. In a famous essay entitled "The Mass Ornament" (1927), critic and social commentator Siegfried Kracauer took the revues to task. The showgirls who performed were, he said, "sexless bodies in bathing suits," not erotic at all.[4] Another critic characterized the revues presented by impresario James Klein at the Komische Oper as "Fleischchaurevuen," saying, "Multiply a nude woman by fifty and you have the main plot of his shows."[5]

Christopher Isherwood's *Berlin Stories*–type of bar with variety entertainment was of course called a cabaret like the movie musical with Liza Minelli as Sally Bowles. The German language has differentiated since the 1950s between *Cabaret,* a strip show, and *Kabarett,* a venue where audiences enjoy social or political satire, but the terms were used interchangeably through the Weimar period. Peter Jelavich, in a seminal study of Weimar cabaret, parses the showgirl revue as one type of performance that belonged to the cabaret culture in the Jazz Era:

> Cabaret was thus not only bounded by dramatic theater, variety shows, and nude dancing; those other types of performance could even be part of the trajectories of individual cabaret troupes. Two further genres much be considered as well: revue and agitprop. Revues were performed on large stages with an abundance of often gaudy production numbers, and held together by something vaguely resembling a plotline. The revue was related to cabaret inasmuch as it comprised a smattering of song and dialogues of a satirical or parodistic nature.[6]

From 1903 until 1913, ten revues were presented each year at Berlin's Metropol-Theater. The city itself was a focus, very upbeat, and the revues touted its modernity and dynamism. There were women in tights and outlandish costumes, and also in military uniforms (a type of production number that continued until 1940). Of the first of these shows at the Metropol, the *Berliner Tageblatt* cited "colorful ballet-girls displaying waists of every size."

The Metropol revues promoted the importance of fashion and the merchandise of the new department stores—both outerwear and underwear. A production number in 1906 showed six silk-clad legs peeking enticingly out of a box, despite the fact a song was being sung about the suffering of home-laborers. A postcard of 1909 shows four young ladies in huge hats and corseted slips, holding tiered petticoats all in white. A show tune for a modest striptease, "'What the Fashionable Lady Needs' [Was die Modedame brache] from *Hallooh! Die grosse Revue!* also showed footwear, stockings, garters, chemises and corsets that the woman of the day was expected to have. It also promoted the types of commodities that were manufactured and retailed in Berlin."[7]

A troupe that did satire could morph into a purveyor of another type performance, nude-dancing. Professor Jelavich writes that the 1920s saw an ongoing sexual revolution in Berlin, that the lifting of censorship allowed the popular arts to treat sexual themes more freely, and that cabaret stages often included "flesh-baring," while tending to mock the nude dancers or kick lines of "Girls."

During the Weimar Republic's early years, numerous entrepreneurs staged shows featuring naked or nearly naked women. For example, the Ballet Celly de Rheidt was started by a demobilized first lieutenant, and starred his wife Cacilie. The code of the spectacles of Cacilie and other women in various stages of undress was "*Schonheitsabende*" (beauty evenings). There is a photograph of men in attendance wearing masks.[8] By 1920, the Celly's dancers appeared with nothing more than transparent scarves or strings of wooden beads on the upper body, and some thin veiling on the hips. The madam of the show was in her thirties but some of the members of the troupe were young teenagers, until the Ballet ran afoul of the law. The use of costumes was not to cover but for dramatic pantomimes. In one Cacilie played a nun falsely accused of breaking vows of chastity, who prostrates herself before a statue of the Virgin Mary, and throws off her clothes. Mary comes alive and blesses the nun, who runs naked to an altar and embraces a crucifix.

As German courts after the Great War ruled that nudity was not obscene in itself, those of conservative views had a hard time persuading the courts to shut a show down; but if the cabaret was small and the audience was in close proximity to the nude dancers, with house lights on and drinks being consumed, a case could be made. Conservatives repeatedly lambasted the nude spectacles; their legality was one more reason to attack the Republic.

A trial of the Ballet Celly de Rheidt for indecency resulted in a ruling that they could continue to perform but the women were ordered to have their breasts and pelvic areas fully covered, or the troupe would be banned from Berlin. The new regulations crippled the Celly and a general crackdown occurred in 1923. The Berlin chief of police wrote to his counterpart in Dresden:

> Women dancers must cover completely their posterior, private parts, and navel with opaque fabrics, so that during dance movements these body parts cannot be revealed in a naked state. Furthermore, the breasts must be covered at least to the extent that the nipples cannot be seen during dance movements.[9]

Just as they would early in casino history in mid–twentieth century America, limitations were dropped if a woman were standing still as a statue. "Although the authorities were supposed to restrain obscenity, they were simultaneously complicit in shaping and sustaining it. Coupling nudity with immobility reinforced a traditional pattern of objectification."[10] The Celly costuming was sometimes louche, its aim to display the body, period. When her troupe did "The Dance of Beauty" they wore short transparent dresses lit by different colored lights, the dancers exposing bare feet or a breast, with Celly herself as a matador disrobing and using her diaphanous garment to tame the beast.

Set and costume designers were often hired from Paris to make the top shows in Berlin sparkle. Some had an audience of two or three thousand in the heyday of 1925–1929. Professor Jelavich describes the part played by American performers, especially African American ones, and other entertainers from abroad such as the line-dancing Tiller Girls, a feature of the Aussstattungsrevuen, Herman Haller's revues at the Theater am Admiralsplatz. Berlin was a center of hundreds of productions in the Weimar period to stem the tide of cinema.

The big productions with eye-popping finales in the 1920s were unbeatable for the sets but less remarkable for costuming. The evocation by James Klein as a major director of Berlin's Jazz Age shows, of the Brandenburg Gate, had a bevy of women in only flowered thongs. Lines of girls had on in their acts imitation police uniforms or outfits for military parade, and a showgirl in one ad photo looks dangerous in an urbane trained gown and incredibly wide hat, holding her mastiff by a leash. And how can one look at a poster for Josephine Baker for her performance at the Theater des Westens in 1928 without awareness that Nazis would come into power five years later?

Some costumes in the photographs from Berlin seem crazier than Ziegfeld's or the Folies Bergère, and to be intentionally vulgar, as if to embody the industrialized mechanistic society. For some costumes an Expressionist stiffness is in evidence. Compared with French shows, there is more metal, the beads are larger, the rhinestone designs less extravagant—as if to assault the senses with modernity rather than beauty. Some of the distinction of the Berlin showgirl costumes in photographs comes from having less froufrou and more angularity. The showgirls often look chilly in monokinis as if they left part of their costumes backstage. Faces were posed to look fierce, sullen or tough, and made up with little red bow mouths. Yet archival photographs of the richly illustrated *Cabaret Berlin: Revue, Kabarett and Film Music between the Wars* show frisky imagination. A bridal finale looks like a garden party (*Es liegt in der Luft*, 1928); in the subcontinental Indian tableau from *Für Dich* (1925) most dancers look vaguely Indian but two wear apparel with the motif of gigantic white gloves that start at the bust and end at the lower leg. Another scene from a Charell revues of 1923, set in front of an ocean liner at night, has 22 young women in bunch satin and tulle evening gowns with big frontal bows, and hats in the style of fezzes adorned with huge rose corsages.

The sets, dazzling and ambitious for often large spaces, enthralled from coordinated large-scale movement, like sailors in cubbies, each looking up at a naked dream girl[11]; or girls coordinated to the letters of a giant backdrop of a typewriter, "typing."[12] Gunter Berghaus writes, "The most extreme forms of ornamentation of the female body occurred in the revues where the girls were employed to represent inorganic objects, such as a picture frame, ivory carvings, jewelry, etc."[13]

Thus the Berlin costumes in the Jazz Era seem to have been grand, inventive and enticing, yet jarring. For example, James Klein studied the revues à grand spectacle in Paris but evoked in his Berlin shows the rhythm and tone of modernity not fantasy and seductive femininity.

The French showgirl costumes' *je ne sais quoi* derived from an attitude towards life—of being able to be serious about total frivolity. The French had a love of spun-sugar fairy tales. Paris had a concentration of artists from many countries. The city was a showcase for art and luxury goods, and the tradition of crafts of dressmaking, feathers, beadwork, embroidering, etc., involved in the music-hall revues. In Berlin the hugely popular urbane entertainment was more topical and responsive to social upheaval. Atina Grossmann writes regarding the so-called Girlkultur that the New Woman

> expressed in dramatic form the discontents of civilization and the ambivalence of modernity. She represents both dancer and salvation: if women's domesticity could somehow be reconciled with wage labor, if rationalization could be made functional for marriage and motherhood, then the restructured economy need not be a disaster for social life, indeed could provide the leisure and consumer goods to improve it.[14]

The costumes in Berlin's showgirl spectacles during the interwar period clash with traditional femininity. They shout out social disquiet to us from the past.

EIGHT

The Icon Is Fixed

"The old Paris is no more (the form of a city changes faster, alas! than a mortal's heart)."—Charles Baudelaire

Usually one thinks of a decline of an art style as an effête period, but showgirl costumes in the world of entertainment were often beautiful, wacky, over the top, artfully absurd, erotic and very expensive creations from the post–World War II period. If these classical and costly shows were, as Mel Gordon sums up, "pretty much done in the late 1930s,"[1] the traditions of effective artifice, and the talents of the artists and artisans from various nations who contributed their talent to the famous Parisian music-halls, made "magnifique" shows even in this period. Paris was decadent and alluring to Americans and watching a spectacle continued to be a safe exercise of lust.

Paris had represented a provocative mix of dissolution on the one hand, and bright lights on the other, for centuries. It was Europe's cultural capital by the time Abigail Adams warned John Quincy Adams to avoid bad influences there. Yet Abigail wrote that she enjoyed the unfamiliar glamour of the Paris Opera. And so the paradoxical lure continued. The fashionable elite came to Paris for cultivation and clothes in the belle époque. Artists and writers came from America for stimulation and to leave prejudice behind in the Jazz Era. Then when the horizons of average Americans broadened after World War II, they flocked to organized entertainment at the "boites" that had evolved from the cabarets that attracted visitors when the Eiffel Tower was built. The music-halls catered to them.

Tourists appreciated French designers, labels and perfumes, the Louvre and the Seine, wines and nearly nude shows. The costumes have to be stunning to live up to the world's romance with Paris. A favorite ballet dancer of the mid–twentieth century, Zizi Jeanmaire, had a showgirl background. She starred in a ballet called *La Croqueuse de diamants* (1950) which inspired the song "Where Do You Go To (My Lovely)?," and her husband, Roland Petit, choreographed—both of them loved the ambience of the music-hall. Her friend Boris Vian once said to her, "You've had it with the tutu? Then go to the music-hall!" The first line of "Where Do You Go To (My Lovely)?" mentioned the dancing of Zizi Jeanmarie, the fashions of Balmain, and hairstyles decorated with "diamonds and pearls."

The French costume tradition at the music-halls was self-aware and proud. For instance, Roland Petit said in about 1970: "As far as I know, even the Ziegfelds were less luxurious than the most modest revue of the Casino!… One could see a dresser constrained

Unused 1930s postcard found in a German soldier's belongings: Paris en Flanant —Bal et Cinéma du Moulin Rouge. Editions d'Art Yvon.

to garnish the back of Marilyn Monroe with safety pins to avoid a catastrophe on the stage." (Not in Paris!) Petit put some blame on the American unions, observing that French costumers enjoyed a certain liberty in their work.[2]

There had to be a commonality among the costumers for the icon to evolve and continue, which was the understanding of the oxymoronic nature of the costumes/show. The frisson, the sparkle, came from opposing visual properties. The costumers gathered all these properties together: fragility that could last through many performances; provocative but tempered, artful but natural, designs; French but with exotic elements; fashionable yet distinct from fashion; and predictable yet modern—transcending the past but with the ability to surprise. Through technical ability and innate wit, the costumers probed the greatest oxymoron of the showgirl spectaculars, the wittily covering yet uncovering of the female body. And that iconic core had its rule of risqué, that no matter if a showgirl wore fifty feet of ostrich feathers, or a gown that could have passed at Versailles in the ancient régime, her costume tantalized and, ultimately, revealed, rather than actually clothed.

In terms of the revue per se, it developed, magnified, professionalized, and became very elaborate. The change in the costumes from the 1890s to the late 1910s when the costume became fixed was more discontinuous. In this period, the ideal female figure altered, the sets with their staircases and swimming pools became more impressive, and the size of the industry burgeoned, magnetizing great artistic talent to the Parisian music-halls.

In the post–World War II period, nothing was added but much endured. The Lido, which opened in 1946, brought flash and glamour and remains one of the top nightclubs in the world. Directors and costumers were working with a waterfall, an ice-skating rink, and a pool that could be used for underwater or tropical scenes. For a time the Lido even had jousting, and two horses; one of which lost his shoe during a show, dove into the audience and injured someone.

One surprising fact is that the Nazi occupation had revived Paris nightlife. "For the Germans," explains Gordon, "Paris was a utopia where you could get anything. There was, for instance, so much homosexual activity in occupied Paris, where in Berlin it would get someone shut up in a concentration camp."[3]

The second most famous French remark, after "Let them eat cake," is attributed to Madame de Pompadour, the ultra-refined mistress to Louis XV, or sometimes to the king himself (this seems to make it more likely that one or the other of them did actually say it). According to Michael Mould's *Routledge Dictionary of Cultural References in Modern French* (2011), Louis was sitting for his portrait by Quentin de la Tour just after the defeat in battle of the French by the Prussians. To coax him out of his hangdog look, Madame de Pompadour said, "Il ne faut pas s'affligier: vous tomberiez malade. Après nous le déluge." [Fretting is only going to make you sick. We are incomparable.]

This was the mood of the showgirl extravaganzas after World War II. Luc Sante suggests that the over-the-topness of this period's costume icon "has its immediate roots in the get-ups worn at some of the big showbizzy interwar Paris brothels, such as Le Sphinx and One-Two-Two."[4] Las Vegas would import them because they were incomparable— no one would ever compete with their live stage sensuality again. The French shows, though, put an emphasis on glamour by contrast to the mechanical polish of the Vegas shows: When a male hand groped toward the costume of Mademoiselle Menard with a tiny glue brush because her cache-sexe had detached, the audience shrieked with delight.[5]

The showgirl gleamed in the imagination of a sobered world order. Hyperbolic costumes continued but the cinema did domesticate things. Movies including *The Prince and the Showgirl* and *Gentlemen Prefer Blondes* had spirited incarnations of the showgirl by Marilyn Monroe, Jane Russell and other stars yet were not very suggestive, positioned at a great distance from the semi-nude tease that the music-halls had pushed for a half-century.

The music-hall revue, Philippe Garner reminds us, "is a hybrid of the performing arts that involves reference to courtly dress and tradition, to fashion, to populist spectacle, and to the circus.... This is a sophisticated amalgam of the camp, the exotic, and the erotic."[6] So the showgirl costume was not invented, it evolved; it became a fantasy of breathtaking materiality that kept off the premises truths about where a woman's casual display of her body can lead.

The staples of high headdresses, flowing side swags or feathers, draped stoles and embellished corsages remained. The influences from which the showgirl costume took form were an amalgamated legacy. At a performance for Louis XIV, writes Garner, "A play by Molière was introduced with a special prelude. The stage was set with fountains. From a large shell within one of these emerged an all-but-naked Madeleine Béjart, the playwright's muse, to recite a prologue."[7]

The showgirl made her appearance, arguably, in the Renaissance with the masque, ballet de cours, and Versailles theatrical, but has left the stage and exists in two dimensions. The last revue before the Moulin Rouge became a cinema was the sketch in three tableaux about Du Barry. The last tableau showed her execution.[8] This was the event that was eliminated from a Mistinguett revue long before but now it was symbolic of a theatrical symbol that had exceeded its time.

Costume design by Freddy Wittop (courtesy Piollet Collection).

After the Germans surrendered in May 1945, and Allied servicemen arrived in Paris, the U.S. government opened four short-lived, huge nightclubs. As I remember tromping from the French hotel where my family lived in 1959 across the Champs Elysées to have waffles with maple syrup or "ain omboogere." I understood the impulse to serve the GIs. Writes Mel Gordon, "the stage entertainment varied from week to week but the high point was always Hit Parade Favorites sung by discreetly attired lines of chorus dancers."[9]

But the U.S. army guidebook to the city in 1946 stated that 40 million spectators had been at the Folies Bergère since the Armistice. The troupes of precision dancers were followed by the "sexy Gallic tableaux." Commenting on the backstage haste, Gordon writes,

> In picture-perfect form or not, they portrayed every kind of wine, aperitif, tree creature, marine animal, or archaic occupation, like the Egyptian priestess, Roman gladiator, and Renaissance courtier. More than one-third of any production was devoted to them. In 1937, Derval defended his barrage of anonymity to his influential cultural critics, "Ah, these nude women, if I got rid of them, I would have to close up shop."[10]

From the vista of the early 1970s, and reminiscent of Ziegfeld's evening gowns, Derek and Julia Parker noted that couture had been for twenty years part of the show: "Whereas most theaters have their manequins nues, the Folies also has its mannequins habillées, whose job has been to show off the magnificent costumes especially designed for the revues, and made in the ateliers in the theater itself."[11]

The tableaux were Gallic but the Americans were invariably saluted. This naturally made for a smoother transit to appearing in Las Vegas, whose casino-based entertainment developed close ties with both the Lido and Folies Bergère in the 1950s. A show called *Allez Lido* in 1981 has its finale on YouTube. It was all glamour, speed, feathers and costumes, formed mostly of gold glittery chain, by Pete Menefee, a star costumer in Vegas, and Fulco. "Lafayette" is hailed and Shirley MacLaine concludes her song, "as the French people say, merci beaucoup." Showgirls sparkled underwater and at the other extreme in consummate masquerade. The Lido 1994 finale "C'est magique" featured costumes that made the dancers raise voluminous side panels of fabric as though they were stick puppets. *Bonheur* (2013) followed a bird-woman to four different worlds in search of happiness and had a panoply of headgear, from bowed contraptions, black feathered hats, and medieval style bennes, to rainbow birds of paradise, as well as head-to-toe cat costumes. A showgirl on an elephant was vaguely Indian yet she evoked Marilyn Monroe. Then the headdresses became stained glass windows in the shape of a reversed heart.

Zaniness built on tradition achieved elegance and equilibrium. Thus the historical overview in 2011 called *50 Years Lido* took the costume motifs from cowgirls, matadors, Iberian dance, military, Russian, tap dance, jazz, cancan, tuxedos, and Sixties mod. In the audience were Maurice Chevalier, Brigitte Bardot, Sophia Loren, and Charles Azenevour. The revue ended with what is a tautology of the post–World War II shows, "Merci beaucoup" in several languages and "nous espérons vous revoir, merci beaucoup," which could be interpreted as, "We speak your language and invite you to return."

My grandchild asked her mother how to use the handle to roll down a window in my car. This dates my car as old-fashioned. My youngest daughter often goes to Paris without having taken particular notice of the Lido or the Moulin Rouge. This rather speaks for the marginality of the showgirl spectaculars.

Daughter Rosalind was going with her boyfriend; naturally I wondered what, being sophisticated young people, they would think of a "semi-nude revue" (see the following for the answer). Her boyfriend was lukewarm about an evening out at a nightclub and her friend from Mauritius, who works in Paris, also had never considered going to any of the revues. All three (ages twenties and early thirties) had a good time and were dazzled. Since "éblouissant" can be considered the fundamental desirable quality of a Lido show, this was good to hear.

An Evening at the Lido
ROSALIND PARRY[12]

The Lido is very old-fashioned, with a velvet rope at the door and ushers in tuxedos. Shorts are a no-no so we sat upstairs in the mezzanine, looking down at a large stage. We sipped champagne. The show was *Paris Merveilles*. There is a flimsy framing plot in which a nerdy blonde in a bun and glasses shows up in Paris. She meets men and women and opens up and by the end is more sexualized. That is the creakiest part of the show: why do the men pull at her and try to undress her? But, the rest is a joyful extravaganza.

It opens with women with ostrich feather bustles. They look like birds from the back. In a pattern that will repeat itself, first half the women descend a staircase in these outfits and bras, then the other half of them come down with the same outfits but no bras. Almost every dance includes that switch from bras to no bras, a little naughty to very naughty. There is a bit of a business chic look going on. Not just the nerdy blonde, who we might assume is a modern business lady, but in the women who come out later, wearing corsets and pencil skirts, or pencil skirts and blazers and no bras, or crisp white shirts open to the navel. Later, more business attire will be made coy, with laced up backs, visible only when the women twirl around. Business in the front, party in the back. More fun later costumes include shiny, almost neon skirts; military jackets over thongs and nothing else; and black cancan dresses with bright pink tulle underneath.

There are also beautiful men in tight spangled pants. One is a shirtless sword swallower. A variety show unfolds throughout the middle of the show. Women emerge as swans, dressed in white with full-sized feathered white swan sculptures on their heads. Black swans also parade out. Then in front the stage opens up, and a platform levels up from the bowels of the theater. On it are women dressed as streams of water, mimicking the movements of the actual fountain that has come up with them. Later the same platform will come up with various, decadent arrangements. The fountain disappears, stagehands mop the floor, and it rises again as a huge chandelier, with women strapped to it, dressed in sexy diamonds and stockings and barely anything else. Then that goes away and later returns as a skating rink, with a seriously talented duo of skaters.

Probably the most creative costumes both come later in the show. In one, the star parades in wearing a huge billowing dress. Underneath that are men, moving the dress around, peeking out now and then. At the end she strips off the skirts, showing just her corset and stockings. The most amusing, though, is the women parading down dressed as flowers in the final number. The flowers are these enormous sculptural headdresses, in all kinds of colors, and the stems are the lengthy legs of the dancers, which are wrapped in diaphanous fabric. Just flowers and see-through fabric, that's the look.

We had a lot of fun!

Tradition has often mandated carefully crafted show programs. For this Lido show, a heavy, colorful program with a chic gold on midnight blue design features three cartoon females naked except for their high heeled boots: one with a top hat, one with the head of a swan and one with a black and gold morning glory where a head would be. The headlessness is reminiscent of the painting at the entrance of Le Chat Noir cabaret. Feathers, the Eiffel Tower and a champagne glass frame the three figures.

The gorgeous and nostalgic feathery costumes ruled in the music-halls until a late-comer to the Paris classy nightclub scene, Alain Bernadin, created something different. Bernadin was a painter and art dealer who had closed an American-style square dancing hall before hitching his star to the nude revue. He took over a series of wine cellars on the Avenue George V just off the Champs-Elysées and founded the Crazy Horse Saloon, the flagship of nude spectacle avant-garde. I used to pass the Crazy Horse sometimes on the way home from work. Guards dressed like Scottish soldiers swept away anybody who lingered out front (reminiscent of the bouncer that Salis hired for the Chat Noir and dressed in the costume of the Swiss Guard). The premises looked mysterious and very quiet in early evening. This came back to me when I heard the line repeated in a perform-ance recorded by Frederick Wiseman in his documentary about the club, "Ce sont des soldats de l'armée érotique."

For Frederick Wiseman to make a documentary of "the Crazy" was unexpected, but perhaps all his projects have been as unexpected as they are riveting. The movie begins and ends with hand shadow play to symbolize the shadow theater background of music-halls at the cabaret Le Chat Noir. A puppeteer pets a kitten, lovers kiss, and a dove files away. Bernadin, the owner until his death, called himself "le prince de l'imaginaire." He drew sketches and asked designers including Paco Rabane to render the costumes.

The in-your-face woman power is ardent. That the dancers practice two hours before each show is palpable. Special effects create costumes of light which Loie Fuller would have delighted in—all kinds of stars, prison bars, leopard spots, checkerboard, filigree, and so forth. There is no need to be French to grasp what it is all about.

In 2017, Chantal Thomass of the French *très cher* lingerie mark created the costumes for a spring show, "Dessous Dessus," emphasizing lace and corsetry. The only parts of the showgirls covered consistently are the feet, which are clad in Louboutin stilettos with the distinctive red soles. (A Louboutin shoe ad has said: "A good shoe is not the one that dresses you but undresses you.") Instead of G-strings or cache-sexes, Bernadin instituted pubic hair trimmed as a four-inch-sided triangle on the Mound of Venus, the nightclub's trademark.

"The Eiffel Tower is lit up like a fille du Crazy," a song pulses, which seems apt. The patterns and colors of illumination are what most of what the dancers wear, similar to what one sees of the Eiffel Tower from afar at night.

Circus and music-hall authority Pascal Jacob is attuned to change and tradition, as his description of working on a revue in 2012, indicates:

> Every project has to start with an idea. For the Lido revue *Paris Merveilles*, the idea was to enhance the spirit of the "Lido woman." But it was also crucial to play with a new vision of feathers, considering the fact that this mythic house has been a feather temple for years. So the costume designer Nicolas Vaudelet decided to work with a young designer, Serkan Cura, a real magician of the feather. Using many different feathers, in terms of length, color, texture, shape and aspect, driven by Nicolas Vaudelet's sketches, Cura created beautiful parures, playing with the ideas of flowers or snowflakes, transforming feathers into fur or petals, creating with each costume a new perception of illusion and beauty.
>
> Vaudelet did a lot of sketches presented to the director Franco Dragone who selected some, and asked him to push other ones, to create at the end of the process, almost two years, a beautiful and coherent display of wonders.[13]

"Wonders" is true. The spray of many fountains caress with blue-lit water, the men's cos-tumes as well as the women's have originality and finesse, and there is a number where dancers hang off a massive chandelier as if they are decorative diamond pendants, stealing

76ᵉ Annee – Nᵒ 4   Prix : 3 fr.   Samedi 22 Janvier 1938

— Oh! m'sieur, soyez gentil... dites a votre ventre de me faire une petite place sur vos genoux.

La Vie Parisienne, **January 22, 1938. "Oh! m'sieur, soyez gentil … dites à votre ventre de me faire une petite place sur vos genoux" (Oh! sir, be so kind … tell your belly to make me a small place on your lap).**

the show vis-à-vis the costume effects. Writes Paul Lewis of the Folies Bergère in 1987, "Mr. Gyarmathy and Mrs. Martini have largely abandoned jokes and skits, concentrating on spectacular set pieces with gorgeous costumes, plenty of topless dancing girls and a sense of dazzling artificialty."[14]

Taking a long view of the current shows, Charles Rearick gives this characterization:

Little has changed in recent years—or even decades. The famous historic cabarets—the Moulin Rouge, the Lido, La Nouvelle Ève—still draw long lines and busloads of tourists every night. In those night spots a performance of the cancan anchors the shows in collective historical memory and assures visitors that they have "seen" a celebrated authentic side of Paris. One of the most famous of the music-halls, however, was not able to continue financially with its traditional formula and introduced a major change in its programming before the end of the twentieth century: the Folies-Bergère, since 1993, has featured musicals, concerts, and stand-up comics instead of variety acts and lavish topical revues with semi-nude show-girls. Other cabarets and "clubs" have broken with the clichéd belle époque tradition by presenting show girls in more up-to-date ways—pole dances, lap dances, and highly choreographed strip shows. The Crazy Horse is the leader in this category. These entertainments depend heavily on tourists, as they are too expensive and not particularly appealing for the French general public. For the French masses who stay home and watch television, there's a Saturday-night favorite billing itself as "Le plus grand cabaret du monde." Bare-breasted show girls in classic dance lines surround the master of ceremonies as he opens the show. The tradition and memory of "gay Paris" live on—and not only for tourists.[15]

I asked photography historian Philippe Garner to opine on the showgirl costume because of his introduction to the most brilliant photo book on the Lido, *Les Girls: Paris 1952–1979*, featuring photographs by Daniel Frasnay.

Costuming: A Commentary

PHILIPPE GARNER[16]

The iconic costume tends to be a design worn by a number of performers at the same time, being more for a decorative lineup than the individual artiste. Thinking back through the evolution of spectacle, I believe that the costume didn't come into focus in the 1920s and 1930s, even though the points come together then—the white headdress, silver rhinestones, bikini or some version of it, high heels, fishnet tights, and stole of feathers. But the icon defined itself in Paris in the postwar years. The Lido was the most characteristic and secondly the Folies Bergère. This "look" became one of the components of Paris's rediscovery of itself as the glamorous center of the world. The image was imagined, then seized on and promoted as part of what was quintessentially French; it became universal.

As an equation of nakedness and acceptability, the showgirl's undress turned eroticism into delightful spectacle. It personalized it. It's a look, whether the wearer is dancing, or parading, or something in between. Of course it has a sexy dimension because the girls are chosen for their fine physique—but not in the least salacious. The stylization makes it sexy and clean: these shows have been spectacles for couples to attend. Thus the costumes weren't an erotic show for male eyes.

There are variations on a theme. Some years ago I saw a show in the French provinces with comedy, music, circus things without animals, and the cream on the top, showgirls, bound it together. It's one of those manifestations that has become classic—Japanese geisha is another—that is frozen as a symbol of culture. The spectacles in Paris have drawn the illustrious—Saint-Laurent, Brigitte Bardot, English royalty. There's nothing tacky about the French version of the iconic look. Could it be kitsch all the same? Yes, it's camp, with very little ironic dimension. Is it vulgar? Yes, but sophisticated. Sophisticated and vulgar are not incompatible.

I am half French and I was always fascinated by the style, glamour, and tradition in

Postcard: Les Apaches du Petit Balcon, Passage Thiéré, le Bastille, 1940.

Paris. The imagery of fashion, style, and spectacle was part of my childhood. I especially came to like the early Crazy Horse, which was an intimate setting and had balletic dance.

According to Charles Rearick, by the 1980s the celebrated nightspots were resting on their laurels, reproducing "set pieces of a legendary past," and playing to tourists.

He has offered a medley of explanations: declining audience interest, dancers no longer getting into the spirit of the shows and not wanting the rigors of training for them, and the emergence of competitors, fresher shows produced by newcomers like Le Paradis Latin (1977).

> Parisians, famously novelty-loving, went for the newer entertainment.... By the late 1980s the most traditional of the showplaces, the Folies Bergère, was unable to fill its worn seats with customers and had to lay off a dozen singers and dancers. Tucked away as it was in a small street near the long-declining Grands Boulevards, the Folies Bergère lacked the association with Montmartre—artistic Bohemian, and Belle-Epoque glamorous—that still bolstered the prestige of the Moulin Rouge.[17]

NINE

The French Connection
in Las Vegas

*"They courted the face on the screen, the face of translucence,
the face of wax on which men find it possible to imprint
the image of their fantasy."*—Anaïs Nin

A troupe of a dozen statuesque Bluebell Girls had their start at the Paris Lido a year after its founding; they would become a starring troupe in Las Vegas for decades. The troupe was the creation of Margaret Kelly Leibovici, "Miss Bluebell," who had an amazing story. An orphan born in Dublin and adopted by an unmarried dressmaker, Margaret took dance lessons to strengthen her weak legs. The nickname "Bluebell" came from her hyacinth blue eyes. She performed as a precision line dancer and in dance movies in the 1930s, and at 22 was choreographing in Paris.

There was a gap in her employment at the Folies Bergère for a time in 1933, when Mistinguett felt the Kelly dancers upstaged her, and Paul Derval, the director for over four decades, let them go. When he brought them back, Margaret Kelly's name was in every program for the next six years.

Kelly married the pianist-composer Marcel Leibovici, who wrote songs for Edith Piaf. A Romanian Jew, Marcel was imprisoned early in the Occupation but escaped. The French Resistance hid him in an apartment building directly across from the Prefecture of Police for several years. Margaret smuggled food to Marcel and when questioned by the Gestapo revealed nothing of her husband's whereabouts. Margaret, still at the Folies Bergère, and by then the mother of the first two of four children, was also interned, in a camp in Besançon, in eastern France, until an Irish diplomat secured her release.

In 1947 she moved to the Lido, the new nightclub of the Clerico brothers. There she formed the Bluebell Girls, a troupe that took a starring role in the revues and would perform worldwide with permanent troupes in Paris, and for nearly 40 years in the Lido de Paris (editions of the revue ran from 1974 to 1991) and at the Stardust Resort and Casino in Las Vegas. Marcel handled the orchestral, business and financial side of their partnership. The costumes were known for their jewel-like sparkle, and the dancers for their height and aplomb.

At the Lido, Kelly also began a long and important collaboration with Donn Arden. Arden was an American who had organized entertainment for the U.S. troops, and was engaged by producers Pierre Louis-Guérin and René Fraday to stay on in Paris and produce shows at the Lido. Arden would have a dual career in Paris and Las Vegas as the most legendary creative producer of revues of the second half of the twentieth century.[1]

Marcel was killed in a road accident in 1961 after which Kelly managed the troupe on her own. Filmmaker François Truffaut was fascinated by the love story of Margaret and her husband, which Truffaut realized with great art in *The Last Metro* (1980). Catherine Deneuve played the Margaret-based character.

In over six decades, Margaret Kelly trained 14,000 Bluebell girls who performed in many countries. In 1970 the Bluebells went topless. The troupe in Las Vegas at the MGM Grand Hotel performed Donn Arden's spectaculars with Kelly's dancers, as a successful hybrid Franco-American show. Kelly was connected with the Lido in Paris and when shows started to be brought in the 1960s to Vegas (the Lido at the Stardust Hotel, the Casino de Paris at the Dunes Hotel, and the Folies Bergère at the Tropicana Hotel), she was a key figure doing casting for the dancers.[2]

Not only productions, cast and choreography but also costumes, jewels and feathers went from Paris to America. For the Lido shows at the Stardust Casino and Hotel, for instance, the jewelry was made by a Parisian jeweler. Arden had already staged several editions of Lido spectaculars in Paris and would stage all 12 editions for the Stardust, until the Lido de Paris closed in 1991. The premises were later used in the movie *Showgirls* (1995).

This 1920s-style costume design is by Jerry Jackson, August 2002 (courtesy Special Collections and Archives, University Libraries, University of Nevada, Las Vegas).

According to Jefferson Graham, author of *Vegas Live and In Person*, Donn Arden came to Las Vegas to put on a show when working on shows for Eastern nightclubs, employed by the Cleveland Mafia. He said he felt "obliged to go. They were the boys and they paid well." They also insisted on fine costumes. "I wouldn't dare use a bunny suit for a costume. It had to be real ermine. I wouldn't dare go to a Lerner's shoe shop and buy shoes. Oh no, the shoes had to be custom made by David Evins and all of this sort of thing, which I loved."[3]

Showgirl costume, New York World Fair, 1939-1940 (New York Public Library).

Arden's first Vegas shows though were not at a big casino but at the Desert Inn. The "Donn Arden Dancers" danced behind the headliner, for example, Danny Kaye, Jack Benny or Betty Grable. The show featured a line of young women "exquisitely costumed and gracefully elegant—but without the special effects that would characterize his later work."[4] This was 1950 when the first fancy nightclubs, including the Sahara, the Sands, the Dunes, the Riviera, and the Fremont sprang up. The celebrity entertainers were polite compared with comedians now, like ventriloquist Edgar Bergen with his wisecracking dummy Charlie McCarthy. Arden hired women for the chorus line who were pretty and not necessarily good dancers because as one former showgirl Jeanie Malone told Graham, "he could *make* you look great—but you had to be a lady, and you had to dress well."[5]

"When good Americans die they go to Paris": Oscar Wilde's character was expressing a prevalent conceit in mid-century America. In movies and fashion, Paris was the epitome of deluxe lifestyle, and tourists brought back tasseled programs from the Folies or the Lido the way they brought cuckoo clocks from Bavaria, Delft pottery from Holland, and kid gloves from Naples. My parents were culturally extremely conservative Protestants, but even they felt that seeing the revues in Paris was unmissable; they took my teenage brother to a show on his 16th birthday, as a rite of passage. The sexy chic of Paris explains why not only the Lido and Folies Bergère opened in 1959 in Vegas but in the summer, "les Girls de Paree" opened at the smaller venue, the Opera House at El Rancho Vegas, headlined by Joe E. Lewis; according to the *Las Vegas Sun*, "The cast received an ovation seldom seen in the Opera House at El Rancho Vegas."[6] French risqué was pushed further when the Folies Bergère opened at the Tropicana Hotel and Casino on Christmas Eve 1959. It was entirely imported from Paris and was continually licensed from the Paris original. This was from 1975 a show of Michel Gyarmathy, the artistic director of the Folies Bergère.

The Paris music-halls were always open to foreign talent. Gyarmathy was a Hungarian Jew who emigrated to Paris at age 25. Paul Derval, then the Folies' artistic director, refused to interview the start-up whose poster Josephine Baker had chosen for one of her revues, with a concept of pink poufs her only cover. Outside the theater Gyarmathy did chalk drawings relating to the classic novel *Manon Lescaut*. Gyarmathy walked over them as he stepped out of his car. "Did you do those?" he said. "Clean off the sidewalk and come in to my office tomorrow with the same drawings on paper." Whereas Arden was fundamentally a producer, Gyarmathy was a costume and set designer. Gyarmathy reveled in creating fairy tale settings of castles and palaces, and outdoor winter grandeur with moonlit icicles and snow. His archives have their most recurring leitmotif as the chandelier, hanging from extravagant sets or balanced on a dancer's head.[7]

The Tropicana show eventually was completely produced in Las Vegas from 1975 until it closed in 2009. Karan Feder, having unique insight based on curating the show's costume archives at the Nevada State Museum, observes: "The 17th edition of the show, which premiered in 1997, contained over 600 theatrical lights, 62 scenery backdrops, a cast of over 100, and approximately 4,000 costume pieces and accessories. The Folies' Parisian bloodlines remained apparent, as the production continued the tradition of the French spectacular."

Through the 1950s and 1960s, while Arden was producing two shows in Vegas, the *Lido* of the Stardust and *Jubilee!* at Bally's, he also ran concurrent shows in Paris, New York, New Jersey, Miami, and Los Angeles. Showgirls arrived, mostly from the French revue scene, often English, who had the right carriage and did not blush. "Chief among

Paris cancan, Le Moulin de la Galette, 1940s.

their talents was the ability to parade around topless, in heels, up and down stairs, with lavish headdresses and elaborate decorations strapped to their backs."[8]

Fast pacing has been a key element of the spectaculars ever since the 1920s. In *And So We Go On*, a 1928 show in a Pathé film of six minutes (available on Youtube), one dancer does a solo with back flips and in another routine a female dancer jumps up onto another. A joke follows of asking if Einstein could count the steps. Pete Menefee has frequently said that Donn Arden brought a Paris show and gave it an American flair, and that the rapid pacing is American.

Both the Tropicana and the Stardust shows became legendary "must sees" for tourists to Las Vegas. The Las Vegas sequence of *The Godfather* (1972) and a scene from Elvis Presley's *Viva Las Vegas* (1964) were filmed at the Tropicana. The movie *Showgirls* was partly filmed on location at the Stardust and its plot revolves around the competition of two showgirls to be the Stardust's top dancer.

Arden contrasted *C'est Magnifique*, the first edition of the Lido show at the Stardust Hotel, with Minsky's. The Lido show was called a spectacular production and the costumes, sets and action were unprecedented. Arden commented that Minsky's, the first topless show in Las Vegas, was different because it was burlesque. "I didn't bring strip tease to America. I brought beautiful nudes done in a classy, elegant way. The Minsky's shows were raucous and bawdy. My shows didn't work that way. They had a touch of class."[9] To Arden it was more provocative to have the nudes semi-covered and to mix the topless and nude with the dressed. The bishop of the local archdiocese told all Catholics to stay away; a bill banning nudes passed in the Nevada State Senate in 1959 but failed to pass in the Assembly.

To cover his performers, Barry Ashton (for his traveling Parisian girlie shows) made rubber sets of breasts. Often, glitter was used to cover nipples: Take eyelash glue and make a circle in the glitter, read the recipe. These were means to avoid entanglement with the law.

Donn Arden also produced two tributes to classic Hollywood, *Hallelujah Hollywood* (in Las Vegas) and *Hello, Hollywood, Hello* (in Reno), which together ran almost 17 years. He was putting the final touches on *Jubilee!* when a disastrous fire occurred at the MGM Grand on November 21, 1981. It killed 85 people and many others were injured. Costumes and scenery were destroyed. Nine months later, the Arden-produced *Jubilee!* opened at Bally's, the MGM Grand's new name.

Jubilee! was the last showgirl revue on the strip when it closed in 2016 after a 34-year run. Bob Mackie and Pete Menefee designed the costumes. A topless "dressed" woman might have 300 chandelier crystals and as many pheasant feathers, and women went through eight to 12 costume changes in a show of about 90 minutes that included the story of Samson and Delilah and the sinking of the *Titanic*.[10] *Jubilee!* had a thousand costumes for "covered" and "uncovered" dancers. The Grand Jewel Box Finale costumes of Bob Mackie were a tribute to Ziegfeld and based on jewel tones—sapphire, emerald, ruby, amethyst, and finally the Bluebells in diamond (white). Ten thousand pounds of Swarovski crystal were said to have been used on the show's costumes, which, according to Pete Menefee, caused a worldwide shortage of rhinestones when *Jubilee!* was in production in 1980.[11] Further evidence of the scale of the spectaculars is that it took 18 people to keep the thousand costumes in shape.

When Pete Menefee came back to update *Jubilee*'s costumes after 30 years, he decided that the pier scene for the sinking of the *Titanic* looked Disneyesque. "Now they look like grown women going to an English tea party.... The designs were drawn in 2½ weeks and constructed in 13—a record."[12] The costumes were made by Silvia's in Las Vegas, with patterns heat-transferred onto fabrics, using computer technology.

The scenery of the spectacular shows, with their on-stage waterfalls and so forth was built in Las Vegas while most of the costumes and even special boots were from Paris. French couture designers like Christian Dior made some of the clothes in the 1980s and 1990s. It further ratified the French connection when Donn Arden created, at the Lido (from Paris) at the Stardust Hotel and *Jubilee!* at Bally's, Paris street scenes, fireworks over the Eiffel Towel, and other ambitious and imaginative themes with the Paris reference. A costumer of the times recalled of Donn Arden that "his creation on the Marquis de Sade theme had costumes half in leather and the other half eighteenth century Marie Antoinette–type dresses."

Michel Gyarmathy directed Paris Folies revue shows in Las Vegas from the first Folies Bergère in Vegas on Christmas Eve 1959 until 1975, an extraordinary cross-cultural association. Gyarmathy spoke to Paul Tabori for *Penthouse* in 1970 about the costumed showgirl icon:

> The boy from Texas who comes to us has, more likely than not, already heard from his father what the Folies Bergère is like. He knows there are staircases, sequined costumes, feathers, and furbelows—and if he does not see all this, he is bound to think that something has gone wrong. So I am forced to stick to these long-established traditions—though I always keep the changes of fashion in mind. I could just as little change the character of the Folies Bergère as a new edition of Grimm's Fairy Tales could make the prince marry one of the Ugly Sisters.[13]

There had already been Folies Bergère productions in the United States, in New York at the Broadway Theater (1939), and the Winter Ballroom in San Francisco (1944), when Barbara Walters' father Lou sold the Latin Quarter in New York and brought the Folies Bergère to the Tropicana. "Las Vegas brought him a new breath, said Walters. "There are so few extravaganzas now and no one did it better than my father."[14] Robin Leach of the *Las Vegas Sun*, noting the French connection, called it "the longest-running Parisian cabaret show."[15] Gyarmathy said in the his candid *Penthouse* interview:

> There is a Folies Bergère revue in Las Vegas—which I have been producing myself for the last seven years. The Casino de Paris also had productions in Las Vegas, and they are all successful. The Americans are wizards at producing their own type of entertainment—but the reason they invite us to work in the States is that only we French can turn out truly Parisian revues. I should say we foreigners—as most of the great Paris spectaculars are produced by what the French call les sales étrangers, the bloody foreigners.[16]

For the performers to look French was a matter of making them appear imperfect:

> A girl, cunningly and lovingly dressed—or undressed, if you like—always has the ways and means to improve and enhance nature. A nude girl has nothing to speak for her except her nudity. Parisian girls, by and large, are charming and delightful and not at all sophisticated as the American girls are. Let me tell you a little anecdote to illustrate my point—to explain why the Parisienne is so popular and ravishing. In our Las Vegas revues only half the company is French—the other half is made up of American girls. This is according to union rules, of course. During the rehearsals it became evident that the American girls were working much harder—it was striking how much more seriously they took their job than my French girls. The management asked me to tell the American girls not to be such eager beavers, to slack off a little, to chatter and gossip, to miss an occasional step, to forget about mechanical precision....
> Too much neatness and efficiency, I think reduce feminine charm—certainly in my business.[17]

The ties with Paris were innumerable and reciprocal. In 1966 Jerry Jackson, from the Midwest, like Donn Arden, was asked to choreograph the hundredth anniversary show of the Folies Bergère in Paris. From 1975 Jerry Jackson did the Paris Latin show at the Tropicana, as artistic director and then costume director when costumes began to be made *in situ*. His costume designs are sophisticated, perfectly in line with the traditional charm but surprising and ebullient. And certain tableaux, like Gyarmathy's of Chinese ivory figures have inspired tableaux in shows in many countries.

Red and black Folies Bergère costume design, 1983, by Jerry Jackson (courtesy Special Collections and Archives, University Libraries, University of Nevada, Las Vegas).

Featuring French Cachet

Las Vegas was inventing itself as the entertainment capital of America and the French music-hall-had the sexy flair the city wanted to project. French cachet continued as part of all the spectaculars for over a half-century, with Parisian imports from the Lido, the Folies Bergère and the Casino de Paris, culminating in the construction of the Paris Hotel on the Strip; the Paris opened in 1999 with fireworks shot from the impressive "toy" Eiffel

Folies Bergère costume, including an elaborate sequin-and-feather headdress (photograph by Karan Feder, courtesy Nevada State Museum Las Vegas).

Tower. That the shows, dancers and costumes had a Parisian stamp was continuously advertised to promote Las Vegas entertaining. A 1960 press release, for example, read, "As the decade ends, the Tropicana brings its second magical show to the Strip. On Christmas Day, it unveils … direct from Paris, FOLIES BERGERE."

It is not known to what extent the owners of a hotel-casino in mid-century Las Vegas might have strategized to exploit the frivolous mood of the Parisian music-hall; perhaps this was merely top entertainment in a non–Puritanical locality, or perhaps there was psychology, that a carefree, sexed up mood was a good ethos for gambling receipts. We know the showgirl spectaculars in Las Vegas had big budgets and longevity, and that the advertising for them carried forth the French cachet consistently. The formula of high kicks, bare breasts, and astonishing costumes and sets was, naturally, an act of audacity that stayed fresh because of all the talent associated with these. A glance at the evolving costumage of one Las Vegas show, at the Tropicana, gives a sense of how the balance shifted from Parisian.

The Folies Bergère came to America in 1959. As the show changed year to year it was known as a new "edition." In 1966 the advertising for the 14th edition fea-

Top: Close-up of Folies Bergère costume headdress (photograph by Karan Feder, courtesy Nevada State Museum Las Vegas). *Middle:* Bra of Folies Bergère costume (photograph by Karan Feder, courtesy Nevada State Museum Las Vegas). *Bottom:* Close-up view of bra from a Folies Bergère costume (photograph by Karan Feder, courtesy Nevada State Museum Las Vegas).

tured the Eiffel Tower with the Paris skyline in the background. The show had a number that featured women nude on top (just a see-through half shirt of beads) with gigantic feathers at rear, back and head, and a panoply of costumes referencing Europe, such as a number with traditional Russian outfits and a set design of a Russian castle, an authentic cancan, and one production number with a traditional European cathedral background (complete with pretend stained windows).

The cancan costumes in the 15th edition of the Folies at the Tropicana in 1975 seem slightly Old West in comparison with those from 1960. The Paris 1920s street bandit scene had an American gangster movie look and an Art Deco background. One number called "Fairytale" was set at Versailles and had eighteenth-century period costumes and wigs along with the huge iconic feathers.

In the 16th edition of the show, Jerry Jackson introduced the "modern Folies," meaning a section where the showgirls danced to current rock songs, by Michael Jackson, Marvin Gaye and David Bowie ("Let's Dance"), as well as a sleek space fashion theme number. Jackson used the French court "Fairytale" number again with a background of hanging vines and flowers. The show began and ended with the classic Parisian showgirl look whereas the middle of the show had the different, contemporary texture. There were fewer feather costumes than the previous edition.

The 17th edition, which premiered in 1997, had a cast of over 100, and about 4,000 costume pieces and accessories. Showcasing the "progress of women," the show took the audience through different decades and included iconic images like the flapper, Rosie the Riveter, and the suffragist. It featured more nudity than previous editions, and was billed that way as well. Of the fabric samples Jackson stapled to drawings many seem synthetic, some probably Lycra and stretch velvet; still a lot of beading and sequins.

In 1984, Jackson was hired by Michel Gyarmathy to choreograph the 100th anniversary of the original Paris "Folies." In 1997, Jackson staged the 80th anniversary of "Casino de Paris" in Paris.

According to Maggie Bukowski, a fashion historian specializing in nineteenth century America who has researched the spectaculars, the Parisian source for the showgirl extravaganzas was still a major advertising point for the 18th edition of the Folies, with a cast that included both French and American showgirls.

The Folies Bergère lasted almost 50 years in Las Vegas. Eventually sequins, beads and themed costumes gained importance with fewer of the huge feathered costumes of the earlier editions. A 2002 memo about changes in the show said that since the outbreak of the bird flu feathers have doubled in cost to import.

The *Lido de Paris* started playing at the Stardust Hotel in 1958 and that show ended in 1991. Before the Lido show arrived, New York impresario Lou Walters, Barbara Walters' father, presented Jayne Mansfield in *French Dressing*, advertised as "a gay Parisian revue with dozens of continental stars and exquisite girls." In early advertising for the Lido as the Folies, the fact that the show was from Paris is hugely important. As the years went on, the French origin was mentioned but is not the most salient fact. What became more important are the changes different iterations go through and the fact that the shows have run so many years.

The particular name of the Lido show when it first played in the U.S., at the Stardust Hotel in Las Vegas, was *C'est Magnifique*. From the *Las Vegas Sun* in 1991: "The Lido posed a couple of historic footnotes, not the least of which was the fact that it brought the first bare breasted female dancers and showgirls to the Las Vegas Stage." The Lido stuck with more traditional showgirl attire—feathers, sequins, beads, but did contain some other costumes such as traditional colorful European peasant and more elaborate court dresses. The Folies at the Tropicana branched out more in terms of costuming. The *People Weekly* of March 18, 1991, noted: "Derived from the original production of 1928, Lido operated on the eternal principle of showcasing women long of limb, sinuous of step, and bountiful of bosom."[18]

Steve Wynn conceived the Bellagio as an alternative destination to Paris, New York, and San Francisco. The cynicism in the media, he said when it opened, about his monumental resort was high: "I wanted to make it impossible for them not to smile. I wanted to wipe the cynicism right off their face.... The opportunities that are afforded by gaming should allow us the freedom to explore the limits of good taste."[19]

The Bellagio opened in 1996. The Paris Las Vegas that opened three years later took the Parisian referent to the limit, with its half-size Eiffel Tower whose back legs descend to the casino floor, two-thirds-size Arc de Triomphe, French pastries, and cartoons of cancan dancers on slot machines.

The circus ghost was still there. William L. Fox, in his study of the meaning of the entertainment, notes, "In the early days of working with tigers in their act, Siegfried and Roy used to turn a young woman into one of the animals, a tidy metaphor for how their routine sublimated the sexy showgirl revues on the Strip into a magic act: exotic women transmuted into exotic cats."[20]

Oscar Wilde in *A Woman of No Importance* (1893) quipped, "Life's aim if there is one is always to be looking for temptations."[21] In the world of showgirl revues, the temptation has been to always go more extravagant.

Most Americans today see a semblance of showgirl costumes in Rockefeller Center in New York, where today the Rockettes do their line dancing and synchronized high kicks in bright glitter. The Rockettes began as the Missouri Rockets in 1925. They were renamed the Roxyettes as performers at the Roxy Theater. Then they became part of the opening show at Radio City music-hall in 1932, and were renamed the Rockettes in 1934. The set and costume designer was the Italian Marco Montodoro who had departed Paris for New York a few years earlier. He replaced Vincent Minnelli.

It is amazing that historical consciousness is such that the Nevada State Museum has archived the *Jubilee!* costumes. Meanwhile Karen Burns, once a dancer in the *Hello, Hollywood, Hello* extravaganza, acquired its costumes which she keeps in repair in her warehouses in Reno:

> My favorite dress was a ball gown in "The Crystal Palace Ballroom on Nob Hill." It was for a scene of elite dancers, lots of wealth and beauty, and we looked like it. All the costumes of six or eight were in tints of chocolate, rust, and muted orange, a brown palace, embroidered with gold sequins and Swarovski crystals. The costumes were floor-length, with a long train held up in one hand and then the other. The men were in tuxedos and we waltzed. That was when I felt the most elegant. I wore the dress and I own it. People don't think of an evening gown in a revue but, today, a celebrity could wear this on the Red Carpet. She would have to be the size. The showgirl had to fit a costume. It could only be altered so much.
>
>   The handwork was incredible. It was done in big workshops but sometimes in the smaller shows costumes were made by performers who had the skill. A female impersonator I knew designed and made his own. I would drive by his house and see him with his friends who came to thread needles and watch soap operas and smoke. It took him 10 hours a day for a week at least to sew on each bugle and teardrop.[22]

Karan Feder, guest curator of costume & textiles at the Nevada State Museum, Las Vegas, is acquainted with the showgirl costumes' structure and embellishment:

> A traditional embellishment employed in cabaret costume is silver plated crystal chain link trim. Each individual rhinestone on the linear trim is encased in a Tiffany mount within a metallic linking system. Some of the rhinestone chain link elements are attached to a wire foundation while others are designed to drape around the curvatures of the female form and to freely move in unison with the dancer. This material is very long lasting and dazzling yet difficult to alter and repair. When any maintenance is called for, the expertise of a seamstress, a solderer, and a welder are required.

Two showgirls in *Fascination*, an outdoor spectacle in Provence, August 18, 1996. Photograph by Philippe Garner.

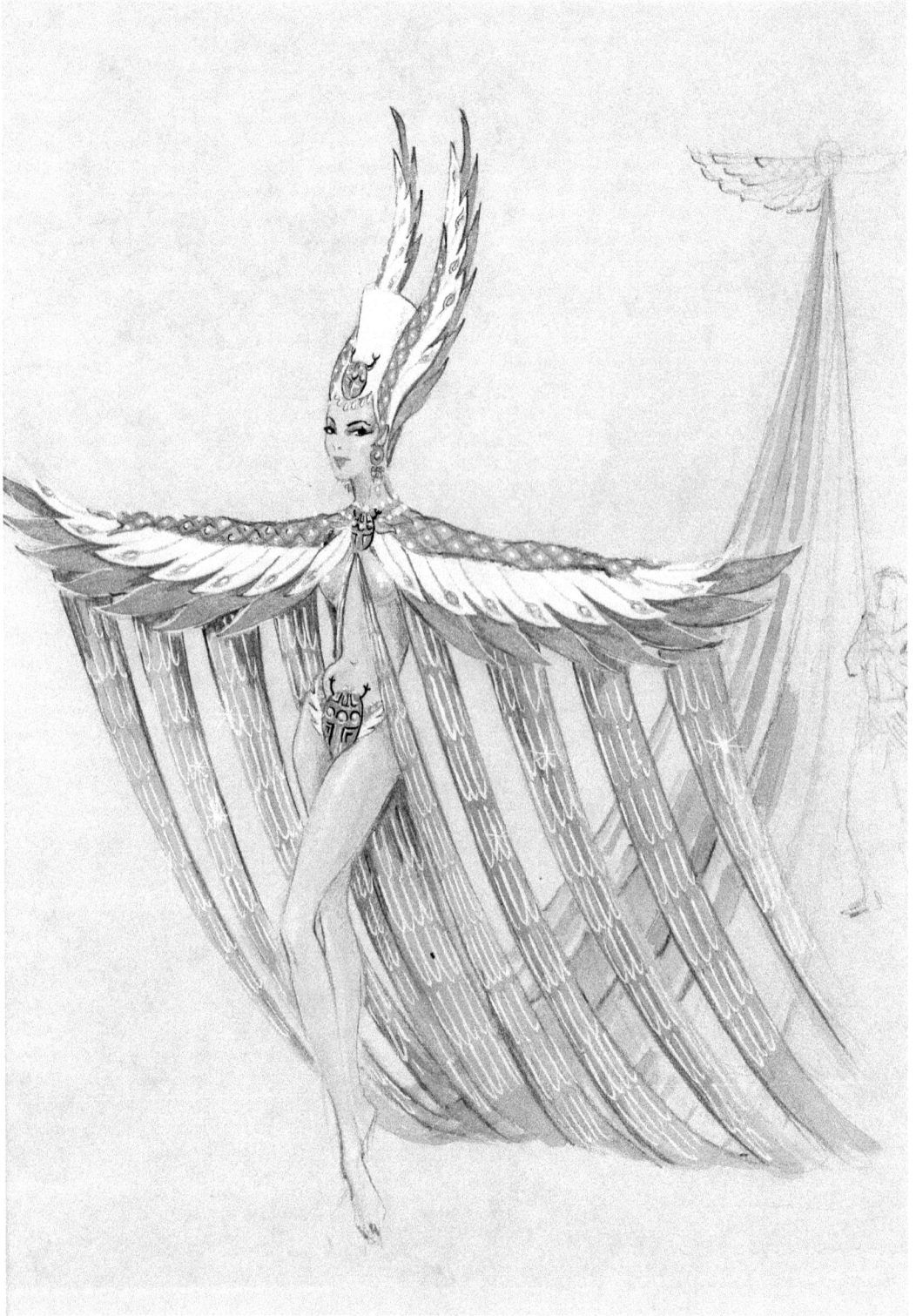

Design in green and white by Bill Campbell for a show at Desert Inn, Las Vegas, c. 1968–1970.

The level of detail used by designers for the Folies Bergère in Las Vegas varied from person to person. Feder notes:

> Three designers all made costumes in the cabaret genre and it's easy to see the difference. The Parisian was more detailed, with a light delicate statement. The showroom in Paris was more intimate and all the artwork could be seen from the front row. For the American setting there was no need for the delicate work anymore. What Gyarmarthy had drawn transferred in a louder, in your face way. A lot had to do with the sheer scale of the stage.

"Paris on the Strip" was the title of an article run by *Showbiz* on April 20, 1997, which mentioned that Jackson staged the 80th anniversary of "Casino de Paris" in Paris.

Design in red by Bill Campbell for a Las Vegas show (courtesy Special Collections and Archives, University Libraries, University of Nevada, Las Vegas).

The *Las Vegas Review Journal* of July 4, 1958, noted: "Those who have seen the show in Paris say it has lost none of the flavor nor any of the zest of its Parisian counterpart, as it was brought here intact from Europe." On September 3, 1958, it was stated: "Never before had such an entertainment event been seen in America! For the first time the gayest of gay shows brought from Paris."

Two Costumers

Pete Menefee had an impressive career as a dancer before designing costumes. In the movie *Mary Poppins* he played one of the chimney sweeps. Designing costumes, like fashion design, is a competitive, fast-paced, demanding business yet Menefee, who has won two Emmys for costume design, was admired for his laid-back creativity.

My Approach to Design
PETE MENEFEE[23]

I have always drawn, since I was a tiny child. I discovered one day in our library that we had a set of maroon books (the encyclopedia) that had four blank pages at the front and four at the back. I got to the G's before my folks discovered what was up. After that, I was supplied with paper....

I never took art classes in school; I was in a college prep class that took doubles in languages and math. It was a surprise that my first design jobs were as a sketch artist. I was staff sketch artist at NBC for a bit. I've no idea where the ideas come from but I've never had a problem designing. I do approach it as a problem to be solved, in design as well as construction. I think I have a very meat and potatoes approach to designing and I am not obsessed with clothing—I'm not one of those designers who have a garage full of costumes. It's always been just a job for me.

Designing with Art and Attitude
BY MISTINGUETT[24]

I've had two great passions in my life, dance and design. Both have haunted me my entire career. When I'm involved with one the other becomes part of the process and I find myself doing both and I'm in heaven. When I design costumes for my choreography everything makes perfect sense.

My work as a dancer, choreographer and an artist combined give me the perfect job, drawing costumes that come to life on stages all over the world.

My only enemy is budget. A bigger budget allows me freedom to create costuming with opulent fabrics, beautiful feathers and lots and lots of sparkle. But on the other hand, a small budget challenges creativity and oftentimes produces some of my best work.

Designing and drawing costumes requires a sense of humor, a point, or an obvious story. Like the moves of the dance, the costume needs to compliment and show the human body in a pleasing way. Line is very important, and movement of the costume is

Mistinguett's showgirl reunion performance, 2009 (photograph by and courtesy of Nasser K).

critical. This is why choreographers make the best costume designers; they know how it feels to move and use the pieces to the max. Nothing is more stunning than a dancer who knows how to work a skirt. And nothing more hideous than a costume that works against the movement.

Once a show is sold and the music is selected, as a choreographer, I design how I want the number to be presented. Nothing you do can be done without the entire show in your head … pacing, timing, color, and budget all have a say in what the costuming will be on the dancers. The attitude of the number is where I start. Strong, lyrical or fun determines what pieces play the most expressive part of the dance.

Elements of the costume that need to be involved with the choreography are the most important part of the planning. If a skirt is involved, then the movement needs to make the most of that skirt to be effective. Making sure that that skirt is made from a fabric that is easy to move and reacts to the movement is first and foremost critical. After that, the rest is easy. Fit, flash and how to maintain the quality of the costume are second to function. Then it becomes a question of style … that's where designers differ the most. To have a "style" that your reviews credit to your work is the highest compliment to your career especially when they recognize it as award-winning. It doesn't get better than that!

The formula of beautiful bodies, lavish costumes and the cancan came to the U.S. first with a touring company of the Folies Bergère. The Tropicana Hotel hired the production and other hotels followed suit—the Stardust Hotel got Donn Arden's *Lido* show and the Dunes Hotel wanted a show and got *Casino de Paris* (this ran from 1963 to 1981), which was owned by the company that owned the Moulin Rouge.

Along the way the laws regulating the public display of nudity determined the costumes that were used. When the Folies Bergère opened at the Tropicana Hotel in 1959, the ban-the-nudes bill failed to pass the Nevada State Assembly.

The lure was the sexuality and level of nudity which had been part of the Paris shows for many years. At first the nudes were not allowed to move but they could be put on discs and the boys would turn them. Then the shows graduated to pasties; these were made of cardboard or buckram with sequins or glitter and could have tassels, and the showgirls could walk. Next they graduated to glue and glitter. Then Barry Ashton, who had brought more class than the old burlesques to the Silver Slipper, did full rubber nude breastplates with embroidery on one side, at the Aladdin. That ended the fight except the showgirls were still not dancing. It was the Lido with the Bluebells, where Miss Bluebell brought covered dancers, nude dancers, and uncovered showgirls who just paraded around. Many of them were girls from the street without dance training and they sometimes couldn't count music.

Once nudity became legal, then, always, bigger was better. Showgirls were constantly having breast modifications with silicone. This became very dangerous, as dangerous as the effect was fabulous. If one girl was big another wanted to be bigger.

There were different types of G-strings. For instance, the bicycle clip, imported from the Folies Bergère, which went up the butt and was a bitch to walk in. It resembled a chastity belt and was made with spring steel and padded to stay in place.

In the 1970s and 1980s no fewer than ten major and five minor shows ran at once in Vegas. The showgirl spectaculars had the more lavish costumes while other venues, like Caesars Palace, had "star policy" where the headlining Hollywood star was the focal point.

Donn Arden's productions competed with Barry Ashton's; if one used rhinestones more, then the other did it; they were always challenging each other. Folco would come from Paris and make changes on designs for a Lido show; the actual costumes continued to be made in Europe. If, say, a costume was caught in scenery, or if four more girls were added, Folco would make the change, then leave. More than one designer would work on a show: sometimes Freddy Wittop did the first half and Folco the second. Pete Menefee did most of the *Jubilee!* show and Bob Mackie did the finale. You could have two or three costume designers but only one set designer because more than one was volatile.

  Certain shows were covered. Then the costume had to be emphatically sexy. Her assets could be pushed up with corset and bra. The costume had to be skin-tight, yet she also had to move.[25]

It was like salt water mixing with fresh. In Las Vegas, many designers created stunning costumes consistent with the French tradition of being dressed fabulously in undress. Eventually even the showgirls' shoes were U.S.–made. The following account of important designers is adapted from the Collection Guide of the University of Nevada Las Vegas Library, courtesy of the director of archives, Su Kim Chung:

> These shows and designers established their own defining style. José Luis Viñas, Folco, Pete Menefee, Bill Hargate, and Bob Mackie, whose costumes for the big French shows of Donn Arden or Frederick Apcar, were international figures in the world of design. Lesser known designers like Josephine Spinedi, who designed for Harold Minsky and Matt Gregory, brought new styles within the context of the traditional showgirl. Spinedi, who designed classic showgirl costumes, also incorporated modern design and fashion, into Matt Gregory's smaller hip shows like *Mad, Mod World*, *The Feminine Touch*, and *Pony Express*. Most of the hotel dance lines were costumed, and changed costumes throughout the show. In many respects, and certainly for the less kinetic lines like the Copa Girls, the costumes and their display were the show. Even for the Donn Arden dancers their costumes often stole the show, and numbers became identified by the costume, not by the music. It reflected the tradition of modeling which formed an integral part of the elaborate French shows, and of Ziegfeld's follies, where statuesque women in ornate hats or headpieces stepped carefully down staircases, or used their accessories like feathered fans to produce an abstract choreographed visual effect.

Just as La Belle Otéro came from Spain and Mata Hari from the Netherlands, talent came from many nations and brought their flair. Vassili Sulich was the principal dancer of the Lido de Paris who crossed over into the U.S. and danced a nude adagio at the Tropicana's Folies Bergère. Vassili Sulich went on to form the Nevada Dance Theater, where he sometimes used motifs and costumes deriving from his native Dalmatia. José Luis Viñas was a Spaniard; he was known for his use of exotic and luxurious textiles and materials including chinchilla, velvet, fox and swan skin.

Salt and Pepper Wedding

Lena Horne and Ella Fitzgerald sang at the Thunderbird Hotel but it was two decades later, not until about 1980, that black women performed as showgirls, in the show *Jubilee!* It is said that when all the dancers were photographed for a billboard, all the faces were painted white, and that after controversy, the MGM Grand Hotel brought the billboard down.

When researching this book, friends took me to the Clark County Heritage Museum to a memorable Christmas exhibition. When I got to the wedding chapel I had déjà vu. It was like a pretty stage set for a movie musical and I'd seen it in a stack of snapshots belonging to Gary Stromberg. He had wed a charismatic dancer named Chelsea Brown in Las Vegas.

The Way We Were
GARY STROMBERG[26]

I met Chelsea in 1968. I was a music publicist at that time representing Ray Charles and Chelsea was the solo dancer who opened Ray's show. We were both very young and just starting our careers. Ray had begun a short tour when I spotted Chelsea, whose bright eyes and stunning smile lit up a room. I immediately set my sights on her and soon made my move. Our relationship got off to a rocky start, though, when she came off stage one night after a performance she didn't think was very good, and she started to cry. I said something stupid, like, "Leave the diva alone," which didn't go over well with her. Soon after, I apologized, and we started dating. The rules for employees of Ray's touring party were that no one was allowed to fraternize with other members of the company, so Chelsea and I had to sneak around to see each other. Late night calls between our hotel rooms led to a clandestine affair.

After the tour ended, Chelsea and I became a couple and she got a new job dancing in Connie Stevens' Las Vegas Hotel Review. We decided to get married. We had only been going together a short time but I was crazy about her. I flew up to Vegas to meet Chelsea and made arrangements for us to get hitched at one of those sleazy factory wedding chapels. Since we were on our own with no family attending the wedding, we needed a witness and "best man." The only person we knew there was Connie Stevens who generously agreed to join us at the chapel.

The wedding, as I recall, was one of the strangest events I've ever been involved in. I arrived at the chapel first, so I could make arrangements with the minister, who turned out to be an old Southern Baptist, decked out in a Madras sports coat, sporting a thick Southern accent. Not the man most likely to bless the marriage of a nice Jewish boy and a lovely African American young woman!

Chelsea arrived with Connie while I was negotiating with the minister. She ducked into a dressing area to change into her wedding dress, not wanting me to see her before the ceremony. When I paid the minister, he escorted me into this tacky little chapel, with all kinds of fake flowers and decorations. After positioning himself on a small stage the minister turned on a pre-recorded version of the Wedding March and waited for the bride to make her entrance.

As my brown-skinned beauty started to walk down the aisle, I saw the minister's jaw drop, shocked at the prospect of marrying a black woman and white man. I looked up at the racist fellow and said to myself, "This is going to be good!" Chelsea had no idea what the minister's feelings about us were, but I sure could tell by the disgusted look on his face. To the minister's credit, he went ahead and performed the brief ceremony, but when he haltingly said, "You may kiss the bride," he winced and turned his head away. I wanted to laugh, but I wanted to kiss Chelsea more, so I ignored this fool.

Connie Stevens had no idea what was going on with the minister; she was just happy to witness our vows. As we made our way outside, Connie ran ahead to the exit, turned, and began yelling "hooray" while throwing rice at us. We all laughed and jumped into a waiting limo I had hired to motor us back to the hotel.

Later that night, I went to see my new wife perform in Connie's lavish show at the Flamingo Hotel. There she was, "the best man" at our wedding, on stage in her gorgeous cerulean blue gown, which drew out the color of her distinctive sky blue eyes, while my new wife and her dancing partner, Cheryl, labored away in their sexy silver sequined bikini costumes and enormous white ostrich feather headpieces which contrasted beautifully with their ebony skin. White three-quarter length gloves and silver stiletto heels completed the ensemble. How they could dance in those shoes baffled me.

Connie had arranged for me to have a ringside seat and midway through the show she stopped to introduce her two young African American dancers, Cheryl Weinberg, who was half black and half Jewish, and the newly married Chelsea Stromberg! The names Weinberg and Stromberg attached to these black beauties drew a huge laugh which Connie really enjoyed. She then called me out to stand and take a bow, as the proud new groom. It was one of the highlights of the show and one of the proudest moments of my life, seeing my new wife on stage, shining like the eventual star I knew she would become.

The newlyweds ended up on the cover of *Ebony* magazine—a Sixties salt and pepper poster couple. Stromberg speaks of Chelsea as a talented dancer but outstanding in terms of charisma, with a smile that reached out to the audience with rare force. Showgirls have not improvised. They are given the costume and may not even touch the headgear that goes at the summit of what they wear. The expressive feature, the exception to the uniform look, is the showgirl's face. She does the makeup herself and the smile is her own. One readily sees things like attitude and spirit in all the close-up photography. Even a blink can be coy or restrained.

"When I don't have my lashes, I feel naked," pop singer Nicki Minaj has said. A contemporary showgirl puts on her lashes with industrial-strength glue, but mid-century performers made their own of paper.

Makeup has made the showgirl larger than life. Applying it in front of a mirror has been an act of placing herself on display. This is an iconic subject for photographing showgirls. "The nude is condemned to never being naked," writes philosopher of art John Berger. "Nudity is a form of dress." The showgirl puts on her nudity with her fake eyelashes, or the red-red lipstick.

And etiquette dictates a glossy smile. Like any physical pose, to maintain it without a break for minutes seems taxing. Showgirls, says Karen Burns, are not, so far as she knows (having performed for two years in *Hello, Hollywood, Hello!* in Reno), instructed about that smile. It is notably wide. It pulls the mouth open and goes sideways—this is no pursed pout. The performer can fix this "muscular" smile more securely than a more natural one that goes up and lights the eyes. The eye makeup helps achieve the impression the smile makes of eagerness to please.

If we consider the smile as making up part of the costume, what distinguishes the smile of a showgirl in a Vegas spectacular from the smile of a music-hall diva? Circus performers have a look of concentration, a tension broken by a flash of smile. The cocottes were too proud of their gorgeous togs to care much about a smile. A Jane Avril or La Goulue looks cheeky in paintings and photographs; the mouth tends to be set in almost a smirk. The frozen sparkle of a 1910 Ziegfeld smile by 1950 was a Hollywood smile of sheer advertisement as if the showgirl leaned out of a Cadillac car. The music-hall performer whose smile was her fortune was Mistinguett. She managed, with it, to say, "I am enjoying myself to the hilt, I am holding nothing back. Whether I appear before you in yards of plumes or dress in an urchin's rags, my smile is unique and imprints itself on you."

TEN

Interpretations

"Femme tu mets au monde un corps toujours pareil. Le tien."
—Paul Elouard, *Tu te Lèves*

Showgirl Fashions in Tennis

The spectacular revues have passed the baton of their glamorous costumes to sports. A high cadre of female tennis players play in sexy nontraditional outfits that incline towards showgirl costumes. Wimbledon, the world's oldest and most prestigious tennis tournament, has maintained an all-white tennis code and a gambit in June 2016 for an ultra-feminine style at the Championships resulted in a clash. That year, all Nike Court female athletes, as per the contracts with their sponsor, were required to wear Nike's short pleated baby doll style dress when they competed at Wimbleton. The outfit got some thumbs down for drawing too much attention to the body when lifting up in a breeze (some athletes also disputed its practicality). Nike recalled the dress.

At the top level of tennis, however, it is no longer accepted that color will distract an opponent. Maria Sharapova received fascinated attention for a red sequined night-play dress at the U.S. Open in 2007.

In particular, Venus and Serena Williams, since becoming the tennis world's super-stars, have tweaked traditions of court attire. Their standout outfits get media coverage and drawings of what Venus, in her EleVen brand, will wear on the courts appear seasons in advance. At the 2010 French Open, Venus wore a low-cut black and red corset held up by spaghetti straps, with a lace flounce skirtlet that looked in photos like half burnt bits of crushed paper. The style referenced the cancan or the Western saloon; complaints were that it looked as if Venus wasn't wearing underwear. *The Sun* (UK) opined: "Perhaps an outfit to reserve for use behind closed doors."

The tiresome question whether Venus had on underwear, raised six months before at the Australia Open, indicates that the media was precisely thinking "showgirl." She wore a canary yellow outfit where an open yellow lattice connected to shimmering metallic short shorts.

If one player creates a stir by being racy in her choice of court wear, another will compete with her. Harking back to the turn of the century, as Venus did in her black and red corset, seems doubly appropriate since the first Ladies Championship at Wimbledon was 1884 and the music-halls were beginning to flourish.

Showgirl Fashions on Ice

What is a showgirl without feathers? Skating ensembles reflect fashion trends and technical advances. Individuals push style forward and sartorial scruples hold them in check.

In the 1990s the showgirl look took off in competitive skating. Brad Griffies was attending the University of Delaware, which had a rink where skaters trained for national and Olympic competitions. He had started sewing for fellow skaters when he was 15, thanks to the prescient gift of a sewing machine from his grandparent. "I was there locally" is how he accounts for his launch from college undergraduate into one of a handful of skating designers at the top level worldwide.

On display in Griffies' workshop in Atlanta, Georgia, are some of his custom-made costumes. One is similar to the dress he created for Gracie Gold, dip-dyed so the ombré fades downwards from pastel blue to midnight blue: "She initially wanted white but when I sent her two the blue convinced her." The cuffs are embellished with six rows of Swarovski crystal beads and the nude mesh over the body-fitting dress blazes with hundreds of rhinestones, each the size of a Pez candy. The finely sewn border could be on the gown of a Byzantine princess.

> In the 1980s and 1990s, everything was sewn on. Now my costumes are unusual as they still involve a lot of hand-sewing…. Sharp crystals would be dangerous if they fell to the ice but the E-6000 glue adheres the rounded ones well to the mesh. Back in the 1980s prongs were used to set the crystals, but a skater could get caught in the metal. To be sure that the dress doesn't pull when put on and taken off over the hips there is a side or back zipper at an angle.
>
> My assistant does the first steps and as designer I do the applique, beading and finish sewing. My vision is to be dramatic, subtle, and sleek.
>
> A choreographer may require strongly themed costuming but that doesn't interest me. I want a sparkling sleek monochromatic look. And I feel with ice—different from a showgirl going down the stairs—that you don't want the costume to take away from the triple or spin. You don't want the dress to wear the skater. You want it to be a frame on a picture.
>
> The showgirl risqué is pure trompe l'oeil. The mesh to the top of the bodice or the neck, forming a teddy, is necessary for comfort and to execute the moves, as the body suits were in the early circuses before they were worn by showgirls for "decency." Everyone has her own look. Even gymnasts all have the same style whereas in skating it's all about personal style. And sleek fit. You can draw out an amazing design on paper but on the body have it be unflattering. Of all types of what you may call showgirl costumes, which all require careful fitting, skating outfits require it the most. The biggest thing is where the skirt is placed on the dress. If not placed just right the total effect is off. Usually I do waist and skirt more at a V, which gives more space to work with on the torso. The French cut, as we call it, covers but lengthens the line.[1]

Griffies' first Olympic costume, for Kimmee Meissner, had very delicate points of reference to belly dance—the chain jewelry on the midriff: The athletic movements performed by the skater mean she can't have heavy decoration or the costume would droop. Once, Griffies reassured a mother whom he felt couldn't afford a costume. "Don't worry," I said, "It's about landing your jumps." "Wrong!" she replied. "Looking sensational makes my daughter skate better."

Sonja Henie (1912–1969) from Norway was the first international athlete superstar. The "Ice Queen" won her first world title in 1927 wearing a white velvet ensemble that ended above the knee. She was the first to show her calves or wear shoulder straps and she changed the women's skating fashion from black skates to white. Henie dressed with glamour on the ice and off. She got very rich in the 1930s and began to wear Van Cleef

& Arpels, and starred in Twentieth Century–Fox films. By 1940 a Henie ensemble appeared to be lowcut strapless nude from the hipbone, but naturally it was overlaid with a fine net teddy. Henie's reputation suffered permanent damage when at the 1936 Olympics in Berlin she gave Hitler a Nazi salute, and later shrugged off her gesture as a lack of interest in world politics.

My parents took our family to the Sonja Henie Ice Review in 1952 in Washington, D.C., because the skater was a phenomenon to see, if no longer a heroine. We sat far up in the bleachers and watched her small figure garbed in costumes of sequins, velvet, ruffles, and little caps, flashing her blades in indefatigable performance. At the time and up until 1990, figure skating was based on figure 8s, but I recall jumps and springs in the Sonja Henie show. A Sonja Henie costumed doll was in many shop windows, wished-for by many little girls.

The 1970s in the skating world were the watershed after which the showgirl look came in. Peggy Fleming's mother made the dress she wore when she won a gold medal at the 1968 Olympics and Dorothy Hamill's mother made outfits for her daughter's early triumphs as well. The demure dresses then had a few pearls on them but did not reflect the rock 'n' roll era.

Laura Sheehy was skating's first dress designer, whose creations were tastefully a-glitter, and she ushered in sequins, puffy sleeves and rhinestones. Elaine Zayat in 1983 and Kristi Yamaguchi a decade later skated in intricately detailed costumes by Laura Sheehy. Sheehy innovated little shoulder pads, and used Lycra fabric instead of jersey, and nude mesh. A skimpy look was somewhat stymied by the so-called "Katerina's Rule," a response by the U.S. figure skating commission to the feather-trimmed skirtless skating costume worn by Katerina Witt for a showgirl-themed number in 1988. The USI rule said that "a skirt covering hips and posterior were required for ladies competition." (In 2003 the skirt part of the rule was dropped.) Soon though, gaudy and/or showgirl-inspired became an option. For example, Yamaguchi skated at the 1992 Olympics in a romantic black costume with gold lace overlay that took off from Venetian Renaissance. This is when the *New York Times* carried an article titled, "Skaters Give Showgirls a Whirl" (February 16, 1992).

Vera Wang in 1994 had her simplified wedding dress in stores and promoted it by giving Nancy Kerrigan a costume that derived from it for the 1998 Olympics in Philadelphia—champagne colored with 11,500 rhinestones. Michelle Kwan wore a two-piece Oriental number in 1996 with beads of jewels around the waist, and two years later at the nationals came on in style-setting simple dress, like a bathing suit, no sleeves, spaghetti straps. The look became very short—and after 2010 longer.

Explains Griffies:

> A skater needs a new outfit each year, as well as two pairs of skates a year and she has to pay for ice time. Whereas a showgirl or ballroom dancer performs where a big part is the outfit, when you skate you primarily want to feel nicely put together.... Young skaters look up to the most brilliant skaters and they want that look. For instance, after a Great Gatsby fringed dress was seen on ice in the 2015 season, a lot of people wanted it. It's an evolution. There's not much change year to year in my designs but after 20 years the aesthetic is different. I never stay in the past but mean always to go forward; you know that everything's already been done, which is something I like because I can look at an idea and ask, how can I make it relevant now?[2]

Just as a wooden placard of a nude beckoned customers to the Au Bon Bock cabaret in Montmartre in the 1880s, billboards advertised "Nudes on Ice! Nudes on Ice" in Las

Vegas in the 1980s. Bill Moore did beautiful costumes for 70s shows like *Ecstasy on Ice*, *Spice on Ice* and *Playgirls on Ice*. The stages were small. *Spy Magazine* reviewed *Nudes on Ice*, which Bill Moore produced with James Arnold; it ran at the Union Plaza Hotel from 1988 to 1990:

> Yes, the skaters are on ice, but no, they're not technically nude: they're topless since total nudity in hotel shows is illegal in Nevada. And to make matters even less nude, only four women out of a coed cast of fifteen are topless. The quartet glides across the stage at the beginning of each number, then skates to the side, clomps off the ice and stands motionless, forming a not technically nude proscenium for the forthcoming entertainment.[3]

Conclusion: Continuance in Paris

Charles Rearick wrote in *Paris Dreams, Paris Memories: The City and Its Mystique* (2011) that celebrated Parisian nightspots naturally play to tourists by, to cite Rearick, reproducing set pieces from another era.

Philippe Garner, formerly deputy chairman of Christie's, though he remains involved with the celebrated auction house as an international consultant. His wife Lucilla trained as a classical dancer and had traveled with a troupe as a showgirl, an itinerant career she abandoned after they met in 1975, putting love over a new contract to dance abroad. Garner makes a thoughtful observation about the "uniform" of the showgirl costume:

> The iconic "showgirl" costume is generally associated with a spectacular line-up of girls, rather than a single artiste. It becomes a uniform, emphasizing the generic ideal rather than the individual.
>
> Thinking back through the evolution of glamorous stage spectacle, I believe that the costume really came into focus in Paris in the 1920s within lavish productions at such venues as the Folies Bergère and the Casino de Paris. The iconic look—the briefest of adornments, often in silver fabric and sparkling rhinestones, elaborated with extravagant, typically white plumage—eventually defined itself, and froze in time, in Paris in the post-war years. It became a symbol of Parisian nightlife. The Lido has proved the most enduring showcase for the quintessential look that has today acquired a universal currency.
>
> As a carefully calibrated equation of near-nakedness and acceptability, the showgirl's undress turned eroticism into delightful spectacle. Of course it has a sensual dimension; the girls are chosen for the fine physiques that they put on display; but it is not in the least salacious. The stylization makes it at once sexy and chaste. The showgirls are a central element of a multi-faceted spectacle that is designed to appeal to both sexes; they are not simply an erotic entertainment for male eyes.
>
> Some years ago, I saw a traveling summer show in a small French village that brought together comedy, music, circus-type acts. The poster feature, the showgirls, provided the crowning moments. I was reminded of how emblematic they were, representing a theatrical genre that has become a classic, like the Geisha girl in Japan, a symbol of a culture. The world-renowned Paris spectacles have drawn illustrious endorsement—think of Yves Saint Laurent designing costumes for Zizi Jeanmaire; and note the numerous celebrities, socialites, artists, and aristocrats who have been prominent among the audiences. The iconic showgirl look is not tacky. Is it kitsch? Yes, I guess so, gloriously kitsch and wonderfully camp. Is it vulgar? Yes, in a way, though sophisticated at the same time; somehow it reconciles these seeming opposites.
>
> I am half French and I have always been fascinated by the traditions of style, elegance, glamour associated with Paris. The imagery of fashion and spectacle was an impactful ingredient of my childhood. As a young man, in the early 1970s, I discovered the girls of the Crazy Horse Saloon. They made an indelible impression, very sexy and very chic—a perfect Parisian cocktail, though these were not traditional "sparkles and feathers" showgirls. I was thrilled some years later to see the showgirls of the Lido—as French as the "Marseillaise" or the Eiffel Tower.

Appendix A:
Fashion and the Showgirl
Cassidy Zachary[1]

The showgirl influence is as pervasive as ever in today's fashion scene. Josephine Baker is a perennial favorite of designers from Marc Jacobs to Miucca Prada, while a myriad of versions of the iconic showgirl costume, with its seemingly infinite glitz and sparkle, can often be found on the runway, be it that of Victoria's Secret or Jean Paul Gaultier. No one, it seems, is immune from the showgirl's charms. But the relationship between fashion and the showgirl is nothing new and when Gaultier sends feathered and bejeweled models down the runway he, like his contemporaries, is drawing upon a rich tradition that extends back over one hundred years.

The entertainment and monetary value of high fashion was not lost on the enterprising impresarios of the expanding music hall industry in the early twentieth century. The showgirl was a natural extension of a relatively new phenomenon at this time that used women stage performers to cultivate the consumer gaze. Just like the fashion model and the department store, recently developed concepts which revolutionized the acts of shopping and viewing fashion, so too were actresses, singers, dancers and showgirls recognized as enticing ways to market fashion to women audiences. In effect, fashion, like sex appeal, was a proven selling point, and in the case of the showgirl, audiences were guaranteed both for the price of one ticket.

The foundation of this symbiotic was laid in the dramatic plays of the belle époque, a time when the theater was *the* place to see and be seen by affluent members of society. This was especially true in Paris, the world epicenter of fashion, where the most prestigious of designers, such as Charles Frederick Worth, Jeanne Paquin and Paul Poiret, dressed a host of celebrity clients on and off the stage. Women audiences attended plays expecting to see a designer's latest work, while critics decried certain plays as being little more than thinly veiled fashion advertisements, so imbedded was the display of fashion in the visual and literary narrative.

Lucile and the Ziegfeld Follies

Just as fashion found its way to the theater, theater made its way into the fashion house by means of the fashion show, a newly instituted concept of the 1900s. France might have been the capital of fashion but it was a British fashion designer, Lady Lucile Duff Gordon, who was one of the fashion show's first creators, and one of its greatest innovators. Known professionally by her first name, Lucile rose to international fame and fortune in the 1910s, with branches of her business in London, Paris, New York City and Chicago by 1915. Part and parcel to her tremendous success was her genius ability to market her work to her clientele in the form of "mannequin parades," as her fashion shows came to be known. Lucile's parades were theatrical productions in their own right, complete with a cast of highly trained models, a stage, dramatic lighting, music and even dancing and storytelling—elements that coalesced to create a spectacle of fashion unlike anything anyone had ever seen.

Lucile moved to New York City at the outbreak of World War I, transporting her fashion show and models to a country where the performance of fashion was nothing new. America's multi-million-dollar clothing industry was based on French, not American designs, and department stores created some of the first public fashion shows in the early 1900s in an attempt to capitalize on the excitement surrounding the latest imports from Paris. Free and open to the public, the shows brought an otherwise exclusive event to the masses while simultaneously cultivating an appetite for the theater of fashion. Lucile would expand upon the public fashion show to great success during her time in the country, where she became *the* fashion authority, a carefully crafted image masterminded by the designer herself.

Lucile ensured the far-reach of her influence by a masterful negotiation of two seemingly opposite concepts: exclusive haute couture fashion and mass, public consumption. In addition to designing for her luxury brand, Lucile was led by a "desire to influence the styles worn by the general public" to partner with Sears & Roebuck in 1916 to create one of the first designer ready-to-wear clothing lines in history.[2] It was this same motivation that prompted Lucile the same year to take her fashion shows to the public in rented theaters, where thousands and not just an affluent few could enjoy her work. Lucile's mannequin parades galvanized the popular imagination and, in addition to her nationally syndicated fashion articles and her monthly column for *Harper's Bazaar,* her celebrity extended across the country; the visionary British designer became an American institution. It was a legacy further cemented through a high-profile relationship with the eminent showman Florenz Ziegfeld, Jr., and their re-invention of the showgirl.

From 1915 to 1921, Lucile designed seven installments of the *Ziegfeld Follies*, in addition to numerous acts for Ziegfeld's upscale nightclub *Midnight Frolic* and three of his musical productions, all the while working on her fashion brand. Her costume and fashion designs were not, in fact, mutually exclusive and from the very beginning of her time at the Follies, entire shows were conceived around the display of Lucile fashions. In 1915, the scene entitled "A Girl's Trousseau" featured showgirls, clothed in the height of 1915 Lucile fashion, walking through life-size Lucile fashion illustrations. It was the *Follies of 1917,* however, that Lucile credited with changing theater history, claiming in her memoirs that it was the first revue to introduce the showgirl "who was there simply to look beautiful and wear beautiful clothes."[3] Lucile was certainly not the sole inventor of the fashionable showgirl—fashion had played a part in both the Shubert Brothers' *The Passing Follies* and *The Ziegfeld Follies* since at least 1912. However, the *Follies of 1917* was original in that it marked the debut of a new *type* of showgirl: it was the first time that Lucile's professional fashion models appeared on the music-hall stage. Wearing clothing of a world-famous fashion designer, the models provided a direct link to the glamorous world of high fashion that had not existed before. This added cachet elevated the otherwise anonymous performer into the spotlight, a place once reserved for headlining celebrity talent.

It was after witnessing one of Lucile's packed public performances with his wife, and Lucile client, Billie Burke, in 1916 that the "maker of stars" Florenz Ziegfeld, Jr., was inspired to transplant Lucile's "scene" and its models directly to the music-hall stage. "He sat there and saw the curtain go up on a scene which might have come out of the Arabian Nights," remembered Lucile, "Dolores, a wonderful and magnificent Dolores, in an Eastern gown of brocade sheathing her slim figure, glimmering like an opal with every movement, walked slowly across the stage.... Hebe, Phyllis and Florence followed her, a lovely trio of walking suits, parasols in their hands.... So the parade went on, three hours of it.... Ziegfeld sat it all out to the end" and implored Lucile: "I have got to have that scene of yours for my Follies.... That girl Dolores is marvelous. She will be the sensation of New York."[4]

The Follies of 1917 featured Lucile models in not one but two scenes inspired by her fashion shows, that of the Arabian Nights and the "Episode of Chiffon." The latter was a bridal scene set in a replica of Lucile's showrooms and starred the model Dolores as the "Empress of Fashion." At six feet tall, the statuesque Dolores cut a striking figure in her Ziegfeld Follies debut which simultaneously marked her departure from Lucile's employ. "The whole of New York paid homage to her beauty," recalled Lucile, "Dolores

"Time Keepers" (Everett Collection).

was fêted and worshipped as though she had been a queen. But she never came back to the showroom again—her days as a mannequin were over."[5] Dolores appeared both on the Follies stage and in fashion magazines across the country including *Vogue* and *Harper's Bazaar* where she was featured alongside her fellow Ziegfeld-Lucile showgirls Hebe and Dinarzade.

Lucile's contributions to the Ziegfeld Follies earned the music hall a reputation for being fashion-forward, something Ziegfeld himself would take credit for two years after Lucile's departure from the company: "As a matter of fact, we not only influence but often lead the fashions,"[6] Ziegfeld told *Ladies' Home Journal* in 1923. "It has been my custom to bring back from Paris every year anywhere from twelve to twenty-four gowns, hats and cloaks.... Not the things that are shown to American buyers, but things ahead of the style.... We put the short skirt into every day wear."[7] Of course, the "short skirt" Ziegfeld referred to at the time extended below the knees but indeed, many of today's most ubiquitous articles of women's clothing find precedence in the costumes of late 19th and early 20th century performers, the stage a safe place for experimentation and daring. Showgirls, but also circus performers, dancers, singers and actresses, were the first to wear any length of shortened skirts, shorts, pants and bikinis years before women were brave enough to take the styles from the stage to the streets.

Thanks in no small part to Lucile, the *Ziegfeld Follies* continued to maintain its fashionable associations throughout the 1920s with the full support of *Women's Wear Daily* who regularly reported on the "fashions" seen in the production and on its performers of the stage. So pervasive was Ziegfeld's connection to fashion that in 1931 (one year before he died), he was hired as art director for the Gold Fabrics Corporation. His debut collection of textile designs was entitled "Glorifying the American Girl," in which all of the prints were "inspired directly by some of the Follies beauties who are considered typically American."[8]

Erté

Of course, the Ziegfeld Follies was not the only production to cultivate an intimate relationship with high fashion during this period, nor was Lucile the most famous designer to partner with the music-hall stage. Just as the size and spectacle of the Follies grew throughout the 1910s and 20s, so too did the revue à grand spectacle of post–World War I Paris, which came with its own set of star performers and designers. The most famous of the latter was none other than the "father of Art Deco" himself, the Russian-born Romain de Tirtoff, or as he is most widely known and celebrated, Erté. Despite working right up to his death in 1990 at the age of 97, Erté's name remains synonymous with the 1920s, a period during which he produced a prolific amount of work for both the theater and fashion.

It was while working for the world-renowned fashion designer Paul Poiret that Erté undertook his first costume design job, co-designing the smash hit play *Le Minaret* in 1913 with José Zamora, another Poiret employee. Poiret was given the design credit but the boldly outlined seductresses found in the production's costume illustrations are one hundred percent Erté, his signature style already well developed by this period. After leaving Poiret's employment in 1914, Erté was hired as a designer for American departments stores Henri Bendel and B. Altman and Company, as well as an illustrator for both

Vogue and *Harper's Bazaar*, the latter almost immediately securing an exclusive contract with the in-demand artist to combat competition. From 1915 until 1936, Erté's works appeared in full, vibrant colors on over two hundred covers of the magazine and his designs in black and white within its pages.

Fashion and fantasy merge in Erté's fashion illustrations; each have a story to tell, be it the Queen Amphitrite hunting for the perfect swimming costume or the Goddess Orithyia longing for a new evening gown. One illustration to the next is occupied by regal Amazonian beauties with bold Grecian profiles who appear swathed in lush draped brocade or glittering lamé fabrics. Dripping in tassels of roses or ropes of pearls, they demand the reader's attention; their heavily made up expressions present a posed nonchalant seduction that is as captivating as it mystical. These illustrations earned Erté the magazine's praise as "the foremost designer of original fashions," but his designs were always more fantastical than realistic.[9] While Erté enjoyed a career in fashion throughout his entire life, his most dramatic, magical work was always to be found on the stage.

Beginning in 1916, Erté's beguiling reveries took flight in the French music-halls owned by theater doyenne Madame Rasimi who gave the young artist unbridled artistic expression in his set and costume designs. It was for Rasimi's 1917 revue *Gobette of Paris* that he first worked with the famed performer Mistinguett: "I designed lavish costumes for her, with long trains and huge feather head-dresses, which she had never worn before."[10] Indeed, Mistinguett's name became synonymous with over-the-top costumes and skyrocketing plumed headwear, but it was a look she adopted from another performer: the incomparable and ever-fashionable Gaby Deslys.

Fashion Icons: Gaby Deslys and Josephine Baker

Gaby Deslys is perhaps best remembered today for her role in introducing the first American jazz band to Europe during World War I in the revue *Laissez le Tomber* in which she starred at the Casino de Paris. "It was the birth of the 'Music-hall' as we now know it," recalled Mistinguett of the revue, "with its profusion of ostrich feathers, satins, nudes, monumental sets and spectacular transformation scenes."[11] An internationally renowned performer in her day, Deslys is responsible for setting the standard for the colossal feathered headwear we most associate with the showgirl today. Extravagant displays of dress were an essential and integral component of Deslys' image that she cultivated through high-profile collaborations with famous costume and fashion designers including Étienne Drian and Lucile. "Though it is true that I never imitated anybody," said Mistinguett, "this did not prevent me from eyeing what Gaby Deslys bought, and buying what she had her eye on."[12]

Deslys' theatrical costumes and personal clothing garnered worldwide media attention, but it was her headwear for which she became the most famous. In an article simply entitled "Hats," *The Green Book Magazine* recounted the power of Gaby's mountainous millinery in a 1916 Irving Berlin revue: "When Gaby stepped out at the opening of *Stop! Look! Listen!* New York gasped at the first millinery confection. Throughout the performance it continued to gasp. It has seen plenty of hats in its day, but never such extraordinary headdresses as Gaby of the Lilies wore."[13] Deslys exclaimed to *Theatre Magazine* in 1916: "My hat ... is the soul of my costume.... It is me, my personality, my individuality; not a covering for the head, but an ornament; my whole theory of proper dressing—

wearing something that no one else wears."[14] Deslys' outstanding headwear, worn on and off the stage, defined her career until her untimely death in 1920, but her legacy continues to endure in the costumes of performers such as Cher, Lady Gaga, and of course, the showgirls of the remaining Parisian revues.

Where millinery defined the look of one music-hall star, a very specific skirt defined that of another. The banana skirt worn by Josephine Baker in *La Revue Negre* at the Casino de Paris in 1925 remains the single most iconic costume of Baker's career—and arguably the entire history of the music-hall. However, the *dance sauvage* performances and costumes of Baker's early career largely overshadow her embodiment of high fashion, glamour and sophistication maintained until her death. Baker arrived in Paris in 1925, wearing the same, rather unassuming clothes she wore while an unknown chorus girl in New York City: "a checkered dress with pockets held up by two checkered suspenders over my checkered blouse"[15] but the city, and most specifically the avant-garde designer Paul Poiret, transformed her. In her memoirs, Baker remembered Poiret sculpting a dress directly on her body out "of the most beautiful silvery material I had ever seen.... It looked like a flowing river. Monsieur Poiret poured the gleaming torrent over me, rolled me up in it, draped it about my body, pulled it tight, ordered me to walk, then loosened it around my legs. I felt like a sea goddess emerging from the foam."[16]

Poiret was only the first of many designers to participate in Baker's life-long love affair with high fashion. "All the great designers—Paul Poiret, Edward Molyneux, Jean Patou—were fighting to dress her," recalled Ada "Bricktop" Smith, Baker's contemporary and friend. "She had an apartment right around the corner from the nightclub, and one day I went there and the clothes were piled high on the floor, and I said, 'Josephine, why don't you hang these clothes up?' 'Oh, no, Brickie,' she said, 'they are going to take them away tomorrow and bring another pile.'"[17]After a very public fallout with Poiret over reportedly unpaid bills in 1926 (Poiret sued her for over $200,000 and lost), Baker had her pick from designers eager to work with the sensation of Paris. Collaborations with Madeleine Vionnet, Jean Patou and the luxury fur company Fourrures Max helped to secure Baker's high fashion image, as did her appearances in fashion magazines such as *Femina* and *Vogue*.

Baker licensed her name to a variety of beauty products and was even credited with starting the fad for tan skin in the 1920s. In 1932, *Vogue* asked its readers, "WAS it Josephine Baker who made us all crave brown skins or wasn't it? Certainly, we can't deny that it was that very summer when she first swang from the roof of the Folies-Bergère … that all smart women began furling their parasols and deciding that it would be amusing to be brown."[18] The article acknowledges Baker's influence while simultaneously revealing the racist stereotypes that would follow Baker throughout her career, and ultimately undermine the transfer of her European success to America, her home country. Similar commentary haunted her 1936 debut at the Ziegfeld Follies, but it did not deter *Women's Wear Daily* from extolling Baker's fashionable virtues: "Through her 10 years residence in Paris *la Baker* has cultivated a definite sense of chic, and a reputation for a certain sophistication of style, so that what she wears may be regarded as news."[19]

As Baker's career progressed, so too did her commitment to high fashion, reaching its apex in the 1940s and 1950s with high fashion royalty Balenciaga and Dior. Towards the end of her life, Baker adopted a more utilitarian, practical aesthetic in her private life but her commitment to an elegant, public image remained undeterred. In the 1970s, Baker reportedly agreed to do a documentary with *Folies Bergère* (1985) author Charles

Castle, but on one condition: "I learned that she would require a new wardrobe of clothes to be designed by either Jacques Faths, Christian Dior or Pierre Balmain," remembered Castle.[20] The costs of haute couture combined with Baker's astronomical appearance fee led to the film's derailment but Castle was "greatly excited when a year later she opened at the London Palladium, but this time with a new act, filled with glamour and glitter, feathers and fantasy; her artistry and magic undiminished, she took London by storm."[21]

Glamorous to the very end, Baker performed in a crystal-studded bodysuit and feathered turban just two years before her death, at the now famous "Battle of Versailles" of 1974, a title given by the press to a charity event at the Versailles palace that pitted American against French fashion designers. Baker might have performed for her adopted country of France, but her legacy was on full display in the American fashion show where an unprecedented ten black models appeared, a way paved in no small part by Baker herself. "The appearance of this glamorous black woman, who had defied American racism to find fame abroad was particularly overwhelming to the young black models who were still coming into their own beauty and their own maturity," wrote Robin Givhan in her book *Battle of Versailles* (2015). "Baker's life story had inspired [model] Amina Warsuma, in particular to come to Europe (not America!) to pursue her dream."[22]

Baker's tremendous legacy exists today, not just in the iconic imagery associated with history's most famous showgirl but in black performers *and* models everywhere. The irony that a recent fashion collection inspired by Josephine Baker had only two black models—out of 43—makes a rather ironic statement in revealing that fashion still has a long way to go.

The Showgirl Immortal: Fashion's Model and Muse

Scholars credit the 1930s demise of the spectacular music-hall revue to the advent of the film musical, a new genre that co-opted all the spectacle of the stage for the silver screen. It was a natural progression for the showgirl as author Linda Mizejewski points out in her book *Ziegfeld Girl* (1999): "The Ziegfeld showgirl legend was destined for Hollywood, which—with the advent of sound cinema in 1927—would both immortalize and displace her."[23] However, the genre "would in the long run glorify her as exuberantly as the original Ziegfeld shows, ensuring her presence in popular culture for decades."[24] Indeed, today fashion designers from Bob Mackie to Jean Paul Gaultier, from Marc Jacobs to Prada take inspiration from the showgirl—if not the Ziegfeld Girl in particular, then the codified costume of feathers, sequins and towering heels and headwear that have long been associated with the showgirl performer throughout history.

"The Sultan of Sequins" Bob Mackie has built a fifty-plus year career out of a reverence for showgirl aesthetics. Before venturing into fashion design in the 1980s, Mackie worked for over twenty years as a costume designer for the stage and screen. His designs with his life partner Ray Aghayan for the film *Lady Sings the Blues* earned the duo an Oscar nomination in 1973, but it was the glitz and glamour of the Las Vegas showgirl on which Mackie would stake his reputation, designing costumes for two Las Vegas revues: the Ziegfeld Follies–inspired *Hallelujah Hollywood* and *Jubilee!*, the latter only recently closed in 2016 after a 34-year run. Mackie's famous Starlett O'Hara "curtain" design for Carol Burnett in a *Gone with the Wind* parody on *The Carol Burnett Show* in 1976 has gone down in theater history as one of the funniest, and most enduring, costumes of all time, but it is his designs for another performer, in particular, to which Mackie's name remains synonymous: Cher.

"When Mr. Mackie finally opened a design studio on Seventh Avenue in 1982," wrote *The Wall Street Journal* in 2005, "his fashion shows with themes such as 'Viva Las Vegas' in 1990 made him the most theatrical designer of New York's fashion week."[25] These theatrical associations proved a double-edged sword, according to Mackie: "Nobody felt they could discover me, since they already knew who I was. I had a lot of wearable clothes in my [fashion] collection, but what they thought of me was what I put on [Cher]."[26] Mackie's collaboration with Cher began in 1971 with *The Sonny & Cher Show* and continues to this day. He can be credited with the most memorable and controversial looks of the fashion maverick's career, including the notorious "Mohawk Warrior" ensemble worn to the 1986 Oscars: "Bob kept saying 'are you sure you want to do this?'" Cher remembered years later. "Raymond (Aghayan) called me Bob's Barbie doll.... There was nothing he designed that I wouldn't wear.... He'd walk the line between fashion and costume and that's my favorite place to go."[27] In 2001, the Council of Fashion Designers of America (CFDA) honored Mackie with a special award for his "Fashion Exuberance," presented to him by another long-time client, Diana Ross.

Mackie is only the most famous of several prominent contemporary designers to have toed the line between fashion and costume design in their reverence for the showgirl. The showgirl made repeated appearances in the fashion collections of John Galliano during his tenure at Christian Dior. For the Fall 2002 Couture collection, Galliano sent "skimpy showgirl dresses and hugely extravagant feathered headdresses" down the runway and again in his 2003 Fall/Winter collection, both over-the-top displays for which the designer remains distinguished.[28] In 2006, Galliano was aptly chosen by performer Kylie Minogue to design the costumes for her "Showgirl" tour. Like Galliano, any number of Thierry Mugler's designs find precedence in the showgirl costume. For his Fall/Winter 1997 collection, when Mugler needed to transform model "Eva Herzigova into a showgirl with a vast collar of scarlet plumes, he went to Madame Nicole who holds court at M. Fevrier."[29] Galliano similarly employed Février, the esteemed feathersmith of the theater trade, in his first showgirl extravaganza for Dior the same year: "When Nadja's arm was transformed into the head of a circus pony ... it was Février who supplied the ostrich mane and aigrette headdress," wrote *Vogue*.[30] In the same article, Madame Nicole reveals her special connection to fashion: "I really specialize in shows—the Lido, the Moulin Rouge, the Folies Bergère. Normally it's Lemarié for fashion, but when they need very spectacular things they come to me."[31]

The showgirl tradition is most deeply ingrained in the work of French fashion designer Jean Paul Gaultier, however, whose admiration for the performer began as a small child. "I dreamed of working on a revue ever since I was a little boy and I saw opening night of *Les Foliés-Bergère* on my grandmother's TV," he told *Women's Wear Daily* in 2016. "I got in trouble at school the next day because I was sketching girls in feathers and fishnets."[32] He continued: "Then I did a revue with my teddy bear at home. I pretended he had breasts. The first cone bra I did was for my teddy bear, not for Madonna. I had a strawberry box for the stage, and I put a lot of feathers on my teddy bear for the headdress. I used feathers from my cleaning brush for the finale."[33] Gaultier landed his first job in fashion at the age of 17 after sending in gold and sequin covered fashion sketches to Pierre Cardin. As indicated by collections such as Paris and Its Muses for haute couture Fall/Winter 2000–2001 and Punk Cancan, haute couture Spring/Summer

2011, glitz and sparkle have remained a staple of his work ever since. In perhaps the highest exemplar of his showgirl admiration, Gaultier has created his very own revue. Gaultier's *Fashion Freak Show* is set to open in 2018 at the very place that ignited his passion, the Folies Bergère: "Eccentric, scandalous, provocative, exuberant and funny as ever, Jean Paul Gaultier is shaking up Paris once again by inventing a new kind of entertainment between a revue and a fashion show." Shaking up Paris? Yes. Inventing a new kind of entertainment? I think Lucile and Florenz Ziegfeld might beg to differ but they would certainly be proud.

Appendix B:
The Costume of Costumes

Tracy Jenkins Yoshimura[1]

Everyone can bring to mind an image for the word "showgirl," but from where does this image spring? For many, their first encounter with a showgirl is on film. Iterations of her appear in countless movies, beginning with the earliest ones that depicted versions of the showgirl and her environs as more-or-less direct translations of scenes from the elaborate stage revues where she was born. In this very brief and subjective survey, I will highlight a small number of iconic showgirl costumes from feature-length films from the nineteen teens to the nineties. All have in common the "exposition of female glamour," in the apt phrase of this book's author, through a display of the nearly-nude body in costumes that are by turns sexy, gaudy, inventive, sparkly, and—almost always—feature a headdress.

Theda Bara embodies the "exotic" temptress/showgirl, and in pre–Hays Code Hollywood boasted some of the most revealing costumes captured onscreen. An American, she was promoted by the studio as foreign-born and most often typecast as a vamp from distant times and places. Few of her films survive, but fortunately there are numerous photographs of her characters dressed as versions of the showgirl. Of the many costumes for her starring role in *Cleopatra* (1917, directed by J. Gordon Edwards), I will describe two that are striking for their level of undress. The first comprises a bra top of metallic coiled openwork snakes encircling each breast and deftly covering (biting?) the nipple while revealing much of the surrounding flesh. A heavy linked chain extends up from each snake over the shoulder and hangs down the back. The headpiece is another metallic snake that winds around the head in a band with the asp/cobra rearing up at the forehead, attached to which are long pyramid-shaped earrings. Below Cleopatra's bare midriff is a skirt of what appear to be sheer stiff lamé strips arranged like the flaps of a carwash. She wears a belt which culminates in a vertical pendant of jewel-encrusted metallic plates at center, providing the necessary opacity. She is barefoot but wears a band around one calf, as well as a single armband.[2]

Another of Cleopatra's ensembles can be glimpsed in motion in a tantalizing film clip of a few seconds. She wears a "bra" of two sequined conical discs, in the manner of oversized pasties whose method of attachment may only be guessed at (a not uncommon feature of Bara's tops). A draped cloth of silk chiffon or tulle, attached at one shoulder and extending to the ground, is lavishly embellished with a sequined and beaded lozenge motif ending in a sheer train with stylized floral embroidery, which Bara as Cleopatra wields like a veil, perhaps alluding to Salome's dance. Large feathered earrings are the sole adornment on the head, notwithstanding the actress's heavy-lidded kohl-rimmed eyes. Her feet are bare, and she wears a single close-fitting bracelet.[3]

Bara describes those days in an uncredited interview on YouTube: "We worked awfully hard on making those pictures. For instance, we had no research department at the studio; I worked myself for months with the curator of Egyptology at the Metropolitan Museum of Art. It was great fun, though." One longs to know what the curator described that was translated thus.

If there is a quintessential American showgirl character, she is Ziegfeld's dancer, and quite literally so, as a number of women left the Follies for careers in Hollywood. In her illuminating chapter, "The Ziegfeld Girl and Hollywood Cinema," Linda Mizejewski observes that "[t]he Ziegfeld showgirl legend was destined for Hollywood, which—with the advent of sound cinema in 1927—would both immortalize and displace her."[4] Motion pictures democratized entertainment of a type previously only seen on stage, and the advent of talking pictures made it possible to reproduce a stage show for a fraction of the ticket price.[5] Interestingly, Florenz Ziegfeld, Jr., disliked Hollywood, and was unable to capitalize on his own filmic depictions of the showgirl, even as dozens of successful

Sitting Pretty (1933), directed by Harry Joe Brown (Paramount Pictures/Photofest).

films would be made based on his legend and on his famous dancers. He spent hand-somely to make the "perfect record of the perfect revue," only to have the result, *Glorifying the American Girl* (1929, directed by Millard Webb), fall flat in reproducing the spectacle of the Follies' live performances despite its opulent and authentic costumes. The static proscenium was retained, the flesh-and-blood showgirls onscreen now one step further removed from the audience. The most successful costume moments are those in the first minutes, when women across America pause in their daily drudgery to transmogrify into showgirls, each ensemble a form-fitting but, by showgirl standards, modest embel-lished gown paired with the requisite high heeled shoes and an enormous feathered head-piece. These dissolves are one of the few instances in which the technology of film is exploited, and even so one can imagine a similar effect being achieved in the theater via scrims.

The person who would unite the showgirl and cinema in an indelible visual spectacle is choreographer/director Busby Berkeley. The former Ziegfeld apprentice took unique advantage of what the camera is capable of without skimping on the sumptuousness and inventiveness of showgirl costumes and tableaux. *Gold Diggers of 1933* (1933, directed by Mervyn LeRoy, numbers created and directed by Busby Berkeley, costumes by Orry-Kelly) opens with perhaps the most literal embodiment of a song in film, "We're in the Money." Seen only from the shoulders up, Ginger Rogers' character Fay Fortune wears a boa of gold coins over a top whose straps are made up of the same coins. Her fellow dancers hold shield-sized coins aside their heads, which are adorned with small brimless caps ringed in coins, dangling coin earrings, and coin-strap tops. Fay's body is revealed in full in a coin bra top and cache-sexe of a large coin surrounded by smaller ones like flower petals, while the dancers are invisible behind her but for their arms holding up the shield-coins in the manner of a Hindu goddess. The dancers wear the same top and one larger coin cache-sexe (all have nude stockings and no apparent underwear). The showgirls part into two rows for the main event, a large sparkling dollar sign that opens to a parade of fashionably coin-clad showgirls, each in a unique ensemble that employs gold lamé and currency. The first is a long dress and matching wrap of draped lamé, sec-ond a bra and tap pants of coins with a single elbow-length glove attached to a small lamé train, third a high-low hem chiffon slip dress with coin trim and a large coin-festooned disc held at the head, fourth a beach-ready look of large-brimmed hat and single coin drop earrings, fifth a cap-sleeved coin top with a coin covered cap, last a lamé dress whose top is cut in two strips from shoulder to waist, just covering the breasts, long body-hugging skirt, and matching cap. Here Berkeley is restrained in his use of dramatic camera angles, especially his signature aerial shots of the geometric arrangement of women's bodies, which we are treated to later in the film; instead he employs the close-up to establish the individuality of the dancers and to highlight the lyrics sung by Rogers.

Parallel to the aforementioned spectacles that borrow both costume and scene from the stage revues are films that depict a grittier cabaret setting. *The Blue Angel* (1930, directed by Josef von Sternberg, costumes by Tihamer Varady) is one of the earlier and arguably most famous of these. Marlene Dietrich plays Lola Lola, the star of a cabaret who drives a professor to madness and ruin. She is introduced to the audience perform-ing a song in which she refers to herself as "Naughty Lola," while wearing a dark or black sequined off-the-shoulder corselet trimmed in stiff tulle at top and bottom. Shoulder straps emerge above and garters below, the latter of which hold up sheer black stockings that catch the stage lights as she strolls about defiantly. In her hair is a matching sequined butterfly. As she turns her back we see a gigantic bow of light-hued satin at her rear, which she gathers up wearily like a tail on her way to sitting on a café chair and drinking a compatriot's mugful of beer. The bow serves as napkin as she rises to begin the next verse. For this number, the one which lures the hapless professor, she is dressed in a light-colored satin bodice and beribboned caged panniers through which one can glimpse her legs; on her head is a curly white wig and tiny tricorn hat with sequined trim. The full vulgarity of the pantomime is revealed as she turns around and the dress is entirely backless, exposing her ruffled white drawers, black bra straps, and black knee-high socks. It is the later ensemble of a short black satin dress with a wide silver belt, sheer gartered stockings, white/silver heels, and gleaming white/silver satin top hat and cuffs, however, that one identifies with the film and the character. The dress's skirt is flipped up to reveal ruffled white drawers as she lifts her knee to her chest, but the more surprising element may be the hat, in this case obviously created for the ensemble but in proportion and silhouette identical to the fashionable man's accessory on which it is based. Dietrich would be costumed entirely in white-tie menswear by Travis Banton in *Morocco* later that year, so perhaps it was inevitable that the top hat would enter the showgirl movie lexicon not by having been kicked off the heads of cancan audience members, but placed on the heads of the women vying for agency in the Hollywood films of the mid–twentieth century.

By the 1950s, the archetypal Hollywood showgirl incorporates elements of cabaret-style costume into her look, in particular the sequined corselet or bustier and panties, fishnet stockings, and top hat or bowler hat in place of the

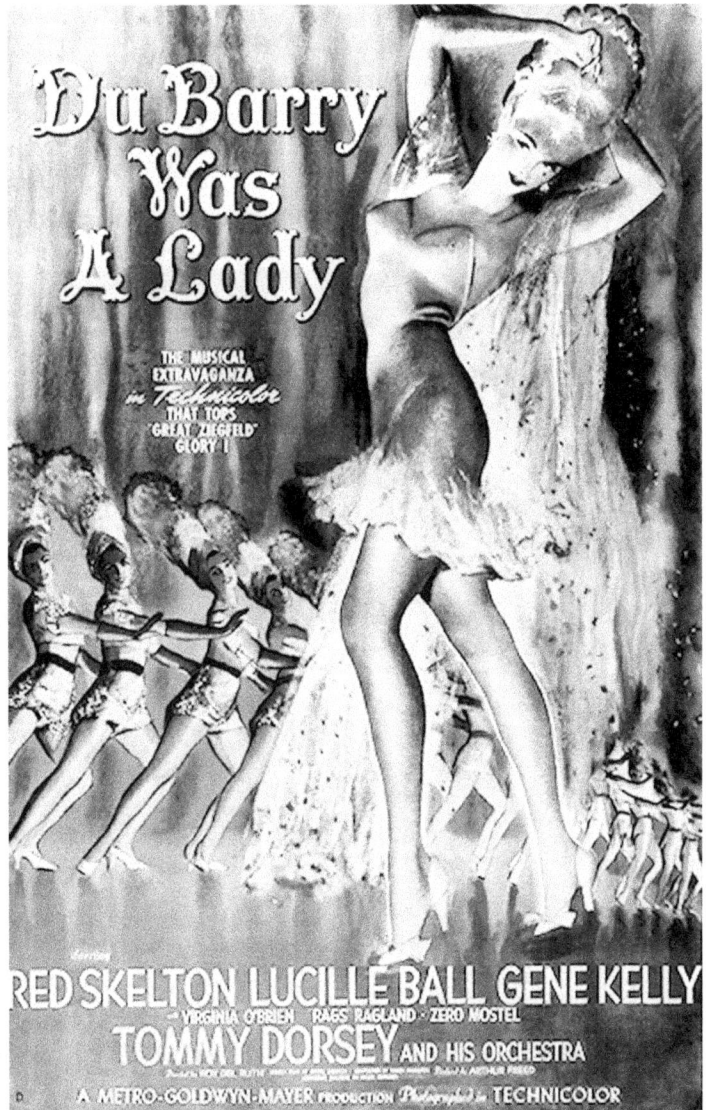

American poster for *Du Barry Was a Lady*, the 1943 MGM musical (Everett Collection).

lavish but somewhat immobilizing feathered headpiece that was the earlier signifier. For *Gentlemen Prefer Blondes* (1953, directed by Howard Hawkes, costumes by Travilla), versions of the movie poster take liberties to replace the headpiece that is part of the actual film's ensemble with, or if no headpiece was present, to add, a top hat, or create an entirely fictitious costume in order to feature a top hat. All of these costumes are variations on a theme similar to the gold and red corselets, shoulder-length red gloves, red top hats with sequined bands, and red satin shoes Rosalind Russell and Marilyn Monroe wear in one poster. No top hats appear in the film on the heads of the women, except in a poster advertising their performances in Paris, and on the accompanying promotional table cards that Monroe's character, Lorelei Lee, shows her future father-in-law to establish her identity. One wonders if the formerly risqué—now completely acceptable—revealing of limbs is given a renewed shot of transgression by the gendered implications (and nod to Weimar Germany) of men's hats on nude-ish women. Or perhaps unable to inject franker depictions of sex into the Hays Code–era films, putting female bodies and male garments in intimate proximity sufficed.

After 1968, the Hays Code is repealed and the showgirl may discard her coyness and perform sexuality as overtly as she or the audience desires. *Cabaret* (1972, directed by Bob Fosse, costumes by Charlotte Flemming) is set in Berlin in 1931, and incorporates

Marilyn Monroe in *The Prince and the Showgirl* (1957), co-starring and directed by Laurence Olivier (Photograph © DILTZ/Bridgeman Images)

polygamy, homosexuality, and abortion into the story. The opening musical number "Willkomen," introduces the cabaret girls and their promiscuity immediately ("Every girl here is a virgin," is met with laughter from the audience). The stage is set. The showgirl costume appears throughout in many guises, notably on the faux "Tiller Girls," who are costumed in fuchsia and black corselets with simulated sequin laces, diamond-shaped cutouts at the navel, gartered black stockings, bowler hats with flowers, and canes. They wear bright red lipstick, dangling gold earrings, and black lace chokers. Golden feathers have migrated down to the dancers' posteriors, to which they are attached with a sequined flower, and where they shed with each thrust of the hips. Later in the number the hats are turned around on the head, the flowers are ripped off and the brims yanked down to form helmets. Canes become rifles and the dancers goose-step around the stage in imitation of soldiers. Liza Minelli's character, Sally Bowles, wears the ultimate version of the cabaret showgirl costume. Deceptively simple, all in low-sheen black, it comprises a button-down vest with plunging neckline, matching shorts with sequined merkin (an artificial covering of hair for the pubic area), garters and stockings, beaded choker, lace-up mid-heeled boots, and a bowler hat with a purple band. The costume is essentially a drag version of a corselet, and adding the female sex as an appliqué on top of Sally's own is a subtly witty and disturbing detail. The merkin is easy to miss on a first glance, but once seen cannot be forgotten.

If the early showgirl films look quaint to modern viewers, and anesthetize them to the struggles of women striving to become dancers but risking exploitation, or worse, *Showgirls* (1995, directed by Paul Verhoeven, costumes by Ellen Mirojnick) strips one of

Gina Gershon and Elizabeth Berkley in *Showgirls* (1995), directed by Paul Verhoeven (Bridgeman Images).

any illusions, most pertinently for our topic, those of an early twentieth century revue-style showgirl costume. Elizabeth Berkley's character, Nomi Malone, gets her big break in the form of a coveted audition for a Las Vegas show. Her first performance is as part of a large cast on a stage crafted to look like an active volcano, which will erupt at the end of the number. She is outfitted in a mesh gold slip mini dress, held by rhinestone straps, and completed with metallic gold thong underwear. The athleticism of the performance requires the dancers to be barefoot; Nomi is lifted, tossed, and pulled from one partner to the next. The dress is completely untailored, and her body within it is as unconstrained as the dance. It ends with the dancers flung to the ground as the volcano erupts, and as she is heaving from the exertion, we see a close-up of her makeup: red eye shadow dotted with sequins that evokes cave paintings and tribal self-adornment. In "Slave," set in the present day, the mandate is bondage, and all of the female dancers appear topless from the beginning. They wear black latex studded bodysuits that outline and expose the breasts, thigh-high patent leather boots with fishnet stockings held by garters, shiny biker hats, and black bobbed wigs. The bodysuits have multi-strapped necks in the style of Jean-Paul Gaultier or Versace, but err on the side of fetish rather than fashion. Some women (and men) ride the perimeter in motorcycles and jackets. The star showgirl is lowered from the ceiling, her hands bound, while men unmask her and tear off her silver leather top and miniskirt, revealing a skimpier version of the other women's costumes, a harnessed cup-less bra and thong panties with thigh-high boots, and a leather and metal choker. The men perform simulated sex acts on her; she breaks free and dances provocatively with another woman whom she dominates and leads off-stage as the performance ends. Movies mirror the decades in which they were made, and *Showgirls* gives us the Vegas where the grand tradition ended up, and ended, for the United States.

The Hollywood showgirl of any era reflects both our enduring ideas about what constitutes her, and, inevitably, her own time. Edward Maeder, in addressing historical costume design in film, notes that "[p]eople in each age create a style that is the acceptable and comfortable aesthetic for their day.... Our vision is so influenced by contemporary style that we cannot be objective, and the result is always an interpretation."[6] Hollywood showgirl costume is, ultimately, a costume *of* costumes. And possibly a more accurate representation than most, as showgirl attire lends itself to the exaggeration and caricature that can mar the accuracy of film costume of everyday attire.

If pressed for a favorite depiction of showgirl costume in film, the truest answer is "the one I will see next." In the meantime, two spectacular creations come to mind for different reasons. The first, in *Male and Female* (1919, directed by Cecil B. DeMille, uncredited costumes by Paul Iribe and Clare West), enrobes Gloria Swanson's character in a two-part halter gown of chiffon and pearls, featuring embroidery and beadwork in a peacock-feather motif which extends into a lengthy train, and a coordinating pearl-fringed skirt, worn with pearl armbands. The headdress is a white peacock imperiously perched on Swanson's head, complete with dangling pearl "earrings," the bird's plumage of white feathers fanning out at the back in high showgirl style. The Babylonian fantasia that provides the excuse for this finery is itself an excuse to enact a painting by Gabriel Cornelius Ritter von Max, *The Lion's Bride*, of a lion laying its paws across a supine woman in a cage. Such a tableau vivant, as we have learned, was designed to elevate nudity to high art and thus sidestep obscenity laws. It is a feature of stage revues that survives little on the screen. The costume fulfills the mandate of both a genuine showgirl and one as imagined by Hollywood, with her fantastical feathered headdress and exuberant embodiment of exotica. The fact that Swanson performed the scene with an actual lion only adds to the associations with other live spectacles, like circuses, and their showgirls.

The second essential showgirl costume comes from the imagination of one of Hollywood's—and fashion's—most celebrated and versatile designers, Gilbert Adrian. *Madame Satan* (1930, directed by Cecil B. DeMille, costumes by Adrian) generated press for Adrian before it hit theaters. A Los Angeles newspaper ran a story about one of the film's costumes having achieved a record in the quantity of cloth used, more than "any so far made in all the world." It was called "Confusion," and was the product of the designer's desire to "see just how much material we could get into a single costume."[7] Adrian's attempts to show up Paris notwithstanding, the gown is a showgirl's dream. It was made for extra Marie Valli, who wears it during a costume ball scene.

> The dress is fashioned from 2,000 yards of silk net, one of the lightest materials known, fastened into 200 balls. Each ball required 30 feet, or 10 yards, of material. The balls are arranged to billow around Miss Valli more or less like an airy pink cloud, now hiding, now revealing the wearer—hence, *confusion*. "It is not a gown which will be generally copied," Adrian said, "else husbands of wives who wore it would spend half their time chasing loosened pink balls around the boudoir, and under the bed."[8]

It is as delightfully absurd a confection as it sounds. Valli wears a nude rhinestone-studded bra and panties connected by a vertical strip down the center, over nude stockings. On her head is a several-foot-high studded headdress that rises narrowly up and at the top fans out into a circle of curved spokes around the head, in the manner of a fountain spraying water. Instead of water issue the pink puffballs described above, linked by long silver ribbons. The effect is not dissimilar to a six-foot-high poodle's ear with a scantily-clad woman at the center, and has all of the ethereal volume, requisite sparkle, and kooky sex appeal that the best Hollywood showgirl costumes exemplify.

Chapter Notes

Introduction

1. The etymologies are from the Oxford English Dictionary.

2. Laurence Senelick, *Cabaret Performance: Sketches, Songs, Monologues, Memoirs* (Baltimore, MD: Johns Hopkins University Press, 1993), 25.

3. John Kendrick, "A History of Cabaret," Musicals 101.com.

4. Howard B. Segel, *Turn of the Century Cabaret: Paris, Barcelona, Berlin, Munich, Vienna, Crakow, Moscow, St. Petersburg, Zurich* (New York: Columbia University Press, 1987), xiv.

5. Charles Rearick, personal communication, June 3, 2017.

6. Stephen Gundle, "Mapping the Origins of Glamour: Giovanni Baldini, Paris and the Belle Epoque," *Journal of European Studies*, 29.3 (Sept. 1999), 3.

7. Gundle, "Mapping the Origins of Glamour," 4.

8. From his in-depth knowledge, Pascal Jacob compares the genre to a growing plant: "Le music-hall est un élégant buisson, aux racines profuses et parfois très profondes, qui plangent aux sources de divertissement." *Music Hall! Du Mans à Macao* (Magellan & Cie, 2013), 33.

9. Daniel Frasnay, *Les Girls; Paris 1952–1979* (London: Greybull Press, 2005), 4.

Chapter One

1. Jean Prasteau, *La Merveilleuse Aventure du Casino de Paris* (Paris: Editions Denoiel, 1975), 84.

2. Irena Lexova, *Ancient Egyptian Dance* (Mineola, NY: Dover, 2007), 61.

3. Trenton Hamilton, *The History of Western Dance* (New York: Britannica Educational Publishing, 2016), 9.

4. Larissa Bonfante, "Nudity as a Costume in Classical Art," *American Journal of Archaeology* Vol. 93, 4 (October 1989), 546.

5. Larissa Bonfante, *Etruscan Dress* (Baltimore, MD: Johns Hopkins University Press, 1975), 21.

6. Peter O'Connell, "Hyperides and Epopteia: A New Fragment of the Defense of Phryne," *Greek, Roman and Byzantine Studies* Vol. 53 (2013), 90–116, grbs.library. duke.edu.

7. Bonfante, *Etruscan Dress*, 24.

8. Adrian Goldsworthy, *Antony and Cleopatra* (New Haven, CT: Yale University Press, 2010), 266.

9. Tom Holland, *Dynasty: The Rise and Fall of the House of Caesar* (New York: Knopf Doubleday, 2015), 332.

10. Adrian Goldsworthy, personal communication, spring 2017.

11. Carol Van-Driel-Murray, "Putting Some Flesh on the Bones: Leather Bikinis and Body Size," in Rob Collins and Frances McIntosh, eds. *Live in the Limes: Studies of the People and Objects of the Roman Frontiers Presented to Lindsay Allason-Jones on the Occasion of Her Birthday and Retirement* (Oxford: Oxbow Books, 2014), 206–216.

12. Patricio Pensabene and Enrico Gallocchio, "The Villa de Casale of Piazza Armerina," www.penn.museum/ documents/publications/expedition/PDF./53-2.

13. Paolo Cesaretti, *Theodora: Empress of Byzantium* (New York: Vendome, 2004), 93.

14. Paolo Cesaretti is a professor of Byzantine civilization, Roman history, and Greek literature at the University of Bergamo (Italy). He has published critical editions and annotated translations of Byzantine philological, historical, and hagiographical texts, monographs, and biographies including *Theodora: Empress of Byzantium* (Vendome, 2004).

15. Richard Wellington Husband, "The Prosecution of Morena," *The Classical Journal*, 12, 2 (Nov. 1916), 113. http://www.jstor.org/stable/3287856.

16. Sarah Maza, "The Rose-Girl of Salency: From Theatricality to Rhetoric," *Private Lives and Public Affairs: The Causes Celebres of Prerevolutionary France* (Berkeley, CA: University of California Press, 1993), 68–76.

17. The painting depicts the custom of registering a dowry. The male domain at the right shows men in charge and emotionally reserved. At the left the distaff figures are emotionally unrestrained; the bride-to-be is a ploy but presumed happy.

18. Henry C. Shelley, *Old Paris: Its Social, Historical and Literary Associations* (Boston: L.C. Page, 1912), 300. He said of the Fair of St. Ovide, "the principle amusement it offered its patrons was nothing more than a gallery of young women arrayed in garments which were intended to caricature the fashions of the day."

19. Maza, "The Rose-Girl of Salency," 79–80.

20. The philosophes used descriptions of this violent practice to support their criticism of the social order. It could refer to the right to deflower, or the custom of the noble's putting a naked leg on the bed, *décuissage* or *jambage*. Dana Marie Chase, *Deflowering the Garden: Le Droit du Seigneur and La Fontaine*, se17.bowdoin. edu/files/ChaseCahiersIX (2004), 78–79.

21. Domenico da Piacenze, *Fifteenth-Century Dance and Music,* commentator and translator A. William Smith (Hillside, NY: Pendragon Press, 1995), Vol.1, ch.3, lines 45–48. Alston Purvis, Peter Rand, and Anna Winestein, *The Ballets Russes and the Art of Design* (New York: Monacelli Press, 2009).

22. It seems that Leonardo da Vinci may have found creating costumes and "machines" for his patrons' extravaganzas fatiguing. For Duke Ludovico of Milan he did a stage set in the form of a half-egg decorated with gold inside, dotted with lights (stars), and the seven planets mounted in slots; dressing people also to represent the planets. Sherwin B. Noland, *Leonardo da Vinci* (New York: Penguin, 2005), 44–45.

23. John Shearman, *Mannerism* (New York: Pelican, 1967), 105.

24. Mary Clarke and Clement Crisp, *The History of Dance* (New York: Crown, 1981), 122.

25. Pomona, in Roman mythology a wood nymph who protected fruit trees and gardens, fit dessert as the Golden Fleece fit with lamb and Atalanta (whose arrow first wounded the Catydonian Boar) with a dish of wild boar. Cohen, 6.

26. Mysylph.com2012-catherine-de-medici-and-the-ballet-comique-de-la-reine.

27. Hamilton, *The History of Western Dance,* 34–35.

28. Nicolas de Saint-Hubert, *La Manière de composer et faire réussir les ballets,* with introduction by Marie-Francoise Christout (Geneva: Editions Minkoff, 1993), 20.

29. Saint-Hubert, *La Manière,* 9.

30. Clare McManus, *Women on the Renaissance Stage* (Manchester, UK: Manchester University Press, 2002), 6.

31. Barbara Ravelhofer, "The Early Stuart Masque: Dance Costume and Music," *Early Modern Literary Studies* 15.1 (2009–10), purl.oclc.org/emis/15-1/mickrave, 161.

32. Jean Wilson, "Everlasting Spring: The Literary and Political Aspects of Country House Revels," *Times Literary Supplement,* March 3, 2017, 29.

33. Roy Strong, *Art and Power: Renaissance Festivals, 1450–1650* (Berkeley: University of California Press, 1984), 157.

34. Sarsnett was silk for lining a garment.

35. McManus, *Women on the Renaissance Stage,* 109.

36. Ravelhofer, "The Early Stuart Masque," 172–181.

37. Ulinka Rublack, *Dressing Up: Cultural Identity in Renaissance Europe* (New York: Oxford University Press, 2011), 222.

38. Ravelhofer, "The Early Stuart Masque," 173.

39. McManus, *Women on the Renaissance Stage,* 127.

40. Antonia Fraser, *Marie Antoinette: The Journey,* 179.

41. A. Fraser, *Marie Antoinette,* 175.

42. A. Fraser, *Marie Antoinette,* 150.

43. Four, *Memoirs of Madame la Tour du Pin,* ed. and trans. by Felice Harcourt (London; Trafalgar Square, 1985), 17–18.

44. Lynn Hunt, "The Many Bodies of Marie Antoinette," *Eroticism and the Body Politic,* ed. Lynn Hunt (Baltimore, MD: Johns Hopkins, 1990), 126.

45. Lynn Hunt, personal communication, February 2017.

46. Flora Fraser, *Emma, Lady Hamilton* (New York: Knopf, 1987), 106.

47. Selma Jean Cohen, *Dance as Theater Art: Source Readings in Dance History from 1581 to the Present,* 2nd ed. (Trenton, NJ: Princeton Book Co., 1992), 36.

48. Carol Lee, *Ballet in Western Culture: A History of Its Origins and Evolutions* (New York: Routledge, 2002), 51.

49. Claude-Francois Ménestrier, *Des Ballets anciens et modernes selon les règles du théâtre* (Paris: René Guignard, 1982, 252–253.

50. Jean-Georges Noverre, *Lettres sur la Dance, sur les Ballets et les Arts, Vol. 1, 1803* (St. Petersburg: Jean Charles Schnoor, 1803), ii. https://ia600304.us.archive.org/1/items/lettressurladans01noveuoft/lettressurladans01noveuoft_bw.pdf.

51. Caroline Pichler, *Memorabilia from My Life,* vol. 1 (Munich, 1914), 181.

52. "Maria Viganò," de.wikipedia.org/wiki/Maria_Viganò.

53. Jane Merrill and Keren Ben-Horin, *She's Got Legs: A History of Hemlines and Fashion* (Atglen, PA: Schiffer Publishing, 2014), 149.

54. Cohen, *Dance as Theater Art,* 5.

55. Thomas Curson Hansard, *Cobbett's Parliamentary History of England: From the Earliest Period to the Year 1803,* Vol. 33 (London: Hansard, 1806–1820), 1307.

56. Judith Chazin-Bennahum, *The Lure of Perfection: Fashion and Ballet, 1780–1830,* Vol. 33 (Routledge, 2005), 152–154.

57. Nathalie Lecomte, "The Female Ballet Troupe of the Paris Opera from 1700 to 1725," trans. Régine Astier, in *Women's Work: Making Dance in Europe before 1800,* ed. Lynn Matluck Brooks (Madison: University of Wisconsin Press, 2007), 106.

58. Lecomte, "The Female Ballet Troupe," 107.

59. Lecomte, "The Female Ballet Troupe," 117.

60. Chazin-Bennahum, *The Lure of Perfection,* 160.

61. Chazin-Bennahum, *The Lure of Perfection,* 222–224.

62. Valerie Steele, ed., *Dance in Fashion* (New Haven, CT: Yale University Press, 2014), 31.

63. W. Macqueen-Pope, *Gaiety: Theater of Enchantment* (London: W.H. Allen, 1949), 44–45.

64. Abigail Adams to Mary Smith Cranch, February 20, 1785, *Letters of Mrs. Adams,* Founders.archives.gov.

65. Mercy Warren to Winslow Warren, December 13, 1781, *Letters of Mrs. Adams,* Founders.archives.gov. Also Charles Warren, "A Young American's Adventures in England and France During the Revolutionary War (Winslow Warren)," *Massachusetts Historical Society Proceedings,* Vol. 65 (1940), 61.

66. Washington Irving, May 20, 1805, *Journals and Notebooks,* 409.

67. Abigail Adams to Mary Smith Cranch, December 9, 1784, *Letters of Mrs. Adams,* 1:258.

68. William L. Chew III is professor emeritus of history at Vesalius College, Brussels. He is working on a book about Thomas Jefferson's travels in France.

69. Thomas Handasyd Perkins, March 27, 1795, *Memoir of Thos. Handasyd Perkins Containing Extracts from His Diary and Letters,* ed. Thomas G. Cary (Boston: 1856), 69.

70. William Lee, *A Yankee Jeffersonian: Selections from the Diary and Letters of William Lee of Massachusetts Written from 1796–1849,* ed. Mary Lee Mann (Cambridge, MA: 1958), February 18, 1796, 13.

71. Washington Irving to Alex Beebee, September 19, 1804, 1:80.

72. Maria Bayard, *Diary of a Tour of England, Scotland, and France. Cathedrals, Art Galleries, Economic and Social Conditions (1814–1815),* March 24, 1815, Rare Books and Manuscripts Division, the New York Public Library, Astor, Lenox and Tilden Foundations.

73. American Wanderer, *The American Wanderer*

through Various Parts of Europe, in a Series of Letters to a Lady, Interspersed with a Variety of Interesting Anecdotes (Dublin: B. Smith, 1777), 99.

74. Abigail Adams to Mrs. Cranch, February 20, 1785, *Letters of Mrs. Adams*, 279.

75. "Fêtes des fous," http://compilhistoire.pagespersoorange.fr/fetefous.html.

76. Charles Castle, *The Folies-Bergère* (London: Methuen, 1982), 92.

77. Mel Gordon, *Horizontal Collaboration: The Erotic World of Paris, 1920–1946* (Port Townsend, WA: Feral House, 2015), 156.

78. https:/journalepicurien.com/tag/sarah-brown/.

79. Castle, *The Folies-Bergère*, 96.

80. Melissa McCaffrey, "Revelry and Debauchery in Turn of the Century Paris," Rectoversoblog.com/2015/09/08.

81. Marie-Aude Bonniel, "Le Carnaval de Paris de 1896: V'la le boeuf gras qui passé," LeFigaro.fr.

82. Carl Jung, *The Collected Works of C.G. Jung*, Vol. 7, 192, para. 305.

83. Earnoldbennett.blogspot.co.uk/2012/11/musical/evening.

84. Mel Gordon, personal communication, March 31, 2017.

85. Michele Majer, ed., *Staging Fashion, 1880–1920* (Bard Graduate Center, Yale University Press, 2012), 28–29.

86. Pierre Véron, column in *Le Monde Illustré*, July 30, 1881, in Lenard R. Berlanstein, *Daughters of Eve: A Cultural History of French Theater Women from the Old Regime to the Fin de Siècle* (Cambridge, MA: Harvard University Press, 2001), 112.

87. Majer, ed., *Staging Fashion*, 38.

88. Early on, lovers regularly bought the stage costumes or the accessorizing jewelry for star showgirls, but Spinelly apparently felt that her wearing a dress was payment enough to the costumer. She and Erté quarreled and he did not work for her again (Erté, *Things I Remember: An Autobiography* [New York: Sevenarts, 1975], 53).

89. Ernest Hemingway, *A Moveable Feast* (New York: Scribner, 1964), 18.

90. Michael B. Miller, *The Bon Marché: Bourgeois Culture and the Department Store, 1869–1920* (Princeton, NJ: Princeton University Press, 1994), 169.

91. Miller, *The Bon Marché*, 172.

92. Colin Jones, *Paris: The Biography of a City* (New York: Viking, 2004), 354–355.

93. Sarah Gutsche-Miller, *Parisian Music-Hall Ballet, 1871–1913* (Rochester, NY: University of Rochester Press, 2015), 40.

94. Valerie Steele, *Paris Fashion: A Cultural History* (New York: Oxford University Press, 1988), 161.

95. Andrea Stuart, *Showgirls* (London: Cape, 1996), 78.

96. Laurence Senelick, "Eroticism in Early Theatrical Photography," *Theater History Studies*, Vol. 11 (1991), 12.

97. Edmond Deschaumes, *Le Mal du Théâtre* (Paris: E. Dentu, 1888), 195–196.

98. Debora L. Silverman, *Art Nouveau in Fin-de-Siècle France: Politics, Psychology, and Style* (Berkeley: University of California Press, 1989), 71.

99. George Jean Nathan in Susan A. Glenn, *Female Spectacle: The Theatrical Roots of Modern Feminism* (Cambridge, MA: Harvard University Press), 156n3.

100. Gloria Groom, ed., *Impressionism, Fashion &*

Modernity (Chicago, IL: The Art Institute of Chicago; distributed by Yale University Press, 2012), 33.

101. Jane Merrill and Keren Ben-Horin, *She's Got Legs: A History of Hemlines and Fashion* (Atglen, PA: Schiffer Publishing, 2014), 136.

102. Marine Costille, *Spectacles au Music-Hall: Le Cas de Quatres Salles Parisiennes, 1917–1940* (Histoire, 2016), 65. dumas-0147493.

103. Robert Bresson, *Bresson on Bresson: Interviews, 1943–1983*, 217.

104. Michael B. Miller, personal communication.

105. Emile Zola, *Au Bonheur des Dames*, trans. Brian Nelson (New York: Oxford University Press, 2008), 410–411.

106. Rachel Steir, *Striptease: The Untold History of the Girlie Show* (New York: Oxford University Press, 2004), 44.

107. Bram Dijkstra, *Idols of Perversity: Fantasies of Feminine Evil in the Fin-de-Siècle Culture* (New York: Oxford University Press, 1986), 386.

108. Dijkstra, *Idols of Perversity*, 386.

109. Richard Ellman, *Oscar Wilde* (New York: Vintage, 1988), 343.

110. Oleg Grabar in Holly Edwards et al., *Noble Dreams, Wicked Pleasure: Orientalism in America, 1870–1930* (Princeton, NJ: Princeton University Press, 2000), 46–47.

111. Roger Leong, *From Russia with Love: Costumes for the Ballets Russes, 1909–1933* (Canberra: National Gallery of Australia, 1998), 68.

112. Holly Edwards, "A Million and One Nights: Orientalism in America, 1870–1930," in Edwards et al., *Noble Dreams*, 40.

113. Juliette Drouet to Victor Hugo, February 8, 1847. Parismuseescollections.paris.fr/en/node/211548.

114. Andrea Deagon, "The Image of the Eastern Dancer: Flaubert's Salome," *The Best of Habibi: A Journal for Lovers of Middle Eastern Dance*, published by Shareen El Safy, 1992–2002.

115. "Histoire d'automates," Visitors Booklet, Theatre des Sablons, culture.theatredessablons,com/media/EXPO SutomatesLivretAdult_A5.

116. Ellman, *Oscar Wilde*, 343.

117. Edwards et al., *Noble Dreams*, 47.

118. Jane Pritchard, *Diaghilev and the Golden Age of the Ballets Russes* (London: Victoria & Albert Museum, 2015), 65.

119. Liane de Pougy, *My Blue Notebooks*, trans. Diane Athill (New York: Harper & Row, 1979), 34–35.

120. Toni Bentley, *Sisters of Salome* (New Haven, CT: Yale University Press, 2002), 31.

121. Jacques-Charles, *Cent Ans de Music-Hall* (Paris: Editions Jeheber, 1956), 60.

122. Herbert R. Lottman, *Jules Verne: An Exploratory Biography* (New York: St. Martin's, 1996), 273.

123. http://cdn.history.com/sites/2/2016/01/Getty Images-85139181.j pg.

124. Delabere P. Blaine, *Encyclopedia of Rural Sports*, 13 and 233.

125. Cindy Crank, "Victorian Horse-Drawn Hearses, Plumes, Pomp and Processions," November 19, 2012, Horses and History blog, Horse-Canada.com.

126. Paul Bouissac, *Semiotics at the Circus* (Berlin: De Gruyter Mouton, 2011), 58.

127. Doris Eaton Travis, *The Days We Danced: The Story of My Theatrical Family from Florenz Ziegfeld to Arthur Murray and Beyond* (Norman: University of Oklahoma Press, 2003), 67.

128. Castle, *The Folies-Bergère,* 22–23.

129. Paul Derval, *The Folies Bergère,* trans. Lucienne Hall (London: Methuen, 1955), 7–8.

130. Castle, *The Folies-Bergère,* 33.

131. Pascal Jacob, personal communication.

132. Julian Neuville, "Un peu d'histoire … Le body," *Le Monde,* July 20, 2014, http://www.lemonde.fr/mode/article/2014/06/20/un-peu-d-histoire-le-body_4441468_1383317.html.

133. Translation from 17emesiecle.free.fr/Babiole.

134. J.M. Barrie, *Peter Pan,* www.gutenberg.org/files/16/16-h/16h.htm.p35.

135. To the question of whether Madeleine Béjart was in fact naked, the historian Jean-Claude Bologne answers (translated): "An engraving shows he scantily dress in a necklace and two bracelets: classic cunning to dissimilate the neckline and wrists of a maillot." Jean-Claude Bologne, *Histoire de la Pudeur* (Paris: Olivier Orban, 1997), 233.

136. Lucy Fischer, "Invisible by Design: Reclaiming Art Nouveau for the Cinema." *Film History,* Vol. 25, 1–2 (2013), 58.

137. Fischer, "Invisible by Design," 64.

Chapter Two

1. Jones, *Paris,* 374.

2. "Moulin-Rouge: La Goulue" (1891) at the Metropolitan Museum of Art. The cancan dancer wears a cheerful polka-dotted red blouse, red stockings, petticoats and a black ribbon around her neck. Behind are ten partial figures, all but two men in top hats and the two women in hats with plumes like deadly hooks. In the foreground the man who makes a rude gesture with his crooked thumb towards the white petticoats is emblematic of the devil character in a puppet show—the top hat concealing any horns.

3. Miller, *The Bon Marché,* 172.

4. Laurence Senelick, "Sexuality and Gender," in *A Cultural History of Theatre in the Age of Empire (1800–1920),* edited by Peter Marx (New York: Bloomsbury Publishing, 2017), 12.

5. Susanna Barrows, ed., *Pleasures of Paris: Daumier to Picasso* (Boston: Museum of Fine Arts, 1991), 25.

6. Barrows, ed., *Pleasures of Paris,* 25.

7. Castle, *The Folies-Bergère,* 22.

8. Dominique Kalifa, *La Culture de Masse en France, vol. 1: 1860–1930* (Paris: Editions La Découverte, 2001), 43.

9. Arthur Pougin, *Dictionnaire Historique Et Pittoresque Du Théâtre Et Des Arts Qui S'y Rattachent* (Paris, 1885), 598.

10. On the price of a night out being difficult for poorer people, Professor Rearick offered a qualification: "The entry price and drink prices at the top (the better?) music-halls and cabarets kept out the poor, yes. At the lowest level in poor neighborhoods there were inexpensive drinking places (cabarets or guinguettes or estaminets) where the poor nursed along a drink in the evening. The café or cabaret (local neighborhood simple place) was better lighted and warmer than the apartments of the poor. Now we're into the messy difficulty of the word 'cabaret.' It can mean a place where a show was presented (as in Kurt Weill's sense and the musical *Cabaret*), but in French it also meant a bar or tavern, a drinking place" (personal communication, August 18, 2017).

11. Charles Rearick, *Pleasures of the Belle Epoque: Entertainment & Festivity in Turn-of-the-Century France* (New Haven, CT: Yale University Press, 1985), 104, 110.

12. Mel Gordon, *Horizontal Collaboration,* 44.

13. Derval, *The Folies Bergère,* 52.

14. Projecting in magazine ads radiant health, Billie Burke endorsed many goods in her career, including Cutex nail polish, Lux soap, and Royal Gelatin but, observes William DeGregorio, "it was her early advertisements for beauty products that laid the foundation for an enduringly appealing image" (Majer, ed., *Staging Fashion,* 172).

15. Emma Elizabeth Crouch, *The Memoirs of Cora Pearl: The English Beauty of the French Empire* (London: George Vickers, 1886), 188.

16. Joanna Richardson, *The Courtesans: The Demi-Monde in 19th Century France* (New York: World Publishing, 1967), 53–54.

17. Richardson, *The Courtesans,* 56–57.

18. Sima Godfrey, "Baudelaire, Gautier, and une toilette savamment composée," *Modernity and Revolution in Late Nineteenth-Century France,* eds. Barbara T. Cooper and Mary Donaldson-Evans (Newark: University of Delaware Press, 1992), 82.

19. Richardson, *The Courtesans,* 58.

20. J-P Worth, *A Century of Fashion* (Boston: Little, Brown, 1928), 101.

21. Polly Binder, *The Truth about Cora Pearl* (London: Weidenfeld & Nicolson, 1986), 139.

22. M.R. Kessler, *Sheer Presence: The Veil in Manet's Paris* (Minneapolis: University of Minnesota Press, 2004), 40.

23. Cora Pearl (pseud.; Derek Parker), *Grand Horizontal: The Memoirs of a Passionate Lady,* ed. William Blatchford (New York: Stein & Day, 1980), 108–109.

24. Philip Dennis Cate, personal communication, February 16, 2017.

25. Mariel Oberthur, *Cafes and Cabarets of Montmartre* (Salt Lake City, UT: Gibbs M. Smith, 1984), 55.

26. Bernard Denvir, *Toulouse-Lautrec* (London: Thames and Hudson, 1991), 83–84.

27. Emile Goudeau, *Dix Ans de Bohème* (Paris: Librairie Illustrée, n.d.), 263.

28. Segel, *Turn of the Century Cabaret,* 21.

29. Charles Cros recited at Le Chat Noir. His "Hareng Saur" (1872), composed for his son at bedtime, became the prototype for deadpan "monologues fumistes" of the 1880s. The last stanza reads, "J'ai composé cette histoire—simple, simple, simple,/Pour mettre en fureur les gens—graves, graves, graves,/Et amuser les enfants—petits, petits, petits."

30. Phillip Dennis Cate, personal communication.

31. Steven Moore Whiting, "Music on Montmartre," in Philip Dennis Cate and Mary Shaw, eds., *The Spirit of Montmartre: Cabarets, Humor, and the Avant Garde, 1875–1905* (New Brunswick, NJ: Rutgers University Press, 1996), 160.

32. Goudeau, *Dix Ans de Bohème,* 263.

33. Goudeau, *Dix Ans de Bohème,* 156. The café-concert didn't have the intellectual patina of the cabaret, but rather was more like a sideshow attraction. The public came and went, wearing whatever they wished, for a "pint." Meanwhile, says Dominique Kalifa in his work on French mass culture, "L'érotisation du spectacle progress également, qui exhibe les corps féminins" (*La Culture de Masse en France, vol. 1: 1860–1930* [Paris: Editions La Découverte, 2001], 39).

34. Charles Rearick is the author of books on French

culture and Paris and is a professor of history, emeritus, at the University of Massachusetts–Amherst.

35. Segel, *Turn of the Century Cabaret,* 59.

36. Segel, *Turn of the Century Cabaret,* 23.

37. Charles Rearick, *Pleasures of the Belle Epoque* (New Haven, CT: Yale University Press, 1985), 30.

38. Cate and Shaw, eds., *The Spirit of Montmartre,* 39.

39. Luc Sante, *The Other Paris* (New York: Farrar, Straus, Giroux, 2015), 169.

40. "Marché des Dos" [The Pimps' March].

41. Eugen Weber, *France, Fin de Siècle* (Cambridge, MA: Harvard University Press, 1985), 38.

42. Julia Frey, *Toulouse-Lautrec: A Life* (New York: Viking, 1994), 278.

43. Peter Leslie, *A Hard Act to Follow: A Music Hall Review* (New York: Paddington Press, 1978), 59.

44. Richard Thomson, Phillip Dennis Cate and Mary Weaver Chapin, *Toulouse-Lautrec and Montmartre* (Princeton, NJ: Princeton University Press, 2005), 6.

45. Sante, *The Other Paris,* 169.

46. Sante, *The Other Paris,* 169.

47. Sue Roe, *In Montmartre: Picasso, Matisse, and Modernism in Paris, 1900–1910* (New York: Penguin, 2015), 11–12.

48. Alain Weill, *120 Ans de Moulin Rouge* (Paris: Seven sept, 2010), 30.

49. Jacques Pessis and Jacques Crépineau, *The Moulin Rouge* (New York: Alan Sutton, St. Martin's Press, 1990), 23.

50. Jane Avril, *Mes mémoires* (Paris: Phébus, 2005).

51. Weill, *120 Ans de Moulin Rouge,* 24–25.

52. Weill, *120 Ans de Moulin Rouge,* 24–25.

53. Yvette Guilbert, *The Song of My Life* (London: G.G. Harrap & Co., [1929]), 74.

54. Jonathan Conlin, *Tales of Two Cities: Paris, London and the Birth of the Modern City* (Berkeley, CA: Counterpoint, 2013), 164.

55. Conlin, *Tales of Two Cities,* 164.

56. Early patents were in Dresden, Germany (1899), and the U.S. (Mary Phelps Jacob, 1914). Syracuse's *Evening Herald* in March 1893 already called a boned band made to be worn with the Directory-style slip-like dresses a brassiere. The O.E.D. references a British Columbian advertisement of 1911 for a brassiere of "fine cambric, lace and embroidery trimmed."

57. Weill, *120 Ans de Moulin Rouge,* 45.

58. Pessis and Crépineau, *The Moulin Rouge,* 64.

59. John Simon, "How Sex Killed Frank Wedekind," *The New York Times,* November 18, 1990, www.nytimes.com/1990/11/18/books.

60. This is quoted in Martin Seymour-Smith, *The New Guide to Modern World Literature* (New York: P. Bedrick Books, 1985), 561–562. Seymour-Smith states that the line is from one of Wedekind's songs he sang on his deathbed.

61. Mel Gordon, personal communication, winter 2017.

62. Frank Wedekind, *Diary of an Erotic Life,* ed. Gerhard Hay; trans. W.E. Yuill (Cambridge, MA: Basil Blackwell, 1990), 125–126.

63. Wedekind, *Diary of an Erotic Life,* 141–142.

64. Vanessa R. Schwartz is a professor of art history, history and French at the University of Southern California, where she is director of visual studies research. Her transatlantic histories of entertainment are *Spectacular Realities: Early Mass Culture in Fin-de-Siècle Paris* (University of California, 1999) and *It's So French! The Belle Epoque that Never Ended: Frenchness and the Cancan Film of the 1950s* (University of Chicago, 2007).

65. "The History of the Can-Can," CBS News, October 11, 2015.

66. Conlin, *Tales of Two Cities,* 141.

67. Conlin, *Tales of Two Cities,* 160.

68. Weill, *120 Ans de Moulin Rouge,* 444.

69. Conlin, *Tales of Two Cities,* 169–170.

70. Richard Balducci, *Les Princesses de Paris: L'Age d'or des cocottes* (Paris: Editions Hors Collection, 1994), 105–106.

71. Rae Beth Gordon, *Dances with Darwin, 1875–1910: Vernacular Modernity in France* (New York: Routledge, 2009), 55.

72. Laurence Senelick, "Eroticism in Early Theatrical Photography," *Theater History Studies,* Vol. 11 (1991), 22.

73. Prasteau, *La Merveilleuse Aventure,* 44–45.

74. Rozsika Parker, *The Subversive Stitch: Embroidery and the Making of the Feminine* (London: I.B. Tauris, 2010), 15.

75. Charles Rearick, *Paris Dreams, Paris Memories: The City and Its Mystique* (Stanford, CA: Stanford University Press, 2011), 13–14.

76. Paul Derval, *The Folies Bergère,* 8.

77. https://www.histoire-image.org/etudes/cecile-sorel-comedie-francaise-couvent-passant-music-hall-cinema.

78. James Gardiner, *Gaby Deslys: A Fatal Attraction* (London: Sidgwick & Jackson, 1986), 10.

79. Pougy, *My Blue Notebooks,* 66.

80. Mary Louise Roberts, *Disruptive Acts: The New Woman in Fin-de-Siècle France* (Chicago: University of Chicago Press, 2017), 79.

81. Rachel Mesch, *Having It All in the Belle Epoque: How French Women's Magazines Invented the Modern Woman* (Stanford, CA: Stanford University Press, 2013), 151.

82. Larolyn Sinsky, "Loie Fuller," The Modernism Lab at Yale University, 2010.

83. Richard Nelson Current and Marcia Ewing Current, *Loie Fuller, Goddess of Light* (Boston: Northeastern University Press, 1997), 99.

84. Current and Current, *Loie Fuller,* 60–61.

85. Current and Current, *Loie Fuller,* 39.

86. Angenette Spalink, *Loie Fuller and Modern Movement* (Thesis for a Master of Arts, Bowling Green State University, 2010), 31.

87. Susan Griffin, *The Book of the Courtesans: A Catalogue of Their Virtues* (New York: Broadway Books, 2001), 88.

88. Ian Graham, *Scarlet Women: The Scandalous Lives of Courtesans, Concubines, and Royal Mistresses* (New York: St. Martin's, 2016), 17.

89. Laurence Senelick, "Sexuality and Gender," *A Cultural History of Theatre in the Age of Empire (1800–1920),* ed. Peter Marx (New York: Bloomsbury Publishing, 2017), 2.

90. Castle, *The Folies-Bergère,* 51–52.

91. Gutsche-Miller, *Parisian Music-Hall Ballet,* 181–182.

92. Balducci, *Les Princesses de Paris,* 49.

93. Dijkstra, *Idols of Perversity,* 246.

94. Balducci, *Les Princesses de Paris,* 49.

95. Gardiner, *Gaby Deslys,* ix.

96. Jacques-Charles, *Cent Ans,* 187.

97. Jacques Damase, *Les Folies du Music-Hall: A History of the Paris Music-Hall from 1914 to the Present Day,* trans. Tony White (London: Hamlyn, 1962), 9.

98. Gardiner, *Gaby Deslys,* 170.

99. Balducci, *Les Princesses de Paris,* 26.

100. "Leona Dare's Trapeze," *New York Times*, June 9, 1879, from *The London News*, May 29, 1879.

101. Elaine Showalter, ed., *Daughters of Decadence: Women Writers of the Fin-de-Siècle* (Rutherford, NJ: Rutgers University Press, 1993), 267.

102. Lela F. Kerley is a cultural historian, one of whose specialties is the history of leisure in early Third Republic France. These ideas are developed in chapter seven of her book *Uncovering Paris: Scandals and Nude Spectacles in the Belle Epoque* (LSU Press, 2017).

103. Mary Louise Roberts, *Disruptive Acts: The New Woman in Fin de Siècle France* (Chicago, IL: University of Chicago Press, 2002), 70.

104. Ann Hollander, *Seeing Through Clothes* (Berkeley: University of California Press, 1993), 195, 213.

105. Colette, *Mes Apprentisages* (Paris: Ferenczi, 1936), 195.

106. Robin W. Doughty, *Feather Fashions and Bird Preservation: A Study in Nature Protection* (Berkeley: University of California Press, 1974), 8n14.

107. "Le bal des ardents," February 21, 2017, http://www.histoires-de-paris.fr/bal-ardents/.

108. "Quelque chose sans un pli sans une tache;/J'emporte malgré vous/et c'est … mon panache." Act VI, Sc. 5, http://www.gutenberg.org/files/1256/1256-8.txt.

109. Doughty, *Feather Fashions*, 12.

110. Amicorum of Johannes Thomas Ortel in Rublack, 224, Brit. Libr. Eg. 12225, 234.

Chapter Three

1. Robert C. Allen, *Horrible Prettiness: Burlesque and American Culture* (Chapel Hill: University of North Carolina Press, 1991), 96.

2. Leslie, *A Hard Act to Follow*, 27.

3. Prints and Photographs Division, Library of Congress.

4. Parker, *The Subversive Stitch*, 23.

5. Doug Reside is curator of the Billy Rose Theatre Division of New York Public Library for the Performing Arts.

6. Allen, *Horrible Prettiness*, 116.

7. Lewis A. Erenberg, *Steppin' Out: New York Nightlife and the Transformation of American Culture, 1890–1930* (Chicago, IL: University of Chicago Press, 1994), 75.

8. Fanny Pryor's father, a New York judge, relented and she wed MacMonnies. LC Bull. Vol. 56, 9 (May 1997).

9. Erenberg, *Steppin' Out*, 116–117.

10. Erenberg, *Steppin' Out*, 214–21.

11. Henry Voigt is an eminent collector of old American menus starting from the 1840s. He serves on the board of the Ephemera Society, belongs to the Grolier Club and lives in Wilmington, Delaware.

12. Michael Lasser is a teacher, theater critic, and writer. His longer article on Ziegfeld, as captivating and insightful as any biography, appeared in *The American Scholar*, Summer 1994, as "The Glorifier: Florenz Ziegfeld and the Creation of the American Showgirl."

13. This is largely covered in Linda Mizejewski's book *Ziegfeld Girl: Image and Icon in Culture and Cinema* (Durham, NC: Duke University Press, 1999). Professor Mizejewski is an author and professor of women's gender, and sexuality studies at Ohio State University.

14. Rachel Shteir, *Striptease: The Untold History of the Girlie Show* (New York: Oxford University Press, 2006), 30.

Chapter Four

1. Jacques-Charles, *Cent Ans de Music-Hall* (Paris: Editions Jeheber, 1956), 186.

2. Angelo Luerti, *Non Solo Erté* (Venice, Italy: Guildo Tamori Editore, 2005), 21.

3. Jacob, *Music Hall!*, 65.

4. After a fire destroyed the Casino de Paris's auditorium it was rebuilt with a glass pool that could be raised to the level of the stage. Before the Clerico brothers took over the Lido, it had a combination supper club and pool type formula preserved in old news movies: clients in evening dress smoke and drink, other clients in fashionable maillots and belted stripe-topped bathing suits dive into the pool where opera singers float in a gondola. For example, see https://www.youtube.com/watch?v=S90hi7wVcRk.

5. Shteir, *Striptease*, 2.

6. Castle, *The Folies-Bergère*, 235.

7. Castle, *The Folies-Bergère*, 236.

8. Leslie, *A Hard Act to Follow*, 180.

9. Luerti, *Non Solo Erté*, 27.

10. Luerti, *Non Solo Erté*, 263.

11. Martin Pénet, *Mistinguett: La Reine du Music-Hall* (Paris: Editions Du Rocher, 1995), 644.

12. Mel Gordon, personal communication, March 31, 2017.

13. "Introducing Gertrude Hoffman," Brooklyn Public Library, April 14, 2011.

14. Jacques-Charles, *Cent Ans de Music-Hall*, 79.

15. Parker, *The Subversive Stitch*, 43.

16. Castle, *The Folies-Bergère*, 64.

17. The descriptions of individual artists very active between the wars is with the help of Sabine Piollet and Angelo Luerti.

18. Gary Chapman lives in Stroud, Gloucestershire (UK), and teaches sugar craft and cake decorating around the world. He is the author most recently of *Classic Fabric Flowers* and *Dolly Tree: A Dream of Beauty*.

19. Jean Claude Bologne, *Histoire de la Pudeur* (Paris: Olivier Orban, 1997).

20. Jacques-Charles, *Cent Ans de Music-Hall*, 79.

21. Sabine Gouin Piollet is an authority on French theater and music hall costumes from 1920 to 1940 and administers the Piollet Collection.

Chapter Five

1. Castle, *The Folies-Bergère*, 98.

2. Berlanstein, *Daughters of Eve*, 210.

3. Prasteau, *La Merveilleuse Aventure*, 69–70.

4. Castle, *The Folies-Bergère*, 97.

5. Rearick, *Paris Dreams, Paris Memories*, 34–35.

6. Pascal, personal exchange.

7. Andrea Stuart, *Showgirls* (London: Cape, 1996), 8.

8. Heather Dawkins, *The Nude in French Art and Culture, 1870–1910* (New York: Cambridge University Press, 2002), 11.

9. Fanny Trollope, *Domestic Manners of the Americans*, 5th ed. (London: Richard Bentley, 1839), 103.

10. Lela F. Felter-Kerley, "Dressing Down: Nudity in Belle Epoque Theatrical Entertainment," *Journal of the Western Society for French History*, Vol. 32 (2004), 295.

11. Castle, *The Folies-Bergère*, 67.

12. Kalifa, *La Culture de Masse*, 44.

13. Parker, *The Subversive Stitch*, 38.

14. Kalifa, *La Culture de Masse*, 47.

15. Leslie, *A Hard Act to Follow*, 159.

16. F. Berkely Smith, *How Paris Amuses Itself* (New York: Funk & Wagnalls, 1903), 24–28; in Whiting, 30.

17. No authentication of the quote has been located (pers. communication with Pat Shipman).

18. Pat Shipman, *Femme Fatale: Love, Lies and the Unknown Life of Mata Hari* (New York: HarperCollins, 2007), 146.

19. Shipman, *Femme Fatale*, 165.

20. Shipman, *Femme Fatale*, 180.

21. Shipman, *Femme Fatale*, 149.

22. Shipman, *Femme Fatale*, 149.

23. Shipman, *Femme Fatale*, 155.

24. Shipman, *Femme Fatale*, 153.

25. "From the time that I was a child I loved men: a strongly built male brought me to a state of ecstasy" (Shipman, *Femme Fatale*, 170).

26. Patricia A. Tilburg, "Colette's Republic: Work, Gender, and Popular Culture and the Nude in the French Music-Hall, 1904–1914," *Radical History Review*, Vol. 98 (2007), 141.

27. Tilberg, "Colette's Republic," 148.

28. Tilberg, "Colette's Republic," 67.

29. Leon Worth, "Ingres, Marquet, Colette Willy," *Paris Journal*, May 2, 1911; in Tilberg, "Colette's Republic," 73–74.

30. Colette, *Collected Stories*, ed. Robert Phelps, trans. Martin Secker and Warburg Ltd. (New York: Farrar Straus Giroux, 1983 [orig. 1958]), 118.

31. Colette, *Mitsou and Music-Hall Sidelights*, trans. Anne-Marie Callimachi (New York: Farrar, Straus and Cudahy, 1957), 211–215.

32. Pougy, *My Blue Notebooks*, 77.

33. Angelo Luerti from Milan is an avid researcher on the history of costume and poster art for the music-hall of the years between the two wars. He is the author of the volumes *Not Only Erté* and *Charles Gesmar, 1900–1928*.

34. "Mistinguett, la Légende du Music-Hall," interview with Martin Pénet on RTL published Nov. 3, 2014. The images discussed are in the author's *La Reine du Music Hall* (Paris: Editions du Rocher, 1995).

35. Pénet, *La Reine du Music Hall*, 386.

36. Cocteau's picture in Pénet, *La Reine du Music Hall*.

37. Pénet, *La Reine du Music Hall*, 449–450.

38. Josephine Baker and Jo Bouillon, *Josephine*, trans. Mariana Fitzpatrick (New York: Harper & Row, 1976), 85.

39. Derval, *The Folies-Bergère*, 64–65.

40. Castle, *The Folies-Bergère*, 191.

41. Alicja Sowinska, "Dialectics of the Banana Skirt: The Ambiguities of Josephine Baker's Self-Representation." *Michigan Feminist Studies*, Vol. 19 (Fall 2005–Spring 2006), http://hdl.handle.net/2027/spo.ark5583.0019.003.

42. Lydia Crowson, "Cocteau and 'Le Numéro Barbette,'" *Modern Drama*, Vol. 19, 1 (Spring 1976), 79–87, 83.

43. Crowson, "Cocteau and 'Le Numéro Barbette,'" 79–87, 83.

Chapter Six

1. The aigrettes were chic and original. Madame Poiret was photographed in a Directoire-transparent lampshade tunic, harem pants, and a little cap from which a white aigrette sprang about 18 inches into the air.

2. Pascal Jacob is a renowned circus arts author and historian who writes about jugglers, acrobats, circus animals, and the American and Parisian circuses. His *His-*

toire du cirque was published in 2002 by Editions de la chene.

3. Jacques-Charles, *Le Journal d'une Figurante: Roman de moeurs du music-hall* (Paris: Gallimard, 1933), 48–49.

4. Famed choreography Roland Petit choreographed the song for "La Revue" at the Casino de Paris in 1969, buying the music-hall the next year. See https://www.youtube.com/watch?v=DRfgebr5BBo.

5. "'Jubilee!' at Bally's Las Vegas Gets New Costumes," June 22, 2011, https://www.youtube.com/watch?v=ewEXpLH5uAs.

6. Lisa Townsend Rodgers, "Showgirl Regalia on Display," February 11, 2016, vegasseven.com/galleries/showgirl/regalia-display/.

7. Grant Philipo, personal communication, December 2016.

8. Burkhard Bilger, "Feathered Glory," *The New Yorker*, September 25, 2017, 70.

9. Bilger, "Feathered Glory," 68.

10. Eric Charles-Donatien, a Parisian born in Martinique, is a *plumassier* designer. Among his clients are fashion designers Roger Vivier, Dior, Margiela, Vera Wang, Yves Saint Laurent, Jean Paul Gautier, and the English milliner Stephen Jones. He has his own company, MOYE & DA of made-to-measure accessories. In Paris he is seen wearing his own feather designs.

11. Jacques-Charles, *La Revue de ma vie* (Paris: Librairie Artheme Fayard, 1958), 233–234.

12. Castle, *The Folies-Bergère*, 220.

13. Leimomi Oakes, thedreamstress.com/2017/02.

14. Leimomi Oakes, thedreamstress.com/2017/02.

15. American Duchess Historical Costuming, blog. americanduchess.com/2012/04/.

16. Marion Brégier, www.blogger.com/profile/116373057258748200625.

17. Parker, *The Subversive Stitch*, 170.

18. Roger Leong, *From Russia with Love: Costumes for the Ballets Russes, 1909–1933* (Canberra: National Gallery of Australia, 2000), 8.

19. Jean-Baptiste Drachkovitch worked with the founders of the sequin company as an embroiderer for 20 years before becoming the company's director in 2010.

20. Jessica Schiffer, "The Surprising History of Sequins," November 14, 2015, www.whowhatwear.com/the-history-of-sequins.

21. "Du Moulin Rouge à Lucky Luke: Clairvoy, chausseur des artistes," *L'express*, April 24, 2014, https://www.lexpress.fr/actualites/1/actualite/du-moulin-rouge-a-lucky-luke-clairvoy-chausseur-des-artistes_1511160.html.

22. Mathieu Labonde, "Mode: Clairvoy, botte secrète sure meseure, *Le Parisien*, April 4, 2014, http://www.leparisien.fr/magazine/plaisir/mode-clairvoy-botte-secrete-sur-mesure-03-04-2014-3737741.php.

23. Lulu from Montmartre, www.lulufrommontmartre.com/2014/04/visite_de_l'atelier_clairvoy_le_bottier_des_stars.

Chapter Seven

1. Mel Gordon, *Voluptuous Panic: The Erotic World of Weimar Berlin* (Port Townsend, WA: Feral House, 2008), 62–63. *Gesamtkunstwerk* refers to a totality of art forms, an ideal theater, the word having been used to describe Wagnerian opera.

2. Gunter Berghaus, "Girlkultur: Feminism, Americanism, and Popular Entertainment in Weimar Germany," *Journal of Design History*, Vol. 1, No. ¾ (1988), 200.

3. Eric D. Weitz, *Weimar Germany: Promise and Tragedy* (Princeton, NJ: Princeton University Press, 2013), 50.

4. Weitz, *Weimar Germany*, 272, 312.

5. Berghaus, "Girlkultur," 199.

6. Peter Jelavich, *Berlin Cabaret* (Cambridge, MA: Harvard University Press, 1993), 3.

7. Jelavich, *Berlin Cabaret*, 157.

8. Lori Munz, *Cabaret Berlin: Revue, Kabarett, and Film Music Between the Wars* (Hamburg: Edel Classics GmbH, 2005), 37.

9. Jelavich, *Berlin Cabaret*, 163.

10. Jelavich, *Berlin Cabaret*, 163.

11. The scene "Wovon matrosen traumen" from Eric Charell's revue *Fur Dich*. Wolfgang Jansen, *Glanzrevuen der Zwanziger Jahre* (Berlin: Edition Hentrich Berlin, 1987), 76.

12. Jansen, *Glanzrevuen der Zwanziger Jahre* 75.

13. Berghaus, "Girlkultur," 219*n*99.

14. Atina Grossmann, "Girlkultur or Thoroughly Rationalized Female: A New Woman in Weimar Germany?," *Women in Culture and Politics: A Century of Change*, eds. Judith Friedlander, Blanche Wiesen Cook, Alice Kessler-Harris and Carroll Smith-Rosenberg (Bloomington: Indiana University Press, 1986), 76.

Chapter Eight

1. Mel Gordon, personal communication, spring 2017.

2. Prasteau, *La Merveilleuse Aventure*, 296.

3. Mel Gordon, conversation, March 3, 2017.

4. Luc Sante, personal communication, May 21, 2017.

5. Castle, *The Folies-Bergère*, 112.

6. Phillip Garner, in a personal exchange.

7. Ibid.

8. Jacques-Charles, *La Revue*, 149.

9. Mel Gordon, *Horizontal Collaboration*, 189–190.

10. Mel Gordon, *Horizontal Collaboration*, 110.

11. Parker, *The Subversive Stitch*, 46.

12. Rosalind Parry is a lecturer at Princeton University, where she received her PhD in 2018. She has written about print, design, and architecture for *Raritan*, *Literary Imagination*, and *T—The New York Times Style Magazine*.

13. Pascal Jacob, personal communication.

14. Paul Lewis, *The New York Times*, July 7, 1987.

15. Charles Rearick, personal communication, October 16, 2017.

16. Philippe Garner, after a career as auctioneer at Sotheby's, became the international head of photography and twentieth century decorative arts at Christie's and now is Christie's deputy chairman of photography.

17. Charles Rearick, *Paris Dreams, Paris Memories: The City and Its Mystique* (Stanford, CA: Stanford University Press, 2011), 122.

Chapter Nine

1. Information on producer Donn Arden comes largely from Special Collections, UNLV, Donn Arden Papers, 2001–5, Biography.

2. Joanne L. Goodwin, *Changing the Game: Women at Work in Las Vegas, 1940–1990* (Reno and Las Vegas: University of Nevada Press, 2014), 81.

3. Graham, *Scarlet Women*, 25.

4. Special Collections, Donna Arden Papers, Biography, 20601–5a.

5. Graham, *Scarlet Women*, 23.

6. *Las Vegas Sun*, August 1, 1959.

7. "Les Archives de Michel Gyarmathy," by Adrien Bernadin, June 23, 2012, online.

8. Erika Kinetz, "The Twilight of the Ostrich-Plumed, Rhinestone-Brassiered Las Vegas Showgirl," *New York Times*, August 13, 2006—ANCE.

9. Graham, *Scarlet Women*, 37.

10. Diane Palm, "Trapped in Time," NPR, February 13, 2016.

11. Pete Menefee quote, July 13, 2011, Las Vegas blog.

12. Lisa Townsend Rodgers, "Showgirl Regalia on Display," Vegasseven.com, http://vegasseven.com/galleries/showgirl-regalia-display/.

13. "A Life of Folies—Michel Gyarmathy," interview by Paul Tabori, *Penthouse*, Vol. 1, 9 (May 1970).

14. "One Costume, Sexier than Ever," interview with Barbara Walters on KNPR, August 5, 2015, knpr.org/knpr/2015-08/one-costume-sexier-ever.

15. Robin Leach, "Folies Bergere Gets New Lease on Life with Museum Exhibit," *Las Vegas Sun*, August 20. 2017, https://lasvegassun.com/vegasdeluxe/2016/jun/08/folies-bergere-gets-new-lease-on-life-with-exhibit/.

16. "A Life of Folies—Michel Gyarmathy," interview.

17. "A Life of Folies—Michel Gyarmathy," interview.

18. Maggie Bukowski, personal communication, May 2017.

19. KLAS Las Vegas Steve Wynn Bellagio Grand Opening Tour & Interview, https://www.youtube.com/watch?v=nLsK4BSZon8.

20. William L. Fox, *In the Desert of Desire: Las Vegas and the Culture of Spectacle* (Reno: University of Nevada Press, 2005), 117.

21. Lord Illingworth is the rake who speaks the line in Act Three (Oscar Wilde, *The Plays* [London: Methuen, 1907], 156).

22. Karen Burns, personal communication, December 2016.

23. Pete Menefee is a multiple Emmy Award–winning costume designer for shows including *Jubilee!*, *Splash*, and *Hello, Hollywood, Hello!* He danced as a chimney sweep in the film *Mary Poppins*.

24. Mistinguett produces, directs and costumes showgirl revues. She also does nonpareil showgirl art.

25. A costume designer who preferred to stay anonymous.

26. Gary Stromberg is a legendary publicist who in the rock 'n' roll era represented musicians including the Rolling Stones, the Doors, Pink Floyd, Muhammed Ali, Barbara Streisand, Three Dog Night, Elton John, Crosby, Stills & Nash, and Steppenwolf.

Chapter Ten

1. Brad Griffies, personal communication.

2. Brad Griffies, personal communication, summer 2016.

3. Jack Barth and Ian Michaels, "Nudes on Ice," *Spy Magazine*, May 1989, 80–81.

Appendix A

1. Cassidy Zachary is a fashion historian and author living in Albuquerque, New Mexico, where she also works as a costumer in film and television.

2. "Lady Duff Gordon Models for Mail Order Distribution," *Women's Wear*, August 18, 1916, 55.

3. Lady Duff Gordon, *A Woman of Temperament* (Attica Books, 2012), 188. Originally published as *Discretions and Indiscretions* by the London publisher Jarrolds Ltd. in 1932.

4. Lady Duff Gordon, *A Woman of Temperament*, 187.

5. Lady Duff Gordon, *A Woman of Temperament*, 187.

6. "Beauty, Fashion and the Follies," *Ladies' Home Journal*, March 1923, 16.

7. "Beauty, Fashion and the Follies," *Ladies' Home Journal*, March 1923, 16.

8. "Pure Dye Crepe Prints and Sports Cloth for Glorifying American Girl," *Women's Wear Daily*, October 28, 1931, 8.

9. "Designs by Erté of Paris," *Harper's Bazaar*, April 1917, 62.

10. Erté, *Things I Remember: An Autobiography* (New York: Sevenarts, 1975), 42.

11. Mistinguett, *Mistinguett, Queen of the Paris Night* (London: Elek Books, 1954), 104.

12. Mistinguett, *Mistinguett*, 104.

13. "Hats," *The Greenbook Magazine*, April 1916, 621.

14. "Hats," 621.

15. Marcel Sauvage, *Les Mémoires de Joséphine Baker* (Paris: Kran, 1927), 84.

16. Josephine Baker and Jo Bouillon, *Josephine*, trans. Mariana Fitzpatrick (New York: Harper and Row, 1977), 52.

17. Jean-Claude Baker and Chris Chase, *Josephine: The Hungry Heart* (New York: Random House, 1995), 120.

18. "Vogue's Eye View of the Mode," *Vogue*, July 1, 1932, 21.

19. "Turquoise as a Perfect Background," *Women's Wear Daily*, February 3, 1936, 30.

20. Castle, *The Folies Bergère*, 189.

21. Castle, *The Folies-Bergère*, 190.

22. Robin Givhan, *The Battle of Versailles: The Night American Fashion Stumbled into the Spotlight and Made History* (New York: Flatiron Books, 2015), 185.

23. Mizejewski, *Ziegfeld Girl*, 136.

24. Mizejewski, *Ziegfeld Girl*, 136.

25. Teri Agins, "The Sultan of Sequins Opens His Vault," *Wall Street Journal*, Eastern Edition, New York, November 17, 2005, D.8.

26. Agins, "The Sultan of Sequins."

27. Frank De Caro, *Unmistakably Mackie: The Fashion and Fantasy of Bob Mackie* (New York: Rizzoli Universe, 1999), 67.

28. "Fashion Scoops," *Women's Wear Daily*, October 3, 2002, 5.

29. Hamish Bowles, "Vogue's View," *Vogue*, October 1, 1997, 143.

30. Bowles, "Vogue's View."

31. Bowles, "Vogue's View."

32. "The Year in Fashion: They Said It," *Women's Wear Daily*, December 14, 2016, 58.

33. Henry Alford, "Fashionista Paris," *New York Times*, September 28, 2008, TR1.

Appendix B

1. Tracy Jenkins Yoshimura is a fashion historian whose interests include the history of retail, the fashion system, and exhibition making. She is an associate collections manager at the Costume Institute at the Metropolitan Museum of Art, where she helps care for the collection.

2. https://digitalcollections.nypl.org/items/a279769 a-7c83-c2f6-e040-e00a18063659.

3. https://digitalcollections.nypl.org/items/510d47 da-0c1f-a3d9-e040-e00a18064a99.

4. Mizejewski, *Ziegfeld Girl*, 136.

5. Mizejewski, *Ziegfeld Girl*, 140.

6. Edward Marder, *Hollywood and History: Costume Design in Film* (Los Angeles: Los Angeles County Museum of Art; London: Thames and Hudson, 1987), 9.

7. Howard Gutner, *Gowns by Adrian: The MGM Years 1928–1941* (New York: H. N. Abrams, 2001), 64.

8. Gutner, *Gowns by Adrian*, 64–66.

Bibliography

Allen, Robert C. *Horrible Prettiness: Burlesque and American Culture*. Chapel Hill: University of North Carolina Press, 1991.

Baker, Josephine, and Jo Bouillon. *Josephine*. Translated by Marianne Fitzpatrick. New York: Harper, 1977.

Balducci, Richard. *Les Princesses de Paris: L'Age D'or des Cocottes*. Paris: Editions Hors Collection, 1994.

Baral, Robert. *Revue: The Great Broadway Period*. New York: Fleet, 1962.

Barrows, Susanna, ed. *Pleasures of Paris: Daumier to Picasso*. Boston: Museum of Fine Arts, 1991.

Bell, Robert. *Ballets Russes: The Art of Costume*. Canberra, A.C.T.: National Gallery of Australia; London: Thames & Hudson, 2011.

Bentley, Toni. *Sisters of Salome*. New Haven, CT: Yale University Press, 2002.

Berghaus, Gunter. "Girlkultur: Feminism, Americanism, and Popular Entertainment in Weimar Germany." Vol. 1, No. ¾ (1988), 193–219. Published by Oxford University Press on behalf of Design History Society. http://www.jstor.org/stable/1315711.

Berlanstein, Lenard R. *Daughters of Eve: A Cultural History of French Theater Women from the Old Regime to the Fin de Siècle*. Cambridge, MA: Harvard University Press, 2001.

Binder, Polly. *The Truth About Cora Pearl*. London: Weidenfeld & Nicolson, 1986.

Bologne, Jean-Claude. *Histoire de la Pudeur*. Paris: Olivier Orban, 1997.

Bonfante, Larissa. *Etruscan Dress*. Baltimore, MD: Johns Hopkins University Press, 1975.

_____. "Nudity as a Costume in Classical Art." *American Journal of Archaeology*, Vol. 93, no. 4 (October 1989).

Bonniel, Marie-Aude. "Le Carnaval de Paris de 1896: V'la le Boeuf Gras Qui Passé." *Le Figaro.fr*

Bouissac, Paul. *Semiotics at the Circus*. Berlin: De Gruyter Mouton, 2011.

Castle, Charles. *The Folies-Bergère*. London: Methuen, 1982.

Cate, Phillip Dennis, and Mary Shaw, eds. *The Spirit of Montmartre: Cabarets, Humor, and the Avant-Garde, 1875–1905*. New Brunswick, NJ: Rutgers University Press, 1996.

Cesaretti, Paolo. *Empress of Byzantium*. New York: Vendome, 2004.

Chazin-Bennahum, Judith. *The Lure of Perfection: Fashion and Ballet, 1780–1830*. London: Routledge, 2004.

Chew, William L., III. "'Straight Sam' Meets 'Lewd' Lewis: American Perceptions of French Sexuality, 1775–1815." In *Revolutions and Watersheds: Transatlantic Dialogues, 1775–1815*. Edited by W.M. Verhoeven and Beth Dolan Kautz. Atlanta: Rodopi, 1999.

Clarke, Mary, and Clement Crisp. *The History of Dance*. New York: Crown, 1981.

Cohen, Selma Jeanne. *Dance as a Theater Art: Source Readings in Dance History from 1581 to the Present*, 2nd ed. Trenton, NJ: Princeton Book Company, 1992.

Colette. *Mes Apprentisages*. Paris: Ferenczi, 1936.

Colette. *Mitsou and Music-Hall Delights*. Translated by Raymond Postgate and Anne-Marie Callimachi. New York: Farrar, Straus & Cudahy, 1957.

Conlin, Jonathan. *Tales of Two Cities: Paris, London and the Birth of the Modern City*. Berkeley, CA: Counterpoint, 2013.

Costille, Marine. *Spectacles au Music-Hall: Le Cas de Quatre Salles Parisiennes, 1917–1940*. Histoire, 2016. dumas-0147493.

Costume Designs for French Music-Halls, 1910–1963. Houghton Library of Harvard University MS Thr 1134.

Crouch, Emma Elizabeth. *The Memoirs of Cora Pearl: The English Beauty of the French Empire*. London: George Vickers, 1886.

Current, Richard Nelson, and Marcia Ewing Current. *Loie Fuller, Goddess of Light*. Boston: Northeastern University Press, 1997.

Curtis, Thomas Quinn. "A Revamped Show and a New Boite on Paris Night Scene." *International Herald Tribune*, January 2, 1969.

Damase, Jacques. *Les Folies du Music-Hall: A History of the Paris Music-Hall from 1914 to the Present Day, etc.* Translated by Tony White. London: Anthony Blond, 1962.

Dawkins, Heather. *The Nude in French Art and Culture: 1870–1910*. London: Cambridge University Press, 2002.

De Caro, Frank. *Unmistakably Mackie: The Fashion and Fantasy of Bob Mackie*. New York: Rizzoli Universe, 1999.

Denvir, Bernard. *Toulouse-Lautrec*. London: Thames and Hudson, 1991.

Derval, Paul. *Folies Bergère*. Translated by Lucienne Hill. London: Methuen, 1955; Editions de Paris, 1954.

Deschaumes, Edmond. *Le Mal du Théâtre*. Paris: E. Dentu, 1888.

Dijkstra, Bram. *Idols of Perversity: Fantasies of Feminine Evil in Fin-de-Siècle Culture*. New York: Oxford University Press, 1986.

Doughty, Robin W. *Feather Fashions and Bird Preserva-*

tion: A Study in Nature Protection. Berkeley: University of California Press, 1975.

Duff Gordon, Lady Lucy. *A Woman of Temperament.* Attica Books, 2012. Originally published as *Discretions and Indiscretions* by the London publisher Jarrolds Ltd. in 1932.

Edwards, Holly. *Noble Dreams, Wicked Pleasures: Orientalism in America, 1870–1930.* Princeton, NJ: Princeton University Press, 2000.

Ellis, Havelock. *The Dance of Life.* New York: Modern Library, 1929.

Ellman, Richard. *Oscar Wilde.* New York: Vintage, 1988.

Eltis, Sos. *Acts of Desire: Women and Sex on Stage, 1800–1930.* New York: Oxford University Press, 2013.

Erenberg, Lewis A. *Steppin' Out: New York Nightlife and the Transformation of American Culture, 1890–1930.* Chicago, IL: University of Chicago Press, 1994.

Erté. *My Life/My Art: An Autobiography.* New York: E.P. Dutton, 1989.

_____. *Things I Remember: An Autobiography.* New York: Sevenarts, 1975.

Felter-Kerley, Lela F. *Uncovering Paris: Scandals and Nude Spectacles in the Belle Époque.* Baton Rouge: Louisiana State University Press, 2017.

Ferguson, Priscilla Parkhurst. *Paris as Revolution: Writing the Nineteenth Century City.* Berkeley: University of California Press, 1994.

Fox, William L. *In the Desert of Desire: Las Vegas and the Culture of Spectacle.* Reno: University of Nevada Press, 2005.

Fraser, Flora. *Emma, Lady Hamilton.* New York: Knopf, 1987.

Frasnay, Daniel. *Les Girls: Paris 1952–1979.* Los Angeles, CA: Greybull, 2005.

Frey, Julia. *Toulouse-Lautrec: A Life.* New York: Viking, 1994.

Gardiner, James. *Gaby Deslys: A Fatal Attraction.* London: Sidgwick & Jackson, 1986.

Givhan, Robin. *The Battle of Versailles: The Night American Fashion Stumbled into the Spotlight and Made History.* New York: Flatiron Books, 2015.

Glenn, Susan A. *Female Spectacle: The Theatrical Roots of Modern Feminism.* Cambridge, MA: Harvard University Press, 2002.

Goldsworthy, Adrian. *Antony and Cleopatra.* New Haven, CT: Yale University Press, 2010.

Goodwin, Joanne L. *Changing the Game: Women at Work in Las Vegas, 1940–1990.* Reno and Las Vegas: University of Nevada Press, 2014.

Gordon, Mel. *Horizontal Collaboration: The Erotic World of Paris, 1920–1946.* Port Townsend, WA: Feral House, 2015.

_____. *Voluptuous Panic: The Erotic World of Weimar Berlin.* Port Townsend, WA: Feral House, 2006.

Gordon, Rae Beth. *Dances with Darwin, 1875–1910: Vernacular Modernity in France.* New York: Routledge, 2009.

Graham, Ian. *Scarlet Women: The Scandalous Lives of Courtesans, Concubines, and Royal Mistresses.* New York: St. Martin's, 2016.

Graham, Jefferson. *Vegas, Live and in Person.* New York: Abbeville, 1989.

Graves-Brown, Carolyn. *Dancing for Hathor: Women in Ancient Egypt.* London: Bloomsbury Academic, 2010.

Griffin, Susan. *The Book of the Courtesans: A Catalogue of Their Virtues.* New York: Broadway Books, 2001.

Guilbert, Yvette. *The Song of My Life.* London: G.G. Harrap & Co., [1929].

Gundle, Stephen. "Mapping the Origins of Glamour: Giovanni Baldini, Paris and the Belle Epoque." *Journal of European Studies,* Vol. 29, no. 3 (September 1999).

Gutner, Howard. *Gowns by Adrian: The MGM Years, 1928–1941.* New York: H.N. Abrams, 2001.

Gutsche-Miller, Sarah. *Parisian Music-Hall Ballet, 1871–1913.* Rochester, NY: University of Rochester Press, 2015.

Hamilton, Trenton. *The History of Western Dance.* New York: Britannica Educational Publishing, 2016.

Harris, Lynette, ed. *The Belly Dance Reader Book, One.* Fairfax, GA: Gilded Serpent, 2012.

Hickman, Katie. *Courtesans: Money, Sex and Fame in the Nineteenth Century.* New York: William Morrow, 2003.

Holland, Tom. *Dynasty: The Rise and Fall of the House of Caesar.* New York: Knopf Doubleday, 2015.

Hollander, Ann. *Seeing Through Clothes.* Berkeley: University of California Press, 1993.

Hunt, Lynn. "The Many Bodies of Marie Antoinette; Political Pornography and the Problem of the Feminine in the French Revolution." *Eroticism and the Body Politic.* Edited by Lynn Hunt. Baltimore, MD: Johns Hopkins University Press, 1991.

Jacob, Pascal. *Music Hall! De Mans à Macao.* Paris: Magellani & Cie, 2013.

Jacques-Charles. *Cent Ans de Music-Hall.* Paris: Editions Jeheber, 1956.

_____. *Le Journal d'une Figurante: Roman de moeurs du music-hall.* Paris: Gallimard, 1933.

_____. *La Revue de ma vie.* Paris: Librairie Artheme Fayard, 1958.

Jelavich, Peter. *Berlin Cabaret: Studies in Cultural History.* Cambridge, MA: Harvard University Press, 1999.

Jones, Colin. *Paris: The Biography of a City.* New York: Viking, 2004.

Kalifa, Dominque. *La Culture de la Masse en France, 1860–1930.* Paris: Editions de la Découverte, 2001.

Kessler, M.R. *Sheer Presence: The Veil in Manet's Paris.* Minneapolis: University of Minnesota Press, 2004.

Lasser, Michael. "The Glorifier: Florenz Ziegfeld and the Creation of the American Showgirl." *The American Scholar,* Summer 1994.

Lee, Carol. *Ballet in Western Culture: A History of Its Origins and Evolutions.* New York: Routledge, 2002.

Leong, Roger. *From Russia with Love: Costumes for the Ballets Russes, 1909–1933.* Canberra: National Gallery of Australia, 2000.

Leslie, Peter. *A Hard Act to Follow: A Music Hall Review.* New York: Paddington Press, 1978.

Levenstein, Harvey. *Seductive Journeys: American Tourists in France from Jefferson to the Jazz Era.* Chicago, IL: University of Chicago Press, 2000.

Lexova, Irena. *Ancient Egyptian Dances.* Translated by K. Haltmar. Mineola, NY: Dover, 2000.

Lucie-Smith, Edward. *Sexuality in Western Art.* London: Thames & Hudson, 1991.

Luerti, Angelo. *Charles Gesmar, 1900–1928: L'Affichiste Attitré de Mistinguett* Milan: Angelo Luerti, 2009.

_____. *Non Solo Erté: Costume Design for the Paris Music Hall 1918–1940.* Vicenza: Guido Tamoni Editore, 2005.

Mackrell, Alice. *Art and Fashion: The Impact of Art on Fashion and Fashion on Art.* London: Batsford, 2005.

Macmillan, Margaret. *Paris 1919: Six Months That Changed the World.* New York: Random House, 2001.

Macqueen-Pope, W. *Gaiety: Theater of Enchantment.* London: W. H. Allen, 1949.

Maeder, Edward. *Hollywood and History: Costume Design in Film.* Los Angeles: Los Angeles County Museum of Art; London: Thames and Hudson, 1987.

Majer, Michele, ed. *Staging Fashion, 1880–1920: Jane Hading, Lily Elsie, Billie Burke.* Bard Graduate Center, Yale University Press, 2012.

Maza, Sarah. *Private Lives and Public Affairs: The Causes Célèbres of Prerevolutionary France.* Berkeley: University of California Press, 1993.

McManus, Clare. *Women on the Renaissance Stage: Anna of Denmark and Female Masquing in the Stuart Court (1590–1619).* New York: Manchester University Press, 2002.

Ménestrier, Claude-François. *Des Ballets anciens et modernes selon les règles du théâtre.* Paris: René Guignard, 1982.

Merrill, Jane, and Keren Ben-Horin. *She's Got Legs: A History of Hemlines and Fashion.* Atglen, PA: Schiffer, 2014.

Mesch, Rachel. *Having It All in the Belle Époque: How French Women's Magazines Invented the Modern Woman.* Stanford, CA: Stanford University Press, 2013.

Miller, Michael B. *The Bon Marché: Bourgeois Culture and the Department Store, 1869–1920.* Princeton, NJ: Princeton University Press, 1994.

Mistinguett. *Mistinguett, Queen of the Paris Night.* London: Elek Books, 1954.

Mizejewski, Linda. *Ziegfeld Girl: Image and Icon in Culture and Cinema.* Durham, NC: Duke University Press, 1999.

Mordden, Ethan. *Ziegfeld: The Man Who Invented Show Business.* New York: St. Martin's, 2008.

Munro-Miller, Jennifer. *In the Flesh: The Representation of Burlesque Theatre in American Art and Visual Culture.* Diss., University of Southern California, 2010. digitallibrary.usc.edu/cdm/ref/collection/p15799coll1271/id/396449.

Munz, Lori. *Cabaret Berlin: Revue, Kabarett, and Film Music Between the Wars.* Hamburg: Edel Classics, 2005.

Noland, Sherwin B. *Leonardo da Vinci.* New York: Penguin, 2005.

Noverre, Jean-Georges. *Lettres sur la Dance, sur les Ballets et les Arts, Vol. 1, 1803.* St. Petersburg: Jean Charles Schnoor, 1803.

Oberthur, Mariel. *Cafés and Cabarets of Montmartre.* Salt Lake City, UT: Gibbs M. Smith, 1984.

Oesterley, W.O.E. *The Sacred Dance: A Study in Comparative Folklore in the Ancient World.* London: Cambridge University Press, 1927; rep. Dover, 2002.

Parker, Derek, and Julia Parker. *The Natural History of the Chorus Girl.* New York: Bobbs-Merrill, 1975.

Parker, Rozsika. *The Subversive Stitch: Embroidery and the Making of the Feminine.* London: I.B. Tauris, 2010.

Pearl, Cora [pseud.]; Derek Parker. *Grand Horizontal: The Memoirs of a Passionate Lady.* Edited by William Blatchford. New York: Stein & Day, 1980.

Pénet, Martin. *Mistinguett: La Reine du music hall.* Paris: Editions du Rocher, 1995.

Pessis, Jacques, and Jacques Crépineau. *The Moulin Rouge.* New York: Alan Sutton, St. Martin's, 1990.

Pichler, Caroline. *Memorabilia from My Life,* vol. 1. Munich, 1914.

Pougy, Liane de. *My Blue Notebooks.* New York: J.P. Tarcher/Putnam, 2002.

Prasteau, Jean. *La Merveilleuse Aventure du Casino de Paris.* Paris: Editions Denoiel, 1975.

Prendergast, Christopher. *Paris and the Nineteenth Century.* Manchester, UK: Blackwell, 1992.

Pritchard, Jane, and Geoffrey Marsh, eds. *Diaghilev and the Golden Age of the Ballets Russes, 1909–1929.* London: Victoria & Albert Museum, 2005.

Purvis, Alston, Peter Rand, and Anna Winestein. *The Ballets Russes and the Art of Design.* New York: Monacelli Press, 2009.

Ravelhofer, Barbara. *The Early Stuart Masque: Dance, Costume, and Music.* New York: Oxford University Press, 2006.

Rearick, Charles. *Paris Dreams, Paris Memories: The City and Its Mystique.* Stanford, CA: Stanford University Press, 2011.

_____. *Pleasures of the Belle Époque: Entertainment & Festivity in Turn-of-the-Century France.* New Haven, CT: Yale University Press, 1985.

Ricci, Franco Maria. *Umberto Brunelleschi: Fashion-Stylist, Illustration, Stage and Costume Designer.* Edited by Laura Casalis. Translated by Katherine Benita Wells. New York: Rizzoli International Publications, 1979.

Richardson, Joanna. *The Courtesans: The Demi-Monde in Nineteenth Century France.* Edison, NJ: Castle Books, 2004.

Roberts, Mary Louise. *Disruptive Acts: The New Woman in Fin-de-Siècle France.* Chicago: University of Chicago Press, 2006.

_____. "Rethinking Female Celebrity: The Eccentric Star in Nineteenth Century France." In *Constructing Charisma: Celebrity, Fame, and Power in Nineteenth-century Europe.* Edited by Edward Berenson and Eva Giloi. New York: Berghahn Books, 2010.

Roe, Sue. *In Montmartre: Picasso, Matisse and the Birth of Modernist Art.* New York: Penguin, 2014.

Rose, Phyllis. *Jazz Cleopatra: Josephine Baker in Her Time.* New York: Vintage, 1991.

Rublack, Ulinka. *Dressing Up: Cultural Identity in Renaissance Europe.* New York: Oxford University Press, 2011.

Saint-Hubert, Monsieur de. *La manière de Composer et de Faire Réussir les Ballets.* Introduction and Notes by Marie-Francoise Christout. Geneva: Editions Minkoff, 1993.

Sante, Luc. *The Other Paris.* New York: Farrar, Straus, Giroux, 2015.

Sauvage, Marcel. *Les Mémoires de Joséphine Baker.* Paris: Kran, 1927.

Schwartz, Vanessa R. *It's So French! Hollywood, Paris, and the Making of Cosmopolitan Film Culture.* Chicago: University of Chicago, 2007.

_____. *Spectacular Realities: Early Mass Culture in Fin-de-Siècle Paris.* Berkeley: University of California Press, 1999.

Segel, Howard B. *Turn of the Century Cabaret: Paris, Barcelona, Berlin, Munich, Vienna, Cracow, Moscow, St. Petersburg, Zurich.* New York: Columbia University Press, 1987.

Senelick, Laurence. *Cabaret Performance: Sketches, Songs, Monologues, Memoirs.* Baltimore, MD: Johns Hopkins University Press, 1993.

_____. "Eroticism in Early Theatrical Photography." *Theater History Studies,* Vol. 11 (1991).

_____. "Sexuality and Gender." In *A Cultural History of Theatre in the Age of Empire (1800–1920).* Edited by Peter Marx. New York: Bloomsbury Publishing, 2017.

Shapiro, Barbara Stern. *Pleasures of Paris: Daumier to Picasso.* Boston: D.R. Godine; Museum of Fine Arts, 1991.

Shelley, Henry C. *Old Paris: Its Social, Historical, and Literary Associations.* Boston: L.C. Page, 1912.

Shipman, Pat. *Femme Fatale: Love, Lies and the Unknown Life of Mata Hari.* New York: HarperCollins, 2007.

Shteir, Rachel. *Striptease: The Untold History of the Girlie Show.* New York: Oxford University Press, 2004.

Showalter, Elaine, ed. *Daughters of Decadence: Women Writers of the Fin-de-Siècle.* Rutherford, NJ: Rutgers University Press, 1993.

Silverman, Debora. *Art Nouveau in Fin-de-Siècle France: Politics, Psychology, and Style.* Berkeley: University of California Press, 1992.

Smith, F. Berkely. *How Paris Amuses Itself.* New York: Funk & Wagnalls, 1903.

Sos, Eltis. *Acts of Desire: Women and Sex on Stage, 1800–1930.* New York: Oxford University Press, 2013.

Sowinska, Alicja. "Dialectics of the Banana Skirt: The Ambiguities of Josephine Baker's Self-Representation." *Michigan Feminist Studies,* Vol. 19 (Fall 2005–Spring 2006). http://hdl.handle.net/2027/spo.ark5583.0019.003.

Spalink, Angenette M. *Loie Fuller and Modern Movement.* Master's Thesis, Bowling Green State University, 2010.

Steele, Valerie. *Paris Fashion: A Cultural History.* New York: Oxford University Press, 1988.

_____, ed. *Dance and Fashion.* New Haven, CT: Yale University Press, 2014.

Strong, Roy. *Art and Power: Renaissance Festivals, 1450–1650.* Berkeley: University of California Press, 1984.

Stuart, Andrea. *Showgirls.* London: Cape, 1996.

Swift, Mary Grace. *A Loftier Flight: The Life and Accomplishments of Charles-Louis Didelot, Balletmaster.* Middletown, CT: Wesleyan University Press, 1974.

Thomson, Richard, Phillip Dennis Cate, and Mary Weaver Chapin. *Toulouse-Lautrec and Montmartre.* The National Gallery of Art in association with Princeton University Press, 2005.

Tilburg, Patricia A. *Colette's Republic: Work, Gender, and Popular Culture in France, 1870–1914.* New York: Berghahn Books, 2009.

_____. "Triumph of the Flesh: Women, Physical Culture and the Nude in the French Music-Hall, 1904–1914." *Radical History Review,* Vol. 98 (2007).

Travis, Doris Eaton. *The Days We Danced: The Story of My Theatrical Family from Florenz Ziegfeld to Arthur Murray and Beyond.* Norman: University of Oklahoma Press, 2003.

University of Georgia, Hargrett Rare Book and Manuscript Library—Paris Music Hall Designs. http://www.libs.uga.edu/hargrett/selections/paris/gallery.html.

Uusitalo, Maarit. *Inigo Jones Costume Design and Symbols in a Stage Costume in Late Renaissance Court Masque.* Master's thesis, Aalto University, 2012. optika_id_732_uusitalo_maarit_2012.

Weber, Eugen. *France, Fin de Siècle.* Cambridge, MA: Belknap Press of Harvard University Press, 1988.

Wedekind, Frank. *Diary of an Erotic Life.* Edited by Gerhard Hay. Translated by W.E. Yuill. Cambridge, MA: Basil Blackwell, 1990.

Weill, Alain. *120 Ans de Moulin Rouge.* Paris: Seven Sept, 2010.

Weitz, Eric D. *Weimar Germany: Promise and Tragedy.* Princeton, NJ: Princeton University Press, 2007.

Whiting, Steven Moore. *Satie the Bohemian: From Cabaret to Concert Hall.* New York: Oxford University Press, 1994.

Zola, Émile. *Au Bonheur des Dames [The Ladies' Paradise].* Translated by Brian Nelson. New York: Oxford University Press, 2008.

Index

Numbers in **bold italics** indicate pages with illustrations

www.ingramcontent.com/pod-product-compliance
Lightning Source LLC
Chambersburg PA
CBHW080550270326
41929CB00019B/3254